韩刚 编著

CATTI&MTI
笔译必背词汇应试训练题库

清华大学出版社
北京

内容简介

本书旨在为备考全国翻译专业资格考试（CATTI）和翻译硕士专业学位（MTI）入学考试的考生提供独家原创的词汇题应试技巧和词汇选择/替换训练题库。编者根据CATTI和MTI考试中词汇题目的普遍特点将所选词汇分别编入选择题和替换题，共设计640道词汇考查题，涉及2500多个中高难度的单词，适合参加翻译类考试的考生在考前一个月进行突击模考练习。训练题库配有详细的答案解析和参考译文，帮助考生快速理解句意结构并牢固掌握相关词汇。

本书封面贴有清华大学出版社防伪标签，无标签者不得销售。

版权所有，侵权必究。举报：010-62782989，beiqinquan@tup.tsinghua.edu.cn。

图书在版编目（CIP）数据

CATTI & MTI笔译必背词汇应试训练题库 / 韩刚编著. —北京：清华大学出版社，2024.3
ISBN 978-7-302-65231-1

Ⅰ.①C… Ⅱ.①韩… Ⅲ.①英语–翻译–词汇–资格考核–自学参考资料 Ⅳ.①H315.9

中国国家版本馆CIP数据核字（2024）第035935号

责任编辑：陈 健
封面设计：何凤霞
责任校对：赵琳爽
责任印制：丛怀宇

出版发行：清华大学出版社
网　　址：https://www.tup.com.cn，https://www.wqxuetang.com
地　　址：北京清华大学学研大厦A座
邮　　编：100084
社 总 机：010-83470000
邮　　购：010-62786544
投稿与读者服务：010-62776969，c-service@tup.tsinghua.edu.cn
质量反馈：010-62772015，zhiliang@tup.tsinghua.edu.cn

印 装 者：三河市君旺印务有限公司
经　　销：全国新华书店
开　　本：185mm×260mm　　印　张：18.25　　字　数：413千字
版　　次：2024年4月第1版　　印　次：2024年4月第1次印刷
定　　价：49.80元

产品编号：105100-01

前　言

本书旨在为备考 CATTI（全国翻译专业资格考试）和 MTI（翻译硕士专业学位）的考生提供独家原创的词汇应试训练题库，适合广大考生在考前一个月进行突击模考练习。本书所列训练词汇均精选自编者本人多年外刊阅读所积累的中高难度词汇，绝非东拼西凑之作！

编者根据全国翻译专业资格考试和翻译硕士专业学位入学考试中词汇题的测试特点将所选词汇分别编入选择题和替换题，共设计有 640 道词汇题目，涉及 2500 多个中高难度的单词。在编写过程中，编者逐题逐词查阅英文权威词典，借用或改写外刊原句或词典例句，并为每道题目提供了参考译文，帮助考生快速理解句意结构并牢固掌握相关词汇。

本书仅给训练题目中的易读错或较生僻的单词标注了读音，以此节约读者的查阅时间。在甄选单词词义时，侧重选择有关单词的常考词义而略去常见通用词义，以此突出测试重点并减轻读者记忆负担。此外，针对一些较生僻的词义，本书精选典型例句并为较难理解或较为典型的例句配备译文，而读者通常可以驾驭的例句则没有配备译文，以此来帮助读者提高自学自修的主动性和自觉性。

希望各位读者在完成本书所有词汇训练题目后能够切实增强 CATTI、MTI 以及其他各类英语考试的应试信心，并在今后阅读英语报纸杂志或文献时做到游刃有余，取得事半功倍的效果！

完稿于 2023 年 12 月

目 录

第1章　词汇选择应试三原则 /1

原则1："背单词无 shortcut" /1

原则2："解语义重 logic" /1

原则3："记搭配乃 priority" /4

第2章　词汇选择训练题库 /9

Practice 1　/9　　　　　　Practice 9　/25

Practice 2　/11　　　　　 Practice 10　/27

Practice 3　/13　　　　　 Practice 11　/29

Practice 4　/15　　　　　 Practice 12　/31

Practice 5　/17　　　　　 Practice 13　/33

Practice 6　/19　　　　　 Practice 14　/35

Practice 7　/21　　　　　 Practice 15　/37

Practice 8　/23　　　　　 Practice 16　/39

第3章　词汇替换应试三原则 /41

原则1："厘清结构找逻辑" /41

原则2："语义排除巧提速" /43

原则3："细微差别看搭配" /47

第4章　词汇替换训练题库 /51

Practice 1　/51　　　　　 Practice 9　/67

Practice 2　/53　　　　　 Practice 10　/69

Practice 3　/55　　　　　 Practice 11　/71

Practice 4　/57　　　　　 Practice 12　/73

Practice 5　/59　　　　　 Practice 13　/74

Practice 6　/61　　　　　 Practice 14　/76

Practice 7　/63　　　　　 Practice 15　/78

Practice 8　/65　　　　　 Practice 16　/80

第 5 章　词汇选择训练题库答案与译文 /83

Practice 1 /83　　　　　　Practice 9   /132

Practice 2 /88　　　　　　Practice 10 /138

Practice 3 /94　　　　　　Practice 11 /143

Practice 4 /101　　　　　 Practice 12 /149

Practice 5 /107　　　　　 Practice 13 /155

Practice 6 /113　　　　　 Practice 14 /161

Practice 7 /119　　　　　 Practice 15 /167

Practice 8 /126　　　　　 Practice 16 /173

第 6 章　词汇替换训练题库答案与译文 /181

Practice 1 /181　　　　　 Practice 9   /233

Practice 2 /187　　　　　 Practice 10 /239

Practice 3 /194　　　　　 Practice 11 /246

Practice 4 /200　　　　　 Practice 12 /253

Practice 5 /207　　　　　 Practice 13 /259

Practice 6 /213　　　　　 Practice 14 /266

Practice 7 /220　　　　　 Practice 15 /272

Practice 8 /226　　　　　 Practice 16 /279

第 1 章
词汇选择应试三原则

原则 1："背单词无 shortcut"

没有词汇量而奢谈解题技巧就是无本之木、无源之水。一定要有扎实的词汇量基础,那么多辅助背单词的书籍或 app,您不好好"择善而从之"吗?

此外,平时阅读文章遇到单词需要查词典时,务必要查该单词的多个词义和例句,扩充单词不同的使用场景。如果使用电子词典,建议选择附带同义词和反义词的词典,这样通过查阅一个单词的词义,可以解决同义替换、近义词辨析、反义词识别等多个词汇考试难题,同步丰富自己的英文写作词汇库。

原则 2："解语义重 logic"

无论题目怎么变化,万变不离其宗:该填动词的绝不用名词,该用形容词的绝不能用副词,张冠切不可李戴,词性绝不能混淆。您不得辨析词性、理顺逻辑后再做选择吗?

词汇选择题目是在句子语境中选择适合的单词,不是单纯地考查词义,还涉及单词词性是否合适、逻辑是否合理,选择时需要全方位思考判断。示例如下:

示例 ❶

The nuclear station _____ water from the dam for cooling.
A. resources　　　　B. searches　　　　C. researches　　　　D. sources

解题步骤

Step 1. 明确句意逻辑:该核电站从大坝那里 _____ 水来进行冷却。按照逻辑,空格处应该是"取水、抽水"之意。

Step 2. 选项逐个辨析:从四个选项中选择符合"取水、抽水"搭配的动词。

词汇量较大的读者很容易选出正确答案 D,但是这是基于对每一个单词词性和词义的精准掌握作出的选择。对于词汇量不足以及对单词词义掌握不全面的读者来说,必须查清记牢每一个单词不常用的词性和词义。比如:你知道 resource 和 source 都可以作动词使用吗?词义是什么?搭配是什么?不要只是停留在某一道题目上,而是要深究每一个选项是否有自己的学习盲点。以下是词汇选择题目"追根究底"式的学习示范。

* **选项 A**

resource 既可以作动词,也可以作名词,**名词使用居多**。

1

resource 作名词使用时，词义为：资源；财力（a supply of sth. that a country, an organization or a person has and can use, especially to increase their wealth）。

该单词还有一个常考名词词义，即勇气；才智；谋略（personal qualities such as courage and imagination that help you deal with difficult situations）。由该词义衍生的形容词 resourceful 也是常考点，词义为：机敏的；足智多谋的；随机应变的（good at finding ways of doing things and solving problems, etc.）。

resource 作动词使用时，使用搭配 ~ sb. with sth.，词义为：向……提供资金（或设备）（to provide a person or an organization with the things that they need in order to operate effectively, especially money），如：

The school must be properly resourced with musical instruments and audio equipment.

一定要为这所学校妥善配备乐器和音响设备。

*选项 B

search 既可以作动词，也可以作名词，**动词使用居多**。

常用表达：search some place for sth./sb.，词义为：搜索；搜寻；搜查；查找（to look carefully for sth./sb.; to examine a particular place when looking for sb./sth.），如：

The police searched the woods for the missing boy.

警察为寻找这名失踪的男孩搜查了树林。

She searched her mind for the man's name, but she couldn't remember it.

她努力回想这个人的名字，但就是记不起来。

*选项 C

research 既可以作动词，也可以作名词，**名词使用居多**。

research 作及物动词使用，词义为：对某一个对象进行详细研究，特别是为了获取新信息或获得新认知（to study a subject in detail, especially in order to discover new information or reach a new understanding），如：

She's researching into possible cures for AIDS.

她正对艾滋病可能的治愈方式进行研究。

Journalists are frantically researching the new prime minister's background, family, and interests.

记者们正对这位新首相的背景、家庭和兴趣进行疯狂的调查研究。

*选项 D

source 既可以作动词，也可以作名词。

作动词使用时，常用表达 ~ sth. (from...)，词义为：（从……）获得某物（to get sth. from a particular place），如：

The produce used in our restaurant is sourced locally.

我们餐厅尽可能采用当地采购的食材。

示例 ❷

Linda Yaccarino began her first day as Twitter's new chief executive officer, replacing Elon Musk, the social-media company's _____ owner, in the role.

A. mercenary   B. monetary   C. mercurial   D. momentous

解题步骤

Step 1. 明确句意逻辑：Linda Yaccarino 接替 Elon Musk 担任 Twitter 的 CEO，而 Elon Musk 是这家社交媒体公司 _____ 的所有人。空格处需要一个形容词来修饰马斯克，他是什么样的人？性格特点如何？有什么样的管理风格？解答此题不仅需要考虑词义本身，还需要基本的常识储备，即对马斯克本人要有起码的认知。

Step 2. 选项逐个辨析：从四个选项中选择可以修饰人的词，该词必须符合逻辑和常识。词汇量较大并且知识面较广的读者很容易选出正确答案 C。各选项详细剖析如下：

* **选项 A**

mercenary 作名词使用时，词义为：雇佣兵（a soldier who will fight for any country or group that offers payment）；作形容词使用时，词义为：只为金钱的，唯利是图的（interested only in the money or other personal advantages that you can get from something）。当初马斯克收购 Twitter 时是纯粹为了钱吗？在本题目语境下为什么要谈及马斯克唯利是图呢？这就需要知识面作为支撑进行判断排除。

* **选项 B**

monetary 只用作形容词，词义为：货币的，钱的（尤指一国的货币）（connected with money, especially all the money in a country）。显然该词不适合本选项语境。

* **选项 C**

mercurial（[mɜː(r)ˈkjʊəriəl]）的词根是 mercury，词义为：多变的；善变的；变幻莫测的（often changing or reacting in a way that is unexpected）。对马斯克有所了解的人——特别是了解他收购 Twitter 前后所做决定的人——都会确定该选项为合理选项，但前提是了解该单词的词义。

* **选项 D**

momentous 的词义为：重要的；意义深远的；不朽的（very important and having a great influence, especially as the result of years of work），用来形容事件而非人，由此可直接排除。

在仔细对比分析四个选项后，大部分读者会在 B 和 C 中做选择，至于最终选择哪个就要在常识基础上结合具体语境作出判断。当然，如果对 B 和 C 选项的词义都不清楚就只能是"听天由命"了。

示例 ❸

A record 12.9m Chinese highschoolers will start the feared gaokao exams on Wednesday. They will solve equations, _____ English sentences, and write about disparate topics (last year's papers mentioned fireworks, Covid tests and Go, a board game).

A. sparse   B. parse   C. parsley   D. parch

解题步骤

Step 1. 明确句意逻辑：高考考生参加高考时要解方程式、_____ 英文句子并根据不同（语文）试卷给出的各不相同的题目写作文。这道题目考查的就是基本常识：高考英语试题考查学生分析英文句子的能力。从这个方向出发去找选项就容易多了。

Step 2. 选项逐个辨析：四个选项形近，需要从中选出匹配"分析、理解"词义的单词。不过，四个选项的单词词性不一，有的根本不能作动词，可以直接排除；有的词义不符，也可以直接排除。正确选项为 B。各选项详细剖析如下：

* 选项 A

sparse 是形容词，词义为：稀少的；稀疏的；零落的（only present in small amounts or numbers and often spread over a large area）。词性不符，直接排除。

* 选项 B

parse 作及物动词使用，词义为：（对句子）作语法分析；作句法分析（to divide a sentence into parts and describe the grammar of each word or part）。该词完全符合本题目语境逻辑，是正确选项。

* 选项 C

parsley 是名词，词义为：欧芹；荷兰芹（a plant with curly green leaves that are used in cooking as a herb and to decorate food）。词性不符，直接排除。

* 选项 D

parch 作及物动词使用，词义为：使（土地）极干燥（to make an area of land very dry）。词义不符合本题目语境，直接排除。

原则 3："记搭配乃 priority"

单词的词义固然重要，但放在词组中的词汇可能就让学生"雾里看花"了。词汇"嫁娶"这样的大事，您不得要知道对方家里的成员关系吗？

很多词汇选择题目通过词组搭配的形式出现，这时考查的重心往往不是单词的基本词义，而是引申义或者词组搭配的整体含义。对于这样的题目就需要平时留意掌握大量的词组搭配。

示例 ❶

While retail energy prices are coming down, food prices are still rising at double-digit rates. That may have led consumers to expect higher inflation, which may in turn _____ into wage negotiations.

A. flow　　　　　B. factor　　　　　C. feed　　　　　D. fill

解题步骤

Step 1. 明确句意逻辑：能源零售价下降而粮食价格仍然攀升。这或许让消费者有通胀继续攀升的预期，而这种预期反过来又会 _____ 有关工资的谈判。破解此题需要具有基本常识，既然有通胀预期，人们自然希望工资会随之上涨，即通胀预期会导致有关提高工资的谈判。从这个逻辑层面去做选择事半功倍。

Step 2. 选项逐个辨析：需要从四个选项中选出匹配"导致、造成"词义的单词。各选项详细剖析如下：

* **选项 A**

flow into... 流进；流入（to rush into something in a smooth, fluid manner, as of a liquid）。该选项不符合语境，直接排除。

* **选项 B**

factor 构成的词组正确用法为：factor sth. in/factor sth. into sth.，意思是"将……因素考虑在内、在……时要考虑到某因素"（to include a particular fact or situation when you are thinking about or planning something）。该词义与本选项逻辑不符，直接排除。

* **选项 C**

feed into sth. 的解释包括：将（钱、数据等）……放入机器等之中（to insert or input something into something, such as a machine）；（河流等）流入（海洋）（to empty into another body of water, as of a river, tributary, etc.）；导致、造成、转换为……（to contribute, relate, or segue into sth.）。

该词组的第三个释义与本题逻辑相符，是正确选项。

* **选项 D**

没有 fill into... 的搭配，可直接排除。fill 的常见搭配为：fill sth. (with sth.)，意为使遍及；弥漫；布满；照满（If a smell, sound or light fills a place, it is very strong, loud or bright and easy to notice.）。fill sb. (with sth.)，意为使充满（感情）（to make sb. have a strong feeling）。

示例 2

South Africa's _____ power cuts—a product of years of corruption and mismanagement at the state-owned electricity utility—astonish outsiders and frustrate locals.

A. revolving　　　B. circulating　　　C. rolling　　　D. alternating

解题步骤

Step 1. 明确句意逻辑：国有电力公司多年的腐败和管理不善造成了南非的 _____ 断电，这让外界人士震惊，也让当地民众失望。此处需要一个形容词与 power cuts 进行搭配，考查常识和词组积累。

Step 2. 选项逐个辨析：需要从四个选项中选出可以与 power cuts 匹配并符合语境的单词。各选项详细剖析如下：

* **选项 A**

revolving 的词义为：旋转的（able to turn in a circle），如：旋转门。在英文中没有 revolving power cuts 的搭配，故直接排除。

* **选项 B**

circulating 的词义为：流通的，循环的（go around or through something）。在英文中没有

circulating power cuts 的搭配，故直接排除。cyclical power cuts 是正确搭配，意思为：轮流拉闸限电或轮流停电。

* 选项 C

rolling 的词义为：规则的；周而复始的（done in regular stages or at regular intervals over a period of time）。词组搭配 rolling power cuts 的意思为：轮流拉闸限电或轮流停电（Rolling power cuts, also known as cyclical or rotating power cuts, are planned grid shutdowns during which individual districts, and the electricity consumers connected to them, are disconnected from the power grid for a certain period of time. This means that electricity will only be available in regular intervals and in certain districts.）。"轮流拉闸限电或轮流停电"也可以用 rolling blackout 表示。由此，选项 C 是正确答案。

* 选项 D

alternating 有"交替的，轮流的"这一词义（happening or coming one after another, in a regular pattern；happening on one day, week, etc. but not on the day, week, etc., that immediately follows），但**不存在 alternating power cuts 的搭配**，因此该选项颇具迷惑性，不能因为单词词义相符就贸然选择，要看搭配才行。如："食品安全"是 food safety，"粮食安全"是 food security，不能因为 safety 和 security 有"安全"这一词义就想当然地胡乱搭配。此外，英文中有 alternating current 的搭配，意思为：交流电（流）（an electric current that changes its direction at regular intervals many times a second）。

示例 3

Happy people appear better able to cope with practical problems because they know when to change _____ or give up.

A. tact　　　　　　B. tack　　　　　　C. cause　　　　　　D. coarse

解题步骤

Step 1. 明确句意逻辑：快乐的人似乎在应对实际问题时能力更强，这是因为他们知道何时要改变_____或者选择放弃。从常识逻辑来看，应对问题时需要解决办法，方法行不通就要变通，也就是改变策略或方法，变通也不行就只能放弃。因此，正确选项应该包含"策略、方法、方式"的词义。

Step 2. 选项逐个辨析：需要从四个选项中选出可以与 change 搭配、带有"改变策略或方法"之意的单词。各选项详细剖析如下：

* 选项 A

tact 的词义为：（处事、言谈等的）老练，圆通，得体，乖巧（the ability to deal with difficult or embarrassing situations carefully and without doing or saying anything that will annoy or upset other people）。change tact 是一种误用，没有这种搭配（When referring to a change in direction, position, or course of action, the correct phrase is to change tack. This is in reference to the nautical use of tack which refers to the direction of a boat with respect to sail position. This phrase has long been confused as "change tact" but this is technically incorrect.）。此外，change one's tactics 是正确搭配，意思为改变策略。

* 选项 B

tack 的词义为：方针；方法；思路（the way in which you deal with a particular situation; the direction of your words or thoughts）。change (one's) tack 是正确搭配，意思为：改变方法；改变思路（to try a different method to deal with the same problem）。选项 B 是正确答案。

* 选项 C

cause 的词义为：原因；起因（the person or thing that makes sth. happen）；（支持或为之奋斗的）事业，目标，思想（an organization or idea that people support or fight for）。没有 change cause 的搭配，直接排除。

* 选项 D

coarse 是形容词，"change _____"需要名词进行搭配，因此直接排除该选项。coarse 的词义为：粗糙的，粗织的（rough）；粗鲁无礼的，粗俗的（尤指涉及性的）（rude and offensive, especially about sex）。该选项其实是一个迷惑选项，正确搭配为 change course，意思为改变航线；改变方向；改弦更张（to start doing something completely new or different）。

总结

知其然还要知其所以然，知其义更要知其用。无论是形近词还是意近词，不要只靠背单词解决问题，只有放到"广泛阅读文章"的"照妖镜"里才知道谁是妖魔谁是神仙。

第2章
词汇选择训练题库

Practice 1

There are 20 incomplete sentences in this practice. Below each sentence, there are 4 choices marked by letters A, B, C and D respectively. Choose the word which best completes each sentence. There is only **ONE** right answer.

1. Although tobacco ads are prohibited, companies _____ the ban by sponsoring music shows.
   A. get through   B. get across   C. get around   D. get over

2. People of all backgrounds are _____ by the city's deterioration under his watch.
   A. irked   B. itched   C. inundated   D. intoxicated

3. Fans of the plucky prime minister in the period drama were _____ when the third season ended in 2013.
   A. beset   B. overwhelmed   C. bereft   D. exhilarated

4. After seven weeks of losses, American stocks were _____ with bear-market territory, but in recent days they appear to have turned a corner.
   A. flirting   B. fighting   C. fudging   D. filled

5. So far redundancies have been largely _____ to startups and newly listed firms, while sackings at established tech companies have been modest.
   A. attributed   B. confined   C. contributed   D. contrived

6. He praised my work and in the same _____ told me I would have to leave.
   A. vein   B. lens   C. tone   D. breath

7. It seems the stars have _____ for the team to finally take home the championship trophy this year.
   A. crossed   B. risen   C. fallen   D. aligned

8. As the stock markets of the world have gotten a little more _____, individual investors are balking at upping the ante.
   A. intrepid   B. tepid   C. limpid   D. lucid

9 The world is on the _____ of a demographic reversal.
   A. front		B. door		C. cusp		D. corner

10 Sam was _____ to the fact that he would never be promoted.
   A. subjected		B. subordinate		C. surrendering		D. resigned

11 Linda is entirely too rude; it's time you put her in her _____.
   A. shoes		B. closet		C. place		D. seat

12 Enrolment in Catholic schools has _____ since the 1960s but recently ticked up in the pandemic.
   A. ballooned		B. spiked		C. bottomed out		D. cratered

13 India and America had inaugurated a Trade Policy Forum in 2009, but let it _____ in 2018; now it is reconvening with renewed enthusiasm.
   A. lapse		B. collapse		C. eclipse		D. flip

14 Terrified to see him thus, the child clung to him and _____ him to be calm.
   A. besought		B. brawled		C. bereaved		D. bedeviled

15 Fighting has _____ the region since November 2020.
   A. blazed		B. blundered		C. blighted		D. brandished

16 History suggests that rapid monetary tightening often _____ a recession, but the Fed knows that runaway inflation would be even worse.
   A. precedes		B. predates		C. prevails over		D. prefaces

17 Other parts of the country were also _____ by pandemic-induced restrictions on free movement and gathering.
   A. trammeled		B. subjected		C. obscured		D. subtracted

18 He was a major advocate of a 2003 Swiss law under which animals are to be treated as _____ beings, not personal property.
   A. sensual		B. sentient		C. sentimental		D. sensory

19 He added the _____ that all the figures in the survey were suspect.
   A. caveat		B. caviar		C. cavalcade		D. cavil

20 How much damage might a stronger yuan _____?
   A. afflict		B. inflict		C. affect		D. elicit

Practice 2

*There are 20 incomplete sentences in this practice. Below each sentence, there are 4 choices marked by letters A, B, C and D respectively. Choose the word which best completes each sentence. There is only **ONE** right answer.*

1. Timbuktu _____ images of gold and Saharan caravans, but the Malian desert city was also a flourishing centre of knowledge.

    A. conjures up   B. evokes up   C. brings up   D. covers up

2. The shortage prompted President Biden to _____ the Defense Production Act to ensure manufacturers have the necessary supplies for baby formula production.

    A. embrace   B. evoke   C. elicit   D. invoke

3. In 1998, he moved to New York City, where he became a _____ in literary and social circles, popping up at parties, events and in the media.

    A. fix   B. fitting   C. fixture   D. fissure

4. When he first bought his apartment, he provided a 30 percent down payment with money _____ together from his parents' retirement funds.

    A. scrapped   B. scraped   C. scribed   D. scripted

5. The country's social credit system punishes _____—such as failure to repay loans—by limiting an individual's ability to travel, get their children into school or borrow from banks in the future.

    A. infractions   B. refractions   C. fractions   D. factions

6. "The end of an era" will become a(an) _____ as commentators assess the record-setting reign of Queen Elizabeth II.

    A. refrain   B. exhortation   C. maxim   D. epitome

7. Britons' unquestioning deference to the crown had been supplanted by the _____ of emotions ranging from loyal and often affectionate tolerance to unbridled hostility.

    A. gamut   B. gambit   C. gauntlet   D. gauge

8. Thanks to these literary works, he has grown in _____ in recent years, becoming comfortable in his own skin.

    A. statute   B. stature   C. caricature   D. couture

9. The government has deployed _____ fiscal stimulus, while households and firms have continued to spend and invest.

    A. judicial   B. judiciary   C. judicious   D. judgemental

10 In recent years, he has taken on several of the queen's duties, from foreign trips to _____, where people are granted knighthoods.

    A. investitures   B. investments   C. dentures   D. ventures

11 Taking your hat off at the door may seem like a _____ to a more genteel age.

    A. backfire   B. backlash   C. throwback   D. blowback

12 In the past, simple, succinct design has influenced our five senses as much as has _____ design. This will remain true in the future.

    A. exterior   B. ebullient   C. elaborate   D. exuberant

13 After a _____ of mass shootings, many Americans are fed up.

    A. deluge   B. divulgence   C. divergence   D. disposition

14 Racked by allegations of corruption, he has fallen from _____.

    A. grief   B. grievance   C. grace   D. glory

15 If we have to sit through another _____ lecture today, I'm going to need another cup of coffee!

    A. mind-boggling   B. mind-blowing   C. mind-bending   D. mind-numbing

16 The campaign was so divisive that even though he won the election it was a _____ victory.

    A. pyrrhic   B. pioneering   C. pompous   D. puritanical

17 There has been much talk of America nearing "peak inflation". The hope was that price pressures, though still high, were about to start _____. But the peak looks more like a plateau—and an elevated one at that.

    A. dissipating   B. dispersing   C. diffusing   D. dissecting

18 Staff shortages caused by _____ of ground and air crew during the pandemic have already caused some airlines to forgo adding even more capacity to meet the surging demand.

    A. dismissals   B. decimation   C. dissolution   D. desolation

19 In August BTS, a South Korean boy band, will see their single "Dynamite" travel to space _____ of South Korea's first lunar orbiter.

    A. courtesy   B. because   C. aboard   D. comprised

20 In the heyday of globalization, multilateral organizations and global corporations seemed to be _____ nation-states.

    A. eclipsing   B. mimicking   C. trailing   D. emulating

Practice 3

*There are 20 incomplete sentences in this practice. Below each sentence, there are 4 choices marked by letters A, B, C and D respectively. Choose the word which best completes each sentence. There is only **ONE** right answer.*

1 With his legion of fans, Mr. Musk will command a gigantic megaphone and be free to plug his own investments, pooh-pooh sound health regulations and _____ down critics.

    A. shut   B. silence   C. show   D. shout

2 Most of the _____ has been monitored by the World Bank, to make sure the money goes to national funds and not into people's pockets.

    A. restitution   B. destitution   C. institution   D. constitution

3 In good times, executives _____ about what their companies might become.

    A. rave   B. ravel   C. gravel   D. gavel

4 Lying in state is observed by many countries. In Britain it is the _____ of sovereigns, their consorts and select prime ministers.

    A. conserve   B. preserve   C. reserve   D. subserve

5 In death as in life, the queen _____ the royal family a little further into the modern world.

    A. hoaxes   B. coaxes   C. plies   D. pries

6 These draconian measures have met a backlash. Other investors are _____ too, not least those with funds still trapped in the country by capital controls.

    A. livid   B. limpid   C. lucid   D. lurid

7 He was careful to say that the _____ effects of the subprime mess might not be as great as those of previous crises.

    A. malign   B. malignant   C. malicious   D. malevolent

8 The games industry could also indirectly help resurrect Sri Lanka's _____ tourism industry.

    A. moribund   B. mundane   C. morbid   D. mortal

9 People can have all sorts of _____ about the report, but we're just trying to be an unbiased source of information.

A. constipation B. consternation C. constellation D. convocation

10 Investors are now concentrating on what the bank will do next after a _____ fall in its share price.

A. capricious B. precipitous C. contemptuous D. callous

11 You have to learn how to take criticism in _____ if you want to be successful in this business.

A. stroke B. stride C. stalk D. stack

12 The disastrous consequences of the British government's mini-budget of September 23rd continue to _____ through febrile markets.

A. reverberate B. rebut C. repulse D. reverse

13 This policy has _____ consumer spending on everything from cheap eateries to high-end jewelry.

A. enthralled B. throbbed C. thrashed D. throttled

14 These small errors do not seriously _____ from the book.

A. distract B. detract C. subtract D. retract

15 Banks are already becoming more _____ to national governments as the latter extend their economic lifelines.

A. besought B. beholden C. bereft D. bedeviled

16 Davos is easy to mock. Pampered insiders _____ on the fate of billions of less fortunate folk.

A. pundit B. portend C. pontificate D. potion

17 This courtly poetry came out of the idea of _____ and courtly love that you might associate with knights in shining armor.

A. cavalry B. chivalry C. clove D. crony

18 As the _____ goes, music stepped in where words failed.

A. truism B. altruism C. gravitas D. fortuitous

19 Weaker digital-ad spending continues to _____ growth at its social-media core.

A. crimp B. crumple C. crinkle D. crease

20 The government refused to _____ with the rebels.

A. barley B. parley C. parlor D. parlay

Practice 4

There are 20 incomplete sentences in this practice. Below each sentence, there are 4 choices marked by letters A, B, C and D respectively. Choose the word which best completes each sentence. There is only **ONE** right answer.

1. The European Central Bank's top _____ will convene in Frankfurt on Thursday to decide how much to raise interest rates.

    A. branch   B. brass   C. behemoth   D. bandit

2. They _____ playfully over whose team was better.

    A. spared   B. spurred   C. sparred   D. speared

3. Mother is devoted to Dad although they _____ all the time.

    A. squabble   B. square   C. squirrel   D. scribble

4. They cheated me, but I feel no _____ toward/against them.

    A. rancour   B. raucous   C. rapport   D. capricious

5. Their endorsement was enough to give her the job she _____.

    A. craved   B. braved   C. raved   D. staved

6. His speech raised the _____ that he could use such a weapon in Ukraine.

    A. spectacle   B. spectacles   C. spectre   D. scepter

7. Truss has adopted the _____ of her hero, Margaret Thatcher.

    A. manor   B. morale   C. mantle   D. mores

8. Smartphones connect billions of people to the Internet's _____ of information and services.

    A. plethora   B. pantheon   C. plankton   D. phantom

9. The two cultures were so utterly _____ that she found it hard to adapt from one to the other.

    A. disparate   B. eclectic   C. dialectic   D. diaspora

10. They are _____ in all their business dealings to prevent fraudulent practices.

    A. circumspect   B. circumvent   C. circumlocutory   D. circumstantial

15

11. COP27, the United Nations' annual climate summit, began in Egypt with delegates agreeing to discuss whether to pay poor countries for the damages they have _____ from climate change.

    A. maintained   B. retained   C. sustained   D. stained

12. Videos circulating on social media showed an overturned truck, ransacked food provisions and _____ between outraged residents and health officials.

    A. altercations   B. alterations   C. alliterations   D. iterations

13. The company offers a _____ atmosphere to work in.

    A. congenial   B. congenital   C. consensual   D. conjectural

14. Shoppers also _____ physical stores during the Double 11 shopping festival.

    A. tonged   B. gonged   C. thronged   D. pronged

15. His life seemed stuck in _____; he could not go forward and he could not go back.

    A. limbo   B. libido   C. jumbo   D. patio

16. The firm's share price has nosedived this year as investors fret over its expensive _____ into streaming services.

    A. fodder   B. forgery   C. foray   D. forlorn

17. During his previous tenure, he was _____ with turning Disney into one of the world's most formidable content-and-technology powerhouses.

    A. crowned   B. craved   C. credited   D. chanted

18. There's a sense of _____ at having completed a race of such length.

    A. elevation   B. altitude   C. elation   D. magnitude

19. Long-term contracts with gas and electricity suppliers have _____ the blow this year—but in 2023 the full effect of energy price rises will be felt.

    A. fashioned   B. cushioned   C. dealt   D. wreaked

20. He claimed that he signed the confession under _____.

    A. duel   B. duo   C. duress   D. caress

Practice 5

*There are 20 incomplete sentences in this practice. Below each sentence, there are 4 choices marked by letters A, B, C and D respectively. Choose the word which best completes each sentence. There is only **ONE** right answer.*

1 The goal of the policy is to encourage people sitting on large gains in the value of their homes to _____ up to newer and larger apartments.

  A. live B. step C. measure D. trade

2 Millions of people have only limited access to electricity, water and heat after Russian missiles _____ much of Ukraine's energy infrastructure.

  A. pulsated B. plundered C. pulverized D. pampered

3 Rio Tinto agreed to pay _____ for its destruction of ancient Aboriginal rock structures in Western Australia while building an iron ore mine in 2020.

  A. restoration B. restitution C. reinstatement D. reinstallation

4 Their wealth is so vast that by distributing even a small fraction of it, they skew the public agenda toward the kind of social change they can _____ —the kind that doesn't threaten them or their class.

  A. mouth B. foot C. stomach D. arm

5 Elon Musk launched a _____ against Apple on Twitter, the social-media platform he now owns.

  A. diatribe B. scribe C. conscribe D. ascribe

6 Some firms will _____ data to gain government subsidies.

  A. message B. mirage C. montage D. massage

7 He has not been _____ about the details of his contract.

  A. upcoming B. up-and-coming C. forthcoming D. foregoing

8 He began a second _____ as chief executive a week ago.

  A. stench B. skint C. stint D. clench

9 Artificial intelligence has already _____ humans at Chess and Go. Now it can routinely win at Diplomacy, which for some aficionados is a truer marker of game-playing ability. Play demands collaboration but also allows for double-crossing.

  A. trailed B. trounced C. entrenched D. entranced

10 He paid for ex-girlfriends' abortions despite his _____ support for a ban on the procedure.

    A. avowed   B. acclaimed   C. disavowed   D. disclaimed

11 Twitter shut its office in Brussels, sparking fears among EU officials that the social-media platform will not follow EU rules on _____ online speech, as the fallout from Elon Musk's takeover continues.

    A. modulating   B. undulating   C. moderating   D. collating

12 This generation has been weaned _____ computer games. But I have to get the kids to read or play outside instead.

    A. off   B. off of   C. on   D. away from

13 Emmanuel Macron will be treated _____ the works, including a state banquet at the White House.

    A. with   B. for   C. to   D. as

14 Stormont, Northern Ireland's parliament, has been _____ in an eleventh-hour attempt to form a government.

    A. recouped   B. recalled   C. rehashed   D. revamped

15 Earlier in October the company left Russia empty-handed after the Russian government _____ some of its Russian assets.

    A. expropriated   B. appropriated   C. approbated   D. corroborated

16 These die-hard fans became _____ and violent after their team's loss.

    A. truculent   B. translucent   C. transient   D. truant

17 He hurried into retirement several senior figures of a more moderate political _____.

    A. stripe   B. strip   C. strap   D. staple

18 Analysts want to see how the theme parks are holding _____ amid a fragile American economy.

    A. on   B. back   C. out   D. up

19 The indebted property developer, whose troubles are _____ of the country's broader economic problems, has to meet the regulator's conditions for avoiding a permanent delisting.

    A. emblematic   B. epitome   C. emphatic   D. endemic

20 I don't want to be one of those elders who _____ young people's form of communication.

    A. castigate   B. cascade   C. castrate   D. constipate

Practice 6

*There are 20 incomplete sentences in this practice. Below each sentence, there are 4 choices marked by letters A, B, C and D respectively. Choose the word which best completes each sentence. There is only **ONE** right answer.*

1. The 1990s vogue for radically minimalist interiors sprung from early 20th-century modernism and a zero tolerance, among some of its exponents, for _____ elements.

    A. existential　　　B. extraneous　　　C. extricable　　　D. exogenous

2. For decades, mental health has been one of the most overlooked areas of public health. Anxiety and depression are the most common _____.

    A. afflictions　　　B. inflictions　　　C. disinclinations　　　D. dispositions

3. John Ruskin, a British art critic, wrote that the traces of damage on a building—"the golden stain of time"—could _____ them with grandeur.

    A. imbue　　　B. imbibe　　　C. immerse　　　D. indulge

4. But, so far at least, the much-feared _____ of Wall Street talents hoping to dodge pay curbs has proved a paper tiger.

    A. exile　　　B. emigration　　　C. exodus　　　D. exhilaration

5. Power shifts have been a big theme of the past week, with much attention at the Davos business _____ being focused on India and China.

    A. jumbo　　　B. jamboree　　　C. combo　　　D. ensemble

6. Politicians of all stripes _____ against the failure of posh universities to enroll a greater number of students from poor families.

    A. flout　　　B. flush　　　C. fulminate　　　D. flounder

7. Wildfires in northern Spain _____ around 1,100 hectares of woods, amid a heatwave that is sending temperatures to near record highs.

    A. incinerated　　　B. incarcerated　　　C. incarnated　　　D. inculcated

8. Mr. Tata said he had once viewed the US, with its _____ consumers and obsession with large cars, as unsuitable for the diminutive Nano.

    A. exacting　　　B. extracting　　　C. excruciating　　　D. expropriating

9. That achievement earned him many honours for services to horology, but it was only the beginning of a long _____ to get his idea accepted.

    A. slog　　　B. snog　　　C. smog　　　D. swag

19

10. Multinationals tend to cut their overall tax bills by reporting profits in low-tax jurisdictions. But change is _____.

A. afoot B. afloat C. aboard D. afoul

11. In theory, such a provision would reduce the gains to firms from _____ away profits to havens.

A. siphoning B. piping C. transforming D. teleporting

12. Britain might have to join Norway and the Netherlands in banning English bulldogs—and _____ a national symbol to exile.

A. condemn B. condone C. confine D. compress

13. Iran will cut off electricity to its 118 authorised crypto-mining firms, hoping to _____ the country's strained power network.

A. relieve B. relive C. revive D. retrieve

14. Police officers have the power to stop him at customs checkpoints if the _____ who has deliberately avoided due payments tries to leave the country.

A. loafer B. sloth C. deadbeat D. waster

15. Life in cities has become less tolerable as censorship tightens—and Western sanctions _____.

A. bite B. batter C. backfire D. backlash

16. The hotel has been _____ of short-term staff ever since the local college closed.

A. starved B. dearth C. deficit D. insufficient

17. There was no doubt that, _____ the few Cassandras who correctly prophesied gloom and doom, the industry had failed colossally.

A. notwithstanding B. nevertheless C. although D. while

18. President Joe Biden asked Congress for a three-month suspension of the federal fuel tax as Americans _____ with soaring petrol prices and high inflation.

A. reckon B. reconcile C. respond D. realign

19. This is still likely to be a relatively _____ recovery by historical standards.

A. subdued B. subsistent C. extant D. existential

20. Britain's economy is powered by its consumers' willingness to spend. So economists _____ earlier this year when talk of a cost-of-living crisis sent British shoppers into a funk.

A. shuddered B. shattered C. smashed D. shriveled

Practice 7

*There are 20 incomplete sentences in this practice. Below each sentence, there are 4 choices marked by letters A, B, C and D respectively. Choose the word which best completes each sentence. There is only **ONE** right answer.*

1. Technological advances in reinforced concrete and steel frames _____ the need for internal load-bearing walls, resulting in spacious, open-plan interiors.

    A. obliterated B. accentuated C. oscillated D. obviated

2. This weekend the _____ at Glastonbury Music Festival will watch more than 3,000 artists perform on over 100 stages.

    A. punters B. punks C. pundits D. porters

3. Does friendship cause _____ to converge, or do pre-existing scented similarities lead to friendship?

    A. odours B. aromas C. fragrances D. stenches

4. Wimbledon, Britain's annual tennis tournament known for its archaic traditions, has long been _____ in the tennis world.

    A. distinctive B. distinct C. differentiated D. discordant

5. Abandoning the Cold War mindset is not to _____ arms control treaties concluded in that era.

    A. abrogate B. corroborate C. apprehend D. renege

6. If you can't stay the _____ when things get a bit messy, then you just aren't cut out for this line of work.

    A. course B. concourse C. cause D. coarse

7. He urged his friends to show their "pecs" to Peter, in a jibe intended to mock his _____ for shirtless photo opportunities.

    A. predilection B. petulance C. pendulum D. proposition

8. Americans will be stuck with wallet-_____ petrol prices for a while yet.

    A. guzzling B. fizzling C. sizzling D. fuddling

9. Environmentalists believe cutting the supply of fossil fuels is necessary to _____ America toward greener energy.

    A. pilot B. pioneer C. pivot D. pirate

10. Paying attention to small details _____ for a more enjoyable trip.

    A. makes B. heads C. gravitates D. opts

11 The heads of the European Central Bank, Federal Reserve and Bank of England urged rapid action to tackle inflation, _____ it become entrenched.

   A. lest   B. unless   C. until   D. even if

12 Ever since he was a little boy, it's been the Marine Corps or _____ for Tom.

   A. bust   B. burst   C. otherwise   D. not

13 If you set the bar too high and you already feel as if you're slipping, don't _____ yourself. After all, it happens to most of us.

   A. berate   B. beseech   C. beget   D. bemoan

14 The order was an unusually bold step for the regulator, which has come under fire in recent years for not being more _____ with automakers.

   A. assertive   B. obsessive   C. attentive   D. aligned

15 I tried to hide my scars under my clothes. Children in school _____ from me. I was a figure of pity to neighbors and, to some extent, my parents.

   A. recoiled   B. retreated   C. retrenched   D. retraced

16 It is now believed to possess dozens of nuclear devices and appears _____ to carry out a seventh nuclear test.

   A. poised   B. positioned   C. braced   D. predestined

17 Her father puts a lot of _____ in her ability to get the job done.

   A. belief   B. stock   C. premium   D. credit

18 Critics have warned that G20 could _____ into another international body long on talk but unable to produce concrete results.

   A. devolve   B. revolve   C. involute   D. dissolve

19 Fruit, vegetables and meat are luxuries for most people, and malnutrition shows in the splotchy skin, sunken cheekbones and _____ frames of the many people I encountered across the country during my years reporting on the ground.

   A. gaunt   B. gauntlet   C. taunt   D. saunter

20 I've seen the nurses in the Democratic People's Republic of Korea dump syringes in a wash basin and _____ them in disinfectant for reuse.

   A. rinse   B. flush   C. clear   D. cleanse

Practice 8

There are 20 incomplete sentences in this practice. Below each sentence, there are 4 choices marked by letters A, B, C and D respectively. Choose the word which best completes each sentence. There is only **ONE** right answer.

1 For years, the national leader has _____ against greed and corruption in the country's financial sector, making an example of a few prominent figures along the way.

    A. roiled   B. routed   C. railed   D. rowed

2 Hand-drawn posters that lined the walls of her rural clinic suggested eating two bulbs of raw garlic, drinking liquor fortified with an egg and sliced ginseng or sipping _____ water with sliced spring onions and sugar to ward off colds and the flu.

    A. tepid   B. insipid   C. limpid   D. trepid

3 In the _____ of its deadly 1990s famine, the Democratic People's Republic of Korea made an unprecedented appeal for international food aid.

    A. throes   B. thrust   C. thrashing   D. event

4 Ukraine, which is one of the world's leading grain exporters, has accused Russia of blocking its ships, _____ a global food crisis.

    A. extricating   B. exacerbating   C. espousing   D. eliciting

5 The pandemic has _____ supply chains and curbed household incomes, and extreme weather has hurt yields in many breadbaskets. The result was a jump in the number of undernourished people in 2021.

    A. warped   B. wrapped   C. wrenched   D. wrung

6 More than $100bn of direct damage has already been _____ on Ukraine's infrastructure.

    A. put   B. effected   C. inflicted   D. afflicted

7 The gunman was charged with murder and attempted murder and _____ into a psychiatric ward.

    A. remanded   B. reprimanded   C. consigned   D. confined

8 A British citizen _____ to death by a court in east Ukraine appealed against the sentence.

    A. condoned   B. conferred   C. condemned   D. incarcerated

9 The lean years helped to stop the city's historic buildings being replaced by the concrete utopias _____ of modernist planners.

    A. loved   B. liked   C. favored   D. beloved

10 The IMF reckons that Ukraine's GDP could shrink by more than a third this year, a blow on a/an

_____ with America's Great Depression in the 1930s.

 A. balance   B. equilibrium   C. par   D. equity

11. It has been an _____ wait for survivors, desperate for news of relatives and friends they have not been able to contact.

 A. excruciating   B. exhilarating   C. exfoliating   D. esoteric

12. Their many years of research have finally _____ in a cure for the disease.

 A. concluded   B. condescended   C. convoluted   D. culminated

13. He was not the only tycoon to find himself in the government's _____ as part of the government's campaign against corruption.

 A. conflagration   B. cross hairs   C. chessboard   D. agenda

14. _____ from a poor farming village in eastern Cambodia, he was a child prodigy who at 14 won admission to a prestigious university in the country.

 A. Emanating   B. Deriving   C. Hailing   D. Originating

15. The country barely has enough electricity to run elevators in the capital city, and most people don't have computers, much less access to the Internet, but the country has long been home to many of the world's _____ and most aggressive hackers.

 A. gravest   B. tersest   C. savviest   D. sexist

16. To most people, to say that the country holds down the value of its currency to boost its exports is to state the _____.

 A. evident   B. apparent   C. obvious   D. palpable

17. Talented students are carefully screened and _____ from an early age.

 A. broomed   B. crooked   C. groomed   D. swooned

18. For all the permanence of the road's landmarks, its people were less grounded, with _____ control over the city's future.

 A. scant   B. skanky   C. stingy   D. smug

19. The digital world loves to _____ in its own jargon, and one of its most popular phrases today is " cloud computing".

 A. relish   B. revel   C. indulge   D. engage

20. Power was restored within a few hours, but the blackout was a worrying _____ of what may be to come.

 A. foretaste   B. foreshadow   C. forestall   D. foretell

Practice 9

There are 20 incomplete sentences in this practice. Below each sentence, there are 4 choices marked by letters A, B, C and D respectively. Choose the word which best completes each sentence. There is only **ONE** right answer.

1. Firing three ministers and shuffling another three might be a sign of a _____ policy shift.
   A. seismic   B. sanguine   C. sumptuous   D. sensuous

2. He lives with his family in a _____ apartment but has built a six-story mansion in his native village in Guangdong.
   A. crunchy   B. clumpy   C. ungainly   D. cramped

3. The country has a _____ social safety net. He can't remember the last time he enjoyed a proper holiday.
   A. pliant   B. pending   C. patchy   D. pervious

4. He _____ no thoughts of leaving, saying that this is his home.
   A. entertains   B. enjoys   C. envelops   D. engages

5. _____ rents and a business slowdown have forced artisan families from their old shops.
   A. Porous   B. Punishing   C. Unexacting   D. Taxing

6. The country he left was desperately poor. Only twice in his childhood was his belly fully _____.
   A. turfed   B. sated   C. glutted   D. gutted

7. Not to be outdone, Amazon, the world's largest online retailer, has unveiled plans for its own _____ into the mass e-book market.
   A. forage   B. rummage   C. foray   D. grope

8. His heart _____ as the plane lifted into the air.
   A. stumped   B. lumped   C. thumped   D. cramped

9. They prefer custardy egg tarts with Portuguese _____.
   A. prance   B. provenance   C. providence   D. precedence

10. Disappointing test results, which _____ a desired university spot, occupied her mind.
    A. prefaced   B. precluded   C. portended   D. placated

11 The Toyota Camry has long been hailed as reliability _____.

    A. representative   B. typical   C. incarnate   D. illustrative

12 HSBC, Hong Kong's most venerable bank and an early _____ of globalization, was accused of closing an account linked to illegal crowdfunding.

    A. paragon   B. predicament   C. python   D. preamble

13 The paper examines how the decision to quit gold or to _____ to it affected trade policies.

    A. cleave   B. clove   C. cursive   D. conducive

14 India will overtake China to become the most populous country sometime in 2023. Each already weighs in at 1.4bn residents. Indian population has been growing at a faster rate for decades, _____ slowing recently.

    A. while   B. even though   C. albeit   D. however

15 Like other CEOs, he is also facing strengthening economic _____, as US companies brace themselves for a possible recession.

    A. tailwinds   B. backfire   C. backlash   D. headwinds

16 Security and the drugs trade will also be discussed, as manufacturing of fentanyl, a synthetic opioid frequently involved in overdoses in America, _____ in Mexico.

    A. procreates   B. proliferates   C. pollinates   D. procrastinates

17 The candidates are scrabbling over similar territory: slashing taxes, increasing defence spending—and distancing themselves from the _____ and chaos of the Johnson era.

    A. sleaze   B. sneeze   C. squeeze   D. smaze

18 He is trying to _____ support for his plans to revive the economy and reform the health and education systems.

    A. clutter   B. sputter   C. muster   D. mutter

19 When the German government suggested recently that a suspension of Russian gas exports to Europe could cause a global financial crisis, it seemed a tad alarmist. But that dark _____ is looming ever larger.

    A. spectacle   B. stake   C. spook   D. specter

20 For a supposedly meritocratic game, football has developed a strong protectionist _____.

    A. smack   B. streak   C. steak   D. sleek

Practice 10

There are 20 incomplete sentences in this practice. Below each sentence, there are 4 choices marked by letters A, B, C and D respectively. Choose the word which best completes each sentence. There is only **ONE** right answer.

1. Abe Shinzo, the former Japanese prime minister, was pronounced dead nearly six hours after the assassination. An outpouring of _____ from world leaders demonstrated Mr Abe's imprint on geopolitics.

   A. attributes   B. tributaries   C. tributes   D. alms

2. The executive order expands access to medication abortion, contraception and emergency medical care. It also convenes volunteer lawyers to provide legal counsel and promotes _____ and public education.

   A. outreach   B. outcrop   C. offshoot   D. off-limits

3. "Revenge travelling" is a term used to describe pent-up demand for _____ after time spent at home in the pandemic.

   A. takeaways   B. anyways   C. getaways   D. walkaways

4. Inflation has ripped through low and middle-income countries. It now exceeds the official target in every big emerging economy _____ one: China.

   A. bar for   B. barring for   C. bar   D. barring from

5. The superhero film does not _____ thunderous applause: The eccentric plotting comes at the expense of narrative urgency.

   A. warrant   B. grant   C. approve   D. vet

6. Companies that bet on rare earths as a hot commodity play are canceling investments or switching attention to other metals like gold as prices of rare earths have _____ to gravity this year.

   A. subscribed   B. subjected   C. succumbed   D. resorted

7. Games and team sports are _____ under the classification of "recreation".

   A. consumed   B. assumed   C. subsumed   D. presumed

8. Floods are striking Australia with increasing ferocity. As waters subside, residents face a difficult choice: leave, or prepare for yet more _____.

   A. innuendos   B. insinuations   C. inundations   D. implosions

9. The outcome of the election remains _____.

A. doubtful   B. delightful   C. conceited   D. amenable

10 The dispute was settled without _____ to law.
A. lieu   B. litany   C. recourse   D. concourse

11 The painting had just been stolen in real life and the joke for movie viewers was that Dr. Smith had been behind the _____ all along.
A. heist   B. heresy   C. heirloom   D. harassment

12 Though our funding was cut, we decided to _____ on with our work and try to finish the project on our own.
A. drag   B. linger   C. insist   D. solider

13 Britons have a positive opinion of the queen; every single age group thinks of her _____.
A. fairly   B. fanatically   C. fraternally   D. favourably

14 Efforts to reach a settlement resume today after a two-week _____.
A. hiccup   B. hitch   C. hiatus   D. hideout

15 As we're becoming more informed about what we buy, our interiors are becoming more considered. We're using fewer elements to _____ a comfortable, practical, stylish home.
A. navigate   B. conceive   C. curate   D. culminate

16 Water shortages will force farmers to let irrigated cropland turn _____.
A. wallow   B. hallow   C. fallow   D. mellow

17 As the pandemic continues to rage across the globe, some practice football games have been held to keep _____ at bay.
A. readiness   B. rareness   C. rustiness   D. rottenness

18 The odds are _____ against the Ukraine, but it would not be the first time that the country has mounted a surprise defence against a stronger opponent.
A. stocked   B. smacked   C. stacked   D. slacked

19 The country is used to sabre-rattling from its _____ neighbour, but this is the largest incursion since January.
A. covetous   B. convincing   C. ingenuous   D. compelling

20 The dollar-a-day definition of global destitution made its _____ in the bank's 1990 *World Development Report*.
A. debunk   B. debut   C. debacle   D. denigration

Practice 11

There are 20 incomplete sentences in this practice. Below each sentence, there are 4 choices marked by letters A, B, C and D respectively. Choose the word which best completes each sentence. There is only **ONE** right answer.

1. Electronic records can _____ with 80% of paper files and reduce the need for office space.

   A. dispose   B. dispense   C. deal   D. dovetail

2. With 581 medals at _____—nearly twice the number available at the most recent Olympics—the South-East Asian Games can claim in one sense to be the world's biggest sporting event.

   A. store   B. grab   C. stake   D. grasp

3. Repairs to the house had made deep _____ into their savings.

   A. inroads   B. infringement   C. encroachment   D. ramifications

4. Not all of Europe's economy is in _____. Its service sectors, especially in the sunny southern parts, are basking in the reopening of hotels and restaurants.

   A. shambles   B. sham   C. ramble   D. preamble

5. Decades of civil war had left the country resembling a _____ of warring fiefdoms.

   A. gaggle   B. gag   C. giggle   D. gurgle

6. As the number of infections surpassed 100 today, Lebanese have opted to stay home and leave the streets _____.

   A. deserted   B. dispersed   C. departed   D. defected

7. In newspaper articles she consistently _____ those in authority who overstepped their limits.

   A. upbraided   B. upended   C. usurped   D. upcycled

8. The party has once again _____ around him as its nominee for governor.

   A. coalesced   B. coerced   C. clobbered   D. cluttered

9. Thanks to a sharp rise in home-working, passenger numbers on the London Underground are likely to _____ expectations.

   A. undercut   B. underscore   C. undershoot   D. underlie

10. All things _____, the euro-zone economy is in better shape than it should be.

    A. told   B. considered   C. calculated   D. counted

11. The dollar continued to take the _____ of investors' ire over the situation in the US.

    A. side   B. advantage   C. inflammation   D. brunt

12. In the US, consumers have _____, housing starts have crashed and a double-dip recession is possible.

    A. retrenched   B. entrenched   C. retreated   D. withdrawn

13. She has been playing the best tennis of her life this year, and she is poised to _____ a hat trick if she wins French Open next month.

    A. pull off   B. put off   C. push on   D. put on

14. Right now, many people are _____ back to the stagflation of the 1970s.

    A. harking   B. evoking   C. stretching   D. rolling

15. I always keep a few thousand dollars in a separate savings account to fall back on if we ever find ourselves in a _____ financially.

    A. band   B. bind   C. bondage   D. bond

16. In America we've divided along regional, educational, religious, cultural, generational and urban/rural _____, and now the world is fragmenting in ways that often seem to mimic our own.

    A. frontiers   B. fronts   C. fringes   D. lines

17. We in the West _____ to a series of universal values about freedom, democracy and personal dignity.

    A. turn   B. refer   C. subscribe   D. cater

18. Public opinion still seems to be behind Mr. Bates at this time, much to her _____.

    A. consternation   B. constipation   C. connivance   D. countenance

19. Ms Truss's critics regard her as an oddity and a lightweight, not least for her _____ of Thatcher's legacy.

    A. invocations   B. provocations   C. convocations   D. concoctions

20. When she was just a child, she was diagnosed with diabetes and told it would _____ her dream of becoming a detective.

    A. scupper   B. scrape   C. sundry   D. sunder

Practice 12

*There are 20 incomplete sentences in this practice. Below each sentence, there are 4 choices marked by letters A, B, C and D respectively. Choose the word which best completes each sentence. There is only **ONE** right answer.*

1 There is not a _____ of truth in the report.

   A. vestige   B. vintage   C. vantage   D. visage

2 As Copenhagen gears up to host the UN climate-change _____ in December, Denmark is keen to parade its green credentials.

   A. jubilee   B. jamboree   C. carousal   D. bender

3 The weapons program of the Democratic People's Republic of Korea has _____ four of President Biden's predecessors, each of whom wielded combinations of various incentives and sanctions, ultimately failing to halt the production of nuclear warheads and missiles.

   A. vexed   B. vindicated   C. fixated   D. flexed

4 The alarming pictures on news bulletins and front pages are likely to _____ against cool-headed response from the government.

   A. mitigate   B. militate   C. militarize   D. mutate

5 A healthy project is in a constant state of _____ between bugs and feature development.

   A. triage   B. tiara   C. trance   D. truant

6 _____ a cowboy hat and speaking with a country twang, he is a real-life bull-rider.

   A. Showcasing   B. Squelching   C. Sporting   D. Sweltering

7 These data we have collected will _____ our decision-making going forward.

   A. warrant   B. justify   C. inform   D. navigate

8 President Joe Biden—eager to avoid a rise in unemployment swelling the _____ of the uninsured—duly stepped in.

   A. rank and file   B. ranking   C. ranks   D. rankers

9 Hundreds of people _____ on a district of the city where many Syrians live. The mob threw stones at homes and cars. They also ransacked shops.

   A. descended   B. ascended   C. cringed   D. fringed

10. Although retired, he remains the _____ chairman of the company.

    A. titular   B. tenure   C. adjunct   D. informal

11. Afghanistan's past four decades have _____ its inhabitants for rapid reversals of fortune.

    A. reinforced   B. bolstered   C. steeled   D. consolidated

12. Health policy is _____ in Britain, so Northern Ireland, Scotland and Wales move at a different pace.

    A. dissolved   B. devolved   C. dissolute   D. debauched

13. For the vote to be valid, a _____ of at least one-third of the voting rights of shares outstanding is required.

    A. quotation   B. quotient   C. quorum   D. qualm

14. Are too many people putting their kids in extracurricular math classes so that now your children can't get into honors courses unless they do these classes? Or is it impossible for my child now to become class _____?

    A. victorious   B. voracious   C. valedictorian   D. valediction

15. The more virulent variant of the virus is taking _____ across America.

    A. place   B. shape   C. hold   D. traction

16. These countries are where those long-term gains in health and well-being are most _____.

    A. renounced   B. announced   C. denounced   D. pronounced

17. They are accused of propping up the _____ and insurgents.

    A. deport   B. depot   C. despot   D. despondent

18. Roosevelt made his papers public of his own _____, but more recent presidents have not had a choice in the matter.

    A. violation   B. concord   C. volition   D. virulence

19. Think of a heavy work load as an exciting opportunity to push yourself, learn new skills and show your _____.

    A. mettle   B. kettle   C. nettle   D. fettle

20. That grim prognosis came in a report Tuesday from the World Bank, which warned that the grinding crisis in Ukraine, supply chain chokeholds, and dizzying rises in energy and food prices are _____ a growing toll on economies all along the income ladder.

    A. exercising   B. extracting   C. exacting   D. extolling

Practice 13

*There are 20 incomplete sentences in this practice. Below each sentence, there are 4 choices marked by letters A, B, C and D respectively. Choose the word which best completes each sentence. There is only **ONE** right answer.*

1. In some Central Asian countries, a significant chunk of the economy _____ remittances that citizens working in Russia send back home.

    A. constitutes　　　B. composes　　　C. comprises　　　D. consists

2. Import growth was sluggish because of _____ domestic demand.

    A. tepid　　　B. trepid　　　C. limpid　　　D. lucid

3. More rapid increases in living costs _____ further escalating social unrest.

    A. mean　　　B. risk　　　C. cause　　　D. trigger

4. The World Bank, founded in the shadow of World War II to help rebuild _____ economies, provides financial support to low- and middle-income nations.

    A. raged　　　B. raved　　　C. ravaged　　　D. rummaged

5. Typically, Honda insists on at least two suppliers of parts, partly to protect against any industrial action that might _____ production.

    A. cripple　　　B. crimple　　　C. crumple　　　D. crumble

6. Government protection includes _____ the impact of rising food and energy prices as well as ensuring that low-income countries have sufficient supplies of vaccines.

    A. flaunting　　　B. blunting　　　C. denting　　　D. blundering

7. The movie is an affirmation of the durability of an approach to moviemaking _____ on curiosity, democratic principles and the idea that people can speak for themselves.

    A. predicted　　　B. predicated　　　C. prefabricated　　　D. prescribed

8. As a fashion icon and a model, she emits an _____ of celebrity.

    A. aurora　　　B. antic　　　C. aura　　　D. alms

9. It was during this formative three-year period that her interest in film _____.

    A. furbished　　　B. blemished　　　C. bred　　　D. burgeoned

10. Russia's blockade of Ukraine's ports has _____ global food prices surging and exacerbated world hunger.

| A. caused | B. driven | C. triggered | D. sent |

11. In recent years, some designers have cultivated maximalism, welcomed by many as a joyful, exuberant _____ to uptight minimalism.

| A. anecdote | B. antithesis | C. antidote | D. antiseptic |

12. Public speaking still tops most people's list of biggest fears, and there have been _____ few improvements over the years.

| A. cheaply | B. preciously | C. rarely | D. precious |

13. "Climate" _____ macro, long-term trends; "weather" is what's going on outside your window.

| A. detonates | B. denominates | C. demarcate | D. denotes |

14. I bet, in a couple of years, that phrases like coworking and couch surfing and time banks are going to become a part of everyday _____.

| A. vernacular | B. exemplar | C. semblance | D. resemblance |

15. The film is _____ with interludes concerning the Wild West, animal training and child stars.

| A. sprinkled | B. showered | C. splashed | D. sweltered |

16. To strike a balance between cooling inflation and _____ recession, the ECB will probably stick to its pre-announced plan of raising rates by a modest 0.25 percentage points.

| A. containing | B. controlling | C. courting | D. curbing |

17. His efforts to steal the 2020 election _____ in the riot.

| A. came | B. manifested | C. culminated | D. culled |

18. On Monday GlaxoSmithKline will _____ off its consumer-health unit—which hawks pharmacy mainstays like toothpaste and anti-inflammatories—as a separate company, called Haleon.

| A. sell | B. take | C. run | D. spin |

19. Over the past two years vaccine-makers have proved that, with enough funding, they can _____ wonders.

| A. make | B. create | C. work | D. invent |

20. Surprisingly, it is Europe that keeps breeding private companies worth more than $1bn (the definition of a "unicorn"), _____ the downward trend in the tech industry.

| A. building | B. buoying | C. bucking | D. backing |

Practice 14

*There are 20 incomplete sentences in this practice. Below each sentence, there are 4 choices marked by letters A, B, C and D respectively. Choose the word which best completes each sentence. There is only **ONE** right answer.*

1. The survey found that higher-calorie, energy-_____ foods are the better bargain for cash-strapped shoppers.

   A. intensive   B. efficient   C. dense   D. conserving

2. Many of polyclopropanated (POP) fuels have energy densities greater than 40 megajoules per litre, which is more _____ than most widely used aviation fuels.

   A. positive   B. portent   C. potent   D. potential

3. To become commercially _____ this biofuel must be scaled up in a cost-effective manner.

   A. variable   B. verifiable   C. viable   D. veritable

4. They describe her as hard-working and dutiful, _____ rather than metropolitan.

   A. polished   B. pompous   C. provincial   D. proverbial

5. A greater threat is a _____ of the spring and summer of that year, when commodity prices soared.

   A. reprisal   B. reprise   C. reprieve   D. repetitive

6. The factory closure put the lives of thousands of workers in _____.

   A. limbo   B. jumbo   C. lump   D. fiasco

7. Competition for talent in Silicon Valley is now reaching fever _____.

   A. punch   B. patch   C. pitch   D. pouch

8. As America starts to grapple with its out-of-control spending habits, we as a nation really should _____ with our education costs.

   A. reckon   B. reconcile   C. remunerate   D. recoup

9. There are regulations _____ the use of electronic devices on board a plane while it is landing.

   A. prescribing   B. proscribing   C. conscribing   D. circumscribing

10. She had an _____ affair with her boss.

A. illegal   B. unlawful   C. illicit   D. outlawed

11 The military will _____ the document before releasing it, blacking out sections that are classified.

A. redact   B. tamper   C. doctor   D. remediate

12 The state-run financial conglomerate has been _____ by heavy weather in housing and capital markets.

A. clobbered   B. clogged   C. cloistered   D. cankered

13 The group's chief executive announced his resignation in June after a successful ten-year _____. His successor will take over a ship that is yet to be steadied.

A. stent   B. stint   C. stunt   D. skit

14 Reality always look better in slow motion. Even the most _____ events can seem like the most dramatic moment of an action film.

A. hodgepodge   B. humdrum   C. dillydallying   D. rumble-tumble

15 Travellers are returning to the air with a _____ after pandemic lockdowns.

A. vengeance   B. revenge   C. avenge   D. retribution

16 Some banks, particularly big, international ones, shy away, fearing that profiting from the poor could _____ of exploitation.

A. smell   B. smack   C. smirk   D. shirk

17 Chess has a rich history of _____ exploits—Mr Carlsen himself was a teenage prodigy.

A. precocious   B. preoccupied   C. copious   D. capricious

18 Despite East Timor's longstanding ambitions for such projects, international financing has not been _____.

A. foregone   B. foregoing   C. forthcoming   D. forlorn

19 Police _____ most of the demonstrators in a small area near the station.

A. corralled   B. collated   C. enthralled   D. foraged

20 Faced with a _____ of questions and criticism, the young girl says she "was totally and utterly stressed", but not surprised.

A. barrel   B. burrow   C. barrage   D. furrow

Practice 15

*There are 20 incomplete sentences in this practice. Below each sentence, there are 4 choices marked by letters A, B, C and D respectively. Choose the word which best completes each sentence. There is only **ONE** right answer.*

1. A web designer says her beliefs about marriage _____ her from creating websites for unorthodox weddings.

    A. prelude   B. preamble   C. preclude   D. pummel

2. Prosecutors allege that Mr Braun and his accomplices doctored accounts to _____ banks and other creditors.

    A. disclaim   B. dupe   C. dope   D. reclaim

3. They want to end Gome's previous, _____ expansion by closing unprofitable stores and opening new ones in a more carefully targeted way.

    A. hapless   B. haphazard   C. mishap   D. haply

4. Viewed through the _____ of 9/11, heightened security at airports is critical to deterring terrorism.

    A. axis   B. prism   C. plasma   D. pixel

5. Western policymakers _____ at the thought of getting bogged down in another bloody counter-insurgency operation in Somalia.

    A. rejoice   B. relish   C. recoil   D. retract

6. I am going to _____ the candidates at the English exam.

    A. insulate   B. insinuate   C. invigilate   D. inundate

7. Companies' verdicts on their own products can't be taken as gospel. The _____ is on scientists, regulators and public-health agencies to fill in the gaps in knowledge.

    A. omen   B. levy   C. onus   D. adage

8. "The world's factory", an _____ often applied to the country, is a designation that now makes some businesses nervous.

    A. epitome   B. epithet   C. epiphany   D. epitaph

9. Australia's central bank said that King Charles Ⅲ would not _____ on the country's new five-dollar

note. A motif honouring Aboriginal culture will take the king's place.

   A. profile　　　　B. portray　　　　C. feature　　　　D. delineate

10. On February 1st the country's security services raided the home of a well-known oligarch—earning _____ from the commission for taking the issue of graft seriously.

   A. plunders　　　B. plaudits　　　C. pundits　　　D. ponders

11. She bears a/an _____ resemblance to her best friend.

   A. cunning　　　B. canny　　　C. uncanny　　　D. conundrum

12. South Africans are tired of homilies from a president who has tarnished his own reformist _____.

   A. credits　　　B. credulity　　　C. credentials　　　D. creed

13. The _____ of South Sudan from the rest of the country was going to be a messy divorce.

   A. cessation　　　B. cession　　　C. secession　　　D. session

14. He maintained a _____, yearslong relationship with his coach.

   A. congenital　　　B. congenial　　　C. amicable　　　D. hereditary

15. Nvidia, an American chip designer, is the _____ seller of shovels in a gold rush. Its share price ran up in 2016 as interest in Bitcoin and artificial intelligence created new demand for its products.

   A. commensurate　　　B. consumable　　　C. consummate　　　D. consolable

16. Just when it seemed life was going well, she was _____ by a devastating illness.

   A. blindfolded　　　B. blindsided　　　C. sidelined　　　D. sidestepped

17. He has parroted the committee's talking points in the past about how the expansion of NATO _____ the country's attack on its neighboring country.

   A. dictated　　　B. warranted　　　C. informed　　　D. underlined

18. McKinsey is reportedly planning to lay off 2,000 staff, in one of its biggest-ever _____.

   A. mulls　　　B. culls　　　C. dulls　　　D. nulls

19. It would be wrong for a national leader to _____ on all the pledges he or she makes to avoid conflict.

   A. renegade　　　B. renege　　　C. invalidate　　　D. negate

20. The police believe the suspect was planning to _____ from Hong Kong by sea.

   A. abstain　　　B. hail　　　C. abscond　　　D. refrain

Practice 16

*There are 20 incomplete sentences in this practice. Below each sentence, there are 4 choices marked by letters A, B, C and D respectively. Choose the word which best completes each sentence. There is only **ONE** right answer.*

1 Corruption in public life is _____ evidence of the absence of the rule of law.

　A. palatable　　B. potable　　C. palpable　　D. pliable

2 The crisis has reached such a force that it renders the existing resolution mechanisms _____.

　A. defect　　B. disinfect　　C. defunct　　D. disaffected

3 A New York resident for over 30 years, the Oscar-winning composer has been convalescing in Japan since last November because of a diagnosis of rectal cancer, discovered just after he went into _____ after several years of treatment for throat cancer.

　A. admission　　B. permission　　C. submission　　D. remission

4 It took a combination of _____ and desperate pleas to local officials to get my wife to a hospital for a prenatal checkup.

　A. blister　　B. bluster　　C. blush　　D. blemish

5 Many people are struggling to even book a plane ticket, _____ by high prices and a lack of direct flights.

　A. stoked　　B. slammed　　C. stymied　　D. swirled

6 *The Wager*, published this week, takes its name from a British frigate that _____ off the coast of Patagonia in 1741.

　A. found　　B. founded　　C. foundered　　D. floundered

7 Some mushrooms look _____ but are in fact poisonous.

　A. innocuous　　B. nocturnal　　C. diurnal　　D. immaculate

8 EU energy ministers agreed to a cap on gas prices after weeks of disagreement. Germany had opposed the cap, but _____.

　A. rebutted　　B. rebuked　　C. relented　　D. refrained

9 Lionel Messi, widely considered the best player in the world in recent years, has at last secured a prize at the FIFA World Cup that had long _____ him.

　A. elicited　　B. eluded　　C. excluded　　D. exalted

10 He claimed that he never meant to fool anyone—he just couldn't resist the praise and _____ of the roaring crowd.

　A. adulteration　　B. alteration　　C. adulation　　D. aberration

11. Consumers tend to reward companies that show consistency in sticking to principles, rather than just _____ to the latest fad.

    A. pampering   B. pandering   C. pondering   D. portending

12. The shares of companies that pulled out of the country soon after it invaded its neighboring country outperformed those of companies that _____, or chose to stay.

    A. doodled   B. drooled   C. dawdled   D. dwindled

13. Designed to provide Shanghai with meat whose _____ it could trust, this facility was one of the three biggest slaughter houses in the world.

    A. providence   B. provenance   C. precedence   D. prevalence

14. As she presided over a shrinking empire, _____ stability and continuity was arguably her most essential job as sovereign.

    A. profiling   B. precipitating   C. precluding   D. projecting

15. The boxy utility vehicles, which have four-wheel drive and the ground clearance to crawl over rocks and _____ streams, matched the unfussy capability of a monarch who trained in driving and maintaining military vehicles with the Auxiliary Territorial Service at the end of World War II.

    A. forge   B. forage   C. ford   D. fjord

16. Elizabeth was an 18-year-old princess when she received her first beloved corgi, Susan, the _____ of all her corgis (and dorgis, after a dachshund made its way into the lineage) to come.

    A. progenitor   B. posterity   C. proprietor   D. propensity

17. Although brooches have pretty much fallen out of favor, they remained a _____ of her wardrobe for decades.

    A. fitting   B. fixture   C. furbish   D. burnish

18. Nothing that the princess wore was a mistake. Everything was _____ and meticulously planned according to occasion, duty, hosts, guests, custom and formality.

    A. frantically   B. fanatically   C. fiendishly   D. forensically

19. Local residents say the tourists—who tend to travel in groups of two dozen or more—are too noisy, are snarling traffic and are _____ public spaces by squatting and dining on boxed lunches outdoors.

    A. blinding   B. blighting   C. brandishing   D. belying

20. For a period of time, the older generation has generally regarded the majority of post-80s or 90s youth as a spoiled generation, who often indulge themselves in social networks, _____ consumption and hyper-individualism.

    A. confidential   B. contemptuous   C. conspicuous   D. condescending

第 3 章
词汇替换应试三原则

原则 1："厘清结构找逻辑"

厘清句子结构，分析句子整体逻辑脉络。基础语法能力是核心，思维逻辑习惯是关键！如果连基本句子结构都搞不清，怎么能知道哪个词可以上演"狸猫换太子"的戏码呢？

示例 ❶

Rich city kids have unfair advantages: Government spending on schools is tilted towards cities, and free education ends after the age of 15.

A. skewed　　　　　B. gravitated　　　　　C. weighting　　　　　D. inclined

解题思路

词汇量大的读者可以直接关注词组 tilt sth. towards…/be tilted towards…，意思为：使……向……倾斜；青睐……；倾向于选择……（to cause something to lean or slope slightly toward someone, something, or some direction；to favor choosing someone or something）。词汇量小的读者就要分析全句句意：经济条件好的城市里的孩子拥有不公平的优势：财政教育支出向城市 ＿＿＿＿，而免费教育只提供到 15 周岁。此处梳理出"倾斜"的含义并不困难。

选项分析

* 选项 A

词组 **be skewed (towards somebody/something)** 的意思为：以某种或许不正确或不公平的方式向某个群体或地方倾斜（directed towards a particular group, place, etc. in a way that may not be accurate or fair），与本题目语义完全吻合，是正确答案。

* 选项 B

词组（主语是 sb.）**gravitate towards…**（人）受……吸引；倾向于选择……（to be attracted to or move toward something），采用的是主动语态，没有 be gravitated towards 的用法，因此该选项是错误的。有关 gravitate towards 词组使用的更多案例如下：

例句 1：With a growing demand, consumers are likely to gravitate toward the newest smart phone models.
　　　　随着需求量的增长，消费者很可能倾向于选择最新款智能手机。

例句 2：The rich around the world tend to gravitate to the same status symbols: mansions, yachts, art, private jets and wine.
　　　　世界各地的富豪倾向于选择同样的彰显身份的象征：豪宅、游艇、艺术品、私人飞机和葡萄酒。

例句 3: When investing in stocks, we assume that, over time, people will gravitate toward the best companies.

我们认为，随着时间的推移，人们投资股市时会倾向于选择最优秀的公司。

* 选项 C

词组 **be weighted in favour of/towards sb./sth.** 的意思为：以一种可能会带来优势或劣势的方式组织安排某事；向……倾斜（to organize something in a way that is likely to produce an advantage or disadvantage），而选项 B 构成的词组 be weighting towards... 必须改为 be weighted towards... 才是正确的。

* 选项 D

词组 **be inclined to do sth.** 的意思是：有……倾向；很可能做某事（tending to do sth; likely to do sth.），英文中不存在 be inclined towards... 的搭配，因此是错误的。

> 示例 ❷
>
> The New York city recorded its worst-ever air quality as smoke from wildfires in central Canada <u>enveloped</u> the region in hazy smog.
>
> A. encircled　　　B. cordoned　　　C. corralled　　　D. shrouded

解题思路

词汇量大的读者可以直接关注词组 envelop sb./sth. (in sth.)，意思为：包住；裹住；盖住；将……笼罩在……之中（to wrap sb./sth. up or cover them or it completely）。词汇量小的读者就要分析全句句意：加拿大中部野火产生的烟雾将纽约市 _____ 在雾霾之中，该市的空气质量创下有史以来最差纪录。由此不难推断，需要替换的词应该包含"笼罩"之意。

选项分析

* 选项 A

encircle 的用法为：~ sb./sth.，意思为：环绕；围绕；包围（to surround sb./sth. completely in a circle），强调"环绕、包围"而非烟雾对城市的"全方位笼罩"，不符合语境，直接排除。

* 选项 B

cordon 的用法为：~ sth. off，意思为：设置警戒线将……围起，封锁（If people in authority, such as the police, cordon off a building or area, they put something around it in order to stop people from entering it.），与本题目语义不符，直接排除。

* 选项 C

corral 的用法为：~ sth.，意思为：把（马或牛）赶入围栏（或关进畜栏）（to force horses or cows into a corral）；~ sb.，意思为：把（一群人）集中起来关在一起（to gather a group of people together and keep them in a particular place）。该选项与本题目语义不符，直接排除。

* 选项 D

shroud 的用法为：~ sth. in sth.，意思为：覆盖；隐藏；遮蔽（to hide something by covering or surrounding it），与本题目语义吻合且符合词组搭配习惯，是正确选项。

示例 3

The bank warned that rising borrowing costs in rich countries posed an additional <u>challenge</u> for the world's poorest economies.

A. whirlwind　　　B. headwind　　　C. tailwind　　　D. leeward

解题思路

该题目可直接关注词组 pose a challenge for sb., 意思为：对……构成挑战。该句句意为：该银行警告称，富裕国家的借贷成本上升给世界上最贫穷的经济体带来了额外的挑战。正确选项要带有"挑战、威胁"等含义。

选项分析

* 选项 A

whirlwind 的词义为：旋风；旋流（a very strong wind that moves very fast in a spinning movement and causes a lot of damage）；一片忙乱（a situation or series of events where a lot of things happen very quickly），不符合本题目语义，直接排除。

* 选项 B

headwind 的词义为：逆风；顶风（a wind that is blowing towards a person or vehicle, so that it is blowing from the direction in which the person or vehicle is moving），引申指（形成）阻力，与"（构成）挑战"意思接近，是正确选项。

* 选项 C

tailwind 的词义为：顺风（a wind that blows from behind a moving vehicle, a runner, etc.），是 headwind 的反义词，不符合本题目语义，直接排除。

* 选项 D

leeward 的词义为：背风面；下风（the side or direction that is sheltered from the wind），不符合本题目语义，直接排除。

原则 2："语义排除巧提速"

根据句子的具体语境，从语义角度排除一些干扰选项。出题者的心思请别猜，当初出题目时人家也是绞尽脑汁想出干扰项的，您需要做的就是跟出题者做个心理逆向推理游戏，难道这不好玩吗？

示例 1

Emerging market and developing economies today are struggling just to cope—deprived of the <u>wherewithal</u> needed to create jobs and deliver essential services to their most vulnerable citizens, the report said.

A. approach　　　B. conception　　　C. funds　　　D. stature

解题思路

wherewithal 对绝大多数读者而言都是一个生僻词，不过在做词汇替换题目时可以根据上下文推测此处的大致含义或逻辑，语义不符合语境或逻辑的选项可直接排除。本句句意为：报告称，如今的新兴市场和发展中经济体只是在苦苦支撑，它们被剥夺了创造就业机会和向最弱势公民提供基本服务所需要的_____。从语义和逻辑角度来看，这些国家或地区经济都陷入了困境，造成的结果就是没有财力（资金）来做什么事情，因此空缺处的含义应该是"资源、资金等"。wherewithal 的常见表达为 the ~ (to do sth.)，意为（做某事的）所需资金，必要的设备，所需技术（the money, things or skill that you need in order to be able to do sth.）。

选项分析

* 选项 A

approach 的词义为：（待人接物或思考问题的）方式，方法，态度（a way of dealing with sb./sth.; a way of doing or thinking about sth. such as a problem or a task），与本题目语境不符，直接排除。

* 选项 B

conception 的词义为：构思；构想；设想（the process of forming an idea or a plan），与本题目语境不符，直接排除。

* 选项 C

fund 的词义为：资金；现款（money that is available to be spent），完全符合本题目语境，是正确答案。

* 选项 D

stature 的词义为：声望；名望（the importance and respect that a person has because of their ability and achievements），与本题目语境不符，直接排除。

示例 ❷

She is part of a phenomenon attracting growing attention in the city: young people <u>leaving</u> high-pressure, prestigious white-collar jobs for manual labor.

A. supplanting　　　B. substituting　　　C. replacing　　　D. trading

解题思路

词组积累较多的读者可能会直接找到测试的核心为 leave A for B，本题目语境下的意思为：辞掉某种工作或行业而选择了新的工作或行业（to quit or abandon one's job or career to take up a different job, company, or kind of career；如：He left a lucrative marketing career for a chance to act on Broadway.）。全句句意为：一种现象正在该市引起越来越多的关注，她正是其中一员：年轻人辞掉压力大、地位高的白领工作，选择去干体力活。题目考查点在于"以 A 代替 B 或将 A 替换为 B"的正确表达方式。

选项分析

* 选项 A

supplant 的用法为：supplant sb./sth. 或被动语态 be supplanted by，意为取代，替代（尤指年老者或落后于时代的事物）（to take the place of sb./sth., especially sb./sth. older or less modern），没有 supplant A for B 的搭配，直接排除。

* 选项 B

substitute 的常用搭配为：substitute A for B，即用 A 代替 B。

例句：You can substitute oil for butter in this recipe.

这道菜中你可以用食用油代替黄油。

A substitutes for B，即 A 取代 B。

例句：Computers can't substitute for human interaction.

计算机不可能取代人类互动。

substitute A with B，即用 B 来代替 A。

例句：I took out the words "he" and "his" and substituted them with "they" and "their".

我删除了"he"和"his"，替换成了"they"和"their"。

本题目是放弃 A 而选择 B，如果选用 substitute 的话，应该是 substitute B for A，否则语义恰恰相反，是错误选项，直接排除。

* 选项 C

replace 的常用搭配为：replace sth./sb. 代替；取代（to take the place of something, or to put something or someone in the place of something or someone else）。

例句：Tourism has replaced agriculture as the nation's main industry.

旅游业已经取代农业成为这个国家的主要产业。

replace A with B 与 substitute A with B 同义。

例句：The factory replaced most of its workers with robots.

这家工厂用机器人取代了大多数工人。

英文中没有 replace A for B 的搭配，因此是错误选项，直接排除。

* 选项 D

trade A for B 的意思是"将 A 换成 B 或拿 A 换取 B"，如：trade my office desk for a conference table（将咖啡桌换成会议桌）；trade power for money（权钱交易）。该选项从语义和词组搭配上都与题目基本吻合，是正确答案。

> **示例 ❸**
>
> Long working hours and domineering managers are common. The economy is slowing, dimming the prospect of <u>upward mobility</u> for a generation that has known only explosive growth.
>
> A. social climbing　　B. vertical mobility　　C. social mobility　　D. an achieved status

解题思路

词组积累较多的读者应该立刻明白 upward mobility 的含义，即社会地位和经济地位上升的流动性（movement or the ability to move to a higher social class）。从这个语义上去找同义词组即可。本题目句意为：工作时间长和上司霸道专横很常见。经济正在放缓，让以前只知道爆炸式经济增长的这代人实现向上流动的前景变得黯淡。

选项分析

* 选项 A

social climbing 这个词组容易让人望文生义，词典上也明确标注是 disapproving，即贬义词。这个词组的含义是：通过与更高社会阶层人士套近乎、讨好巴结而尽力提高自己的社会地位（the act of trying to improve your social position by being very friendly to people from a higher social class）。该选项与题目语境不符，直接排除。

* 选项 B

vertical mobility 的意思是"纵向社会流动"，包含了"向上和向下流动"两层含义（Vertical mobility refers to the movement from one level on the social hierarchy to another. It involves either "upward mobility" or "downward mobility."），因此，该选项与 upward mobility 不能直接画等号，直接排除。

* 选项 C

social mobility 与 vertical mobility 相同，都包含了"向上和向下流动"两层含义（Social mobility is the movement of individuals, families, or groups through a system of social hierarchy or stratification.），因此，该选项与 upward mobility 不能直接画等号，直接排除。

* 选项 D

achieved status 的意思是"自致地位"，即通过自己的成就努力争取获得的社会地位，或者指一个人在一生中通过知识、能力、技巧等取得的结果（An achieved status is one that is acquired on the basis of merit; it is a position that is earned or chosen and reflects a person's skills, abilities, and efforts.），由此可以判断，该选项与 upward mobility 最为接近，是正确答案。

此外，与 achieved status 相对的表达是 ascribed status（先赋地位），即通过承袭得到的社会地位，而在某些社会中，也指一个人从出生起就被赋予无法改变的社会地位（An ascribed status is not earned, but rather is something people are either born with or had no control over.）。

原则3："细微差别看搭配"

有些词的语义只有细微差别,需要平时积累并在考试时仔细辨别,同时词组搭配也至关重要。练就火眼金睛当然离不开平时阅读时的细心积累,否则,您不就是现场随意搭配吗?

示例 1

Rather than trying even harder to compete, some young people find the traditionally less <u>coveted</u> career route attractive.

A. hankered　　B. yearned　　C. craved　　D. cherished

解题思路

词组积累较多的读者应该知道 covet 是及物动词,词义为:渴望;贪求(尤指别人的东西);觊觎(to want sth. very much, especially sth. that belongs to sb. else)。替换词也必须是带有近似含义的及物动词。本题目句意为:有些年轻人不愿更积极努力地参与竞争,而是发现传统上不那么令人垂涎的职业路径富有吸引力。在选择替换词时既要把握词义的细微差别,也要确保搭配合理、语法正确。

选项分析

* 选项 A

hanker 是不及物动词,首先即可排除;该单词的常用搭配是:hanker after/for sth. 渴望,热切希望拥有(尤指无法得到或不该拥有的东西)(to have a strong wish for something, especially if you cannot or should not have it)。

* 选项 B

yearn 是不及物动词,首先即可排除;该单词的常用搭配是:yearn for sth./yearn to do sth. 渴望(to wish very strongly, especially for something that you cannot have or something that is very difficult to have)。

* 选项 C

crave 是及物动词,词义为:渴望,切盼,渴求(to have a very strong feeling of wanting something),与 covet 可以替换使用,是正确选项。

* 选项 D

cherish 是及物动词,词义为:珍爱;钟爱;爱护(to love sb./sth. very much and want to protect them or it),即本身已经拥有而不是渴求拥有,这与本题目不符,直接排除。

示例 2

She developed anxiety from her heavy workload, but was too busy to <u>decompress</u>.

A. unfurl　　B. unleash　　C. uncoil　　D. unwind

解题思路

本题目句意清晰：繁重的工作让她患上了焦虑症，但又忙得无暇减压。正确选项应该带有"减压、放松"的含义。

选项分析

* 选项 A

unfurl 的词义为：（使卷紧的东西）打开，展开（When sth. that is curled or rolled tightly unfurls, or you unfurl it, it opens），与本题目语义不符，直接排除。

* 选项 B

unleash 的搭配为 unleash sth. (on/upon sb./sth.)，词义为：发泄；突然释放；使爆发（to suddenly let a strong force, emotion, etc. be felt or have an effect），与本题目语义不符，直接排除。

* 选项 C

uncoil 的词义为：（使盘卷的东西）展开，打开；拉直（to become or make sth. straight after it has been wound or twisted round in a circle），与本题目语义不符，直接排除。

* 选项 D

unwind 除了有"解开，打开，松开（卷绕之物）"（to undo sth. that has been wrapped into a ball or around sth.）的词义之外，还有"放松，轻松"（to stop worrying or thinking about problems and start to relax）的词义，这与本题目语义吻合，是正确选项。

示例 ❸

The glut of college graduates has started to flatten wages for that group.

A. galore　　　　B. surfeit　　　　C. flood　　　　D. horde

解题思路

本题目句意清晰：大学毕业生过剩已开始压低该群体的工资。正确选项应该带有"过剩"的含义并且符合语法规则。

选项分析

* 选项 A

galore 是形容词，而本题目需要一个名词进行替换，可直接排除。galore 的词义为：大量；很多（in large quantities），做后置定语，如：lend money galore（出借大量的资金）、cite examples galore（引用大量的例子）、consultations galore（大量的磋商）等。

* 选项 B

a surfeit of sth. 的意思是：过量（an amount that is too large），从语义和语法上都与本题目吻合，是正确选项。

* 选项 C

a flood of sb./sth. 的意思是：大批、大量（的人或事物）（a very large number of things or people that appear at the same time），与本题目中"过多"的含义不符，直接排除。

* 选项 D

a horde of sb. 的意思是一大群人（a large crowd of people），与本题目中"过多"的含义不符，直接排除。

> **总结**
>
> 这种考试题虽然名义上是词汇替换，实则考查了英文句法结构、逻辑分析能力、干扰排除技巧和词组搭配积累。考生只有不断通过广泛而有效的阅读才能"兵来将挡，水来土掩"，真正做到胸有成竹！

第4章
词汇替换训练题库

Practice 1

There are 20 sentences in this practice. In each of them one word is underlined, and below each sentence, there are 4 choices marked by letters A, B, C and D respectively. Choose the word that can replace the underlined part without causing any grammatical error or changing the basic meaning of the sentence. There is only **ONE** right answer.

1. Emerging nations will experience the harshest setback, with the blows from the pandemic still reverberating.

   A. resonating   B. resounding   C. lingering   D. leveraging

2. She calls mahjong a superficial, pointless game, and was a bit taken aback to hear her own 29-year-old daughter had taken it up.

   A. frolicsome   B. frisky   C. facetious   D. frivolous

3. The film isn't so much an allegory or fantasy as a witty philosophical speculation on some elemental human issues.

   A. fable   B. metaphor   C. allegation   D. preamble

4. Even as the plot grows more ominous, the film director maintains a lightness of touch and a visual playfulness that keeps the movie securely in the realm of pop pleasure.

   A. portentous   B. pretentious   C. preposterous   D. presumptive

5. For decades, Walt Disney has been striving to reimagine the typical amusement park as a theme park, an idealized salute to America's past and a nod to an experimental vision for its future.

   A. revise   B. retool   C. rework   D. redefine

6. Derelict urban sites have been cleared and tidied into new public spaces. Brutalist structures associated with the Yugoslav era have been reimagined as exhibition venues.

   A. Decrepit   B. Discreditable   C. Discreet   D. Immaculate

7. He expertly unpicked the significant features of each painting.

   A. unshackled   B. unraveled   C. unloaded   D. undone

8. He made an oblique reference so that we couldn't figure out what he really meant.

   A. diagonal   B. slanted   C. implicit   D. grotesque

9 She is not a fluent public speaker while he is polished, albeit sometimes prickly.

  A. spiky   B. spiny   C. thorny   D. wiry

10 Overall, the storyline is intriguing, if sometimes rambling.

  A. confused B. riveting C. compounded D. contraband

11 The messiness might provide some reassurance that the sovereign wealth funds hardly seem to have nefarious agendas.

  A. nebulous B. tenuous C. reprehensible D. apprehensible

12 Europe's feuding leaders could hash out a deal to put the single currency and the zone's banking system on a sustainable footing.

  A. thrash out B. hammer C. churn out D. shush

13 She's a slow and methodical worker, and her drawings reflect the extra care she takes.

  A. organized B. mechanical C. systemic D. maculate

14 The committee's aim has plainly been to sketch out the contours of a potential federal prosecution of Mr Trump.

  A. silhouette B. outline C. periphery D. fringe

15 Thursday's hearing will dissect the former president's inaction over the course of the day.

  A. dichotomize B. confect C. bisect D. parse

16 Geek culture has lost some of its lustre in the past three years, thanks to a glut of films set within the Marvel Cinematic Universe.

  A. glutton B. viscosity C. gluten D. superfluity

17 The firm is cagey about what, exactly, it will do with these data, and insists that it will not violate anyone's privacy.

  A. reticent B. renascent C. recalcitrant D. refractory

18 The committee will have to decide if there is enough criminal culpability to indict Mr Trump.

  A. arraign B. arrange C. allege D. assert

19 The upshot was that Asia swapped dependence on external financing for dependence on external demand.

  A. outcome B. cause C. highlight D. takeaway

20 Tech stocks keep tanking, and yet unicorns are born every day.

  A. fueling B. buoying C. folding D. unfolding

Practice 2

*There are 20 sentences in this practice. In each of them one word is underlined, and below each sentence, there are 4 choices marked by letters A, B, C and D respectively. Choose the word that can replace the underlined part without causing any grammatical error or changing the basic meaning of the sentence. There is only **ONE** right answer.*

1. Her conspiratorial comments and sly winks make her obnoxiously smug.
   A. slog   B. snob   C. snub   D. self-important

2. The passage recapitulates the version he offers in his prologue.
   A. reveals   B. divulges   C. reviews   D. discloses

3. His speech was received with rapture by his supporters.
   A. raptor   B. elation   C. rupture   D. elevation

4. After putting in the hard work of patience and penitence, the month is finished off with optimism.
   A. repentance   B. reparation   C. reticence   D. retribution

5. On Monday, when the leader went on television with his Green Book in hand, his diatribe was incoherent but familiar.
   A. tirade   B. bluster   C. charade   D. blush

6. I heard some of the audience heckle me with loud whistles.
   A. barrack   B. harangue   C. berate   D. botch

7. When I signed on as a candidate, I had no idea I'd have to pander to every group out there to gain their support.
   A. ponder   B. hanker   C. cater   D. crater

8. Banks are already becoming more beholden to national governments as the latter extend their economic lifelines.
   A. beleaguered   B. bewildered   C. indebted   D. genteel

9. Some were well behaved, while others were impudent.
   A. imprudent   B. brash   C. indolent   D. brazen

10. In fact, the real threat comes from overly chummy links between a state and its multinationals.
    A. congenial   B. congenital   C. cunning   D. crafty

53

11. Plans for a new airport have <u>foundered</u> because of budget cuts.

    A. floundered   B. flopped   C. pranced   D. sundered

12. If many companies are reluctant to leave, the local government is just as <u>loath</u> to lose the companies and their tax revenue.

    A. loathe   B. louche   C. disincentive   D. disinclined

13. While WASP-96b is highly unlikely to be home to anything living, using the same techniques could reveal whether smaller, rocky worlds orbiting other stars are <u>inhabitable</u>.

    A. habitable   B. inhospitable   C. unlivable   D. unviable

14. What he did at the meeting <u>raised his boss's hackles</u>.

    A. riled his boss   B. rattled his boss   C. rumbled his boss   D. rambled his boss

15. He returned to Washington in the late 1970s and becomes an <u>obsequious</u> academic, finally hammered into submission.

    A. ingratiating   B. reverent   C. deferential   D. proud

16. Quite suddenly, after the long search for a quantum mechanics, there existed two competing and seemingly <u>antithetical</u> versions.

    A. antiseptic   B. unequivocal   C. axiomatic   D. opposite

17. While Mr. Biden and lawmakers tried to build support for the bill by describing the chips found in everything from refrigerators to thermostats to cars as the "oil" of the 21st century, the phrase was already <u>hackneyed</u> three decades ago.

    A. stale   B. tacky   C. baleful   D. baneful

18. African countries struggle with <u>unenviable</u> decisions about how to prioritise COVID-19 vaccinations relative to perennial needs, such as jabs against tetanus and measles.

    A. undesirable   B. underwhelming   C. unsavoury   D. unassuming

19. The method has long been used by horticulturalists to propagate plants, particularly <u>finicky</u> flora like orchids.

    A. faddy   B. pedantic   C. fastidious   D. demanding

20. Listening to his West Point address, I hear <u>exasperation</u> in his voice and the implied words: "Enough already."

    A. vexation   B. fixation   C. exacerbation   D. exaltation

Practice 3

There are 20 sentences in this practice. In each of them one word is underlined, and below each sentence, there are 4 choices marked by letters A, B, C and D respectively. Choose the word that can replace the underlined part without causing any grammatical error or changing the basic meaning of the sentence. There is only **ONE** right answer.

1 America has so far evinced a more laissez-faire approach towards AI regulation than Britain or the EU.

A. evoked　　　B. eluded　　　C. evaded　　　D. exuded

2 Netflix moved online its soirée planned for Friday evening to avoid a ruckus.

A. caucus　　　B. circus　　　C. commotion　　　D. concoction

3 A church representative endorsed the prosecution and condemned the exhibition as blasphemous.

A. prolific　　　B. profane　　　C. pernicious　　　D. pugnacious

4 The DPRK has raised tensions dramatically in Asia by conducting its second nuclear test, earning the opprobrium of the international community.

A. approval　　　B. oppression　　　C. censure　　　D. approbation

5 The rally is forcing some contrarian investors, who bet on a price fall due to large inventories, to capitulate.

A. capitalize　　　B. succumb　　　C. capsize　　　D. sunder

6 He viewed us with a studied indifference.

A. learned　　　B. deliberate　　　C. studious　　　D. guarded

7 Enhancing his reputation for pragmatism, the vice-chancellor of Germany muted his Green beliefs to reignite idled coal-fired power stations.

A. deferred　　　B. mothballed　　　C. insulated　　　D. enclosed

8 The unprepossessing town of Ashford might soon become the biggest Shared Space scheme in the world.

A. uninviting　　　B. palatable　　　C. preposterous　　　D. unpretentious

9 There was always, in her conversation, the same odd mixture of audacity and puerility.

A. purity　　　B. puberty　　　C. immaturity　　　D. immaculacy

10 Indeed, the chaos might provide some reassurance that the sovereign wealth funds hardly seem to have nefarious agendas.

A. emollient　　　B. patronizing　　　C. supercilious　　　D. hidden

11. The prospect of slower economic expansion alongside persistent inflation is leading to a febrile mood in markets.

    A. feverish   B. delirious   C. salacious   D. slinky

12. We carried on talking and finished the meal but his nonchalance made me feel desolate, a little dead.

    A. impassiveness   B. impasse   C. impatience   D. reticence

13. The media organization has shrugged off repeated demonstrations that its scoring system, which rests on unverified data, can be falsified.

    A. gamed   B. tamed   C. tampered   D. tapered

14. Mr Trump's latest anti-democratic diatribe elicited widespread condemnation—but silence from senior Republicans.

    A. tirade   B. tiara   C. triage   D. trance

15. Lawmakers spurned a reform bill championed by a senator for West Virginia.

    A. spurred   B. scorned   C. sparred   D. scarred

16. The costs of many consumer goods are falling as supply-chain issues melt away. Property prices are also weakening, weighed down by elevated interest rates. But relief at any slowdown in inflation will be circumscribed.

    A. circumvented   B. demarcated   C. delineated   D. restricted

17. Unattributed sources told two Belgian media outlets that Ms Kaili had been suborned by Qatar.

    A. subordinated   B. bribed   C. confiscated   D. doped

18. A combination of the Democratic People's Republic of Korea's increasingly brazen missile programme and the conflict between Russia and Ukraine have convinced the Japanese that they can no longer afford to skimp on security.

    A. skip   B. stint   C. stunt   D. swipe

19. So far, the committee hasn't weighed in on the matter, putting advertisers in a dilemma as they put finishing touches on their Olympics plans.

    A. quandary   B. quarry   C. squander   D. squash

20. Those who want to keep Title 42 in place say scrapping it will see even more illicit border-crossings, overwhelming America's already-frazzled asylum system.

    A. frizzled   B. muzzled   C. floundered   D. frayed

Practice 4

There are 20 sentences in this practice. In each of them one word is underlined, and below each sentence, there are 4 choices marked by letters A, B, C and D respectively. Choose the word that can replace the underlined part without causing any grammatical error or changing the basic meaning of the sentence. There is only **ONE** right answer.

1. Nefarious forces had tried to piggyback off the frustrated young people to destabilize the country.
   A. Nonferrous   B. Wicked   C. Nebulous   D. Wacky

2. They went to different universities and their relationship just faded.
   A. sizzled out   B. fizzled out   C. frazzled out   D. muzzled out

3. Officials anticipate a surge of illegal border crossings. Thousands of migrants are already on the move; many have been waiting in northern Mexico for Title 42 to expire.
   A. falter   B. lapse   C. relapse   D. founder

4. Research findings belie the notion that bacteria are simple, silent loners.
   A. betray   B. underlie   C. disprove   D. defy

5. Without a reliable flow of information, businesses and investors from outside the country are left to speculate on just how long it will take for the economy to recover.
   A. Notwithstanding   B. Except   C. Absent   D. Abstaining

6. Underreporting Covid-related fatalities is not unique to India, but the country remains especially inscrutable.
   A. unfathomable   B. uncompanionable   C. impassable   D. unscathed

7. Neither the tariffs nor the export controls have had an appreciable negative effect on our economy.
   A. apprehensive   B. reprehensible   C. palpable   D. plausible

8. Leaders, especially in the United States, believed that more or less free trade would make the world more amenable to our political values and safer for us as a nation.
   A. amicable   B. amiable   C. agreeable   D. acceptable

9. He pledged to his people that he would not cede land to Russia if the countries were to broker a peace deal.
   A. conclude   B. overturn   C. concede   D. transfer

10 The subtitle of this riveting book is Mr Smith's own description of his survival technique.

A. entrancing   B. startling   C. sweltering   D. whimsical

11 Young people view him, aged 61, as a sprightly outsider shaking up Nigeria's venal, sclerotic political class.

A. rigorous   B. righteous   C. spry   D. sprite

12 Last-minute concessions had been made to disaffected groups to win their support.

A. disgruntled   B. untouched   C. untenable   D. disinterested

13 About a dozen foreign companies have concessions to develop lithium deposits, but all such contracts will now be reviewed.

A. indulgence   B. exemptions   C. franchises   D. compromises

14 The House committee investigating the Capitol riot of January 6th 2021 recommended that the Justice Department charge Donald Trump with four federal crimes. They include obstruction of justice, conspiracy to defraud the United States, aid for an insurrection and making false statements to the government.

A. insurgency   B. resuscitation   C. resurrection   D. insinuation

15 The last French spy to hold foreign streaming audiences captive was Malotru, the inscrutable protagonist of *Le Bureau*, a French-language thriller.

A. sprightly   B. enigmatic   C. unscrupulous   D. facetious

16 Jeans can send out a powerful egalitarian message, but are far more likely to be a dress deathtrap for politicians.

A. satirical   B. sartorial   C. sardonic   D. sarcastic

17 Lack of food and ammunition forced the surrender of the rebels.

A. capitulation   B. capitalization   C. decapitation   D. capitation

18 The war has merged into a global contest also aimed at this country.

A. coerced   B. coalesced   C. relapsed   D. congealed

19 Many people in the city now feel his policies have let miscreants operate without consequence.

A. malefactors   B. misfeasance   C. nonfeasance   D. misogynists

20 The jury acquitted her, but I still think she's guilty.

A. requisitioned   B. absolved   C. expropriated   D. relented

Practice 5

*There are 20 sentences in this practice. In each of them one word is underlined, and below each sentence, there are 4 choices marked by letters A, B, C and D respectively. Choose the word that can replace the underlined part without causing any grammatical error or changing the basic meaning of the sentence. There is only **ONE** right answer.*

1 Coming to work drunk put paid to her hopes of promotion.

    A. scrapped   B. scuppered   C. scraped   D. scooped

2 Retail sales in October were down; sentiment indicators for manufacturing and construction remain depressing.

    A. discouraged   B. dispirited   C. depressed   D. disenchanted

3 When asked by a reporter why he'd made such a foolhardy flight, he was ready with a pithy reply: "A man can't just sit around."

    A. patchy   B. pliable   C. terse   D. wordy

4 Athletes will run and swim but will also engage in more offbeat competitions, like obstacle racing and jet-skiing.

    A. downbeat   B. squeamish   C. unconventional   D. eccentric

5 The company refused to be interviewed, but one former employee said discrimination was rife within the company.

    A. prevailing   B. teeming   C. ruinous   D. preeminent

6 I am sure the citizens will feel sad at the rather ignominious end of this great warship.

    A. discreditable   B. dismissible   C. disillusioning   D. disparaging

7 There is a palpable sense of frustration in France with German intransigence, but senior officials dismiss all talk of a downgrade as scaremongering.

    A. insistence   B. perseverance   C. indulgence   D. noncompliance

8 The gunman somehow managed to get past the guards unnoticed.

    A. contrived   B. mulled   C. masterminded   D. mustered

9 Archaeologists still can only surmise as to the origin of Man.

    A. construe   B. deduce   C. defer   D. deplore

10 The local authorities continue to use gentle inducements, rather than force, to coax old people to accept vaccinations.

A. nudge   B. hoax   C. talk   D. prompt

11 This month, the Bank of England wrong-footed markets by declining to deliver an expected rate rise.

A. confounded   B. compounded   C. condoned   D. confirmed

12 I don't like to opine on the stock market, and again I emphasize that I have no idea what the market will do in the short term.

A. dwell on   B. focus on   C. capitalize on   D. weigh in on

13 The current wave of infections sweeping across Europe could necessitate the return of tough restrictions.

A. warrant   B. dictate   C. denote   D. denominate

14 Many observers recoil from this exaltation of a single leader.

A. adulteration   B. adulation   C. admiration   D. alteration

15 If incoming data do not show a slackening in inflation, doves' arguments may become untenable, and a rocky 2022 looms.

A. shaky   B. sketchy   C. sticky   D. shoddy

16 Just after his flight landed in New York City, he unleashed an expletive-laden tirade over the plane's public address system.

A. invective   B. grievance   C. libel   D. exclamation

17 His speech had nothing more to offer than the usual bromides about how everyone needs to work together.

A. sincerity   B. banalities   C. harangue   D. sweet nothings

18 The annual meeting of the World Economic Forum is a study in contrasts—especially between the well-heeled insiders cloistered in Davos and the billions of outsiders about whose fate they pontificate.

A. contemplate   B. deliberate   C. condescend   D. preach

19 Attendance at this year's annual conference was down by perhaps half on previous years, and companies reined in the parties and pizzazz.

A. frenzy   B. paparazzi   C. glitz   D. blitz

20 Lack of progress on the peace deal, outlined recently in a damning report written by UN-appointed observers, means the UN on Thursday is likely to vote to extend an arms embargo and asset freezes.

A. pejorative   B. derogatory   C. censorious   D. well-documented

Practice 6

*There are 20 sentences in this practice. In each of them one word is underlined, and below each sentence, there are 4 choices marked by letters A, B, C and D respectively. Choose the word that can replace the underlined part without causing any grammatical error or changing the basic meaning of the sentence. There is only **ONE** right answer.*

1. The villagers were insistent that the existing mining area should not be enlarged beyond what was given since they were not going to gain anything from this.

    A. adamant   B. admonished   C. affidavit   D. audacious

2. As chairman of the Federal Reserve, Jerome Powell prizes predictability, giving investors ample guidance to prepare them for policy changes.

    A. prefers   B. popularizes   C. puts a premium on   D. ponders over

3. When faced with injustice in society, remaining quiescent is no option for a man of integrity.

    A. acquiescent   B. acquainted   C. accustomed   D. accommodative

4. On Wednesday workers at an Apple's shop in Maryland will begin voting on whether to unionise, but Apple is not taking to the idea.

    A. taking in   B. taking a fancy to   C. reveling in   D. relishing in

5. Traditionally, the country tempers these tales of martial brilliance with more saccharine stories intended to secure popular devotion.

    A. erotic   B. sentimental   C. carnal   D. sanguine

6. He was reluctant to testify, but reportedly did not want to defy a subpoena to appear.

    A. flout   B. flounder   C. flunk   D. denote

7. Fed officials indicated Wednesday that they're ready to begin "tapering"—the process of slowly pulling back the stimulus they've provided during the pandemic.

    A. wind down its debt purchases   B. scale up its bond-buying programme
    C. buy back bonds   D. cut back debt payments

8. On Wednesday, the Fed is set to release its latest economic projections, which investors are likely to parse closely. They may be reassured if the central bank projects a path for interest rate increases that is more moderate than expected.

    A. palliate   B. pore   C. dissent   D. dissect

9. We must be fair competitors and must never denigrate other firms.

    A. negate   B. renege   C. decimate   D. slur

10 There might be currents within atheism, and atheists can argue, but schism isn't the right word.

    A. rupture   B. skepticism   C. cynicism   D. rapture

11 How much of your time goes to trivial, mundane work rather than the challenging stuff you enjoy and that your boss values?

    A. unremarkable   B. morbid   C. masochistic   D. unassuming

12 Studies show that using negative, derogatory words—even as you talk to yourself—can darken your mood as well.

    A. disparaging   B. patronizing   C. supercilious   D. pompous

13 There were no military bands, no massed crowds lining the streets, and none of the pomp and ceremony that will accompany her funeral today.

    A. celebration   B. exaltation   C. circumstance   D. observance

14 Encompassing as many musical genres as it has had members, the freewheeling ensemble's blend of free jazz, blues, swing and R&B, as well as its early embrace of electronic instruments, was avant-garde and esoteric.

    A. unfettered   B. unregulated   C. unchecked   D. untainted

15 Friedman used his polemical powers to win the commission over to his belief in an all-volunteer army.

    A. articulate   B. dialectical   C. satirical   D. amulet

16 Drawing sensible conclusions is harder still in India where national issues are all but drowned out in a cacophony of local politics.

    A. dissonance   B. symphony   C. orchestra   D. cascade

17 An EU without Britain would be more parochial and less liberal. An EU without the euro might not exist at all.

    A. insular   B. proverbial   C. parabolical   D. pariah

18 I hope that our proceedings have the correct blend of amicability and acerbity.

    A. acidity   B. celibacy   C. credulity   D. gullibility

19 His keen grey eyes, impersonal and brusque, flashed upon her half impatiently.

    A. curt   B. brisk   C. grotesque   D. crude

20 The very high traffic levels made the highway a very attractive location for businesses serving travelers, leading to the sobriquet of hot dog highway.

    A. epithet   B. alias   C. pseudonym   D. soliloquy

Practice 7

*There are 20 sentences in this practice. In each of them one word is underlined, and below each sentence, there are 4 choices marked by letters A, B, C and D respectively. Choose the word that can replace the underlined part without causing any grammatical error or changing the basic meaning of the sentence. There is only **ONE** right answer.*

1 The stock market seems unperturbed, but the situation is dicey.

    A. clingy   B. dingy   C. dodgy   D. tacky

2 In the book, he delineates covert operations by American operatives to gain technology or manufacturing techniques that would speed Washington's way.

    A. delimits   B. demarcates   C. depicts   D. conscribes

3 Occasionally, the camera would relent from the president's stolid demeanour and pan across the faces of the cadets in grey.

    A. impassive   B. inexpressible   C. ineffable   D. impassable

4 Some people believe that a broken mirror is an augury of seven years' bad luck.

    A. divination   B. prophesy   C. portent   D. precinct

5 Despite a commitment to a more open government, the public is still being kept in the dark about the inner machinations of the Cabinet.

    A. mechanisms   B. manoeuvring   C. machinery   D. workings

6 His foibles and frustrations were mercilessly dissected by the news media.

    A. faults   B. blemishes   C. blunders   D. bloomers

7 His marriage to Diana, Princess of Wales, which crumbled amid lurid tabloid headlines and mutual charges of infidelity, remains for many the defining event of his public life.

    A. melodramatic   B. lucid   C. ludicrous   D. salacious

8 An ancient activity that accounts for only 8% of world merchandise trade, agricultural trade is the most heavily distorted by misbegotten policies.

    A. half-baked   B. impetuous   C. tactless   D. inept

9 Looking around me I deplore the lack of style and elegance in most modern plays.

    A. deprecate   B. decry   C. bemoan   D. bedevil

10 As America's senate <u>backtracks</u> on a bill to decriminalise cannabis, Germany—with a potential market estimated at $16.6bn—is mulling legalisation.

    A. stands its ground   B. backfires   C. revisits   D. backpedals

11 In a country where restaurants serve snails, fast food is clearly culturally <u>aberrant</u>.

    A. deviant   B. defiant   C. abhorrent   D. opulent

12 Justice is <u>personified</u> as a goddess with her eyes covered.

    A. exemplified   B. typified   C. incarnated   D. epitomized

13 Mr. Biden did <u>allow</u> that "we still have a problem with Covid."

    A. permit   B. presume   C. assume   D. acknowledge

14 Such <u>incendiary</u> claims could easily be dismissed as the rants of a man with a grudge.

    A. flammable   B. inflammable   C. febrile   D. nebulous

15 With pomp and <u>pageantry</u>, on Saturday a 1.3km artificial waterway linking the lake to the Baltic Sea will be unveiled.

    A. circumstance   B. etiquette   C. demeanor   D. deportment

16 India is clearly taking a more <u>strident</u> approach in its engagement with its neighbor.

    A. strenuous   B. stringent   C. aggressive   D. impudent

17 Charles takes the helm of a royal family that has been rocked by a series of upheavals. He has struggled to keep <u>wayward</u> family members in line.

    A. boisterous   B. rowdy   C. willful   D. wishful

18 He will be an active king and he will probably push his <u>prerogatives</u> to the limits, but he won't go beyond them.

    A. privilege   B. license   C. derogatory   D. purgatory

19 In 2007, as financial instruments grew increasingly <u>inscrutable</u>, Mr. Jones became bearish on the whole sector.

    A. impenetrable   B. impermeable   C. impervious   D. impassable

20 Even the most disgusting cigarette packet image may become <u>palatable</u> over time, as seems to have been the case in Canada.

    A. appetizing   B. tempting   C. acceptable   D. detestable

Practice 8

*There are 20 sentences in this practice. In each of them one word is underlined, and below each sentence, there are 4 choices marked by letters A, B, C and D respectively. Choose the word that can replace the underlined part without causing any grammatical error or changing the basic meaning of the sentence. There is only **ONE** right answer.*

1 The researchers intend to study such data with an open mind, reasoning that any results may prove useful.

   A. boffins   B. saffrons   C. buffs   D. muggers

2 Since the German philosopher was driven batty by the cracking of horsemen's whips, one wonders how he would have managed in a cacophonous modern city.

   A. calamitous   B. conundrum   C. dissonant   D. decadent

3 They nodded at every banality about making sacrifices today for a better tomorrow.

   A. latitude   B. altitude   C. platitude   D. solitude

4 *The Treaty of Lisbon* is widely backed not on its merits but because its failure would risk pushing the EU into yet another interminable internal debate.

   A. intermittent   B. impertinent   C. impudent   D. incessant

5 This educational policy could be self-defeating and unrealistic.

   A. self-serving   B. self-effacing   C. counterproductive   D. counterbalancing

6 In any murder mystery film, it pays to watch the boring grey man (or woman) in the corner; quiet, unobtrusive characters can be deadly.

   A. unconstructive   B. unconvincing   C. unsuspecting   D. inconspicuous

7 The Protestant Europe and English-speaking zones have drifted away from the rest of the world cultures and now jut out like some extraneous cultural peninsula.

   A. pertinent   B. inextricable   C. irrelevant   D. inexorable

8 Britain's prime minister is engulfed in recriminations after a bungled mini-budget spooked investors.

   A. botched   B. boggled   C. bundled   D. brawled

9 Contention between rival camps at a political convention is often acrimonious.

   A. spiteful   B. compassionate   C. fiery   D. delirious

10 At every turn he is met with vitriol and condescension.

    A. acrimony   B. animosity   C. amity   D. enmity

11 An analytical, clinical approach to the problem had surprising results.

    A. surgical   B. objective   C. critical   D. subjective

12 There seemed to be a preponderance of Oriental-style dishes, perhaps understandable as many guests were from the Far East.

    A. prevalence   B. preposterousness   C. ponderance   D. provenance

13 On Friday the court will hold another hearing on the injunction.

    A. conjunction   B. interdict   C. intersection   D. adjunct

14 The government continues to fudge the issue by refusing to give exact figures.

    A. dodge   B. hedge   C. fumble   D. flounder

15 The country will get a new president, but the petulantly pugnacious sitting president has no intention of bidding farewell to power.

    A. poignant   B. truculent   C. peevish   D. crabby

16 Once one of Rwanda's richest men, Mr Kabuga is alleged to have bankrolled ethnic Hutu extremists during the genocide.

    A. cashed in on   B. capitalized on   C. financed   D. banked on

17 Yesterday the house of Lehman Brothers fell, they may think, today the head of the I. M. F. will succumb in an ignominious and shocking manner.

    A. shameful   B. sham   C. scam   D. scum

18 There is still a sense of entitlement and inertia, particularly among those who are used to benefiting from the state's largesse.

    A. munificence   B. impasse   C. démarche   D. magnitude

19 What are effective strategies to discredit rumors and correct misinformation?

    A. disgrace   B. debunk   C. dismiss   D. delimit

20 All but the most effusive sentiment about the activity must be kept at bay—hence the profusion of propaganda that has appeared on bridges, on billboards, and in 60-foot-tall flower arrangements.

    A. vociferous   B. ebullient   C. luscious   D. succulent

Practice 9

*There are 20 sentences in this practice. In each of them one word is underlined, and below each sentence, there are 4 choices marked by letters A, B, C and D respectively. Choose the word that can replace the underlined part without causing any grammatical error or changing the basic meaning of the sentence. There is only **ONE** right answer.*

1 Her straggly hair takes away from her otherwise attractive appearance.
   A. detracts   B. distracts   C. deducts   D. discredits

2 You need to overcome this deplorable mendacity, or no one will ever believe anything you say.
   A. subterfuge   B. centrifuge   C. refuge   D. deluge

3 The film is worth viewing, both for its historical import as well as for its artistry.
   A. teleport   B. importance   C. transportation   D. vantage

4 He was almost plaintive in the apology he made for his present policy.
   A. melancholic   B. repetitive   C. candid   D. callous

5 Their crackdown might have been easier to digest had they practised the moral strictures they preached.
   A. constraints   B. statures   C. scriptures   D. caricatures

6 Mr Smith, who is no stranger to legal jeopardy, appears largely unfazed.
   A. unbiased   B. unbridled   C. unruffled   D. untamed

7 What's already been laid bare is that Chelsea is unviable in its current form without the largesse of its billionaire patron, a reflection of a sport whose parlous finances would sink just about any other industry.
   A. precarious   B. petulant   C. preposterous   D. ponderous

8 A year after America's shambolic withdrawal from Afghanistan, Washington should do more to atone for its mistakes.
   A. sham   B. symbolic   C. haphazard   D. hapless

9 Irritated at being thwarted in the share-out of cabinet seats, the former prime minister has wrought havoc.
   A. Iterate   B. Irate   C. Ire   D. Tirade

10 I don't know if they are massaging the numbers—even if they need to massage the figures, the better thing to do would be to massage them within the usual time frame.

A. kneading B. doctoring C. nursing D. accommodating

11. Should politicians in the world's big three economies continue to dither, another global recession is possible.

A. ditto B. vacillate C. ditch D. tether

12. Judges said that the humanitarian group had violated legal requirements by operating outside its geographical remit.

A. permit B. purview C. proxy D. precinct

13. The fragility of this convoluted process became apparent in last year's Covid-induced chip shortage.

A. confluent B. influent C. elaborate D. effectuate

14. After he got out of the bar, he suddenly began to yell drunken gibberish on the sidewalk.

A. gabble B. babble C. bubble D. gaffe

15. His statement leaves the Fed wriggle room to deliver yet another jumbo rate rise if inflation remains uncomfortably high.

A. wiggle B. giggle C. shingle D. swindle

16. The social gathering became rambunctious and out of hand.

A. blistering B. boisterous C. baffling D. bewildering

17. The environmental group's protest by messing with artwork inconveniences the public less directly than its more conventional past activity, such as blocking roads, but also feels more tangential to climate issues.

A. relevant B. tangible C. irrelevant D. intangible

18. Educational diversity is a murky and contested concept, opaque by design and an anodyne way to confront the combustible topic of race.

A. insipid B. neutral C. limpid D. insidious

19. Some of the arguments in favour of shutting the factory are questionable and others downright spurious.

A. bogus B. cavernous C. salacious D. porous

20. His iconoclastic tendencies can get him into trouble.

A. iconic B. ironic C. unorthodox D. ironclad

Practice 10

*There are 20 sentences in this practice. In each of them one word is underlined, and below each sentence, there are 4 choices marked by letters A, B, C and D respectively. Choose the word that can replace the underlined part without causing any grammatical error or changing the basic meaning of the sentence. There is only **ONE** right answer.*

1. The teller's eyes widened as a customer poured thousands of pennies onto the counter, an intentionally obnoxious way to pay a high heating bill.

   A. unpalatable   B. nocturnal   C. rebellious   D. treacherous

2. Police created roadblocks to prohibit people visiting her grave, reacting violently when thousands tried to reach the cemetery anyway.

   A. regardless   B. despite   C. irrespective   D. respectively

3. The student became an Internet celebrity for spoofing his teachers.

   A. parodying   B. spooking   C. rambling   D. carousing

4. With the global economy stuttering, Bangladesh's will too.

   A. moping   B. fluttering   C. faltering   D. coping

5. It was also in this period that crime figures started their inexorable rise and placed the police under immense pressure.

   A. inextricable   B. inevitable   C. immaculate   D. unfathomable

6. In key Senate and gubernatorial races, the former president proffered his endorsements based on loyalty over electability.

   A. fealty   B. realty   C. faculty   D. frailty

7. A lot of viewers complained that there was too much gratuitous sex and violence in the film.

   A. unwarranted   B. wholesome   C. gratis   D. gladiatorial

8. This has proven to be a nutritionally dubious, inexpedient method for losing weight.

   A. expeditious   B. expendable   C. inadvisable   D. indispensable

9. Speaking to Britain's parliament, he echoed Winston Churchill; to the German Bundestag, he invoked the Berlin Wall.

   A. evoked   B. provoked   C. cited   D. incited

10 It is not easy to picture his upbringing in quotidian reality.

　　A. quotient　　　　B. idiomatic　　　　C. custodian　　　　D. commonplace

11 At the height of the boom in ICOs (initial coin offerings) in 2017, Binance rushed to list the flurry of newly launched cryptocurrencies, as other exchanges dawdled.

　　A. dwindled　　　　B. doodled　　　　C. daggled　　　　D. dallied

12 A complete crash across the cryptocurrency sector would probably obliterate his wealth, most of which is held in digital assets.

　　A. oblivion　　　　B. alliterate　　　　C. eliminate　　　　D. delineate

13 With the lifting of Covid-19-induced travel restrictions, many travel sites have been overwhelmed.

　　A. swamped　　　　B. swarmed　　　　C. sweltered　　　　D. smudged

14 They are still instilling terror of the virus with lurid reports of mass death cases in the country.

　　A. sensational　　　　B. sensual　　　　C. sanguine　　　　D. lucid

15 Historically, women did not receive as much education as men, which experts surmise could have increased the risk of getting Alzheimer's for earlier generations.

　　A. gather　　　　B. fret　　　　C. trust　　　　D. assert

16 To placate protesters, he agreed to step down in 2022.

　　A. mollify　　　　B. nullify　　　　C. barricade　　　　D. cascade

17 The film director had previously taken Lawrence to task for his patriarchal pomposity.

　　A. haughtiness　　　　B. propensity　　　　C. epiphany　　　　D. serendipity

18 He was a tall, austere, forbidding figure.

　　A. augur　　　　B. august　　　　C. augment　　　　D. acumen

19 The country, irked by the US's commitments, may find a way to signal its disapproval for Ms. Harris's showboating.

　　A. riled　　　　B. foiled　　　　C. biled　　　　D. beguiled

20 Mr. Spielberg paints a detailed, emotionally intelligent portrait of his postwar Jewish suburban family, but avoids the amber-tinged nostalgia of much boomer-era biography. Funny and wise, the film is one by a consummate showman slowing down to reflect.

　　A. commonplace　　　　B. commensurate　　　　C. adroit　　　　D. profuse

Practice 11

*There are 20 sentences in this practice. In each of them one word is underlined, and below each sentence, there are 4 choices marked by letters A, B, C and D respectively. Choose the word that can replace the underlined part without causing any grammatical error or changing the basic meaning of the sentence. There is only **ONE** right answer.*

1 Now that Billy's famous, I doubt he'll <u>deign</u> to call his own mother.

    A. feign   B. reign   C. condescend   D. denigrate

2 OPEC and its allies, including Russia, agreed to cut oil production in an effort to boost <u>sagging</u> prices.

    A. flagging   B. tagging   C. lagging   D. gagging

3 While environmental groups are still optimistic, even the most <u>strident</u> supporters of the rule change acknowledge that the energy crisis has made the politics challenging.

    A. stringent   B. raucous   C. boisterous   D. committed

4 People <u>gripe</u> about the economy, interest rates and house prices.

    A. grouse   B. rouse   C. snipe   D. carouse

5 The upcoming games will bring joy, and much-needed economic <u>balm</u>, to a country that in recent weeks has endured protests, rocketing food and fuel prices and a change in prime minister.

    A. salve   B. salvation   C. sedition   D. sedation

6 For a period of time, the older generation has generally regarded the majority of post-80s or 90s youth as a spoiled generation, who often indulge themselves in social networks, <u>conspicuous</u> consumption and hyper-individualism.

    A. apparent   B. evident   C. flamboyant   D. explicit

7 Eight Russian soldiers purportedly died after eating pies <u>spiked</u> by a seemingly friendly old lady.

    A. fabricated   B. peddled   C. poisoned   D. prepared

8 For decades Nick Cave has won legions of fans for his rich, deep voice and hauntingly beautiful songs. More recently he has begun to <u>demystify</u> his creative process.

    A. put a human face on   B. put a spin on   C. put a premium on   D. put a damper on

9 The queen is suffering from "<u>sporadic</u> mobility problems".

    A. episodic   B. esoteric   C. elastic   D. elaborate

10 During arguments, he is often demonstrative, waving his arms for emphasis.

  A. affectionate B. emotional C. affected D. emotive

11 Any new standards will have to compete against a plethora of current ones, potentially magnifying the incompatibility that already plagues the industry.

  A. surfeit B. sufficiency C. slew D. string

12 The company only had a nebulous idea of the next model of car they would manufacture.

  A. nebular B. hazy C. succulent D. succinct

13 In April the government ended VAT relief on festival tickets. Revellers at Glastonbury Festival had to shell out £280 for the privilege.

  A. ravers B. benders C. banters D. rangers

14 They've been trying to push through a pay cut for employees for months, but the labor union keeps striking it down.

  A. pierce B. put C. pull D. pitch

15 Debates will only be transmitted by government television channels, allowing him to gag dissident voices.

  A. muffle B. shuffle C. shush D. blush

16 Harry and Meghan accused the royal family of callous and racist treatment.

  A. uncaring B. palliative C. capricious D. uncanny

17 If someone had started giving me prissy hand signals as I started to swear last week, my rage attack would have got a lot uglier.

  A. prim B. prime C. primordial D. pristine

18 He continues to isolate his country from the contagion of foreign ideas.

  A. contamination B. condemnation C. condescension D. convulsion

19 He did not know why, but he felt oppressed by the vague sense of impending calamity.

  A. imminent B. imposing C. imprudent D. immaculate

20 Consumers and businesses seem to have an uncanny ability to keep going despite the country's international pariah status.

  A. cunning B. unkempt C. undue D. eerie

Practice 12

*There are 20 sentences in this practice. In each of them one word is underlined, and below each sentence, there are 4 choices marked by letters A, B, C and D respectively. Choose the word that can replace the underlined part without causing any grammatical error or changing the basic meaning of the sentence. There is only **ONE** right answer.*

1 There is no safety in unlimited technological hubris.

    A. debris   B. device   C. conceit   D. deceit

2 His core beliefs seem closer to the small-state ideology of Ronald Reagan than to Mr Trump's incontinent chauvinism.

    A. inconsistent   B. incompatible   C. unbridled   D. uncanny

3 He doesn't want this story to get into the grubby hands of the tabloid press.

    A. shabby   B. crabby   C. shrubby   D. mucky

4 The two bailiffs muscled him through the door and his frantic shouts echoed through the courthouse for what seemed like an eternity.

    A. hysterical   B. fraught   C. fanatic   D. hectic

5 He knows that Brazilians feeling the pinch could punish him in October, when he is up for re-election.

    A. feeling the crunch   B. feeling the heat   C. feeling out of place   D. feeling groovy

6 Judging by the music festival's enduring success in an era of proliferating festivals, they do a fine job: Tickets are like gold dust.

    A. marketable   B. available   C. attainable   D. accessible

7 In the middle of his speech, he just spaced out and trailed off into an unintelligible murmur.

    A. got disoriented   B. got dispirited   C. got dissipated   D. got disconnected

8 He is raring to get back into politics.

    A. eager   B. hesitant   C. daring   D. avid

9 I feel squeamish at the sight of blood.

    A. queasy   B. squashy   C. tacky   D. skittish

10 Myanmar's generals have no qualms about shedding blood.

    A. quacks   B. quaint   C. misgivings   D. misrepresentation

11 It is increasingly difficult to blame soaring petrol prices on the machinations of the Organisation of Petroleum Exporting Countries.

    A. mechanization   B. collusion   C. reckoning   D. mastermind

12 Some air-traffic controllers may also down tools.

    A. walk out   B. take to the roads   C. walk on   D. take hold

13 Their approach to the problem has been vindicated by the positive results.

    A. showcased   B. subsisted   C. subjugated   D. validated

14 On May 9th he trounced his closest rival for the presidency.

    A. trailed   B. trumped   C. trampled   D. transcended

15 On June 24th the Supreme Court upheld a ruling that cleared Mr Modi of complicity in the 2002 riots.

    A. implication   B. ramification   C. accomplice   D. corroboration

16 India's courts are ever more deferential to the government.

    A. reverent   B. indifferent   C. deterrent   D. deferrable

17 He will attend a summit of the five Caspian coastal countries: Russia, Azerbaijan, Iran, Kazakhstan and Turkmenistan.

    A. pelagic   B. littoral   C. archipelagic   D. peninsular

18 Protections against domestic violence and sexual harassment are still spotty.

    A. speckled   B. dappled   C. obvious   D. doubtful

19 In the name of reconciliation, politicians disavow the militias that once killed on their behalf.

    A. disown   B. denounce   C. recant   D. deny

20 Many seethe at the corruption and incompetence of their leaders, though much venom is directed locally, not at the government per se.

    A. agitate   B. fume   C. fulminate   D. culminate

Practice 13

There are 20 sentences in this practice. In each of them one word is underlined, and below each sentence, there are 4 choices marked by letters A, B, C and D respectively. Choose the word that can replace the underlined part without causing any grammatical error or changing the basic meaning of the sentence. There is only **ONE** right answer.

1 The findings are part of a sweeping effort by the National Highway Traffic Safety Administration to determine the safety of advanced driving systems as they become increasingly commonplace.

A. broad B. swathe C. broader D. wide

2 Automakers were allowed to redact descriptions of what happened during the accidents, an option that Tesla as well as Ford and others used routinely, making it harder to interpret the data.

A. edit B. erudite C. ruse D. coalesce

3 We've gotten so enamored with big tech, and that masks very significant weaknesses elsewhere.

A. smitten B. animated C. enchanted D. smooched

4 Mr Biden has vowed to be tough on the country, and is loth to do something that would be portrayed by Republicans as a capitulation.

A. submission B. habituation C. insinuation D. attenuation

5 They parse social media posts, collect biometric data, track phones, record video using police cameras and sift through what they obtain to find patterns and aberrations.

A. anomalies B. abhorrence C. abstinence D. adherents

6 The golf club is run by a very unfriendly clique.

A. coterie B. community C. conclave D. clandestine

7 The complete analysis of a wine's aroma is extremely complex and expensive.

A. scent B. fragrance C. odor D. nose

8 While some prosecutions had resulted in convictions, others had led to acquittal or dismissal.

A. exoneration B. absolution C. discharge D. acquiescence

9 Cryptocurrency heists have become a highly lucrative yet relatively risk-free way for the country to raise funds to buttress the regime during the pandemic.

A. hackers B. thefts C. deists D. alchemists

10 You are mistaken if you think they will have moral compunction for attacking somebody else's network.

A. qualms B. conjunction C. injunction D. compass

11 They bristle at such statements, mindful that when Wall Street crowns a new emperor it also sets him up for a downfall.

A. recoil B. wince C. frown D. crux

12 Several villages suffered serious <u>privations</u> during their long isolation during the war.

A. deprivations B. privatizations C. conflagrations D. infestations

13 Now, halfway to 2050, the city has entered an uncertain <u>purgatory</u>. Its demise has been proclaimed before.

A. limbo B. libido C. sanctuary D. purgation

14 Having failed to realize their ideals, they sighed sorrowfully for the <u>transience</u> of life.

A. transitoriness B. transcendence C. transmogrification D. translucence

15 The film is a comically <u>poignant</u> portrait of a middle-aged father searching for a son he did not know he had.

A. pugnacious B. pompous C. premeditated D. distressing

16 She eventually found a university spot in Vancouver to study computer science. <u>Unwittingly</u>, she joined a stream of Syrians emigrating for fear of regional conflicts.

A. Unsurprisingly B. Unawares C. Knowingly D. Deliberately

17 After each <u>paroxysm</u> in its neighboring country, its population swelled with refugees.

A. patois B. paradox C. patio D. outburst

18 The city's economic growth is <u>exemplified</u> by the many new buildings that are currently under construction.

A. exfoliated B. exasperated C. epitomized D. exhilarated

19 They besieged the building, shattering glass, twisting metal gates and <u>scrawling</u> anti-war graffiti.

A. scribbling B. scrambling C. scrabbling D. scraping

20 She has decried editorials that <u>demeaned</u> the late Vietnamese leader.

A. disparaged B. demoted C. disenchanted D. bemoaned

Practice 14

There are 20 sentences in this practice. In each of them one word is underlined, and below each sentence, there are 4 choices marked by letters A, B, C and D respectively. Choose the word that can replace the underlined part without causing any grammatical error or changing the basic meaning of the sentence. There is only **ONE** right answer.

1 Out of sympathy, she began to move money about, <u>ostensibly</u> to "lend" from the rich to the poor for a short period.

A. palpably B. avowedly C. seemingly D. allegedly

2 Put bluntly, countries and companies from around the world did not dare snub the often abrasive power by not turning up.

　　A. snob　　　　　B. snatch　　　　　C. snarl　　　　　D. slight

3 Serving as a company director can be perilous. But for an investor, not taking up such a role is often worse.

　　A. precarious　　　B. rickety　　　　C. wobbly　　　　D. precipitous

4 Like some other erstwhile true believers, he became one of most cogent critics of his former faith.

　　A. devoted　　　　B. despicable　　　C. previous　　　　D. posthumous

5 A sprightly 67-year-old who has regular health check-ups abroad, he says he has no plans to leave office.

　　A. lethargic　　　　B. ethereal　　　　C. agile　　　　　D. genteel

6 His reflections on the pointlessness and suffering of war seem particularly prescient today.

　　A. discerning　　　B. judicious　　　　C. prophetic　　　D. illusory

7 Mrs Merkel has been criticised for pressing ahead with the now-mothballed Nord Stream 2 gas pipeline meant to link Germany and Russia.

　　A. deferred　　　　B. conferred　　　　C. deterred　　　　D. buffered

8 The ECB faces an unenviable dilemma: tighten monetary policy to fight inflation, or keep it loose to support a weakening economy?

　　A. ineffable　　　　B. inadvisable　　　C. undesirable　　　D. inevitable

9 The UK Treasury made some half-baked arguments this month about why small institutions can be just as risky as large ones to the system.

　　A. tongue-in-cheek　B. nonchalant　　　C. ill-conceived　　D. half-hearted

10 Given the state's record of fraud and violence, some worried that the result would be a party riven by conflict and disorder.

　　A. rife　　　　　　B. raved　　　　　　C. divided　　　　D. defied

11 The restaurant was patronized by many artists and writers during the 1920s.

　　A. sponsored　　　　B. ensued　　　　　C. frequented　　　D. capitalized

12 At the age of 70 he was forced to recant his beliefs under threat of death by torture.

　　A. disavow　　　　B. dispossess　　　　C. renounce　　　　D. reject

13 Under the auspices of Mr Cook the firm's net profits more than doubled to an estimated $57bn last year.

    A. aegis   B. jaundice   C. guidance   D. angst

14 Examples like this belie the notion that bacteria are simple, silent loners.

    A. underlie   B. underline   C. disprove   D. disapprove

15 Their inflation expectations suggest the Fed, the ECB and the Bank of Japan will all miss their targets for the next decade.

    A. offshoot   B. uproot   C. undershoot   D. scoot

16 Mr Biden directed his officials to devise emergency plans should circumstances change.

    A. consistency   B. convergence   C. contingency   D. confluence

17 In applying for a student visa, an affidavit of support must be submitted from an individual who will assure this opportunity.

    A. confirmation   B. subpoena   C. perjury   D. penury

18 Trading conditions have frankly been diabolical.

    A. atrocious   B. iniquitous   C. heinous   D. acrimonious

19 The negotiation may have been taken out of the cryogenic deep freeze, but whether it will come to life once it has thawed remains unclear.

    A. embryonic   B. cryptographic   C. hyperthermal   D. ultracold

20 The most striking is the visceral dislike of rawness. In the country, the consumption of raw foods was historically viewed as a barbarian habit, and almost everything is still eaten cooked.

    A. indifferent   B. insightful   C. instinctive   D. intellectual

Practice 15

There are 20 sentences in this practice. In each of them one word is underlined, and below each sentence, there are 4 choices marked by letters A, B, C and D respectively. Choose the word that can replace the underlined part without causing any grammatical error or changing the basic meaning of the sentence. There is only **ONE** right answer.

1 Secret intelligence files reveal severe tensions between putative allies who can be drinking tea one day and fighting each other the next.

    A. presumed   B. palliative   C. precluded   D. punitive

2 America and its allies have left the country with their reputations badly damaged.

    A. denigrated   B. reneged   C. denounced   D. dented

3 She said her abrupt decision was prompted by an argument with the police.

    A. inquisition   B. altercation   C. amelioration   D. eutrophication

4 European colonizers, who considered the New World peoples to be heathens, forced them to conform to European ways.

    A. heresies   B. heterodoxies   C. pagans   D. perpetrators

5 Aside from a brief respite of a year or two when he had a council flat, the London streets have been the only home he's known.

    A. lull   B. breather   C. intermission   D. intermezzo

6 It's an amazing camera, but the price is exorbitant!

    A. stratospheric   B. exhilarating   C. hectic   D. exuberant

7 The CEO has been flirting with disaster with her off-the-cuff comments to the press lately.

    A. facing   B. floundering   C. flouting   D. foundering

8 To speak in Washington of a multipolar world is to invite opprobrium.

    A. apprehension   B. approbation   C. condemnation   D. convocation

9 We botched our first attempt at wallpapering the bathroom.

    A. bungled   B. bundled   C. bandaged   D. baffled

10 Part of the editorial is an exhortation to spend less time sending tweets; but a bigger concern is that too many journalists have come to see the Twitter audience as a proxy for the public.

    A. extortion   B. excoriation   C. encouragement   D. exfoliation

11 Today, Asian Americans are not only the scapegoat for duplicitous C.E.O.s. We are also the scapegoat for a fading sense of well-being in a market-driven and hypercompetitive society.

    A. double-dealing   B. dubious   C. pious   D. impervious

12 Most of the restitution has been monitored by the World Bank, to make sure the money goes to national funds and not into people's pockets.

    A. restoration   B. reinstatement   C. resurrection   D. compensation

13 If you were very rich, it would be insensitive to moan to anyone less rich about what a nuisance it was when charities clamour for money.

A. crass   B. discreet   C. discerning   D. cross

14 The National Archives houses passenger manifests from vessels arriving in the United States from foreign ports between approximately 1820 and the mid-twentieth century.

A. fingerprints   B. lists   C. claims   D. manifestos

15 In Arizona, the Bureau of Land Management has begun a program to revive landfills and abandoned mines for renewable energy.

A. reclaim   B. recuperate   C. repurpose   D. recoil

16 This draft law may oblige innocent firms to pay to settle and prevent infringed parties from seeking redress.

A. revenge   B. resolution   C. reparation   D. retribution

17 Many of the protesters said they put their life savings in the banks and are now destitute.

A. despondent   B. dispirited   C. impecunious   D. petulant

18 The government frequently excoriates companies for mishandling data.

A. obliges   B. excises   C. expropriates   D. berates

19 It is rare for industrial assets to be expropriated in Europe these days.

A. appropriated   B. misappropriated   C. embezzled   D. requisitioned

20 These shell companies can shield those using dirty dosh to buy assets, often swanky pads in places like London and Paris.

A. swish   B. swash   C. smashing   D. spooky

Practice 16

There are 20 sentences in this practice. In each of them one word is underlined, and below each sentence, there are 4 choices marked by letters A, B, C and D respectively. Choose the word that can replace the underlined part without causing any grammatical error or changing the basic meaning of the sentence. There is only **ONE** right answer.

1 A spunky woman with the swagger of a 20-year-old, she overcame several hurdles to build the business.

A. fiery   B. feisty   C. plump   D. classy

2 She badgered her neighborhood committee by telephone and text message until they relented.

    A. harassed   B. pestered   C. cudgeled   D. cordoned

3 From today on, visitors must submit to a facial recognition scanner to enter.

    A. resort   B. turn   C. look   D. succumb

4 For many citizens, that lack of recourse has contributed to a sense of resignation.

    A. submission   B. capitulation   C. departure   D. debauch

5 People are far more trusting overall in how government entities handle their personal information and far more suspicious about the corporate sector.

    A. trustful   B. trustworthy   C. trusty   D. trustable

6 Many residents see the handover of data as a necessary trade-off for security and convenience.

    A. compromise   B. complement   C. compliment   D. condiment

7 So nervous was the company about commercial confidentiality that he published his findings surreptitiously under his pseudonym.

    A. superstitiously   B. stupendously   C. furtively   D. figuratively

8 Some studies that extol dairy products as a calcium source have been funded at least in part by the dairy industry.

    A. exclaim   B. exalt   C. extort   D. exude

9 Try visiting a society in turmoil and telling people that they live in an age of rising well-being and receding threats. You are likely to be met with incredulous glares.

    A. incredible   B. unbelieving   C. unbelievable   D. creditable

10 The erosion of secure working-class jobs, as manufacturing work flees overseas and labor unions wither, is thought to have precipitated much of the West's populist backlash.

    A. provoked   B. precluded   C. proclaimed   D. profaned

11 A few opponents of the project have espoused far-fetched theories, or used language that some considered anti-Asian scaremongering.

    A. advocated   B. expounded   C. astounded   D. extricated

12 As diplomatic relations have frayed, American officials have questioned whether seemingly innocuous Russian investments could be used for nefarious purposes.

    A. nebulous   B. tenuous   C. evil   D. vigil

13 Hate can only percolate—and I'm going to call it hate and people are going to cringe and not like that at all—but hate can only percolate underground for so long.

   A. permeate　　　B. perforate　　　C. perspire　　　D. perpetuate

14 Much of what will unfold during the platinum jubilee to mark her 70 years on the throne is objectively ludicrous.

   A. preposterous　　　B. luscious　　　C. succulent　　　D. luxurious

15 Few Britons now recoil at the prospect of King Charles Ⅲ, even if he sometimes seems more a fuddy-duddy uncle than a national patriarch.

   A. desist　　　B. decry　　　C. abominate　　　D. revile

16 Dithering over delivering arms to the country has damaged Germany's international image.

   A. Validating　　　B. Vindicating　　　C. Vacillating　　　D. Verifying

17 These horror movies feature plenty of gore, creepy soundtracks and, of course, monsters galore.

   A. apiece　　　B. aplenty　　　C. apart　　　D. aside

18 His lifestyle can be compared to that of a Persian Gulf monarch or a flamboyant oligarch.

   A. ostentatious　　　B. flagrant　　　C. obnoxious　　　D. fanatic

19 Safety experts are concerned because these systems allow drivers to relinquish active control of the car and could lure them into thinking their cars are driving themselves.

   A. lull　　　B. lurk　　　C. lullaby　　　D. lubricate

20 Setting the theme of the splendid yet intimate-for-a-royal-coronation ceremony, King Charles Ⅲ's first remarks at the beginning of the two-hour spectacle at Westminster Abbey were, "I come not to be served, but to serve."

   A. despondent　　　B. resplendent　　　C. despotic　　　D. spurious

第5章
词汇选择训练题库答案与译文

Practice 1

1 C

A. 渡过难关（to manage to deal with a difficult situation or to stay alive until it is over）

B. get sth. across to sb. 讲清楚；说明；使被理解（to make people understand something）

C. 规避或绕开构成阻碍的权威或规定（to avoid or elude an authority or regulation that constitutes a barrier）

D. 克服，恢复过来（to start to feel happy or well again after something bad has happened to you; to start to forget someone and feel happy again after a relationship has ended）

句子大意： 尽管烟草广告遭到禁止，但是烟草公司还是通过赞助音乐演出来规避这一禁令。

2 A

A. 使烦恼；激怒（to annoy or irritate sb.）

常用搭配：~ sb. (to do sth.); It irks sb. that…

B. 渴望；热望（to want to do sth. very much）

C. 使不胜负荷；使应接不暇（to give or send sb. so many things that they cannot deal with them all）

常用搭配：~ sb. (with sth.)

D. 使醉；使陶醉；使中毒（to make somebody drunk with alcohol or stupefied with drugs or other substances; to make somebody intensely excited or overjoyed, often so much so that the person becomes irrational）

句子大意： 在他当政期间，该市境况日益恶化，这让不同背景的人们都愤怒不已。

3 C

plucky 勇敢的，有胆量的；刚毅的（having a lot of courage and determination）

A. ~ sb./sth. 困扰；威胁（to affect sb./sth. in an unpleasant or harmful way）

B. ~ sb.（感情或感觉）充溢，难以承受（to have such a strong emotional effect on sb. that it is difficult for them to resist or know how to react）

压垮；使应接不暇（to be so bad or so great that a person cannot deal with it; to give too much of a thing to a person）

C. ~ of sth. 完全没有，丧失，失去（某物）（completely lacking sth.; having lost sth.）

感到失落（sad and lonely because you have lost sth.）

83

D. [ɪɡˈzɪləˌreɪt] 使高兴，使兴奋，使激动（to make sb. feel very happy and excited）

句子大意： 这部历史剧中那位有胆有识的首相角色收获了很多粉丝，当该剧第三季于2013年结束的时候，这些粉丝都倍感失落。

4 A

A. 非常接近某种结果（往往是非常不好的结果）（to come very close to some outcome or result, often a very bad one）

B. ~ with sb./sth. 与……一起作战；用……战斗（to use something as a weapon while fighting someone or something）

C. ~ (on) sth. 含糊其词；回避（to avoid giving clear and accurate information, or a clear answer）

D. 充满（be full of sth.）

句子大意： 在经过数周下跌后，美国股市在熊市边缘徘徊。不过，最近几天，股市似乎有所好转。

5 B

redundancy（因劳动力过剩而造成的）裁员，解雇（the situation when sb. has to leave their job because there is no more work available for them）

A. ~ sth. to sth. 把……归因于；认为……是由于（to say or believe that sth. is the result of a particular thing）

B. ~ sb./sth. to sth. 限制；限定（to keep sb./sth. inside the limits of a particular activity, subject, area, etc.）

C. 捐献，捐赠（尤指金钱或物品）；捐助（to give sth., especially money or goods, to help sb./sth.）

D. ~ to do sth.（不顾困难而）设法做到（to manage to do sth. despite difficulties）

~ sth.（克服困难）促成某事（to succeed in making sth. happen despite difficulties）

~ sth. 巧妙地策划；精巧地制造（如机器）（to think of or make sth., for example a plan or a machine, in a clever way）

句子大意： 到目前为止，裁员的情况主要发生在初创企业和新上市公司，老牌科技公司裁员的情况一直较少。

6 D

A. in the same vein 以同样的风格或方式等；同样，同理（放在句首）

B. (look at/discuss/reflect on) sth. through the lens of…，从……方面来（看、讨论、回顾等）。[(look at/discuss/reflect sth.) by utilizing a particular viewpoint or perspective]

C. set the tone for 为……定下调子；为……奠定基调

D. in the same breath 用来表示时间的短促，意为"但紧接着，但同时"，通常与前一段意图或意思相反（used for saying that someone has said two things that cannot both be true; if you talk about two people or things in the same breath, you mention them together）

句子大意： 他称赞了一番我的工作，但紧接着说不得不辞退我。

7 D

A. 常见表达 star-crossed 来自星座占卜，意思是两个情侣的本命星位置交错，所以注定没有好结果（thwarted or opposed by the stars; ill-fated）。如：star-crossed lovers 意为一对天造地设却被外力阻隔的苦命恋人。补充表达：…be written in the stars，指冥冥之中早已注定的、无法改变的事，通常形容爱情。

B. 升起（when the sun, moon, etc. rises, it appears above the horizon）

C. 下落；跌落（to drop down from a higher level to a lower level）

D. The stars have aligned for sb. to do sth. 当前的形势或条件对于做某种活动或事情非常适合；天时到了，好运来了（The current situation or set of conditions is ideal for the prospects of some activity or endeavor.）

句子大意： 看来这支队伍的好运终于到了，今年有望赢得锦标赛奖杯 / 有望锦标赛夺冠。

8 B

up the ante 加码，加大赌注（to try to get a greater advantage from a situation by taking a bigger risk）

A. 勇敢的；无畏的（very brave; not afraid of danger or difficulties）

B. 不冷不热的；微温的（slightly warm, sometimes in a way that is not pleasant）

C. （液体、气体等）清澈的；清澄的；透明的；透光的 [(of a liquid, air, etc.) clear and transparent]（眼睛、心灵等）清澈的；平静的；无忧无虑的 [(of the eyes, a heart, etc.) emotionally calm and composed]

D. 表达清楚的；易懂的（clearly expressed; easy to understand）
（尤指生病期间或病愈后，糊涂状态中或过后）头脑清晰的，清醒的（able to think clearly, especially during or after a period of illness or confusion）

句子大意： 随着全球股市更加低迷，散户股民不敢贸然增加赌注。

9 C

A. 通常用 on the...front，如：on the economic front（在经济方面）；on many fronts（在多个方面）。

B. 常见表达：at the door 在门口等着他人开门（if someone is at the door, they are waiting for you to open the door of a building so they can come inside）

C. on the cusp of... 即将迎来……（on the verge of some beginning point or the start of some major development）

D. ……的拐角（物体表面）之上，如：a vase on the corner of the table.

句子大意： 世界即将迎来一场人口结构的逆转。

10 D

A. 受到，遭受；被……折磨（to make someone experience something unpleasant）

B. 隶属的；下级的；次要的（be subject to the control or authority of someone or something else）
把……置于次要地位；使……从属于（to put someone in an inferior position to someone else; to put something in an inferior position to something else）

C. 向某人投降，如 surrender to sb.（to submit or yield to the power, influence, or authority of someone）
（被迫）放弃，交出（某人或某物）[surrender sb. or sth. to sb. or sth. else (to give up sb. or sth. to sb. or sth. else)]

D. 只好接受；对……听天由命；安于……（If you are resigned to something unpleasant, you calmly accept that it will happen.）

句子大意： 山姆只好接受自己将永远得不到提拔的事实。

11 C

A. 常见搭配 put (oneself) in (someone's) shoes（或者 put oneself in somebody's place/position），意为设身处地、换位思考（to imagine oneself in the situation or circumstances of another person, so as to understand or empathize with their perspective, opinion, or point of view）。

B. 常见搭配 come out of the closet，意为公开承认秘密（尤指因耻辱或尴尬而一直保守着的秘密）；"出柜"（to admit sth. openly that you kept secret before, especially because of shame or embarrassment）。

C. 常见搭配 put one in one's place，意为教训某人，让某人意识到自己的地位或身份，让某人有自知之明（rebuke someone, remind someone of his or her position）。

D. 常见搭配 be in the driving seat，意为担任负责人；处于统领地位（to be the person in control of a situation）。

句子大意： 琳达太粗鲁无礼了，你应该好好调教调教她。

12 D

A. （突然）膨胀，涨大（to suddenly swell out or get bigger）

B. 迅速升值；急剧增值（to rise quickly and reach a high value）

C. 触底反弹（If something such as an economy or price bottoms out, it reaches its lowest level before starting to improve again.）

D. 突然大幅下降（to fail or fall suddenly and dramatically）

句子大意： 天主教学校的在校生数量自20世纪60年代以来出现了大幅下降，但是近来在疫情期间出现了反弹。

13 A

A. 逐步停止或停止一段时间（to stop gradually or for a short time）

B. 突然失败；崩溃，瓦解（to fail suddenly or completely）

C. 使失色；使相形见绌；使丧失重要性（to make sb./sth. seem dull or unimportant by comparison）

D. （使）快速翻转，迅速翻动（to turn over into a different position with a sudden quick movement; to make sth. do this）

句子大意： 印度和美国曾于2009年设立了贸易政策论坛，但2018年停办了一次；如今，人们又满怀热情地重启论坛。

14 A

A.（动词原形为 beseech）~ sb. (to do sth.) 恳求，乞求（to ask sb. for sth. in an anxious way because you want or need it very much）

B. 打斗；闹事（to take part in a noisy and violent fight, usually in a public place）

C. 丧失亲友（If sb. is bereaved, a relative or close friend has just died.）

D. ~ sb./sth. 长期搅扰（to cause a lot of problems for sb./sth. over a long period of time）

句子大意：看到他这样孩子都吓坏了，紧紧依偎着他，求他冷静下来。

15 C

A. 熊熊燃烧（to burn brightly and strongly）

~ sth. (across/all over sth.) 大肆宣扬（to make news or information widely known by telling people about it in a way they are sure to notice）

B. 犯愚蠢的（或粗心的）错误（to make a stupid or careless mistake）

C. ~ sth. 损害；妨害（to spoil or damage sth., especially by causing a lot of problems）

D. ~ sth. 挑衅地挥舞，激动地挥舞（尤指武器）（to hold or wave sth., especially a weapon, in an aggressive or excited way）

句子大意：自 2020 年 11 月以来，战争给这个地区带来了诸多破坏。

16 A

A. ~ (sb./sth.) 在……之前发生（或出现）；（从事件发生顺序上）先于，带来或造成……（to happen before sth. or come before sth./sb. in order）

B. ~ sth.（在日期上）建成时间（或形成时间等）早于……（to be built or formed, or to happen, at an earlier date than sth. else in the past）

C. 压倒，战胜；占优势（to be or prove superior in strength, power, or influence）

D. ~ sth. by/with sth. or ~ sth. by doing sth. 以……为开端；作……的开场白（to say sth. before you start making a speech, answering a question, etc.）

句子大意：从历史上来看，货币政策快速收紧经常会带来衰退，但是美联储清楚通胀的过快上涨会更糟糕。

17 A

A. ~ sb./sth. 限制，束缚，阻碍（某人的活动自由）（to limit sb.'s freedom of movement or activity）

B. ~ sth. (to sth.) 使臣服；使顺从；（尤指）压服（to bring a country or group of people under your control, especially by using force）

C. ~ sth. 使模糊；使隐晦；使费解（to make it difficult to see, hear or understand sth.）

D. ~ (sth.) (from sth.) 减；减去（to take a number or an amount away from another number or amount）

句子大意：对自由流动和聚会采取的防疫限制措施也对该国其他地区人们的出行造成影响。

18 B

A. 感官的；愉悦感官的（connected with your physical feelings; giving pleasure to your physical senses, especially sexual pleasure）

喜欢感官享受的；耽于肉欲的（suggesting an interest in physical pleasure, especially sexual pleasure）

B. 有感觉能力的；有知觉力的（able to see or feel things through the senses）

C. 情感的（而非理性的）（connected with your emotions, rather than reason）

伤感的，充满柔情的；多愁善感的（producing emotions such as pity, romantic love or sadness, which may be too strong or not appropriate; feeling these emotions too much）

D. 与感官有关的，知觉器官的（relating to the senses of sight, hearing, smell, taste, and touch）

句子大意：2003年瑞士颁布一项法律，规定大众应当将动物视为有感知能力的生物而非个人财产。他是此项法案的主要推动者。

19 A

A. 警告，告诫；防止误解的说明，附加说明（a warning that particular things need to be considered before sth. can be done; to qualify with a warning or clarification）

B. （尤指用鲟鱼子腌制的）鱼子酱（the eggs of some types of fish, especially the sturgeon, that are preserved using salt and eaten as a very special and expensive type of food）

C. （参加典礼的）骑马队列，车队（a line of people on horses or in vehicles forming part of a ceremony）

D. 无端指摘，吹毛求疵（the act of arguing or protesting about unimportant details）

句子大意：他附加了一个说明，称这一调查中的所有数据都不足为信。

20 B

A. ~ sb. with sth. 折磨；使痛苦（to affect sb./sth. in an unpleasant or harmful way）

B. ~ sth. on sb. 使遭受打击；使吃苦头（to make sb./sth. suffer sth. unpleasant）

"让某人遭受经济损失"可以是 afflict sb. with financial losses，也可以是 inflict financial losses on sb.。

C. ~ sb./sth. 影响（to produce a change in sb./sth.）

~ sth. 炫耀；做作地使用（或穿戴）（to use or wear sth. that is intended to impress other people）

D. elicit sth. from sb. 从某人那里探出（信息等）（to manage to get information from someone）

句子大意：人民币升值会有多大危害？

Practice 2

1 A

A. 用魔法召唤；想象出；唤起（to create or achieve something difficult or unexpected, as if by magic; to bring something such as a feeling or memory to your mind; to make something appear using magic powers）

B. ~ sth. 引起，唤起（感情、记忆或形象）（to bring a feeling, a memory or an image into your mind）（及物动词，没有 evoke up 的搭配）

C. 提起，提出来（to start discussing a subject）

D. 包庇（某人）；为某人打掩护；掩盖（to hide the truth about something by not telling what you know or by preventing other people from telling what they know）

句子大意：廷巴克图市会让人联想起黄金和撒哈拉的驼队，但位于马里的这座沙漠城市也曾是一个蓬勃发展的知识中心。

2 D

A. ~ sth. 欣然接受，乐意采纳（思想、建议等）；信奉（宗教、信仰等）（to accept an idea, a proposal, a set of beliefs, etc., especially when it is done with enthusiasm）

B. ~ sth. 引起，唤起（感情、记忆或形象）（to bring a feeling, a memory or an image into your mind）

C. ~ sth. (from sb.)（往往困难地）从某人那里获得信息或反应（to get information or a reaction from sb., often with difficulty）

D. ~ sth. (against sb.) 援引，援用（法律、规则等作为行动理由）（to mention or use a law, rule, etc. as a reason for doing sth.）

~ sb./sth. 提及，援引（某人、某理论、实例等作为支持）（to mention a person, a theory, an example, etc. to support your opinions or ideas, or as a reason for sth.）

句子大意：这种短缺情况迫使拜登总统援用《国防生产法案》以确保厂家有必要的原料供给来生产婴儿配方奶粉。

3 C

A.（尤指简单、暂时的）解决方法（a solution to a problem, especially an easy or temporary one）

B. 可拆除装置，附加设备（如煤气灶、灯、搁架）（items in a house such as a cooker, lights or shelves that are usually fixed but that you can take with you when you move to a new house）

C. 某个地方或活动的常客（a familiar or invariably present element or feature in some particular setting, especially a person long associated with a place or activity）

定时举办的体育赛事或节庆活动（a settled date or time especially for a sporting or festive event）

D. [ˈfɪʃər] 裂缝，裂隙；（思想、观点等的）分歧（a long narrow crack or opening, especially in rock; a division into factions of a group or political party）

句子大意：1998 年，他搬到了纽约，在那里成了文学界和社交圈的常客，频频出现在派对、活动和媒体上。

4 B

A. ~ sth. 废弃；取消；报废（to cancel or get rid of sth. that is no longer practical or useful）

B. ~ together（钱等）费力凑齐；积攒（to succeed in getting enough of something, especially money, by making a lot of effort）

C. 做抄写员（to work as a scribe）

D. ~ sth. 为电影（或戏剧等）写剧本（to write the script for a film/movie, play, etc.）

句子大意： 他最初买房时，用父母的退休金凑齐了 30% 的首付。

5 A

A. 犯规；违法（an act of breaking a rule or law）

B.（光、音波等的）折射（the change in direction that occurs when a wave of energy such as light passes from one medium to another of a different density, e.g. from air to water）

C. 分数（a division of a number）

D.（大团体中的）派系，小集团（a small group of people within a larger one whose members have some different aims and beliefs to those of the larger group）

句子大意： 该国用社会信用体系来惩罚不偿还贷款等违信行为，惩罚措施包括从个人出行、子女入学或银行贷款等方面加以限制。

6 A

A. 经常重复的评价（或抱怨）（a comment or complaint that is often repeated）

B. 劝勉激励（the act of strongly encouraging or trying to persuade someone to do something）

C. 格言，箴言；座右铭（a well-known phrase that expresses sth. that is usually true or that people think is a rule for sensible behaviour）

D. [ɪˈpɪtəmi] the ~ of sth. 典型，典范（a perfect example of sth.）

句子大意： 在人们评价伊丽莎白二世女王创纪录的统治历史时，将屡屡使用"一个时代的终结"这一措辞。

7 A

A. [ˈgæmət] 全部；全范围（the complete range of a particular kind of thing）

常用搭配：run the gamut of something（to experience or show the whole range of something）（例句：Jonson has run the gamut of hotel work, from porter to owner of a large chain of hotels.）

B. 开头一招；开局路数（a thing that sb. does, or sth. that sb. says at the beginning of a situation or conversation, that is intended to give them some advantage）

（国际象棋中为获得优势而采取的）开局让棋法（a move or moves made at the beginning of a game of chess in order to gain an advantage later）

C. [ˈgɔːntlət]（中世纪武士铠甲的）金属手套，铁手套（a metal glove worn as part of a suit of armour by soldiers in the Middle Ages）

常用搭配：run the gauntlet of... 遭受质疑、批评或攻击等困难局面（to have to deal with a lot of people who are criticizing or attacking you）

D. ~ (of sth.)（用于估计或判断的）事实，依据，标准（a fact or an event that can be used to estimate or judge sth.）

句子大意： 英国人对王室绝对的顺从态度已经被各种各样的情绪所取代，从忠诚和往往充满深情的宽容到肆无忌惮的敌意。

8 B

(feel) comfortable in (one's) own skin 从容自信（displaying a relaxed confidence in and clear understanding of oneself and one's abilities, especially when presenting oneself to or interacting with other people）

补充表达：live in one's own skin 设身处地，换位思考（to be in sb.'s shoes）

A. 成文法；法令，法规（a law that is passed by a parliament, council, etc. and formally written down）

B. 声望，名望（the importance and respect that a person has because of their ability and achievements）
身高，个子（a person's height）

C. ['kærɪkətjʊə(r)] 人物漫画（a funny drawing or picture of sb. that exaggerates some of their features）
夸张的描述（a description of a person or thing that makes them seem ridiculous by exaggerating some of their characteristics）

D. [kuˈtjʊə(r)] 时装设计制作；时装（the design and production of expensive and fashionable clothes; these clothes）

补充表达：haute couture [ˌəʊt kuˈtjʊə(r)] 高档女子时装（业）（the business of making fashionable and expensive clothes for women; the clothes made in this business）

句子大意： 近年来，他的这些文学作品让他声望不断提高，现在的他从容自信。

9 C

A. 法庭的；法官的；审判的；司法的（connected with a court, a judge or legal judgement）

B. （统称）审判人员；司法部；司法系统（the judges of a country or a state, when they are considered as a group）

C. 审慎而明智的；明断的；有见地的（careful and sensible; showing good judgement）

D. 动辄评头论足的；动辄指责人的（judging people and criticizing them too quickly）

句子大意： 该政府采取了审慎而明智的财政刺激措施，同时家庭和企业也继续消费和投资。

10 A

A. 授权仪式；任职仪式（a public ceremony in which someone is given an official title）

B. （时间、精力的）投入（the act of giving time or effort to a particular task in order to make it successful）

C. 一副牙齿；一副假牙（a partial or complete set of artificial teeth for the upper or lower jaw, usually attached to a plate）

D. （尤指有风险的）企业，投机活动，经营项目（a business project or activity, especially one that involves taking risks）

近年来，他分担了女王的多项职责，包括海外出访以及主持封爵授勋仪式。

11 C

A. ~ (on sb.) 产生事与愿违的不良（或危险）后果（to have the opposite effect to the one intended, with bad or dangerous results）

B. ~ against sth. or ~ from sb.（对社会变动等的）强烈抵制，集体反对（a strong negative reaction by a large number of people, for example to sth. that has recently changed in society）

C. ~ (to sth.) 返祖者；返祖；返祖型的东西（a person or thing that is similar to sb./sth. that existed in the past）

D. 违背初衷的结果（the results of a political action or situation that are not what was intended or wanted）

句子大意：进门脱帽的礼节仿佛让时光倒流，一下子回到了彬彬有礼的年代。

12 C

A. 外面的；外部的；外表的；户外的（on the outside of sth.; done or happening outdoors）

B. 充满自信的；精力充沛的；热情洋溢的（full of confidence, energy and good humour）

C. 复杂的；详尽的；精心制作的（very complicated and detailed; carefully prepared and organized）

D. 精力充沛的；热情洋溢的；兴高采烈的（full of energy, excitement and happiness）
　繁茂的；茁壮的（strong and healthy; growing quickly and well）

句子大意：朴素简洁的设计对感官的影响力并不亚于复杂精美的设计。过去是这样，将来也一样。

13 A

A. 涌现的事物；蜂拥而至的事物（a large number of things that happen or arrive at the same time）

B. 泄漏；暴露（the act of making known something that was secret）

C. 分歧；发散（a difference in the way that two or more things develop from the same thing）

D. 性格；性情（the natural qualities of a person's character）

句子大意：在经历了一连串的大规模枪击案后，许多美国人已经受够了。

14 C

rack sb./sth. 使痛苦不堪；使受折磨（to make sb. suffer great physical or mental pain）

A. ~ (over/at sth.)（尤指因某人去世引起的）悲伤，悲痛，伤心（a feeling of great sadness, especially when sb. dies）

B. ~ (against sb.) 不平的事；委屈；抱怨；牢骚（something that you think is unfair and that you complain or protest about）

C. fall from grace (= fall out of favor)（尤指因做了错事或不道德之事而）失去信任，失去尊重，失去恩宠（to lose the trust or respect that people have for you, especially by doing sth. wrong or immoral）

补充表达：be in sb.'s good graces 为某人所赞同（或喜爱）；得到某人的欢心（to have sb.'s approval and be liked by them）

D. 荣誉；光荣；桂冠（fame, praise or honour that is given to sb. because they have achieved sth. important）

壮丽；辉煌；灿烂（great beauty）

句子大意：他备受腐败指控的折磨，已经失去人心。

15 D

A. 难以想象的；难以理解的；令人惊愕的（very difficult to imagine or to understand; extremely surprising）

B. 非常令人兴奋的；给人印象极深的；非常令人吃惊的（very exciting, impressive or surprising）

C. 致幻的；使极度兴奋的（mind-bending drugs make you see or hear things that are not real）

复杂的，难以理解的（very difficult to understand; complex）

令人难以置信的（reaching the limit of credibility）

D. 非常乏味的；令人厌烦的（very boring）

句子大意：如果我们今天要再听一个无聊乏味的讲座的话，我得要再喝杯咖啡才行！

16 A

A. 惨胜；伤敌一千，自损八百 [(of a victory) won at too great a cost to have been worthwhile for the victor]

常见表达为 a pyrrhic victory（A pyrrhic victory is a victory that comes at a great cost, perhaps making the ordeal to win not worth it. It relates to Pyrrhus, a king of Epirus who defeated the Romans in 279 BCE but lost many of his troops.）

B. 开拓性的；探索性的（introducing ideas and methods that have never been used before）

C. 虚华的；言辞浮夸的（showing that you think you are more important than other people, especially by using long and formal words）

D. 清教徒式的；道德要求极为严格的（having very strict moral attitudes）

句子大意：竞选活动造成严重分裂，因此尽管他赢得了选举，但也只是一场惨胜。

17 A

A.（使）消散，消失；驱散（to gradually become or make sth. become weaker until it disappears）

~ sth. 挥霍，浪费，消磨（时间、金钱等）（to waste sth., such as time or money, especially by not planning the best way of using it）

B. 散开；疏散（人群等）（to move apart and go away in different directions; to make sb./sth. do this）

~ (sth.) 散布；散发；传播（to spread or to make sth. spread over a wide area）

C. ~ (sth.) 传播；弥漫，散射（to spread sth. or become spread widely in all directions）

D. ~ sth. 解剖（人或动植物）（to cut up a dead person, animal or plant in order to study it）

~ sth. 仔细研究；详细评论；剖析（to study sth. closely and/or discuss it in great detail）

句子大意：一直以来广泛流传着有关美国正接近"通胀峰值"的说法。尽管通胀压力依然很大，但人们曾以为这种压力即将开始减退。不过，现在看来，这个峰值更像是一个高位平台。

18 A

A. 解雇；开除；撤职（the act of dismissing sb. from their job; an example of this）

B. 大批杀害，每十个人杀一个 [destroying or killing a large part of the population (literally every tenth person as chosen by lot)]

C. （婚姻关系的）解除；（商业协议的）终止；（议会的）解散（the act of officially ending a marriage, a business agreement or a parliament）

D. 孤寂；悲哀；忧伤（the feeling of being very lonely and unhappy）

废墟；荒芜；荒凉（the state of a place that is ruined or destroyed and offers no joy or hope to people）

句子大意：在疫情期间一些航空公司解雇了地面和空中机组工作人员，造成了如今员工短缺的局面，使得这些航空公司不能通过进一步增加运力来满足不断飙升的出行需求。

19 A

A. courtesy of... 蒙……好意；经由……提供；作为……的结果（used for saying who has provided something, and for thanking them for it; as a result of...）

B. 逻辑不对，不是因为 orbiter 才 travel to space，而是"搭乘" orbiter

C. （aboard 后直接加 the ship/train/plane 等）在（船、飞机、公共汽车、火车等）上（on or onto a ship, plane, bus or train）

D. 包括；包含；由……组成（to have sb./sth. as parts or members）

句子大意：韩国男子团体"防弹少年团"的单曲 Dynamite 将于 8 月份搭乘韩国的第一个绕月轨道卫星进入太空。

20 A

A. 使……（重要性、权势等）丧失，黯然失色，暗淡（to lose importance, power, etc. especially because sb./sth. else has become more important, powerful, etc.）

B. ~ sth. （外表或行为举止）像，似（to look or behave like sth. else）

C. （在比赛或其他竞赛中）落后，失利（to be losing a game or other contest）

D. ~ sb./sth. 努力赶上……；向……看齐（to try to do sth. as well as sb. else because you admire them）

句子大意：在全球化鼎盛时期，多边组织和跨国企业似乎风头盖过了民族国家。

Practice 3

1 D

A. ~ down 关闭；停业；停工；阻止

B. silence 压制；使安静；使不说话。没有 silence down sb. 的搭配。（to make someone or something be quiet; to prevent someone from expressing their views or from criticizing or opposing someone）

C. showdown 摊牌，一决雌雄。没有 show down sb. 的搭配。（an important argument that is intended to end a disagreement that has existed for a long time）

D. ~ down 以喊叫声压倒对方；用叫喊声淹没（to make it difficult to hear what someone says by shouting while they are speaking）

句子大意： 有了庞大的粉丝群，马斯克就相当于拿着一个巨大的扩音器，可以自由宣传自己的投资，对健全的医疗法规嗤之以鼻，并让粉丝发声以盖过批评者的声音。

2 A

A. 归还（真正物主）；归还（赃物等）（the act of giving back sth. that was lost or stolen to its owner）

赔偿；补偿；（通常指）赔款（payment, usually money, for some harm or wrong that sb. has suffered）

B. 赤贫；匮乏（the state of having no money or possessions）

C. （大学、银行等规模大的）机构（a large important organization that has a particular purpose, for example, a university or bank）

慈善机构；社会福利机构（a building where people with special needs are taken care of, for example, because they are old or mentally ill）

D. 身体素质；体格（the condition of a person's body and how healthy it is）

组成；形成（the act of forming sth.）

句子大意： 这笔赔偿款的大部分一直由世界银行（World Bank）进行监控，以确保赔偿款流入国库而非落入个人腰包。

3 A

A. ~ (about sb./sth.) 热烈谈论（或书写）；（热情洋溢地）奋笔疾书（to talk or write about sth. in a very enthusiastic way）

常考同义词：rhapsodize ['ræpsədaɪz] 热情地谈论（或写）（to talk or write with great enthusiasm about sth.）

B. ~ sth. 使更复杂；使更纷乱（to make a situation or problem more complicated）

C. 铺石子（在路上）；使困惑惊讶（to cover or spread with gravel; perplex, confound）

D. 敲小槌（催促通过议案、要求注意等）；敲小槌示意……开始或生效（to bring about or compel by using a gavel; to begin or put into effect by striking a gavel）

句子大意： 光景好的时候，高管们总爱高谈阔论企业的发展前景。

4 B

select 精选的；作为……精华的；优等的（carefully chosen as the best out of a larger group of people or things）

A. (*n.*)（含有大块或整块水果的）果酱，蜜饯（jam containing large or whole pieces of fruit）

(*v.*) ~ sth. 节省；节约（to use as little of sth. as possible so that it lasts a long time）

B. ~ (of sb.) （某人或群体活动、工作等的）专门领域、专属（an activity, a job, an interest, etc. that is thought to be suitable for one particular person or group of people）

C. （动植物）保护区；自然保护区（a piece of land that is a protected area for animals, plants, etc.）

D. 对……有用，促进（to help to further, promote, or bring something about）

句子大意：许多国家都有瞻仰遗容的传统。在英国，只有君主、他们的配偶和某些首相有此殊荣。

5 B

A. ~ sb. 作弄；欺骗（to trick sb. by making them believe sth. that is not true, especially sth. unpleasant）

B. ~ sb. 哄劝；劝诱（to persuade sb. to do sth. by talking to them in a kind and gentle way）

C. 定时往来；定期行驶（to travel regularly along a particular route or between two particular places）

~ sth.（娴熟地）使用（to use a tool, especially in a skilful way）

常见搭配：ply one's craft 施展才华

D. ~ (into sth.) 探听，打听，探查（隐私）（to try to find out information about other people's private lives in a way that is annoying or rude）

句子大意：无论生前还是死后，女王都劝诱皇室成员多向现代世界靠拢一些。

6 A

A. 暴怒的；狂怒的（extremely angry）

乌青色的；青灰色的（dark bluish-grey in colour）

B.（液体、气体等）清澈的；透明的；透光的 [(of a liquid, air, etc.) clear and transparent]

C. 表达清楚的；易懂的（clearly expressed; easy to understand）

D. 俗艳的；花哨的（too bright in colour, in a way that is not attractive）

（故意地）骇人听闻的，令人毛骨悚然的（shocking and violent in a way that is deliberate）

句子大意：这些严苛的措施招致强烈反对。其他投资者——主要是那些资金因资本调控措施而被套牢在该国的投资者——也愤怒不已。

7 A

A.（v.）~ sb./sth.（公开地）诽谤，毁谤，中伤（to say bad things about sb./sth. publicly）

（adj.）有害的；引起伤害的（非主观造成）（causing harm）

B. 恶性的（that cannot be controlled and is likely to cause death）

恶意的；恶毒的（主观故意）（having or showing a strong desire to harm sb.）

C. 怀有恶意的；恶毒的（主观故意）（having or showing hatred and a desire to harm sb. or hurt their feelings）

D. [məˈlevələnt] 有恶意的；有坏心肠的（主观故意）（having or showing a desire to harm other people）

句子大意：他谨慎地表示次级债危机的不利影响可能没有之前的危机那么大。

8 A

A. 行将灭亡的；即将倒闭的；濒于崩溃的（no longer effective and about to come to an end completely）

B. 单调的；平凡的（not interesting or exciting）

C. 病态的；不正常的（having or expressing a strong interest in sad or unpleasant things, especially disease or death）

与疾病有关的（connected with disease）

D. 不能永生的；终将死亡的（that cannot live for ever and must die）

致命的；非常危急的（causing death or likely to cause death; very serious）

句子大意：游戏产业或能间接地帮助斯里兰卡濒于崩溃的旅游业起死回生。

9 B

A. 便秘 [the condition of being unable to get rid of waste material from the bowels easily (= being constipated)]

B. 惊愕；惊恐（a worried, sad feeling after you have received an unpleasant surprise）

C. 星座（a group of stars that forms a shape in the sky and has a name）

一系列（相关的想法、事物）；一群（相关的人）（a group of related ideas, things or people）

D.（尤指教会或大学的）大型正式会议（a large formal meeting, especially of Church officials or members of a university）

句子大意：人们对此报告会有各种惊慌失措的表现，但我们只是在努力提供客观的信息。

10 B

A. [kə'prɪʃəs]（态度或行为）反复无常的；任性的（showing sudden changes in attitude or behaviour）

B. [prɪ'sɪpɪtəs] 突然的；骤然的；急剧的（sudden and great）

草率的；仓促的；贸然的（done very quickly, without enough thought or care）

名词形式为：precipice ['presəpɪs] 悬崖；峭壁悬崖；峭壁（a very steep side of a high cliff, mountain or rock）

C. 蔑视的；鄙视的；表示轻蔑的（feeling or showing that you have no respect for sb./sth.）

D. 冷酷无情的；无同情心的；冷漠的（not caring about other people's feelings or suffering）

句子大意：投资者们现在关注的是该银行在股票暴跌后会采取什么措施。

11 B

A. put sb. off their ~ 扰乱某人；使某人乱了方寸（to make sb. make a mistake or hesitate in what they are doing）

B. 词组固定搭配：take...in (one's) stride 从容应对，对……泰然处之（to deal with a problem or difficulty calmly and not to allow it to influence what you are doing）

get into your ~ 进入状态；开始顺利地做某事（to begin to do sth. with confidence and at a good speed after a slow, uncertain start）

put sb. off their ~ 使分心；拖某人后腿（to make sb. take their attention off what they are doing and stop doing it so well）

C. ~ sb.（非法）跟踪，盯梢（to illegally follow and watch sb. over a long period of time, in a way that is annoying or frightening）

D. ~ (of sth.) 大量；许多；一大堆（a large number or amount of sth.; a lot of sth.）

（尤指工厂的）大烟囱（a tall chimney, especially on a factory）

栈；堆栈 [a way of storing information in a computer in which the most recently stored item is the first to be retrieved (= found or got back)]

句子大意：你必须学会对批评泰然处之才能在这个业务领域取得成功。

12 A

febrile 狂热的（nervous, excited and very active）

A. 有长久深刻的影响；产生广泛影响（to have a strong effect on people for a long time or over a large area）

B. ~ sth. 反驳；驳斥；证明（言论等）错误（to say or prove that a statement or criticism is false）

C. ~ sb. 使厌恶；使反感（to make sb. feel disgust or strong dislike）

~ sb./sth. 拒绝接受；回绝（to refuse to accept sb.'s help, attempts to be friendly, etc.）

D. ~ sth. 颠倒；彻底转变；使完全相反（to change sth. completely so that it is the opposite of what it was before）

句子大意：英国政府9月23日公布的迷你预算计划带来的灾难性后果继续对本已狂热的市场产生广泛影响。

13 D

A. enthral/enthrall 迷惑，吸引住（to make you so interested or excited that you give it all your attention）

B. ~ (with sth.)（有规律地）抽动，抽痛（to feel a series of regular painful movements）

（强烈有节奏地）跳动，搏动，震响（to beat or sound with a strong, regular rhythm）

C. ~ sb./sth.（作为惩罚用棍子等）抽打，连续击打（to hit a person or an animal many times with a stick, etc. as a punishment）

~ sb./sth.（赛事中）轻易击败，一举战胜（to defeat sb. very easily in a game）

D. ~ sb. or sth. 使窒息；勒死（to stop the breath of sb. by compressing the throat; strangle, choke or suffocate in any way）

禁止发声（to silence or check as if by choking）

句子大意：这个政策抑制了从廉价餐馆到高端珠宝等所有行业的消费者支出。

14 B

A. ~ sb./sth. (from sth.) 转移（注意力）；分散（思想）；使分心（to take sb.'s attention away from what they are trying to do）

B. 减少，降低，削弱（质量、价值、重要性等）（to diminish the importance, value, or effectiveness of something—often used with from）

C. ~ (sth.) (from sth.) 减；减去，做减法（to take a number or an amount away from another number or amount）

D. ~ sth. 撤销，收回（说过的话）（to say that sth. you have said earlier is not true or correct or that you did not mean it）

~ sth. 撤回，收回（协议、承诺等）（to refuse to keep an agreement, a promise, etc.）

句子大意：书中虽然有些小错误，但瑕不掩瑜。

15 B

A.（动词原形 beseech）~ sb. (to do sth.) 恳求；哀求；乞求（to ask sb. for sth. in an anxious way because you want or need it very much）

B. be ~ to sb. (for sth.)（因受恩惠而心存）感激；欠人情；受制于……[owing a favor or gift to (someone); having obligations to (someone)]

C. be ~ of sth. 完全没有，丧失，失去（某物）（completely lacking sth.; having lost sth.）

感到失落（sad and lonely because you have lost sth.）

D. ~ sb./sth. 长期搅扰（to cause a lot of problems for sb./sth. over a long period of time）

句子大意：随着各国政府向银行伸出经济援手，银行日益受制于政府。

16 C

A. 行家；权威；专家（a person who knows a lot about a particular subject and who often talks about it in public）

B. ~ sth. 预兆，预示，预告（尤指坏事）（to be a sign or warning of sth. that is going to happen in the future, especially sth. bad or unpleasant）

C. [pɒnˈtɪfɪkeɪt] ~ (about/on sth.) 自以为是地谈论；目空一切地议论（to give your opinions about sth. in a way that shows that you think you are right）

D. 药水；毒液；魔水（a drink of medicine or poison; a liquid with magic powers）

句子大意：达沃斯（世界经济论坛）很容易受到嘲讽。养尊处优的与会者们自以为是地就数十亿穷苦大众的命运高谈阔论。

17 B

A. [ˈkævəlri]（旧时的）骑兵；装甲兵。

B. [ˈʃɪvəlri]（尤指男人对女人的）彬彬有礼，殷勤，体贴（polite and kind behaviour that shows a sense of honour, especially by men towards women）

（中世纪的）骑士制度 [(in the Middle Ages) the religious and moral system of behaviour which the perfect knight was expected to follow]

C. [kləʊv] 丁香（热带树木的干花，形似小钉子，用于烹饪调味，尤用作甜食的香料）（the dried flower of a tropical tree, used in cooking as a spice, especially to give flavour to sweet foods）

a garlic ~/a ~ of garlic 蒜瓣 [one of the small separate sections of a bulb (= the round underground part) of garlic]

D. 好友；密友（a person that sb. spends a lot of time with）

句子大意：这种宫廷诗取材于骑士精神和典雅爱恋，你可能会由此联想到身穿闪光盔甲的骑士。

18 A

A. 不言而喻的道理；自明之理；老生常谈（an undoubted or self-evident truth, especially one too obvious for mention）

B. 利他主义；无私（the fact of caring about the needs and happiness of other people more than your own）

C. ['grævɪtæs] 严肃；庄严（the quality of being serious）

D. [fɔ:(r)'tju:ɪtəs] 偶然发生的；（尤指）巧合的（happening by chance, especially a lucky chance that brings a good result）

句子大意：常言说得好：言语无法表达之时，音乐就派上了用场。

19 A

A. ~ sth. 阻止，妨碍（某事物的发展）（to restrict the growth or development of sth.）

~ sth. 烫发；使（头发）成波形（to make curls in sb.'s hair by pressing it with a heated tool）

B. （只有动词形式）~ (sth.) (up) (into sth.) 压皱；（使）变皱，起皱（to crush sth. into folds; to become crushed into folds）

区分：rumple（有动词和名词两种形式）~ sth. 弄皱；弄乱（to make sth. untidy or not smooth and neat）

C. （有动词和名词两种形式）（尤指皮肤、布料或纸张）变皱，起皱纹（to become covered with or to form a lot of thin folds or lines, especially in skin, cloth or paper）

常考同义词：wrinkle（有动词和名词两种形式）（尤指脸上的）皱纹（a line or small fold in your skin, especially on your face, that forms as you get older）

（布或纸上的）褶皱，皱痕（a small fold that you do not want in a piece of cloth or paper）

D. （有动词和名词两种形式）褶痕；皱痕（an untidy line that is made in cloth or paper when it is pressed or crushed）

（皮肤上，尤指脸上的）皱纹（a line in the skin, especially on the face）

~ (sth.) 弄皱；压褶；（使）起褶子（to make lines on cloth or paper by folding or crushing it; to develop lines in this way）

~(sth.)（皮肤）皱起；使起皱纹（to make lines in the skin; to develop lines in the skin）

句子大意：数字广告支出走弱继续阻碍其核心部门——社交媒体部门的业务增长。

20 B

A. 大麦；大麦粒（a plant grown for its grain that is used for making food, beer and whisky; the grains of this plant）

B.（和某人）和谈，谈判，会谈（to discuss sth. with sb. in order to solve a disagreement）

C. 客厅；会客室（a room in a house, used for entertaining guests）

D. 把……押作赌注（to use a small amount of money to try to win a larger amount of money; to use something that you have in order to get something much better or much more valuable）

句子大意：政府拒绝与叛乱分子和谈。

Practice 4

1 B

A. 分支；分部；分行；分店（a local office or shop/store belonging to a large company or organization）

B. 固定表达 top brass（公司、机构等的）最高负责人，要员，头目（the people who are in the most important positions in a company, an organization, etc.）

C. 超级公司（或机构）（a very big and powerful company or organization）

D. 土匪（a member of an armed group of thieves who attack travelers）

句子大意：欧洲央行的高层将于周四在法兰克福召开会议，商定利率升幅。

2 C

A. ~ sb./sth. (from sth.) 饶恕；赦免；放过（to allow sb./sth. to escape harm, damage or death, especially when others do not escape it）

B. ~ sth. 促进，加速，刺激（某事发生）（to make sth. happen faster or sooner）

C. ~ (with sb.)（多指在友好气氛中）辩论，争论（to argue with sb., usually in a friendly way）

D. ~ sth./sb. 用矛刺；用尖物穿刺（to throw or push a spear or other pointed object through sth./sb.）

句子大意：他们友好地争论谁支持的球队更出色。

3 A

A. 因鸡毛蒜皮的小事争吵、拌嘴（to engage in a bad-tempered argument, often over a trivial matter）

常考同义词：bicker/wrangle

B. ~ sth.（使）打成平局，打平（to make the number of points you have scored in a game or competition equal to those of your opponents）

~ sb. 贿赂；收买；买通（to pay money to sb. in order to get their help）

C.（作动词使用）贮存；贮藏（to hoard or save things）

D. 草草记下，匆匆书写（尤指因时间仓促）（to write sth. quickly and carelessly, especially because you do not have much time）

句子大意：虽然爸妈总是为鸡毛蒜皮的小事争吵，但妈妈还是深爱着爸爸。

4 A

A. （= rancor，形容词形式为 rancorous）怨恨；怨毒（feelings of hatred and a desire to hurt other people, especially because you think that sb. has done sth. unfair to you）

B. 刺耳的；尖厉的（sounding loud and rough）

　粗鲁的，吵闹的，暴力的（rude, noisy, and violent）

C. [ræˈpɔ:(r)] ~ (with sb.)/~ (between A and B) 亲善；融洽；和谐（a friendly relationship in which people understand each other very well）

D. （态度或行为）反复无常的；任性的（showing sudden changes in attitude or behaviour）

句子大意：他们欺骗了我，但我并不怨恨他们。

5 A

A. ~ (for) sth. or ~ to do sth. 渴望；热望（to have a very strong desire for sth.）

B. ~ sb./sth. 勇敢面对；冒（风险）；经受（困难）（to have to deal with sth. difficult or unpleasant in order to achieve sth.）

C. ~ about sb./sth. 热烈谈论（或书写）；（热情洋溢地）奋笔疾书（to talk or write about sth. in a very enthusiastic way）

D. ~ off 防止，阻止发生 [to ward off (something adverse), forestall]

句子大意：他们的认可足以让她获得这个她梦寐以求的工作。

6 C

A. 精彩的表演；壮观的场面（a performance or an event that is very impressive and exciting to look at）

B. 〈正式〉眼镜（eyeglasses）

C. (= specter) ~ (of sth.) 恐惧；恐慌；忧虑（something unpleasant that people are afraid might happen in the future）

D. [ˈseptə(r)]（= sceptre）王权；（帝王的）权杖（a decorated stick that a king or queen carries at ceremonies）

句子大意：他的讲话令人担心他有可能在乌克兰使用这种武器。

7 C

A. 庄园宅第（a large country house surrounded by land that belongs to it）

B. 士气（the capacity of a group's members to maintain belief in an institution or goal, particularly in the face of opposition or hardship）

C.（固定表达）the ~ of sb./sth.（可继承的）责任，职责，衣钵（the role and responsibilities of an important person or job, especially when they are passed on from one person to another）

D. ['mɔːreɪz] 风俗习惯；传统（the customs and behaviour that are considered typical of a particular social group or community）

句子大意： 特拉斯继承了她的偶像玛格丽特·撒切尔的衣钵。

8 A

A. 过量；过剩（an amount that is greater than is needed or can be used）

常考同义词：surfeit ['sɜː(r)fɪt] (of sth.)，过量（an amount that is too large）

B.（一国或一个民族信仰的）众神，诸神（all the gods of a nation or people）

（统称某一领域的）名人，名流（a group of people who are famous within a particular area of activity）

万神庙；先贤祠；伟人祠 [a temple (= religious building) built in honour of all the gods of a nation; a building in which famous dead people of a nation are buried or honoured]

C. 浮游生物（the very small forms of plant and animal life that live in water）

D. 鬼魂；幽灵（a ghost）

幻觉；幻象（a thing that exists only in your imagination）

句子大意： 智能手机将数十亿人与互联网上应接不暇的过量信息和服务连接起来。

9 A

A. ['dɪsp(ə)rət]（与 different 基本同义，语气更为强烈，偏书面语）迥然不同的；无法比较的；不相干的（so different from each other that they cannot be compared or cannot work together）

B. 不拘一格的；兼收并蓄的（not following one style or set of ideas but choosing from or using a wide variety）

常考同义词：heterogeneous [ˌhetərəʊ'dʒiːniəs] 由很多种类组成的；各种各样的（consisting of many different kinds of people or things）

C. 辩证（法）的（using questions and answers as a method of examining something or of finding a solution to a problem）

D.（犹太人的）大流散（the movement of the Jewish people away from their own country to live and work in other countries）

（任何民族或群体的）大移居（the movement of people from any nation or group away from their own country）

句子大意： 这两种文化截然不同，以至于她发现很难适应另一种文化。

10 A

A. ['sɜː(r)kəmˌspekt] 小心谨慎的；考虑周密的；慎重的（thinking very carefully about sth. before doing it, because there may be risks involved）

B. [ˌsɜː(r)kəmˈvent] ~ sth. 设法回避；规避（to find a way of avoiding a difficulty or a rule; to go around something that is stopping you from going where you want）

C. 迂回的，委婉曲折的，拐弯抹角的（using or containing more words than necessary to express an idea）

D. 按情况推测的（containing information and details that strongly suggest that sth. is true but do not prove it）

句子大意：为了避免欺诈的发生，他们处理所有的业务交易都小心谨慎。

11 C

A. ~ sth. 维修；保养（to keep a building, a machine, etc. in good condition by checking or repairing it regularly）

~ sb./sth. 供养；扶养（to support sb./sth. over a long period of time by giving money, paying for food, etc.）

B. ~ sth. 保持；持有；继续拥有（to keep sth.; to continue to have sth.）

C. ~ sth. 遭受；蒙受（to experience sth. bad）

D. ~ sth. 玷污，败坏（名声）（to damage the opinion that people have of sth.）

句子大意：联合国一年一度的气候峰会——《联合国气候变化框架公约》第二十七次缔约方大会（COP27）在埃及开幕，与会代表一致同意将讨论是否就贫困国家因气候变化而遭受的损失进行赔偿。

12 A

A. 争论；争辩（a noisy argument or disagreement）

B. 改变；更改（the act of making a change to sth.）

C. [əˌlɪtəˈreɪʃ(ə)n] 头韵，头韵法（相连单词的开头使用同样的字母或语音）（the use of the same letter or sound at the beginning of words that are close together）

D. [ˌɪtəˈreɪʃ(ə)n] 迭代（the process of repeating a mathematical or computing process or set of instructions again and again, each time applying it to the result of the previous stage）

（计算机）新版软件（a new version of a piece of computer software）

句子大意：社交媒体上流传的视频显示，一辆卡车被推翻，食品供应被抢光，愤怒的居民与卫生官员发生争执。

13 A

A. [kənˈdʒiːniəl] ~ (to sb.) 合意的；适宜的（pleasant because it suits your character）；志趣相投的；合得来的（having a similar disposition, tastes, etc.; compatible; sympathetic）

~ (to sth.) 适合的；适当的（suitable for sth.）

B. 生性的；生就的（existing as part of a person's character and not likely to change）

生来有病的（born with a particular illness）

C. 一致同意的（which people in general agree with）

经双方同意的（which the people taking part have agreed to）

D. 推测的，猜想的（of the nature of, or involving conjecture; speculative）

句子大意： 该公司提供了一个宜人的办公环境。

14 C

A. 用钳子（夹）（to lift or move something with tongs）

B. （n.）锣；奖章；勋章（an award or medal given to sb. for the work they have done）

（v.）打锣；（交通警）鸣锣阻止汽车前进 [to summon (a driver) to stop by sounding a gong]

C. 群集；涌向（to go somewhere or be present somewhere in large numbers）

D. 掘翻（泥土等）；给……装上尖头（叉齿等）（to stab, pierce, or break up with a pronged device）

句子大意： 在双十一购物节（"光棍节"）期间，线下商店也人满为患。

15 A

A. （尤指因等待他人作决定）处于不定状态（a situation in which you are not certain what to do next, cannot take action, etc., especially because you are waiting for sb. else to make a decision）

B. 性欲；性冲动（sexual desire）

C. （n.）大型客机（尤指波音 747）（a large plane that can carry several hundred passengers, especially a Boeing 747）

（adj.）巨型的；巨大的；特大的（very large; larger than usual）

D. ['pætiəʊ]（房屋外面或后面的）露台，平台（a flat hard area outside, and usually behind, a house where people can sit）

句子大意： 他的生活好像陷入了不知所措的境地，进退两难。

16 C

nosedive v. 急剧下降；急转直下；暴跌（to fall suddenly）

A. （马等家畜的）饲料，秣（food for horses and farm animals）

（人或东西）只能是做……的料（people or things that are considered to have only one use）

B. 伪造；伪造罪（the crime of copying money, documents, etc. in order to cheat people）

伪造品；赝品（something, for example a document, piece of paper money, etc., that has been copied in order to cheat people）

C. ~ (into sth.)（从事新职业、活动的）尝试（an attempt to become involved in a different activity or profession）

~ (to/into...) 短途（寻物）；短暂访问（新地方）（a short journey to find a particular thing or to visit a new place）

D. （人）孤苦伶仃的；孤独凄凉的（appearing lonely and unhappy）

（地方）凄凉的；荒芜的（not cared for and with no people in it）

不大可能成功的；难以实现的（unlikely to succeed, come true, etc.）

注意区分 forlorn 与 foregone: a foregone conclusion 必然结果；不可避免的结局（If you say that sth. is a foregone conclusion, you mean that it is a result that is certain to happen.）

句子大意：由于投资者对这家公司以高昂的代价进军流媒体服务领域感到担忧，今年公司股价已经暴跌。

17 C

A. ~ sth. (with sth.)（尤指通过增添成就、成功等）使圆满，使完美（to make sth. complete or perfect, especially by adding an achievement, a success, etc.）

B. ~ for sth. or ~ to do sth. 渴望；热望（to have a very strong desire for sth.）

C. ~ sb. with sth./doing sth. 认为某人对某事有功劳（to say that someone is responsible for something good）

D. 反复唱；反复呼喊（to sing or shout the same words or phrases many times）

句子大意：在他上一任期期间，迪士尼成为世界上最令人敬畏的内容与技术巨头之一，他功不可没。

18 C

A. （某地方的）高度；（尤指）海拔（the height of a place, especially its height above sea level）

（水平或数量的）提高，升高，增加（an increase in the level or amount of sth.）

B. 海拔（the height above sea level）

C. 兴高采烈；欢欣鼓舞；喜气洋洋（a feeling of great happiness and excitement）

D. 巨大；重大；重要性（the great size or importance of sth.; the degree to which sth. is large or important）

震级（the size of an earthquake）

句子大意：跑完那么长距离的赛程后，欢欣之情会油然而生。

19 B

A. （尤指用手工）制作，塑造（to make or shape sth., especially with your hands）

B. ~ sth.（跌倒或碰撞时）起缓冲作用，缓和冲击（to make the effect of a fall or hit less severe）

~ sb./sth. (against/from sth.) 缓和打击（to protect sb./sth. from being hurt or damaged or from the unpleasant effects of sth.）

C. deal sb./sth. a blow 或 deal a blow to sb./sth. 给……以打击；使……受到伤害（to be very shocking or harmful to sb./sth.）

D. ~ sth. (on sb.) 造成（巨大的破坏或伤害）（to do great damage or harm to sb./sth.）

常用搭配：wreak havoc/destruction on sth. 造成巨大破坏（to cause a lot of trouble with something; to ruin or damage something）

与天然气和电力供应商签订的长期合同缓冲了今年能源价格上涨造成的冲击，但到

2023年能源价格攀升产生的影响将会充分显现出来。

20 C

A.（旧时为解决纷争的）决斗（a formal fight with weapons between two people, used in the past to settle a disagreement, especially over a matter of honour）

（双方的）竞争，斗争（a competition or struggle between two people or groups）

B. 一对表演者；搭档（two people who perform together or are often seen or thought of together）

C. [dju'res] 胁迫；强迫（a compulsion, coercion, or pressure to do something; threats used to compel someone to act contrary to his/her wishes or interests）

D. 抚摩；爱抚；亲吻（a gentle touch or kiss to show you love sb.）

句子大意：他声称自己是受到胁迫才签的供状。

Practice 5

1 D

A. ~ up to sth. 不辜负；符合（to be as good as what was expected or promised）

B. ~ up to sb. or sth. 走近或走到……面前（to move in front of or close to someone, something, or some position）

C. ~ up to sb. or sth. 符合；够得上；符合标准（to meet a particular requirement, standard, or expectation）

在质量、能力或技能等方面与……相同或不相上下（to be equal to someone or something in quality, ability, skill, etc.）

D. ~ up to sth. 卖次买好；升级消费层次（to exchange a lower-level product for a specific higher-level product）

（消费上）升级换代 [to trade something in (something, such as an automobile) for something more expensive or valuable of its kind]

句子大意：该政策的目标是鼓励那些坐享房屋价值大幅上涨的人们改善居住条件，"以小换大、以旧换新"。

2 C

A. 有规律地跳动（或发声）；均匀震动（to make strong regular movements or sounds）

~ with sth. 洋溢，充满（激情或活力）（to be full of excitement or energy）

B.（尤指战乱时用武力）抢劫，掠夺（to steal things from a place, especially using force during a time of war）

C. ~ sb./sth. 彻底击败（或战胜）；摧毁（to defeat or destroy sb./sth. completely）

D. ~ sb. 细心照顾，精心护理；娇惯，纵容（to take care of sb. very well and make them feel as comfortable as possible）

句子大意：在俄罗斯用导弹摧毁了乌克兰相当一部分能源基础设施之后，数百万民众的供水、供电和供热保障受到限制。

3 A

A. 整修；修复（the work of repairing and cleaning an old building, a painting, etc. so that its condition is as good as it originally was）

B. 归还（真正物主）；归还（赃物等）（the act of giving back sth. that was lost or stolen to its owner）

赔偿；（通常指）赔款（payment, usually money, for some harm or wrong that sb. has suffered）

常考同义词：reparation（战败国的）赔款（money that is paid by a country that has lost a war, for the damage, injuries, etc. that it has caused）

C. 修复；复原；复职（the act of restoring someone to a previous position）

D. 重新安装（the act of installing again）

句子大意：力拓集团 2020 年在澳大利亚西部开发铁矿时破坏了当地古老的原住民岩洞，日前已经同意出钱修复。

4 C

A. ~ sth. 言不由衷地说（to say sth. that you do not really feel, believe or understand）

B. ~ the bill 负担费用（to be responsible for paying the cost of sth.）

C. ~ sth. 欣赏；欣然接受；喜欢和……相处（to approve of sth. and be able to enjoy it; to enjoy being with a person）

D. 武装；装备（to provide weapons for yourself/sb. in order to fight a battle or a war）

句子大意：他们拥有巨额财富，即便只是分配其中一小部分就可以使得公共议程偏向他们能够接受的社会变革——那种不会威胁到他们或他们所处阶级的变革。

5 A

A. ['daɪətraɪb] ~ against sb./sth.（无休止的）指责；（长篇）抨击，谴责（a long and angry speech or piece of writing attacking and criticizing sb./sth.）

B.（印刷术发明之前的）抄写员，抄书吏（a person who made copies of written documents before printing was invented）

C. [kən'skraɪb] 征募；征用（to pick especially for required military service）

D. ~ sth. to sth. else 归咎于；归功于（to believe or say that something was caused by a particular thing; to believe or say that something was originally written or said by a particular person）

句子大意：埃隆·马斯克在如今收到自己麾下的社交媒体平台推特上发表了一篇抨击苹果的长文。

6 D

A. 向某人传送（电子信息）（to send a text message to sb.）

B. ['mɪrɑːʒ] n. 幻景；海市蜃楼（an effect caused by hot air in deserts or on roads, that makes you think you can see sth., such as water, which is not there）

幻想；妄想（a hope or wish that you cannot make happen because it is not realistic）

C. [mɒn'tɑːʒ] 蒙太奇；剪辑组合物（a picture, film/movie or piece of music or writing that consists of many separate items put together, especially in an interesting or unusual combination)

D. ['mæsɑːʒ] ~ sth. 美化（事实）；虚报（数量）；粉饰（to change facts, figures, etc. in order to make them seem better than they really are）

常考同义词：falsify（~ sth.）篡改，伪造（文字记录、信息）（to change a written record or information so that it is no longer true）

句子大意：部分企业通过编造数据来骗取政府补贴。

7 C

A. 即将发生（或来临）的（going to happen soon）

B. 奋发有为的，积极进取的，崭露头角的（likely to develop, become successful, or become popular soon; gaining prominence and likely to advance or succeed）

C.（人）乐于提供信息的（willing to give information about sth.）

（物）现成的；有提供的（ready or made available when needed）

即将发生（或出版等）的（going to happen, be published, etc. very soon）

D. 上述的；前述的（used to refer to sth. that has just been mentioned）

句子大意：他一直不肯提供有关合同的具体信息。

8 C

A. 臭气；恶臭（a strong, very unpleasant smell）

B. 身无分文的（without any money）

C. ~ as sth. 从事某项工作（或活动）的时间（a period of time that you spend working somewhere or doing a particular activity）

D. ~ sth.（通常表示愤怒、决心或不安时）捏紧，攥紧（拳头等），咬紧（牙齿等）（when you clench your hands, teeth, etc., or when they clench, you press or squeeze them together tightly, usually showing that you are angry, determined or upset）

句子大意：他一周前开始了担任首席执行官的第二个任期。

9 B

aficionado [əˌfɪʃəˈnɑːdəʊ]（某方面的）狂热爱好者，……迷（a person who likes a particular sport, activity or subject very much and knows a lot about it）

A.（在比赛或其他竞赛中）落后，失利，失败（to be losing a game or other contest）

B. ~ sb. 彻底打败；击溃（to defeat sb. completely）

常考同义词：trump（~ sth./sb.）胜过，打败（to beat sth. that sb. says or does by saying or doing sth. even better）

C. ~ sth. 使处于牢固地位；牢固确立（to establish sth. very firmly so that it is very difficult to change）

D. ~ sb. 使狂喜；使入迷（= trance）（if someone or something beautiful or impressive entrances you, you are so attracted by them that you give them all your attention）

句子大意：人工智能在象棋和围棋方面早已完胜人类，如今在 Diplomacy（强权外交 / 外交风云）这款游戏上也屡屡战胜人类。对于一些"外交风云"迷而言，这款游戏可以更加准确地体现玩家的能力。玩这款游戏需要相互配合，但也允许有背叛行为。

10 A

A. ~ that… 声明；公开宣称（to say firmly and often publicly what your opinion is, what you think is true, etc.）

B. 公开称赞某人 / 某事物；给予……高度评价（to praise or welcome sb./sth. publicly）

C. ~ sth. 不承认；否认；拒绝对……承担责任（to state publicly that you have no knowledge of sth. or that you are not responsible for sth./sb.）

D. ~ sth. 公开否认；拒绝承认（to state publicly that you have no knowledge of sth., or that you are not responsible for sth.）

~ sth. 放弃（财产、头衔等的）权利（to give up your right to sth., such as property or a title）

句子大意：尽管他公开宣称支持禁止堕胎，但他曾出钱让数位前任女友堕胎。

11 C

A. ~ sth. 调节（嗓音的大小、强弱、高低等）（to change the quality of your voice in order to create a particular effect by making it louder, softer, lower, etc.）

B. 起伏；荡漾（to go or move gently up and down like waves）

C. ~ (sth.) 审查在线聊天或帖子是否存在不当内容或言辞 [to monitor (the conversations in an online chatroom or posts on a message board) for bad language, inappropriate content, etc.]

D. [kəˈleɪt] ~ sth. 核对、校勘、对照（不同来源的信息）（to collect information together from different sources in order to examine and compare it）

~ sth. 整理（文件或书等）（to collect pieces of paper or the pages of a book, etc. and arrange them in the correct order）

句子大意：埃隆·马斯克收购推特造成的影响仍在持续。推特关闭了位于布鲁塞尔的办事处，这让欧盟官员们担心推特将不会遵守欧盟有关审查在线言论的规则。

12 C

A. wean off sth./wean off of sth./wean sb. off sth. 断绝，放弃；使某人不再依赖……（to slowly or gradually stop doing, ingesting, or consuming something to which one has developed a strong habit or dependency）

B. 意思同 A 选项

C. (be) weaned on sth. 从小就习惯……，养成了对……的依赖（to make someone get used to something when they are young）

D. 同 A 选项：wean away from sth./wean sb. away from sth.（= wean off sth./wean sb. off sth.）

句子大意：这一代人从小就养成了在电脑上打游戏的习惯，不过我还是要让孩子们多读读书或者到户外运动才行。

13 C

the works 一切可用或可有的东西（the entirety of what's available; all the related elements of something）

A. treat sb. with sth.（用某种物质）处理；以……方式对待某人（如：treat sb. with humanity/sincerity/contempt）

B. treat sb. for sth. 医治、治疗某种疾病（如：treat the patient for cancer）

C. treat sb. to sth. 招待，款待；买（可享受的东西）（to buy sth. special that sb. enjoys or arrange it for sb.）

D. treat sb. as sth./sb. else 像对待某人或某事物一样对待某人（如：treat John as his own son）

句子大意：伊曼纽尔·马克龙将会尽享一切礼遇，包括在白宫为他举办的国宴。

14 B

the eleventh hour 紧要关头，千钧一发之际（the critical moment）

Stormont 北爱尔兰议会大厦（常用来代指北爱尔兰议会）（the building in Northern Ireland that is used for meetings of the Northern Ireland Assembly）

A. ~ sth. 收回（成本）；弥补（亏损）（to get back an amount of money that you have spent or lost）

B. ~ sb. 召回某人（to order sb. to return）

~ sth. 收回，召回（残损货品等）（to ask for sth. to be returned, often because there is sth. wrong with it）

C. ~ sth.（稍微改动）重新推出；以新形式表达旧内容（to arrange ideas, pieces of writing or pieces of film into a new form but without any great change or improvement）

D. ~ sth.（通常指）改进外观，翻新（to make changes to the form of sth., usually to improve its appearance）

句子大意：北爱尔兰议会的议员在最后时刻被召回以组建政府。

15 A

A. ~ sth. 征用，没收（私有财产）（to officially take away private property from its owner for public use）

~ sth. 侵占（他人财产）（to take sb.'s property and use it without permission）

近义词：commandeer（战争期间为军事目的而）强征；强占（to officially take someone's property for military use; to take something that belongs to someone else; to take arbitrary or forcible possession of）

B. ~ sth. 盗用；挪用；侵吞（to take sth., sb.'s ideas, etc. for your own use, especially illegally or without permission）

~ sth. (for sth.) 拨（专款等）（to take or give sth., especially money for a particular purpose）

C. [ˈæprəʊˌbeɪt] 认可，批准（to approve officially）

D. 证实，确证（to support with evidence or authority）

句子大意：早在10月份，俄罗斯政府没收了该公司的部分在俄资产，之后该公司两手空空地撤出了俄罗斯。

16 A

A. 爱争吵的；粗暴的；好斗的；寻衅的（tending to argue or be bad-tempered; slightly aggressive; disposed or eager to fight or engage in hostile opposition; belligerent）

B. 半透明的（allowing light to pass through but not transparent）

C. ['trænziənt] 短暂的；转瞬即逝的（continuing for only a short time）

D. 逃学的（absent without permission, especially from school）

偷懒的；混日子的（idle, lazy, or neglectful）

句子大意：这些铁杆粉丝在他们支持的队伍落败后激愤不已、躁动不安。

17 A

A. 种类；类型；观点（a type, category or opinion）

（军装或警服上表示等级的）条，杠（a narrow piece of cloth, often in the shape of a V, that is worn on the uniform of a soldier or police officer to show their rank）

B. （陆地、海域等）狭长地带；带状水域（a long narrow area of land, sea, etc.）

C. 固定东西的带子（a strip of leather, cloth or other material that is used to fasten sth., keep sth. in place, carry sth. or hold onto sth.）

D. 基本食物；主食（a basic type of food that is used a lot）

（某国的）主要产品，支柱产品（something that is produced by a country and is important for its economy）

~ (of sth.) 主要部分；重要内容（a large or important part of sth.）

句子大意：他让几位政治立场较为温和的高级人物匆忙退休。

18 A

A. 尽管面临挑战依然继续存在下去、坚持下去（to continue or persist despite challenges）（如 The company will not be able to hold on if we lose money again this quarter.）

没有"How are you holding on?"的表达。

B. 阻止；抑制（to stop someone or something from moving forward）

C. 继续存活或存在；不退让，坚持到底，负隅顽抗（to continue to survive or endure; to continue to defend a place that is being attacked）

How long will sb. or sth. hold out? 表达某人或某物还能坚持多久/用多久的意思，但没有"How is sb./sth. holding out?"的表达。

D. 保持坚挺或良好的状态（to remain strong or in a fairly good condition）

惯用表达："How are you holding up?"（"你还好吗？"通常是对经历了不幸的人的问候语）

句子大意：分析家们想要看看在美国经济脆弱的大环境下这些主题公园能否挺得住。

19 A

A. 特有的；典型的；有代表性的（that is considered typical of a situation, an area of work, etc.）

B.（要加 the）the ~ of sth. 典型；典范（a perfect example of sth.）

C. 强调的；有力的（an emphatic statement, answer, etc. is given with force to show that it is important）
明确表示的；加强语气的（making it very clear what you mean by speaking with force）

D. 地方性的；（某地或某集体中）特有的，流行的，难摆脱的（regularly found in a particular place or among a particular group of people and difficult to get rid of）

句子大意：这家负债累累的房地产开发商面临的困境是该国整体经济问题的缩影。该公司只有满足监管部门提出的条件才能避免永久退市。

20 A

A. ~ sb./sth./yourself (for sth.) 严厉批评；申斥（to criticize sb./sth. severely）

B. 倾泻；流注（to flow downwards in large amounts）

C. ~ sb./sth. 割除（男子或雄性动物的）睾丸；阉割（to remove the testicles of a male animal or person）

D. 使便秘（to cause somebody or something to become constipated）

句子大意：我不想变成那种批评年轻人沟通方式的老人。

Practice 6

1 B

exponent（观点、理论等的）拥护者，鼓吹者，倡导者（a person who supports an idea, theory, etc. and persuades others that it is good）

A. 关于人类存在的；与人类存在有关的（connected with human existence）

B. 没有直接联系的；无关的（not directly connected with the particular situation you are in or the subject you are dealing with）

C. 摆脱得了的；能救出的；能脱险的（able to be freed or removed from an entanglement or difficulty）

D. [ekˈsɒdʒənəs] 外生的；外源的（originating outside an organism or system）

常考反义词：endogenous [enˈdɒdʒənəs] 内源性的；内生的（having no obvious cause）

句子大意：极简主义室内装修风格起源于20世纪初的现代主义，20世纪90年代逐渐流行起来。有些极简主义的倡导者称，极简主义对不相干的元素零容忍。

2 A

A. 折磨；痛苦（pain and suffering or sth. that causes it）

B. 不可数名词：遭受；强加（痛苦或折磨）（the infliction of pain/suffering）

C. 不情愿；不乐意；无意（a lack of willingness to do sth.; a lack of enthusiasm for sth.）

D. 性格；性情（the natural qualities of a person's character）

~ to/towards sth./~ to do sth. 倾向；意向（a tendency to behave in a particular way）

（财产、金钱的）处置，让与（a formal act of giving property or money to sb.）

句子大意：数十年来，心理健康一直是最不受重视的公共健康领域之一。焦虑和抑郁是最为常见的心理健康问题。

3 A

A. ~ sb./sth. (with sth.) 使充满，灌输，激发（强烈感情、想法或价值）（to fill sb./sth. with strong feelings, opinions or values）

B. ~ (sth.) 喝，饮（酒等）（to drink sth., especially alcohol）

   ~ sth. 吸收，接受（信息等）（to absorb sth., especially information）

C. ~ sb./sth. (in sth.) 使浸没于（to put sb./sth. into a liquid so that they or it are completely covered）

   ~ yourself/sb. in sth.（使）深陷于，沉浸在（to become or make sb. completely involved in sth.）

D. ~ sth. 满足（欲望、兴趣等）（to satisfy a particular desire, interest, etc.）

   放纵；听任（to be too generous in allowing sb. to have or do whatever they like）

   ~ in sth. 参加，参与（尤指违法活动）（to take part in an activity, especially one that is illegal）

句子大意： 英国艺术评论家约翰·拉斯金（John Ruskin）曾写道：建筑物身上遭到破坏的痕迹是"时间的金色污点"，可以让建筑充满壮丽之感。

4 C

A. 流放；流亡；放逐（the state of being sent to live in another country that is not your own, especially for political reasons or as a punishment）

   流亡国外者；被流放者；离乡背井者（a person who chooses, or is forced to live away from his or her own country）

B. 移民；移居外国（the relocation or process of people leaving one country to reside in another）

C. ~ (from…) (to…)（大批人同时）离开（a situation in which many people leave a place at the same time）

D. 愉快；兴奋（excitement and happiness）

句子大意： 业界曾经非常担心华尔街的人才会为逃避薪酬限制而纷纷出走，但至少就目前来看，这不过是虚惊一场。

5 B

A. 大型客机（尤指波音 747）（a large plane that can carry several hundred passengers, especially a Boeing 747）

B. [ˌdʒæmbəˈri] 大型聚会；庆祝会（a large party or celebration）

   童子军大会；女童子军大会（a large meeting of Scouts or Guides）

C. 混合物；（尤指食物的）杂烩，组合餐（a number of different things combined together, especially different types of food）

D. 乐团，剧团，舞剧团（全体成员）（a small group of musicians, dancers or actors who perform together）

句子大意： 实力转移成为上周的一个重要主题：在达沃斯（Davos）经济论坛上，人们纷纷把注意力集中在了印度和中国身上。

6 C

A. ~ sth. 公然藐视，无视（法律等）（to show that you have no respect for a law, etc. by openly not obeying it）

B. 发红；脸红（to become red, especially because you are embarrassed, angry or hot）

~ (sth.) 冲（抽水马桶）（When a toilet flushes or you flush it, water passes through it to clean it, after a handle, etc. has been pressed.）

C. ['fʊlmɪneɪt] ~ against sb./sth. 愤怒谴责；怒斥（to criticize sb./sth. angrily）

D. 不知所措（to struggle to know what to say or do or how to continue with sth.）

困难重重；艰苦挣扎（to have a lot of problems and to be in danger of failing completely）

句子大意：形形色色的政治家都在大肆批评英国名牌大学招收的贫困家庭的学生太少。

7 A

A. ~ sth. 把……烧成灰烬；焚毁（to burn sth. until it is completely destroyed）

B. ~ sb. (in sth.) 监禁；关押（to put sb. in prison or in another place from which they cannot escape）

C. ~ sth. 将（概念或品质）具体化；拟人化（to give a definite or human form to a particular idea or quality）

D. ['ɪnkʌlkeɪt] 反复灌输；谆谆教诲（to cause sb. to learn and remember ideas, moral principles, etc., especially by repeating them often）

句子大意：在西班牙北部，接近历史最高记录的高温天气引发野火，林地过火面积约1100公顷。

8 A

A. （事）需要付出很大努力的；（人）要求严格的（needing or demanding a lot of effort and care about details）

B. （没有形容词形式）提取；抽出；摘出（要点）（to get something from someone who does not want to give it to you; to get the exact information that you need from a lot of information that you have）

C. 极痛苦的；糟糕透顶的（extremely painful or bad）

D. （没有形容词形式）没收（财产等）；征用（土地）；把……据为己有（to take someone's land, money, or possessions and use them for public purposes; to take something that does not belong to you and use it for yourself）

句子大意：塔塔先生说，他曾经认为，美国的消费者比较挑剔，人们也痴迷大型车，这些都不适合小型车 Nano 的发展。

9 A

A. 一段时间的艰苦工作（或努力）（a period of hard work or effort）

B. 接吻爱抚（If two people snog, or if one person snogs another, they kiss and hold each other for a period of time.）

C. 烟雾（烟与雾混合的空气污染物，尤见于城市）（a form of air pollution that is or looks like a mixture of smoke and fog, especially in cities）

D. 被盗货品；赃物（goods that have been stolen）

（挂于窗户等上方的）装饰性布幔（或帷幕）（cloth that is hung in large curved folds as decoration, especially above a window）

句子大意：这一成就是他为钟表业做出的贡献，为他赢得了诸多荣誉，但这只是他为普及自己理念而踏上的漫漫征程的起点。

10 A

A. 计划中；进行中（being planned; happening）

B. （在水上）漂浮（floating on water）

有偿债能力；能维持下去（having enough money to pay debts; able to survive）

C. 在（船、飞机、公共汽车、火车等）上（on or onto a ship, plane, bus or train）

D. run afoul of sth.（= run foul of sth.）（与法律、规章、当权者等）相抵触，有冲突（to do sth. that is not allowed by a law or rule, or to do sth. that people in authority disapprove of）

句子大意：跨国公司倾向于通过在低税率地区报税来减少整体纳税额，但这种情况正在发生变化。

11 A

A. ~ sth.（尤指私自或非法）抽走，转移（钱）（to remove money from one place and move it to another, especially dishonestly or illegally）

B. 用管子将气体或液体转移 [to remove some gas or liquid (from something or some place) using one or more pipes]

C. ~ sth./sb. (from sth.) (into sth.) 使改变外观（或性质）；使改观（to completely change the appearance or character of sth., especially so that it is better）

D. ~ (sb./sth.)（通常见于科幻作品）（被）远距离传送 [(usually in science fiction) to move sb./sth. immediately from one place to another a distance away, using special equipment; to be moved in this way]

句子大意：从理论上来讲，这一条款将减少公司通过将利润转移到避税天堂获得的收益。

12 A

A. ~ sb. to sth. 迫使……接受困境（或不愉快的状况）（to force sb. to accept a difficult or unpleasant situation）

B. ~ sth. or ~ (sb.) doing sth. 容忍；纵容（to accept behaviour that is morally wrong or to treat it as if it were not serious）

C. ~ sb./sth. to sth. 限制；限定（to keep sb./sth. inside the limits of a particular activity, subject, area, etc.）

D. ~ sth. (into sth.) 精简；浓缩；压缩（to reduce sth. and fit it into a smaller space or amount of time）

句子大意：英国可能不得不像挪威和荷兰一样禁止饲养英国斗牛犬，让这一国家象征"流亡国外"。

13 A

A. ~ sth. 减轻（问题的严重性）；缓和，缓解（to make a problem less serious）

B. ~ sth.（尤指在想象中）再次体验，重温（to experience sth. again, especially in your imagination）

C.（使）苏醒，复活（to become, or to make sb./sth. become, conscious or healthy and strong again）

复兴，振兴（to become, or to make something become, active, successful, or popular again）

D. ~ sth. 挽回；找回（to get back sth. that was lost）

句子大意：伊朗将会切断对118家获批加密挖矿公司的电力供应，希望借此缓解该国电网的紧张局面。

14 C

A. 虚度光阴者；游手好闲者；浪子；二流子（a person who wastes their time rather than working）

B. 树懒（南美洲热带动物，行动缓慢）（a South American animal that lives in trees and moves very slowly）

懒散，怠惰（the bad habit of being lazy and unwilling to work）

C. 赖账者；不讲信用的公司（a person or company that tries to avoid paying their debts）

懒人；二流子；身无分文的无业者（a lazy person; a person with no job and no money, who is not part of normal society）

（不与子女同住，也不支付抚养费的）无良父亲，失职父亲（a father who does not live with his children and does not pay their mother any money to take care of them）

D. 浪费……的人；耗费……的东西（a person or thing that uses too much of sth. in an unnecessary way）

废物；饭桶；酒囊饭袋（a person who is useless or no good at anything）

句子大意：如果欠账不还的"老赖"试图离境，警方有权在海关检查站予以阻止。

15 A

A. 产生不良影响（to have an unpleasant effect）

B. 连续猛击；殴打（to hit sb./sth. hard many times, especially in a way that causes serious damage）

C. ~ (on sb.) 产生事与愿违的不良（或危险）后果；适得其反（to have the opposite effect to the one intended, with bad or dangerous results）

D.（只有名词形式）~ (from sb.) against sth.（对社会变动等的）强烈抵制，集体反对（a strong negative reaction by a large number of people, for example to sth. that has recently changed in society）

句子大意：由于审查制度不断加强以及西方制裁开始产生影响，各个城市的生活变得越发让人难以忍受。

16 A

A. ~ sb./sth. of sth.; be starved of/for sth. 极需；缺乏（to suffer the lack of sth.）

B. a ~ (of sth.) 缺乏；不足（a lack of sth.）

C. 不足额；赤字；缺少（the amount by which sth., especially an amount of money, is too small or smaller than sth. else）

D. ~ to do sth. or ~ for sth. 不充分的；不够重要的（not large, strong or important enough for a particular purpose）

句子大意：自从这所地方大学关闭以来，这家酒店一直处于临时工人手不够的状态。

17 A

Cassandra [kəˈsændrə] 灾祸预言家；（希神）卡桑德拉（特洛伊国王的女儿，拥有预言灾祸的能力，但是从来没有人相信她的预言）（a person who predicts that sth. bad will happen）

A.（有 notwithstanding sth. 的搭配）虽然；尽管（without being affected by sth.; despite sth.）

B.（没有 nevertheless sth. 的搭配）尽管如此，不过（despite sth. that you have just mentioned）

C.（后面通常要跟句子）虽然；尽管（used for introducing a statement that makes the main statement in a sentence seem surprising）

D.（常见搭配为 while sb. does sth. 或 while doing…, sb. does…）虽然；尽管（although; despite the fact that…）

句子大意：尽管已经有少数几个灾祸预言家正确预测了该行业的黯淡前景，但毫无疑问，整个行业实则遭受重创。

18 A

A. 应对，处理，将……考虑在内（to deal with someone or something; to cope with someone or something; to prepare for, or take into account someone or something）

B. ~ sth. with sth. 使和谐一致；调和（to find an acceptable way of dealing with two or more ideas, needs, etc. that seem to be opposed to each other）

~ sb./yourself (to sth.) 将就；妥协（to make sb./yourself accept an unpleasant situation because it is not possible to change it）

C. ~ (to sth.) (with sth./by doing sth.) 做出回应（to do sth. as a reaction to sth. that sb. has said or done）

D. ~ sth. 对……进行调整；使适应新形势（to make changes to sth. in order to adapt it to a new situation）

~ yourself (with sb./sth.) 改变观点，改变策略（以与别人相同）（to change your opinions, policies, etc. so that they are the same as those of another person, group, etc.）

句子大意：由于美国民众面临着汽油价格飞涨和高通胀的压力，拜登总统呼吁国会暂停收缴三个月的联邦燃油税。

19 A

A. 不活跃的；低迷的；萧条的（not very busy; with not much activity）

B. 生存的；生计的（existing, or continuing in existence）

C. [ek'stænt] 尚存的；现存的（still in existence）

D. 关于人类存在的；与人类存在有关的（connected with human existence）

句子大意：以历史标准衡量的话，本轮复苏仍可能相对温和。

20 A

funk 恐惧；忧虑（a state of fear or anxiety）

A.（因寒冷、害怕或激动而）发抖，发颤，战栗（to shake because you are cold or frightened, or because of a strong feeling）

B.（使感情、希望或信念等）粉碎，破灭（to destroy sth. completely, especially sb.'s feelings, hopes or beliefs）

C. 捣毁；打败；粉碎（to destroy, defeat or put an end to sth./sb.）

D.（使）枯萎，皱缩（to become or make sth. dry and wrinkled as a result of heat, cold or being old）

句子大意：英国经济由消费者的消费意愿驱动。因此，在今年早些时候，当有关消费成本危机的讨论让英国消费者陷入恐慌时，经济学家们都不寒而栗。

Practice 7

1 D

A. ~ sth. 毁掉；覆盖；清除（to remove all signs of sth., either by destroying or covering it completely）

B. [æk'sentʃueɪt] ~ sth. 着重；强调；使突出（to emphasize sth. or make it more noticeable）

C. ~ (between A and B)（情感或行为）摇摆，波动，变化（to keep changing from one extreme of feeling or behaviour to another, and back again）

D. ~ sth. 消除……；不再需要……（to remove a problem or the need for sth.）

句子大意：随着钢筋混凝土和钢架技术的进步，室内不再需要承重墙，因此空间变得宽敞、开阔起来。

2 B

A. punter 顾客；主顾；客户（a person who buys or uses a particular product or service）

B. 朋克摇滚乐迷（a person who likes punk music and dresses like a punk musician, for example by wearing metal chains, leather clothes and having brightly coloured hair）

小流氓；小混混；小阿飞 [(informal) a young man or boy who behaves in a rude or violent way]

C. 行家；权威；专家（a person who knows a lot about a particular subject and who often talks about it in public）

D.（尤指火车站、机场或旅馆）行李员，搬运工（a person whose job is carrying people's bags and other loads, especially at a train station, an airport or in a hotel）

（医院里的）护工（a person whose job is to move patients from one place to another in a hospital）

句子大意： 本周末，参加格拉斯顿伯里音乐节（Glastonbury Music Festival）的乐迷将会欣赏到 3000 多位艺术家在超过 100 个舞台上呈现的表演。

3 A

A. 气味（the property of a substance that gives it a characteristic scent or smell）

与某人相处融洽或不合（be in good odour or be in bad odour with sb.）

B. 芳香；香味（a pleasant, noticeable smell）

C. 香味；芳香（a pleasant smell）

香水（a liquid that you put on your skin in order to make yourself smell nice）

D. 恶臭；难闻的气味（a strong unpleasant smell）

句子大意： 是友谊让朋友之间的气味相近还是因为"气味相投"才会成为朋友？

备注： 带有"香味"含义的单词辨析

aroma 指一种强烈的、弥漫的香味，如烟叶、咖啡或美味食品散发出的香味。

scent 指天然的淡淡幽香。

perfume 尤指由香精中所散发的香味。

fragrance 特指植物的清新香味。

4 A

A. 独特的；有特色的（having a quality or characteristic that makes sth. different and easily noticed）

B. 清晰的；清楚的；明显的（easily or clearly heard, seen, felt, etc.）

C. 差异化的（clearly different from others）

D. 不一致的；不协调的；不和的（not in agreement; combining with other things in a way that is strange or unpleasant）

句子大意： 温网是英国一年一度的网球赛事，以传承古老传统而闻名，在网球界向来独树一帜。

备注： distinct 和 distinctive 辨析

*distinct 用于描述两个或多个不同事物或事物群体，如：

The book has three distinct parts. 这本书有三个不同的部分。

There are two distinct ethnic groups. 有两个不同的民族。

此外，distinct 也可以修饰 possibility（可能性）或 impression（印象）用以表示强烈、明显，如：

A flight cancellation is a distinct possibility. 航班取消的可能性很大。

We had the distinct impression that they were lying. 我们明显感觉到他们在撒谎。

*distinctive 常用来表达某个人或物具有独有的、区别于其他人或物的特质，如：

He had a distinctive walk. 他走路很有特色。

This wine has a more distinctive flavor than that one. 这种酒的味道比那种酒更独特。

This store sells only the most distinctive chocolates. 这家商店只卖最有特色的巧克力。

5 A

A. ~ sth. 废除，废止，撤销（法律、协议等）（to officially end a law, an agreement, etc.）

B. 证实；使（信仰等）坚定；使加强（to support what someone says by giving information or evidence that agrees with them）

C. ~ sb. 逮捕；拘押（to catch sb. and arrest them）

~ sth. 理解；认识到（to understand or recognize sth.）

D.（不及物动词）~ (on sth.) 违背（诺言）；背信弃义（to break a promise, an agreement, etc.）

句子大意：人们不应将摆脱冷战思维简单地理解为废除冷战时达成的军控条约。

6 A

A. 固定表达：stay the course 坚持到底（to continue attempting or pursuing something difficult to its end or conclusion）

B.（尤指机场或火车站的）大厅，广场（a large, open part of a public building, especially an airport or a train station）

C.（支持或为之奋斗的）事业，目标，思想（an aim or idea that people support or fight for）

D. 粗的；大颗粒的（consisting of relatively large pieces）

粗鲁无礼的，粗俗的（尤指涉及性的）（rude and offensive, especially about sex）

句子大意：如果事情稍有不顺你就坚持不下去了，那就说明你不是干这行的料。

7 A

pecs = pectoral ['pekt(ə)rəl] 胸大肌

jibe (at sb./sth.) 嘲讽；嘲弄；讥讽（an unkind or insulting remark about sb.）

A. [ˌpriːdɪˈlekʃ(ə)n] ~ (for sth.) 喜爱；偏爱；钟爱（If you have a predilection for sth., you like it very much.）

常考近义词1：penchant ['penʃənt] for sth. 爱好；嗜爱（a special liking for sth.）

常考近义词2：proclivity (for sth./for doing sth.)（常指对坏事的）倾向，癖好（a natural tendency to do sth. or to feel sth., often sth. bad）

B. 形容词形式为 petulant: 闹脾气的；爱耍性子的；任性的（bad-tempered and unreasonable, especially because you cannot do or have what you want）

C. ['pendjʊləm] 钟摆（a long straight part with a weight at the end that moves regularly from side to side to control the movement of a clock）

D. 见解；主张；观点（a statement that expresses an opinion）

提议，建议，计划（尤指业务上的）（an idea or a plan of action that is suggested, especially in business）

句子大意：他敦促自己的朋友向皮特秀"肌肉"，以此来嘲讽皮特袒胸拍照的偏好。

8 A

A. ~ (sth.) 狂饮；猛喝；（英式英语）狼吞虎咽 [to drink sth. quickly and in large amounts (In British English it also means to eat food quickly and in large amounts.)]

B.（火等）发出嘶嘶声（When sth., especially sth. that is burning, it makes a sound like a long "s".）

C. 发出（油煎食物的）咝咝声（to make the sound of food frying in hot oil）

D. 使醉；使迷糊；经常过量饮酒（to make a person or mental faculty confused, often through intoxication; to drink too much alcohol regularly）

句子大意：美国民众将在未来一段时间内面临汽油价格居高不下的局面。

9 C

A. ~ sth. (through sth.) 引导；使通过（尤指复杂的地方或系统）（to guide sb./sth. somewhere, especially through a complicated place or system）

~ sth. 试点；试行（to test a new product, idea, etc. with a few people or in a small area before it is introduced everywhere）

B. ~ sth. 当开拓者；做先锋；倡导（When sb. pioneers sth., they are one of the first people to do, discover or use sth. new.）

C. 转变方向或做事情的方式（to change direction; to change the way in which something is done）

常见词组搭配：pivot sb./sth. (to/towards sth.) (away from sth.)；pivot towards doing sth.

D. ~ sth. 盗印；窃用（to copy and use or sell sb.'s work or a product without permission and without having the right to do so）

句子大意：环保人士认为，减少化石燃料供应是推动美国向更清洁能源转型的必要之举。

10 A

A. ~ for... 会产生……的结果，是成为……的好材料（to produce or result in something; to be good material for something）

B. ~ for... 前往；朝……方向走去 [head for (someone or something) to proceed or move toward someone or something]

C. ~ to/towards... 倾向于；受到吸引（to be attracted to someone and go to be with them; to be interested in something and want to do it or to have it）

D. ~ for... 选取；赞成 [to decide to accept (someone or something) from a group of possibilities]

句子大意：注重小细节有助于让旅行变得更加愉快。

11 A

A. 免得；以免（in order to prevent sth. from happening）

B. 除非；除非在……情况下（used to say that sth. can only happen or be true in a particular situation）

C. 到……时；直到……为止（up to the point in time or the event mentioned）

D. 纵然；就算；甚至（used for emphasizing that although something may happen or may be true, another situation remains the same）

句子大意： 欧洲央行、美联储和英格兰银行的行长敦促采取快速行动来抑制通胀，以防通胀"根深蒂固"、积重难返。

12 A

A. 特殊句式：...(somewhere or something) or bust 不去某地或做某事决不罢休，一定要力争……，不成功便成仁（an expression used to indicate that someone will not stop trying until they arrive at a certain place or achieve a certain goal）

B. be bursting to do sth. 急于（或迫切想）做某事（to want to do sth. so much that you can hardly stop yourself）

C. 除此之外（except for what has just been referred to）

例句：The poor sound quality ruined an otherwise beautiful film. 本来是一部优秀的电影，可是却被这糟糕的音质给毁了。

D.（有时用于句末，表示所说非所想）才不是呢（sometimes used at the end of a statement to show that you did not mean what you have said）

例句：That was the best meal I've ever had-not! 那是我吃过的最棒的一餐——是才怪呢！

句子大意： 自从孩童年代起，汤姆就立志非做海军陆战队员不可。

13 A

A. ~ sb./yourself 痛斥；严厉指责（to criticize or speak angrily to sb. because you do not approve of sth. they have done）

B. ~ sb. (to do sth.) 恳求；哀求；乞求（to ask sb. for sth. in an anxious way because you want or need it very much）

C. ~ sth. 引发；导致（to make sth. happen）

D. ~ sth. 哀怨；悲叹（to complain or say that you are not happy about sth.）

句子大意： 如果你为自己定的目标过高，并且已经感觉自己是无法达到的，不要因此而责备自己。毕竟大部分人都会有这种经历。

14 A

A. 坚定自信的；坚决主张的（behaving confidently and not being frightened to say what you want or believe）

B. 着迷的；迷恋的；难以释怀的（thinking too much about one particular person or thing, in a way that is not normal）

C. ~ to sth. 注意的；专心的；留心的（listening or watching carefully and with interest）

~ to sb. 关心的；肯帮忙的（helpful; making sure that people have what they need）

D. ~ sth. (with/to sth.) 使一致（to change sth. slightly so that it is in the correct relationship to sth. else）

123

句子大意：该命令对该监管机构来说是一个不同寻常的大胆举措，近年来，该机构因对汽车制造商不够强硬而受到批评。

15 A

A. 退缩；畏缩（to move your body quickly away from sb./sth. because you find them or it frightening or unpleasant）

~ from sth./from doing sth. or ~ at sth. 对……做出厌恶（或恐惧）的反应（to react to an idea or a situation with strong dislike or fear）

B. 退却；撤退（to move away from a place or an enemy because you are in danger or because you have been defeated）

（由于批评或环境过于恶劣）改变主意，退缩（to change your mind about sth. because of criticism or because a situation has become too difficult）

C. 节约；紧缩开支（to spend less money; to reduce costs）

~ sb. 缩减（人员）（to tell sb. that they cannot continue working for you）

D. ~ sth. 沿原路返回；折回（to go back along exactly the same path or route that you have come along）

~ sth. 重走（别人走过的路线）（to make the same trip that sb. else has made in the past）

~ sth. 追溯；找出；回顾（to find out what sb. has done or where they have been）

句子大意：我试图用衣服遮住伤疤。学校里的孩子都躲着我。邻居们都可怜我，在某种程度上，父母也可怜我。

16 A

A. 有充分准备；准备好；蓄势待发（completely ready for sth. or to do sth.）

泰然自若的；沉着自信的；稳健的（having a calm and confident manner and in control of your feelings and behaviour）

B. be well/ideally/perfectly positioned to do sth. 有充分的能力、条件或资格做某事（to be in a situation in which you will be able to do something successfully）

C. brace oneself for sth./be braced for sth. （针对困难的或令人不快的事物）稳住情绪或做好准备（to physically or mentally prepare oneself for something, typically something that is imminent, in an attempt to limit any adverse impact）

D. ~ (to do sth.) 命中注定的；上天安排的（already decided or planned by God or by fate）

句子大意：据信，它目前拥有几十个核装置，似乎已做好进行第七次核试验的准备。

17 B

A. ~ (in sth./sb.) 相信；信心（a strong feeling that sth./sb. exists or is true; confidence that sth./sb. is good or right）

B. 词组搭配：put stock in... 重视，相信，接受（= place stock in...）（to pay attention to something; to have or invest faith or belief in something; to accept something）

与 stock 有关的其他常考搭配 1：on the stocks 在制作（或建造、准备）中（in the process of

being made, built or prepared）

与 stock 有关的其他常考搭配 2：take stock of sth.（对某情况）加以总结；做出评估；进行反思；盘点（to stop and think carefully about the way in which a particular situation is developing in order to decide what to do next）

C. put a premium on… 格外重视（to place an especially high value on something）

D. do sb. credit 或 do credit to sb. 使值得赞扬（If sth. does credit to a person or an organization, they deserve to be praised for it.）

其他常考搭配：on the credit side（尤用于提及缺点之后）就优点方面而言（used to introduce the good points about sb./sth., especially after the bad points have been mentioned）

句子大意：她的父亲对她完成这项工作的能力很有信心。

18 A

A. 演变成……（to degenerate or deteriorate gradually）

B.（使）旋转

~ around… 以……为主要（考虑）；以……为中心（兴趣）（to have sth. as a primary focus, theme or interest）

C. 内卷（to become complex or inwardly rolled, whorled, or curved）

D. ~ sth. 解除（婚姻关系）；终止（商业协议）；解散（议会）（to officially end a marriage, business agreement or parliament）

~ into laughter, tears, etc. 禁不住（笑起来或哭起来等）（to suddenly start laughing, crying, etc.）

句子大意：批评人士已经发出警告，称二十国集团可能会发展成为另一个长期纸上谈兵但无法形成具体成果 / 雷声大雨点小的国际组织。

19 A

A.（常因疾病、饥饿或忧虑而）瘦削憔悴的（very thin, usually because of illness, not having enough food, or worry）

B.（驾驶等用的）长手套，防护手套（a strong glove with a wide covering for the wrist, used for example when driving）

C. ~ sb. 辱骂；嘲笑；讽刺；奚落（to try to make sb. angry or upset by saying unkind things about them, laughing at their failures, etc.）

D. 悠闲地走；漫步；闲逛（to walk in a slow relaxed way）

句子大意：水果、蔬菜和肉食对大多数人来说都是奢侈品，在对该国进行实地报道的多年里，我在各地见到过许多皮肤上有斑点、面颊深陷、骨瘦如柴的人，这些都是营养不良的表现。

20 A

A.（用清水）冲掉，洗刷（to remove dirt, etc. from sth. by washing it with clean water）

B. ~ (sth.) 冲（抽水马桶）（When a toilet flushes or you flush it, water passes through it to clean it, after a handle, etc. has been pressed.）

（用水）冲走（to get rid of sth. with a sudden flow of water）

C. （使）变清醒，变清晰（If your head or mind clears, or you clear it, you become free of thoughts that worry or confuse you or the effects of alcohol, a blow, etc. and you are able to think clearly.）

D. ~ (sth.) 清洁（皮肤）；清洗（伤口）（to clean your skin or a wound）

句子大意：我看到过朝鲜的护士把注射器倒在水盆里，用消毒剂冲洗干净后重复使用。

Practice 8

1 C

A. 搅浑；搅乱；惹怒（to disrupt sth.; to anger or annoy sb.）

B. 彻底击败；使溃败（to completely defeat someone in a battle, competition, or election）

C. ~ (at/against sth./sb.) 怒斥；责骂；抱怨（to complain about sth./sb. in a very angry way）

D. 吵架；大声争辩（to have a noisy argument）

句子大意：多年来，该国领导人一直怒斥国内金融行业中存在的贪婪和腐败现象，在此过程中树立了一些杀鸡儆猴的典型。

2 A

garlic clove 蒜瓣；garlic bulb 蒜头

A. 不冷不热的；微温的（slightly warm, sometimes in a way that is not pleasant）

不热情的；不热烈的（not enthusiastic）

B. 无味道的；淡而无味的（having almost no taste or flavour）

没有趣味的；枯燥乏味的（not interesting or exciting）

C. （液体、气体等）清澈的；清澄的（clear, transparent, as water or eyes）

D. 惊恐的，胆小的（fearful or apprehensive; timid; timorous）

句子大意：她经营的农村诊所墙上挂着手绘海报，海报上建议人们吃两头生大蒜，喝加了鸡蛋和人参片的酒，或者喝加了小葱片和糖的温水来预防感冒和流感。

3 A

A. （尤指死亡时的）剧痛（violent pains, especially at the moment of death）

in the throes of sth./of doing sth. 意为正在做，正忙于（尤指困难或复杂的活动）（in the middle of an activity, especially a difficult or complicated one）

B. （论据、政策等的）要点，要旨（the main point of an argument, a policy, etc.）

C. 棒打；殴打；痛打（an act of hitting sb. very hard, especially with a stick）

（比赛）大败，惨败（a severe defeat in a game）

D. 如果发生……；倘若……（in case of sth.; if sth. happens）

句子大意：在20世纪90年代致命饥荒最为严重的时候，朝鲜曾前所未有地请求国际社会提供粮食援助。

4 B

A. ~ sb./sth./yourself (from sth.) 解救；挣脱（to free sb./sth. or yourself from a place where they/it or you are trapped）

B. ~ sth. 使恶化，使加剧（to make sth. worse, especially a disease or problem）

C. ~ sth. 支持，拥护，赞成（信仰、政策等）（to give your support to a belief, policy, etc.）

D. ~ sth. (from sb.)（费力地）打探出、诱出（信息或反应）（to get information or a reaction from sb., often with difficulty）

句子大意： 作为粮食出口大国的乌克兰指责俄罗斯封锁该国的运粮船只，称此举加剧了一场全球粮食危机。

5 A

A. ~ (sth.)（使）扭曲，弯曲，变形（to become, or make sth. become, twisted or bent out of its natural shape, for example because it has become too hot, too damp, etc.）

B. be wrapped up in sb./sth. 专心致志于；全神贯注于（to be so involved with sb./sth. that you do not pay enough attention to other people or things）

C. ~ sth. 扭伤（脚踝、肩膀等）（to twist and injure a part of your body, especially your ankle or shoulder）
使痛苦，使十分难过（尤指以致哭喊出声）（to make sb. feel great pain or unhappiness, especially so that they make a sound or cry）

D. ~ sth. (out) 拧出，绞出（衣服等中的水）（to twist and squeeze clothes, etc. in order to get the water out of them）
~ sth. 拧，扭（鸟的脖子，以将其杀死）（If you wring a bird's neck, you twist it in order to kill the bird.）

句子大意： 这次疫情扭曲了供应链并抑制了家庭收入，极端天气也使得许多粮食主产区歉收。在此背景下，2021 年营养不良人口的数量大幅上涨。

6 C

A. ~ sth. on sth. 给予（重视、信任、价值等）（to give or attach a particular level of importance, trust, value, etc. to sth.）

B. ~ sth. 使发生；实现；引起（to make sth. happen）

常见搭配：effect changes

C. inflict sth. on sb. 使遭受打击；使吃苦头（to make sb./sth. suffer sth. unpleasant）

D. 折磨；使痛苦（to affect sb./sth. in an unpleasant or harmful way）

常考搭配：afflict sb. with sth.；"让某人遭受经济损失"可以是"afflict sb. with financial losses"，也可以是"afflict financial losses on sb."

句子大意： 现在乌克兰基础设施遭受的直接损失已经超过 1000 亿美元。

7 A

A. ~ sb. 将（嫌疑人）还押候审（to send sb. away from a court to wait for their trial which will take place at a later date）

B. [ˈreprɪˌmɑːnd]~ sb. (for sth.) 训斥；斥责（to tell sb. officially that you do not approve of them or their actions）

C. ~ sb./sth. to sth.（为摆脱而）把……置于，把……交付给（to put sb./sth. somewhere in order to get rid of them/it）

D.（没有 confine sb. into… 的搭配）~ sb./sth. to sth. 限制；限定（to keep sb./sth. inside the limits of a particular activity, subject, area, etc.）

~ sb./sth. (in sth.) 监禁；禁闭（to keep a person or an animal in a small or closed space）

句子大意： 这个持枪歹徒被指控谋杀和谋杀未遂，已被送入精神病房还押候审。

8 C

A. [kənˈdəʊn]~ sth. or ~ (sb.) doing sth. 容忍；纵容（to accept behaviour that is morally wrong or to treat it as if it were not serious）

B. ~ (with sb.) (on/about sth.) 商讨；协商；交换意见（to discuss sth. with sb., in order to exchange opinions or get advice）

~ sth. (on/upon sb.) 授予，颁发（奖项、学位、荣誉或权利）（to give sb. an award, a university degree or a particular honour or right）

C. 宣判；判处（某人某种刑罚）（to say what sb.'s punishment will be）

~ sb. to sth. 迫使……接受困境（或不愉快的状况）（to force sb. to accept a difficult or unpleasant situation）（如：80 percent of Zimbabweans will be condemned to poverty upon retirement.）

D. ~ sb. (in sth.) 监禁；关押；禁闭（to put sb. in prison or in another place from which they cannot escape）

句子大意： 一位在乌克兰东部被法院判处死刑的英国公民对这一判罚提出上诉。

9 D

搭配考查。

A、B 和 C 选项后的介词都要跟 by 而不是 of，而 be beloved of sb. 是一个固定搭配。

beloved 由 love 变来，被动语态 be loved 合成为一个形容词 beloved，就不再用 be beloved by，而改为 be beloved of sb.，这里 beloved 带有名词的含义，意思是"是某人之爱"。如：

（1）He is beloved of children. 他是儿童之爱＝儿童都喜欢他。

（2）It's a book beloved of children everywhere. 这是受各地儿童钟爱的一本书。

A. not for love or/nor money 决不；无论怎样也不（If you say you cannot do sth. for love nor money, you mean it is completely impossible to do it.）

There's little/no love lost between A and B.（……之间）彼此厌恶，互无好感（They do not like each other.）

B. more like... （提供比以前更准确的数量）差不多，更接近（used to give a number or an amount that is more accurate than one previously mentioned）

more like (it)（更恰当地描述）倒更像是，说……还差不多（better; more acceptable）

C. ~ sb. or sth. 偏袒，偏爱（to give someone an unfair advantage）

D. be beloved of sb. ……所钟爱的；深受……喜爱的（loved very much by sb.; very popular with sb.）

句子大意： 这段萧条时期为阻止城市的历史建筑被现代主义规划者钟爱的混凝土乌托邦取代发挥了作用。

10 C

词组考查。

A. on balance 总的来说（after considering all the information）

B. 平衡；均衡；均势（a state of balance, especially between opposing forces or influences）

C. on (a) par with 与……不相上下 [at the same level or standard as (someone or something else)]

below par 未达标准、要求或预期（below average; not as good as desired, required, or expected）

above par 高于平均水平，优秀（better than average）

D. 公平；公正（a situation in which everyone is treated equally）

句子大意： 国际货币基金组织估计，乌克兰今年的 GDP 可能会萎缩超过三分之一，相当于 20 世纪 30 年代美国大萧条时期的经济萎缩规模。

11 A

A. 极痛苦的；糟糕透顶的（extremely painful or bad）

B. 令人开心激动的（very exciting and enjoyable）

C. （exfoliate 的现在分词形式）磨砂；温和去角质（to wash or rub your face or body in order to remove dead skin cells）

D. [ˌesəʊ'terɪk] 只有内行才懂的；难领略的（likely to be understood or enjoyed by only a few people with a special knowledge or interest）

句子大意： 幸存者在煎熬中等待，急切地想知道那些失联亲友们的消息。

12 D

A. （使）结束，终止（to come to an end; to bring sth. to an end）

B. ~ to do sth. 屈尊；俯就（to do sth. that you think it is below your social or professional position to do）

~ to sb.（对某人）表现出优越感（to behave towards sb. as though you are more important and more intelligent than they are）

C. 卷绕；旋绕（to twist or coil something in folds）

D. ~ (in/with sth.)（以某种结果）告终；（在某一点）结束（to end with a particular result, or at a particular point）

句子大意： 经过多年的研究，他们终于找到了这个疾病的治愈方法。

13 B

A. 大火灾；大火（a very large fire that destroys a lot of land or buildings）

B. be in the cross hairs of sb. 成为别人急于批评或攻击的对象（in a position in which other people are eager to criticize or attack）

C. 国际象棋棋盘（a board with 64 black and white squares that chess is played on）

D. hidden agenda（言语或行为背后的）隐秘意图，秘密目的（the secret intention behind what sb. says or does）

句子大意：他不是唯一一个成为政府反腐运动打击对象的大亨。

14 C

A. ~ sth. 神情或举止表现出……（to express a quality or feeling through the way that you look and behave）

~ from（光，气体等）发出，发散；起源（to come from or out of）

B. ~ from sth. or ~ sth. from sth. 从……导出、获得，来自……（to take, receive, or obtain sth. especially from a specified source）

C. ~ from（人）来自某个地方（to be from a particular place）

D. ~ in some place or from sth. 起源于；发端于（to happen or appear for the first time in a particular place or situation）

~ sth. 创立；创建；发明（to create sth. new）

句子大意：他来自柬埔寨东部一个贫穷的村庄，曾是一名天才儿童，14岁时便考入该国的一所名校。

15 C

A. 严重的；重大的；深切的（very serious and important; giving you a reason to feel worried）

B. 简要的；简短生硬的（using few words and often not seeming polite or friendly）

C. (adj.) 有见识的；通情达理的（having practical knowledge and understanding of sth.; having common sense）

(n.) 实用知识；了解（practical knowledge or understanding of sth.）

D. (adj.) 存在针对女性的性别歧视意味的（referring to women's bodies, behavior, or feelings in a negative way）

(n.) 性别歧视者（a person who treats other people, especially women, unfairly because of their sex or who makes offensive remarks about them）

句子大意：在该国首都，几乎连运行电梯的电力都难以保证，而且大多数人没有电脑，更不用说上网了。然而，长期以来世界上许多最厉害、最具攻击性的黑客都出自该国。

16 C

习语搭配考查。

A. 清楚的；显而易见的（clear; easily seen）

B. 显而易见的；明白易懂的（easy to see or understand）

貌似的；未必真实的（that seems to be real or true but may not be）（如：表面原因 apparent cause）

C. state the obvious 陈述明显的事实；说句明摆着的话；不言自明；毋庸讳言（to tell people things they already know）

明显的；理解的（easy to see or understand）

D. 易于察觉的；可意识到的（that is easily noticed by the mind or the senses）

句子大意：对大多数人来说，该国通过压低本国货币 / 让本国货币贬值来促进出口是不言自明的事情。

17 C

A. 扫地（to sweep with a broom）

B. ~ sth. 使（手指或手臂）弯曲（to bend your finger or arm）

C. 使做好准备；培养；训练（to prepare or train sb. for an important job or position）

D. ~ (over sb.) 对某人花痴；对（某人）神魂颠倒（to feel very excited, emotional, etc. about sb. that you think is sexually attractive, so that you almost become unconscious）

句子大意：有天赋的学生从小就被筛选出来进行精心培养。

18 A

A. 一丁点的；微小的；不足的；欠缺的（hardly any; not very much and not as much as there should be）

常考近义词：scanty 不足的；欠缺的；太少的（too little in amount for what is needed）

B. 令人反感的；令人讨厌的（very unpleasant）

C. 小气的；吝啬的（not given or giving willingly; not generous, especially with money）

D. 沾沾自喜的；自鸣得意的（looking or feeling too pleased about sth. you have done or achieved）

句子大意：尽管这条道路上的地标性建筑都是永久性的，但是这里的人们生活却没有那么稳当，对这座城市的未来几乎没有控制权。

19 B

A. （及物动词）享受；渴望；喜欢（to get great pleasure from sth.; to want very much to do or have sth.）；注意区分 relish sth./doing sth. = revel in sth./doing sth..

B. ~ in... 纵情于；陶醉；酷爱（to enjoy something very much）

常考近义词组：delight in... 很喜欢、欣赏（to derive great pleasure or joy from something or someone）

（例句 1：I delight in your interest in my work. 例句 2：We all delight in James. 例句 3：The happy couple delighted in taking romantic walks through the park.）

C. ~ sth. 满足（欲望、兴趣等）（to satisfy a particular desire, interest, etc.）

~ in sth. 放纵，听任（to allow yourself or someone else to have something enjoyable）

D. ~ sth. 吸引住（注意力、兴趣）（to succeed in attracting and keeping sb.'s attention and interest）

~ (with sth./sb.) 与……建立密切关系并尽力了解（to become involved with and try to understand sth./sb.）

~ (sb.) 与（某人）交战；与（某人）开战（o begin fighting with sb.）

句子大意：数字世界喜欢陶醉在自己的行话中，其中最流行的词汇之一就是"云计算"。

20 A

A. a ~ (of sth.) 预先的体验；预示；征象（a small amount of a particular experience or situation that shows you what it will be like when the same thing happens on a larger scale in the future）

B. （动词，名词形式为 foreshadowing）~ sth. 预示；是……的预兆（to be a sign of sth. that will happen in the future）

C. （动词）~ sth./sb. 预先阻止；先发制人（to prevent sth. from happening or sb. from doing sth. by doing sth. first）

D. （动词）（尤指用魔力）预知，预言（to know or say what will happen in the future, especially by using magic powers）

句子大意：虽然供电在几小时之内就恢复了，但这次停电是未来可能会发生的情况的一次令人担心的预先体验。

Practice 9

1 A

A. 影响深远的；重大的（having a very great effect; of very great size）

地震的；地震引起的（connected with or caused by earthquakes）

B. ~ (about sth.) 充满信心的；乐观的（cheerful and confident about the future）

C. 华贵的；豪华的；奢华的（very expensive and looking very impressive）

D. 愉悦感官的（giving pleasure to your senses）

句子大意：开除三位部长，另外三位部长遭调离职务，这或许代表着将有重大的政策转向。

2 D

A. 硬脆的；爽脆的；松脆的（firm and crisp and making a sharp sound when you bite or crush it）

B. 大而厚重的（big, thick and heavy）

常考近义词：cumbersome/chunky/bulky

C. 笨手笨脚的；（举止）不雅观的，难看的（moving in a way that is not smooth or elegant）

D. 狭窄的；狭小的（A cramped room, etc. does not have enough space for the people in it.）

句子大意：他与家人住在一间狭窄的公寓里，但在广东的老家建了一座六层的豪宅。

3 C

A. 绵软顺从的；柔顺的（soft and giving way to sb., especially in a sexual way）

（人）温顺的；容易摆布的（willing to accept change; easy to influence or control）

常考近义词：pliable 易受影响的；可塑的；容易摆布的（easy to influence or control）

B. 待定的；待决的（waiting to be decided or settled）

即将发生的（going to happen soon）

C. 不完整的；参差不齐的（not complete; good in some parts, but not in others）

零散的；散落的；分布不匀的（existing or happening in some places and not others）

D.（光等）能透过的；可渗透的（able to be penetrated or permeated）

常考近义词：porous/penetrable/permeable

句子大意：该国的社会保障体系不健全，他已经不记得自己上一次享受正常的假期是什么时候了。

4 A

A. ~ sth. 心存，怀有（想法、希望、感觉等）（to consider or allow yourself to think about an idea, a hope, a feeling, etc.）

B. ~ sth. 享有；享受（to have sth. good that is an advantage to you）

C. ~ sb./sth. (in sth.) 包住；裹住；盖住（to wrap sb./sth. up or cover them or it completely）

D. ~ sth. 吸引住（注意力、兴趣）（to succeed in attracting and keeping sb.'s attention and interest）

句子大意：他没有离开的想法，称这里就是他的家。

5 B

A. 多孔的；透水的；透气的（having many small holes that allow water or air to pass through slowly）

B. 要求高的（demanding）（例句：Nevertheless, in the past decade the area has lost a number of corporate tenants to its punishing rents and business rates. 但是，在过去 10 年里，过高的租金和税率迫使一些企业租户离开了这一地区。）

非常困难的；令人筋疲力尽的（extremely difficult or tiring）

C. 要求不高的（not rigorous）

D. 繁重的；费力的；伤脑筋的（needing a great amount of physical or mental effort）

句子大意：高昂的租金和放缓的商业增速迫使靠手艺吃饭的家庭放弃了他们的老店。

6 B

A. ~ sth. 用草皮覆盖（to cover an area of ground with turf）

B. ~ sth. 满足（欲望）（to satisfy a desire）

常考近义词：satiate（~ sb./sth.）满足（to give sb. so much of sth. that they do not feel they want any more）

C. ~ sth. (with sth.) 超量供应；充斥（to supply or provide sth. with too much of sth.）

D. ~ sth. 损毁（建筑物或房屋）内部（to destroy the inside or contents of a building or room）

~ sth. 取出……的内脏（以便烹饪）（to remove the organs from inside a fish or an animal to prepare it for cooking）

句子大意：他离开的时候，这个国家还非常穷。他在童年时代只有两次吃饱过。

7 C

A. （v.）~ (for sth.) 觅（食）（to search for food）

（n.）（牛马的）饲料（food for horses and cows）

B. ~ through sth. 翻寻；翻箱倒柜地寻找；搜寻（the act of looking for sth. among a group of other objects in a way that makes them untidy）

C. ~ (into sth.)（改变职业、活动的）尝试（an attempt to become involved in a different activity or profession）

D. 猥亵；摸 [an act of groping sb. (= touching them sexually)]

句子大意：为了不被超越，全球最大在线零售商亚马逊已经公布了进军电子书大市场的计划。

8 C

A. ~ sb. 把……难住、难倒（to ask sb. a question that is too difficult for them to answer or give them a problem that they cannot solve）

（尤指愤怒或烦恼时）脚步重重地走（to walk in a noisy, heavy way, especially because you are angry or upset）

B. ~ A and B together or ~ A (in) with B 把……归并一起（或合起来考虑）（to put or consider different things together in the same group）

C. 强有力地跳动；怦怦地跳（to beat strongly）

~ (sb./sth.) 重击，狠打；（尤指用拳）捶击（to hit sb./sth. hard, especially with your closed hand）

D. ~ sth. 阻碍，阻止（发展或进步）（to prevent the development or progress of sb./sth.）

常考形容词形式：cramped 狭窄的；狭小的（A cramped room, etc. does not have enough space for the people in it.）

句子大意：飞机起飞时他的心怦怦直跳。

9 B

A. （马的）腾跃；欢跃；昂首阔步（an act or instance of prancing）

B. 原产地；发源地（the place that sth. originally came from）

C. 上帝；苍天；天佑（God, or a force that some people believe controls our lives and the things that happen to us, usually in a way that protects us）

D. ~ (over sb./sth.) 优先；优先权（the condition of being more important than sb. else and therefore coming or being dealt with first）

句子大意：他们更喜欢葡式蛋挞。

134

10 B

A. [ˈprefəs] ~ sth. (with sth.) 为……写序言（to provide a book or other piece of writing with a preface）

~ sth. by/with sth. or ~ sth. by doing sth. 以……为开端；作……的开场白（to say sth. before you start making a speech, answering a question, etc.）

B. [prɪˈkluːd] 使行不通、不可能；阻止（to prevent sth. from happening or sb. from doing sth.; to make sth. impossible）

C. ~ sth. 预兆，预示，预告（尤指坏事）（to be a sign or warning of sth. that is going to happen in the future, especially sth. bad or unpleasant）

D. [pləˈkeɪt] ~ sb. 安抚；平息（怒气）（to make sb. feel less angry about sth.）

句子大意：考试成绩不理想让她无法进入心仪的大学，这件事让她耿耿于怀。

11 C

考查点：这四个选项只有 incarnate 可以做后置定语。

A. ~ (of sth.) 可作为典型（或示例）的（able to be used as a typical example of sth.）

B. ~ (of sth.) 作为……典型的；有代表性的（having the usual qualities or features of a particular type of person, thing or group）

C. (*adj.*) 可作为……典型的（personified or typified）（如：stupidity incarnate）

（通常后置）人体化的；化身的；拟人化的（possessing bodily form, especially the human form）

（如：a devil incarnate）

（*v.*）~ sth.，意思同形容词形式

D. ~ (of sth.) 说明的；解释性的（helping to explain sth. or show it more clearly）

句子大意：丰田凯美瑞长期以来一直被誉为可靠性的典范。

12 A

A. 完人；典范（a person who is perfect or who is a perfect example of a particular good quality）

B. 尴尬的处境；困境；窘境（a difficult or unpleasant situation, especially one where it is difficult to know what to do）

C. 蟒；蚺蛇（a large tropical snake that kills animals for food by winding its long body around them and crushing them）

Python 编程语言

D. 序言；前言；开场白（an introduction to a book or a written document; an introduction to sth. you say）

句子大意：香港最受尊敬的银行、全球化的早期典范汇丰银行被指控关闭了一个与非法众筹活动有关的账户。

13 A

A. ~ to sth./sb.；紧贴；紧挨（to stick close to sth./sb.）

~ sth. 劈开；砍开；剁开（to split or cut sth. in two using sth. sharp and heavy）

~ to sth. 坚信；信守；忠于（to continue to believe in or be loyal to sth.）

B. a garlic ~ or a ~ of garlic 蒜瓣 [one of the small separate sections of a bulb (= the round underground part) of garlic]

C. 连笔的；草书的（with the letters joined together）

D. be ~ to sth. 有助于……的；有益的；有助的（making it easy, possible or likely for sth. to happen）

句子大意：该论文分析了放弃或坚持金本位对贸易政策产生的影响。

14 C

A. sb. does sth. while doing sth. else，意思为"在做某事的同时做另一件事"，与此处逻辑不符

B. 是从属连词，后跟从句

C. albeit（all be it）的英语注释为：although it may be。由于 albeit 这个词本身就包含了主语（it）和谓语动词（be），所以后接的结构就不再有主语和谓语，而是接副词、形容词或介词短语

D. however 不能连接 doing sth.

句子大意：印度将会在 2023 年超越中国，成为世界上人口最多的国家。现在两国人口数都已经达到 14 亿。数十年来，印度人口增速一直快于中国，只是最近有所放缓。

15 D

A. 顺风（a wind that blows from behind a moving vehicle, a runner, etc.）

B. ~ (on sb.) 产生事与愿违的不良（或危险）后果（to have the opposite effect to the one intended, with bad or dangerous results）

C. ~ (from sb.) against sth.（对社会变动等的）强烈抵制，集体反对（a strong negative reaction by a large number of people, for example to sth. that has recently changed in society）

D. 顶风，逆风；不利因素（a wind that blows in the opposite direction to the one in which you are moving）

句子大意：与其他首席执行官一样，随着美国企业纷纷为可能的经济衰退做准备，他也面临着日益强劲的经济逆风。

16 B

A. ~ (sth.) 繁殖；生育（to produce children or baby animals）

B. 迅速繁殖（或增殖）；猛增（to increase rapidly in number or amount）

C. ~ sth. 授粉；传粉（to put pollen into a flower or plant so that it produces seeds）

D. 拖延；耽搁（to delay doing sth. that you should do, usually because you do not want to do it）

句子大意：安全与毒品贸易也在讨论日程之上，因为芬太尼的制造在墨西哥迅猛增长。芬太尼是一种合成阿片类物质，美国的药物滥用问题常常与芬太尼有关。

17 A

A. sleaze（尤指政客或商人的）舞弊，欺诈，违法行为（dishonest or illegal behaviour, especially by politicians or business people）

（尤指涉及性行为的）污秽，肮脏，乌烟瘴气（behaviour or conditions that are unpleasant and not socially acceptable, especially because sex is involved）

B. 喷嚏；喷嚏声（the act of sneezing or the noise you make when you sneeze）

C. 挤压；捏（an act of pressing sth., usually with your hands）

D. 烟霾（a combination of haze and smoke similar to smog in appearance but less damp in consistency）

句子大意：这些候选人的竞选主张比较类似：大幅减税、增加国防开支并避免出现约翰逊时代的违法行为和混乱局面。

18 C

A. ~ sth. (up) (with sth./sb.) 凌乱地塞满；乱堆放（to fill a place with too many things, so that it is untidy）

B. ~ sth. 气急败坏地说；急促而语无伦次地说（to speak quickly and with difficulty, making soft spitting sounds, because you are angry or shocked）

艰难维持，很可能会停歇（If an activity sputters, it continues with difficulty and seems likely to stop.）

C. ~ sth. (up) 找寻，聚集（支持、勇气等）（to find as much support, courage, etc. as you can）

集合，召集，集结（尤指部队）（to come together, or bring people, especially soldiers, together for example for military action）

D. 嘀咕；嘟囔（to speak or say sth. in a quiet voice that is difficult to hear, especially because you are annoyed about sth.）

~ (about sth.)（私下）抱怨，发牢骚（to complain about sth., without saying publicly what you think）

句子大意：他正努力为其经济复苏计划和医疗教育系统改革方案寻求支持。

19 D

A. 精彩的表演；壮观的场面（a performance or an event that is very impressive and exciting to look at）

奇特的现象；出人意料的情况（an unusual or surprising sight or situation that attracts a lot of attention）

B. ~ in sth.（在公司、计划等中的）重大利益，重大利害关系（an important part or share in a business, plan, etc. that is important to you and that you want to be successful）

C. 鬼（a ghost）

间谍；特工（a spy）

D. ~ (of sth.) 恐惧；恐慌；忧虑（something unpleasant that people are afraid might happen in the future）

未来发生不愉快事件的可能性（the possibility of something unpleasant that might happen in the future）

句子大意：德国政府最近表示俄罗斯对欧洲天然气的出口中断可能会引发全球金融危机，这种说法似乎有点杞人忧天。但这种可能性正变得越来越大。

20 B

A. 打巴掌，掴（尤指对小孩的惩戒）（a sharp hit given with your open hand, especially to a child as a punishment）

B. （尤指不好的）性格特征（a part of a person's character, especially an unpleasant part）

C. 牛排（a thick slice of good quality beef）

D. 线条流畅的；造型优美的（having an elegant smooth shape）

阔气的；衣冠楚楚的；时髦的（looking rich, and dressed in elegant and expensive clothes）

句子大意：足球本应是一项精英治理的运动，现在却带有较强的保护主义色彩。

Practice 10

1 C

A. 属性；性质；特征（a quality or feature of sb./sth.）

B. （流入大河或湖泊的）支流（a river or stream that flows into a larger river or a lake）

C. ~ (to sb.)（尤指对死者的）致敬，颂词；悼念；吊唁礼物（an act, a statement or a gift that is intended to show your respect or admiration, especially for a dead person）

（尤指旧时一国向他国交纳的）贡品，贡金 [(especially in the past) money given by one country or ruler to another, especially in return for protection or for not being attacked]

D. [ɑːmz] 施舍物；救济金（money, clothes and food that are given to poor people）

句子大意：在遇刺近6个小时后，日本前首相安倍晋三被宣布死亡。世界领袖纷纷发唁电悼念，表明安倍曾对地缘政治产生重大影响。

2 A

A. 外展服务（the process of an organization building relationships with people in order to advise them, for example about health or financial problems）

B. （岩石）露出地面的部分（a large mass of rock that stands above the surface of the ground）

C. 分支；（尤指）分支机构（a thing that develops from sth., especially a small organization that develops from a larger one）

D. 禁入地区（If a place is off-limits, you are not allowed to go there.）

句子大意：该行政令扩大了药物堕胎、避孕和紧急医疗服务的范围，召集律师志愿者提供法律咨询服务，并推动相关宣传教育活动的开展。

3 C

A. （= takeout）外卖餐馆（a restaurant that cooks and sells food that you take away and eat somewhere else）

外卖的饭菜；外卖食物（a meal that you buy at this type of restaurant）

B. （= anyway）（转换话题、结束谈话或回到原话题时说）不过，总之，反正（used when changing the subject of a conversation, ending the conversation or returning to a subject）

C. 休闲放松的地方；短途度假（a place away from home where you can relax; a short vacation）

D. 轻易取得的胜利（an easy victory）

句子大意："报复性旅游"这一术语是指在疫情期间居家隔离后人们久被压抑的出游需求迸发的现象。

4 C

用法考查。

bar 或 barring 做介词使用，意思为"除……外"，相当于 except for sb./sth.

考点补充：单词 except 有一个特殊用法，即：当句子谓语是单词 do 的任何形式时，那么 except 后面需接动词原形，此时意思与 but 相同（如：She didn't do anything except weep last night.）。

A. 没有这种搭配，常见搭配：except for…

B. 没有这种搭配，常见搭配：except for…

C. bar 作为介词使用，同 barring，意思为"除……外"

D. bar sb. (from sth./from doing sth.) 禁止，阻止（某人做某事）（to ban or prevent sb. from doing sth.）

句子大意：中低收入国家普遍面临通胀压力。通胀水平现已超过除中国之外的所有主要新兴经济体的官方目标。

5 A

A. 使有必要；使正当；使恰当（to make sth. necessary or appropriate in a particular situation）

B.（尤指正式地或法律上）同意，准予，允许（to agree to give sb. what they ask for, especially formal or legal permission to do sth.）

C. ~ sth. 认可；核准（to say that sth. is good enough to be used or is correct）

D. ~ sth. 仔细检查，审查（内容、质量等）（to check the contents, quality, etc. of sth. carefully）

句子大意：没必要为这部超级英雄电影给予雷鸣般的掌声／喝彩：古怪的剧情牺牲了叙事紧迫性。

6 C

A. ~ (to sth.) 定期订购（或订阅等）（to pay an amount of money regularly in order to receive or use sth.）

~ (to sth.) 定期交纳（会员费）；定期（向慈善机构）捐款（to pay money regularly to be a member of an organization or to support a charity）

B. ~ sth. (to sth.); be subjected to sth. 使臣服；使顺从；（尤指）压服（to bring a country or group of people under your control, especially by using force）

C. ~ to sth. 屈服；屈从；抵挡不住（攻击、疾病、诱惑等）（to lose your ability to fight against someone or something, and to allow them to control or persuade you）

D. ~ to sth. 诉诸；求助于；采取（to do something extreme or unpleasant in order to solve a problem）

句子大意：随着今年稀土价格的大幅下跌，那些将稀土当作热门大宗商品下注的企业正纷纷取消在该领域的投资或将注意力转向黄金等其他金属。

7 C

A. ~ sb. (with sth.) 使充满（强烈的感情）（to fill sb. with a strong feeling）

~ sth. 烧毁；毁灭（to completely destroy sth.）

B. ~ sth. 承担（责任）；就（职）；取得（权力）（to take or begin to have power or responsibility）

~ sth. 呈现（外观、样子）；显露（特征）（to begin to have a particular quality or appearance）

C. ~ sth. + *adv.*/prep. 将……归入（或纳入）（to include or place within something larger or more comprehensive; to encompass as a subordinate or component element）

D.（尤指法庭上）推定，假定（to accept that sth. is true until it is shown not to be true, especially in court）

句子大意：游戏和团队体育活动被归类为"休闲活动"。

8 C

A. 暗指；影射（an indirect remark about sb./sth., usually suggesting sth. bad or rude; the use of remarks like this）

B. 旁敲侧击的话；影射；暗示（something that sb. insinuates）

C. 淹没；洪灾（a flood of water）

D. 内爆；股票等爆仓（an occasion when the outer surface of an object breaks violently and falls inward; an occasion when something such as an organization or an economic system is completely destroyed by things that are happening within it）

句子大意：澳大利亚遭受的洪水越来越严重。随着洪水逐渐退去，居民们面临一个艰难的抉择：是离开家园，还是为更多的洪水做好准备。

9 A

A. 仍不明朗，悬而未定（uncertain in outcome）

B. 令人愉快的；宜人的（very pleasant）

C. 自负的；骄傲自大的（having too much pride in yourself and what you do）

D. 顺从的；顺服的（easy to control; willing to be influenced by sb./sth.）

句子大意：选举结果仍不明朗。

10 C

A. in lieu (of sth.) 替代（instead of）

B. ~ (of sth.)（对一系列事件、原因等）枯燥冗长的陈述（a long boring account of a series of events, reasons, etc.）

C. recourse (to sth.) 依靠；求助（a turning to someone or something for help or protection）
追索权；追索补偿 [the right to demand payment from the maker or endorser of a negotiable instrument (such as a check)]

D.（尤指机场或火车站的）大厅，广场（a large, open part of a public building, especially an airport or a train station）

句子大意：这个争端没有诉诸法律就得到了解决。

11 A

A. [haɪst]（对商店、银行贵重物、钱的）盗窃（an act of stealing sth. valuable from a shop/store or bank）

B. ['herəsi] 宗教异端；信奉邪说（a belief or an opinion that is against the principles of a particular religion; the fact of holding such beliefs）

离经叛道的信念（或观点）（a belief or an opinion that disagrees strongly with what most people believe）

C. 传家宝；世代相传之物（a valuable object that has belonged to the same family for many years）

D. 骚扰；折磨人的东西（annoying or unpleasant behavior toward someone that takes place regularly, for example threats, offensive remarks, or physical attacks）

句子大意： 在现实生活中，这幅画当时刚刚被盗，让影片观众觉得好笑的是，史密斯博士居然一直是这起盗窃案的幕后黑手。

12 D

A. 迁延；使拖延（to continue for longer than you want or think is necessary）

B. 流连；逗留；磨蹭（to stay somewhere for longer because you do not want to leave; to spend a long time doing sth.）

~ (on) 苟延残喘；奄奄一息（to stay alive but become weaker）

C. 坚决要求……，（不顾他人反对）坚持某种行为或行动（to demand something firmly and persistently; to continue with some behavior or course of action in spite of the disapproval of others）

D. 迎难而上，咬牙坚持（to continue doing something with determination or resolve, despite difficulties or an unlikely chance of succeeding）

句子大意： 尽管我们的经费遭到削减，但我们决定咬牙坚持下去，争取靠我们自己完成这个项目。

13 D

A. 公平合理地；公正地（in a fair and reasonable way; honestly）

B. 狂热地；疯狂地（in a way that shows that you are extremely interested in something, to a degree that some people find unreasonable）

C.（指志趣相投者）兄弟般地（in a friendly way, like a brother）

D. 正面地；反响好地；赞同地（showing approval）

句子大意： 英国人对女王的评价较为正面；每个年龄段的人都对她怀有好感。

14 C

A. 一连串的打嗝（a series of hiccups）

小问题；暂时性耽搁（a small problem or temporary delay）

B. 暂时的困难（或问题）；故障（a problem or difficulty that causes a short delay）

C. [haɪ'eɪtəs] 间断；停滞（a pause in activity when nothing happens）

D. 藏身处；隐蔽所（a place where sb. goes when they do not want anyone to find them）

句子大意：在中断了两周之后，为达成解决方案进行的努力今天得以重启。

15 C

A. ~ sth. 找到正确方法（对付困难或复杂的情况）（to find the right way to deal with a difficult or complicated situation）

B. 想出（主意、计划等）；构想；设想（to form an idea, a plan, etc. in your mind; to imagine sth.）

C. 策展；负责（博物馆、展览、节庆活动、网站等）内容的遴选；为……策划设计（to be in charge of selecting and caring for objects to be shown in a museum or to form part of a collection of art, an exhibition, etc.; to be in charge of selecting films, performers, events, etc. to be included in a festival; to select things such as documents, music, products, or Internet content to be included as part of a list or collection, or on a website）

D. ~ (in/with sth.)（以某种结果）告终；（在某一点）结束（to end with a particular result, or at a particular point）

句子大意：随着我们对要购买的东西越来越了解，我们对室内装饰也思考得更加周全。我们正在用更少的元素来设计一个舒适、实用又时尚的家。

16 C

A. ~ (in sth.)（为保持凉爽或嬉戏在烂泥、水里）打滚，翻滚（to lie and roll about in water or mud, to keep cool or for pleasure）

~ in sth. 沉湎；放纵（to enjoy sth. that causes you pleasure）

B.（因地位重要或年长而）尊崇（to give something great importance and respect, often because it is very old）

奉为神圣（to make something holy）

C. 休耕的；休闲的（not used for growing crops, especially so that the quality of the land will improve）

D. 醇香的；甘美的（smooth and pleasant）

老练的；成熟的（calm, gentle and reasonable because of age or experience）

句子大意：缺水问题将迫使农民休耕。

17 C

A. ~ (for sth.) 准备就绪（the state of being ready or prepared for sth.）

B. 稀有性；稀少性（the quality of being very unusual and not at all common）

C. 荒疏；荒废；退步（not as good as it used to be, because you have not been practising）

D. 腐烂；脆性（the quality of rotting and becoming putrid）

句子大意：随着疫情继续在全球蔓延，为了防止球技生疏，人们举办了一些足球训练赛事。

18 C

固定表达考查。

The odds are stacked against someone. 机会不大，非常困难，形势极为不利，没有多少胜算（used to describe a situation in which someone does not have a good or fair chance of winning, succeeding, etc.）

反义词组：The odds are stacked in (someone's or something's) favor.

A. ~ sth. (with sth.) 贮备，贮存（食物、书籍等）（to fill sth. with food, books, etc.）

B. ~ sb./sth. 用巴掌打；掴（to hit sb. with your open hand, especially as a punishment）

C. ~ (sth.) (up)（使）放成整齐的一叠（或一摞、一堆）（to arrange objects neatly in a pile; to be arranged in this way）

D. 懈怠；怠惰；偷懒（to work less hard than you usually do or should do）

句子大意：乌克兰获胜概率不大，但这也不是该国第一次对一个更强大的对手发动突袭防卫战。

19 A

sabre-rattling 耀武扬威，武力威胁（a threat of violence or military action）

incursion 突然入侵；突然侵犯；袭击（a sudden attack on a place by foreign armies, etc.）

A. 贪求的；垂涎的（having a strong desire for the things that other people have）

B. 令人信服的；有说服力的（that makes sb. believe that sth. is true）

C. 单纯的；天真的（honest, innocent and willing to trust people）

D. 引人入胜的；扣人心弦的（that makes you pay attention to it because it is so interesting and exciting）
   令人信服的（that makes you think it is true）

句子大意：该国早已习惯了虎视眈眈的邻国进行的武力威胁，但这次的突然侵犯是自1月份以来规模最大的一次。

20 B

A. ~ sth. 批判；驳斥；揭穿……的真相（to show that an idea, a belief, etc. is false; to show that sth. is not as good as people think it is）

B.（演员、运动员的）首次亮相；初次登台（或上场）（the first public appearance of a performer or sports player）

C. [deɪ'bɑːk(ə)l] 大败；崩溃；垮台（an event or a situation that is a complete failure and causes embarrassment）

D. 诋毁；贬损（the act of making a person or a thing seem little or unimportant）

句子大意："一天一美元"的全球贫困定义在世界银行1990年的《世界发展报告》中首次提出。

Practice 11

1 B

A. ~ of sth. 处理；除掉；处置（to get rid of something that you no longer need or want）

B. ~ with sth. 无须；没有……也行；省掉（to no longer use someone or something because you no longer want or need them）（例句：Let's dispense with the formalities and get right down to business. 我们就省去俗套礼节，直接谈正事儿吧。）

C. 处理；对付；应付（to take action to do something, especially to solve a problem）

D. ~ (sth.) (with/into sth.) 吻合；与……吻合（If two things dovetail or if one thing dovetails with another, they fit together well.）

句子大意：电子记录可以取代 80% 的纸质文件并减少对办公空间的需求。

2 C

词组搭配考查。

be at stake 成败难料；得失都可能；有风险（that can be won or lost, depending on the success of a particular action）

A. in store (for sb.) 即将发生（在某人身上）；等待着（某人）（waiting to happen to sb.）

B. up for grabs 提供的；可供争夺的（available for anyone who is interested）

C. go to the stake over/for sth.（此处 stake 的意思是"火刑柱"）为坚持自己的观点（或信仰）甘冒一切危险；为维护自己的观点（或信仰）不惜赴汤蹈火（to be prepared to do anything in order to defend your opinions or beliefs）

D. grasp the nettle 果断地处理棘手问题（to deal with a difficult situation firmly and without hesitating）

句子大意：东南亚运动会共设 581 枚奖牌，是最近一次奥运会奖牌数的近两倍，因此，该运动会从某种意义上可以宣称是世界上规模最大的运动会。

3 A

A. 取得进展，产生效果 [make inroads/an inroad: to start to have a direct and noticeable effect (on something)]（例句：Doctors are making great inroads in the fight against cancer.）

由于某些负面的原因造成……的下降或减少（a decrease or reduction, often caused by something unwelcome）

B. 侵权；侵犯；侵害；违反（a violation, as of a law, regulation, or agreement）

C. 侵害；侵略；侵入；侵占物（any entry into an area not previously occupied; entry to another's property without right or permission）

D.（众多复杂而又难以预料的）结果，后果（one of the large number of complicated and unexpected results that follow an action or a decision）

句子大意：维修房子花了他们不少的积蓄。

4 A

A. 混乱局面；无序的场面；凌乱不堪；一片狼藉（a situation in which there is a lot of confusion）

肮脏（或凌乱）的地方（a place which is dirty or untidy）

B. 假象；假情假意；伪装（a situation, feeling, system, etc. that is not as good or true as it seems to be）

虚假的行为（或感情、言语等）；伪善（behaviour, feelings, words, etc. that are intended to make sb./sth. seem to be better than they really are）

C. 漫步（a long walk for pleasure）

杂乱无章的长篇大论（a long confused speech or piece of writing）

D. 序言；绪论；导言；前言；开场白（an introduction to a book or a written document; an introduction to sth. you say）

句子大意： 欧洲并不是所有的经济部门都不景气。服务业——特别是在阳光灿烂的南欧地区的服务业——正沐浴在酒店餐饮业复工复产的"阳光"中。

5 A

fiefdom 封地；封地主义思想；采邑（an area or organization that someone controls completely）

A. 一群（吵闹的人）（a group of noisy people）

一群（鹅）（a group of geese）

B. （使人不能说话的）封口布；塞口布（a piece of cloth that is put over or in sb.'s mouth to stop them speaking）

禁刊令（阻止公开报道或讨论某事的法令）（an order that prevents sth. from being publicly reported or discussed）

C. 咯咯笑；傻笑（a slight silly repeated laugh）

D. 汩汩声；潺潺声（a sound like water flowing quickly through a narrow space）

（婴儿高兴时发出的）咯咯声（the sound that babies make in the throat, especially when they are happy）

句子大意： 延续数十年的内战让这个国家陷入了军阀割据混战的局面。

6 A

A. ~ sth. 舍弃，离弃（某地方）（to go away from a place and leave it empty）

B. （使）分散，散开；疏散；驱散（to move apart and go away in different directions; to make sb./sth. do this）

C. 离开；离去；起程；出发（to leave a place, especially to start a trip）

D. ~ (from sth.) (to sth.) 背叛；叛变；投敌（to leave a political party, country, etc. to join another that is considered to be an enemy）

句子大意： 今天的感染确诊数量超过 100 人，黎巴嫩人纷纷选择闭门不出，街上空无一人。

7 A

A. ~ sb. (for sth./for doing sth.) 申斥；训斥；责骂（to criticize sb. or speak angrily to them because you do not approve of sth. that they have said or done）

B. ~ sb./sth. 翻倒；倒放；使颠倒（to turn sb./sth. upside down）

C. ~ sb./sth. 篡夺；侵权（to take sb.'s position and/or power without having the right to do this）

D. 变废为宝 [to recycle (something) in such a way that the resulting product is of a higher value than the original item]

句子大意： 她在报纸文章中不断斥责那些越权的当权人士。

8 A

A. ~ (into/with sth.) 合并；联合；结合（to come together and form a group or a single unit）

B. ~ sb. (to do sth.) 强迫；胁迫；迫使（to force sb. to do sth. by using threats）

C. ~ sb./sth. 极大地打击；惩罚；使受到（严重经济损失）（to affect sb. badly or to punish them, especially by making them lose money）

D. ~ sth. (up) (with sth./sb.) 凌乱地塞满；乱堆放（to fill a place with too many things, so that it is untidy）

句子大意：该党再一次团结在他的周围，推举他作为该党的州长提名人。

9 C

A. ~ sb./sth. 削价竞争；以低于（竞争对手）的价格出售（to sell goods or services at a lower price than your competitors）

~ sb./sth. 削弱；使降低效力（to make sb./sth. weaker or less likely to be effective）

B. 在……下面画线；强调（to emphasize something, or to show that it is important）

C. 低于（目标）[to shoot short of or below (a target)]

D. ~ sth. 构成……的基础；作为……的原因（to be the basis or cause of sth.）

句子大意：由于居家办公人员的急剧增加，伦敦地铁的载客量很可能会低于预期。

10 B

A.（词组搭配为 all told 而非 all things told，all told = in total）总计，共有多少（as a complete total）

B. all things considered 从整体来看；总而言之（used for saying that you have thought carefully about all aspects of something before expressing an opinion about it）

C. 没有 all things calculated 的搭配

常考衍生词补充：calculating（= scheming）精明的；精于算计的（good at planning things so that you have an advantage, without caring about other people）

D. 没有 all things counted 的搭配

常考表达补充：count your blessings

知足（to be grateful for the good things in your life）

句子大意：从整体来看，欧元区经济状况好于预期。

11 D

A. take sb.'s side 站在……一边；支持某人

B. take advantage of... 占便宜；充分利用；对……加以利用 [make good use of (something); to profit by (something)]

C. 炎症；发炎（a condition in which a part of the body becomes red, sore and swollen because of infection or injury）

D. bear, take, etc. the brunt of sth. 承受某事的主要压力；首当其冲（to receive the main force of sth. unpleasant）

句子大意：投资者对美国现状感到愤怒，美元继续首当其冲。

12 A

A. 节约；紧缩开支（to spend less money; to reduce costs）

~ sb. 缩减（人员）（to tell sb. that they cannot continue working for you）

B. ~ sth. 使处于牢固地位；牢固确立（to establish sth. very firmly so that it is very difficult to change）

C.（由于批评或环境过于恶劣）改变主意，退缩（to change your mind about sth. because of criticism or because a situation has become too difficult）

D. ~ sth. 收回，撤回，撤销（说过的话）（to say that you no longer believe that sth. you previously said is true）

~ (from sth.) (into sth./yourself) 脱离（社会）；不与人交往（to become quieter and spend less time with other people）

句子大意： 在美国，消费者已紧缩支出，新房开工数大幅下降，美国有可能会陷入双底衰退。

13 A

A. 成功做到了困难或不可思议的事情（to succeed in doing something difficult or unexpected）

B. 推迟，拖延（to delay doing something, especially because you do not want to do it）

C. 在停止一段时之后继续一段旅程；在所剩时间不多时继续赶工做某事（to continue a trip, especially after stopping for a period of time; to continue doing something, especially when you do not have much time）

D. 穿戴（to cover a part of your body with a piece of clothing or jewelry so that you are wearing it）

句子大意： 今年她一直保持着最佳的网球竞技水平，如果下个月在法网中也能获胜的话，将上演帽子戏法。

14 A

A. ~ back to 回想起；追溯到（to remember or talk about something that happened in the past; to be similar to something from the past）

B. ~ sth. 引起，唤起（感情、记忆或形象）（to bring a feeling, a memory or an image into your mind）

常考同义词：invoke（~ sth.）使产生，唤起，引起（感情或想象）（to make sb. have a particular feeling or imagine a particular scene）

C. ~ back to 起源于（主语是 sth.）（originate from）

D. 减少，限制，降低或让……贬值，或者重启以恢复到以前的水平或状态（to reduce, limit, decrease, or devalue something, or reset something to a previous level or status）

句子大意： 现在，很多人都会想起20世纪70年代陷入滞胀时的情形。

15 B

A. 流行音乐乐队（a small group of musicians who play popular music together, often with a singer or singers）

B. in a ~ 陷入困境；难以解决问题（in a difficult or embarrassing position; also, unable to solve a problem）

C. 奴役；束缚（the state of being a slave or prisoner）

D. ~ (between A and B) 纽带；联系；关系；契合（something that forms a connection between people or groups, such as a feeling of friendship or shared ideas and experiences）

句子大意：我通常会在另一个存款账户里留几千美元备用，万一哪天遇到经济困难了还能救一下急。

16 D

A. ~ (of sth.)（学科或活动的）尖端，边缘（the limit of sth., especially the limit of what is known about a particular subject or activity）

B. on all fronts 在各个方面（in every field of endeavor）

C.（地区或群体的）边缘（the outer edge of an area or a group）

D. along/on the lines of 与……大致相近或按照……（加以区分等）（roughly similar or in keeping with）

句子大意：在美国，我们按照地域、教育、宗教、文化、代际和城乡的界限分裂开来，而如今整个世界也在支离破碎，而且经常是以看似模仿我们的方式分割开来。

17 C

A. ~ to 向（人）求助；求助于（to go to someone for help when you are having difficulty dealing with a situation）

B. ~ to 参考；涉及；谈到（to mention someone or something when you are speaking or writing）

C. ~ to 同意；赞成（to agree with an idea）

D. ~ to 投合；满足……的需要（to provide people with something they want or need, especially something unusual or special）

句子大意：我们西方人赞同一系列关于自由、民主和个人尊严的普世价值观。

18 A

A. 惊愕；惊恐（a worried, sad feeling after you have received an unpleasant surprise）

B. 便秘 [the condition of being unable to get rid of waste material from the bowels easily (= being constipated)]

C. 共谋；纵容；默许（help in doing sth. wrong; the failure to stop sth. wrong from happening）

D. 面容；脸色；面部表情（a person's face or their expression）

句子大意：令她惊愕不已的是，公众舆论目前似乎仍倾向于贝茨先生一边。

19 A

oddity 古怪反常的人（或事物）（a person or thing that is strange or unusual）

lightweight 无足轻重的人（或事）；没有影响力的人（或事）（a person or thing of little importance or influence）

A. 提及，援引（某人、某理论、实例等作为支持）（the act of mentioning a person, a theory, an example, etc. to support your opinions or ideas, or as a reason for sth.）

B. 挑衅；刺激；激怒（the act of doing or saying sth. deliberately in order to make sb. angry or upset; something that is done or said to cause this）

C.（尤指教会或大学的）大型正式会议（a large formal meeting, especially of Church officials or members of a university）

召集会议（the act of calling together a convocation）

D.（古怪或少见的）混合物，调和物，调配品（尤指饮料或药物）（a strange or unusual mixture of things, especially drinks or medicines）

句子大意：特拉斯的批评人士认为她古怪反常、没有多少影响力，主要是因为她援引撒切尔的思想理论来支持自己的观点。

20 A

A. ~ sth. 使泡汤；使成泡影（to cause sb./sth. to fail）

B. 擦坏；刮坏；蹭破（to rub sth. by accident so that it gets damaged or hurt）

C. 各式各样的；杂费的；各种各样的（sundry things or people are all different from each other and cannot be described as a group）

D. ~ sth./sb. (from sth./sb.)（尤指强制地）分开，使分离，割裂（to split or break sth./sb. apart, especially by force）

常考同根词：asunder (*adv.*) 分离；化为碎片；分开地（into pieces; apart）

常见搭配：tear/cut/split sth. asunder

句子大意：她在儿童时代就被确诊患有糖尿病并且被告知这将使她成为侦探的梦想化为泡影。

Practice 12

1 A

A. 残留部分；遗迹（a small part of sth. that still exists after the rest of it has stopped existing）

（通常用于否定句）丝毫，一点儿（usually used in negative sentences, to say that not even a small amount of sth. exists）

B. 特定年份（或地方）酿制的酒；酿造年份（the wine that was produced in a particular year or place; the year in which it was produced）

C. 优势；优越的地位（a position giving a strategic advantage, commanding perspective, or comprehensive view）

D. ['vɪzɪdʒ]（人的）脸，面容（a person's face）

句子大意：这份报告中没有一句是真话。

2 B

A.（尤指25周年或50周年的）周年纪念，周年大庆，周年庆祝（a special anniversary of an event, especially one that took place 25 or 50 years ago; the celebrations connected with it）

B. [ˌdʒæmbəˈriː] 大型聚会；庆祝会（a large party or celebration）

C. 欢乐喜庆的酒宴；闹饮（a wild, drunken party or celebration）

D.（一段时间）狂饮作乐，大量吸毒（a period of drinking a lot of alcohol or taking a lot of drugs）

句子大意：当哥本哈根紧锣密鼓地筹备12月份将要召开的联合国气候变化大会时，丹麦渴望展示自己的绿色环保业绩。

3 A

A. ~ sb. 使恼火；使烦恼（to annoy or worry sb.）

B. ~ sb. 澄清（责难或嫌疑）；证明（某人）无罪（责）（to prove that sb. is not guilty when they have been accused of doing sth. wrong or illegal）

C. ~ on sth. 凝视；只注意……（to focus exclusively on something）

D. ~ (sth.) 屈伸，活动（四肢或肌肉，尤指为准备体力活动）（to bend, move or stretch an arm or a leg, or contract a muscle, especially in order to prepare for a physical activity）

句子大意：朝鲜的武器计划一直是令拜登总统的四位前任烦恼不已的问题。四位前任总统都曾采用胡萝卜加大棒的做法，但最终都未能阻止朝鲜制造核弹头和导弹。

4 B

A. ~ sth. 减轻；缓和（to make sth. less harmful, serious, etc.）

B. ~ against 妨碍；产生（尤其为负面）作用或影响（to have an influence, especially a negative one, on something）

C. ~ sth. 使具有军事性质；武装化（to make sth. similar to an army）

D.（使）变异，突变（to develop or make sth. develop a new form or structure, because of a genetic change）

句子大意：新闻快报与报纸头版上触目惊心的图片可能会妨碍政府做出冷静的回应。

5 A

A. [ˈtriːɑːʒ] 患者鉴别分类；伤员鉴别分类（the sorting of and allocation of treatment to patients and especially battle and disaster victims according to a system of priorities designed to maximize the number of survivors）

问题诊断分类法（the process of examining problems in order to decide which ones are the most serious and must be dealt with first）

B. [tiˈɑːrə] 冠状头饰（女子用，如公主在正式场合戴的镶有宝石的王冠式头饰）（a piece of jewellery like a small crown decorated with precious stones, worn by a woman, for example a princess, on formal occasions）

C. 昏睡状态；催眠状态（a state in which sb. seems to be asleep but is aware of what is said to them, for example if they are hypnotized）

出神；发呆（a state in which you are thinking so much about sth. that you do not notice what is happening around you）

D. 无故旷课者，逃学者（a child who stays away from school without permission）

句子大意：一个健康的项目应该不断在缺陷故障和功能开发之间进行诊断鉴别。

6 C

twang [twæŋ] 鼻音（通常指方言）

A. 展示（本领、才华或优良品质）（to show someone or something in a way that attracts attention and emphasizes their good qualities）

B. ~ sth. 制止；压制；遏制（to stop sth. from growing, increasing or developing）

C. ~ sth. 得意地穿戴；夸示；故意显示（to have or wear sth. in a proud way）

D. 中暑，热得没气力（to be affected in an uncomfortable way by extreme heat）

句子大意：他得意地戴着一顶牛仔帽，说话带有乡村地区的鼻音，是一位活生生的牛仔。

7 C

A. 使有必要；使正当；使恰当（to make sth. necessary or appropriate in a particular situation）

B. 证明……正确（或正当、有理）（to show that sb./sth. is right or reasonable）

C. ~ sth. 对……有影响，作为……的依据或参考（to have an influence on sth.）

D. ~ sth. 找到（对付困难或复杂的情况）的正确方法（to find the right way to deal with a difficult or complicated situation）

句子大意：我们搜集的这些数据将会成为今后决策的依据。

8 C

A. 普通士兵（the ordinary soldiers who are not officers）

普通成员（the ordinary members of an organization）

B. 地位，排名，排位（尤指在体育运动中）（the position of sb./sth. on a scale that shows how good or important they are in relation to other similar people or things, especially in sport）

C. the ~ of sb. 某类人组成的群体、队伍（all the people within a group, organization, etc.）

D. 兵；出身行伍的军官（a commissioned officer promoted from the ranks）

句子大意：拜登总统迫切想要通过避免失业人数增加来防止未投保人群的大幅增加，因此进行了适度干预。

9 A

A. ~ on 降临；……蜂拥而至（to arrive and begin to affect sb./sth.; to arrive or attack in a sudden or overwhelming manner）

~ from 源自于，传承，带有……血统（to come down from a source, derive; to pass by inheritance）

B. 上升；升高；登高（to rise; to go up; to climb up）

C. 畏缩；怯退（to move back and/or away from sb. because you are afraid）

D. ~ sth. 构成……的边缘、边界（to form a border around sth.）

句子大意：数百人突降该市的叙利亚人聚居区，这些暴民向房屋和汽车投掷石头，还洗劫了商店。

151

10 A

A. ['tɪtʃələr] 名义上的；有名无实的（having a particular title or status but no real power or authority）

标题的；被用作标题的（the titular character of a book, play, film/movie, etc. is the one mentioned in the title）

B. （尤指重要政治职务的）任期，任职（the period of time when sb. holds an important job, especially a political one; the act of holding an important job）

（尤指大学教师的）终身职位，长期聘用（the right to stay permanently in your job, especially as a teacher at a university）

C. ['ædʒʌŋkt] 非正式、非全职的（not completely or permanently a part of the staff where you work）

D. 不拘礼节的；友好随便的；非正规的（relaxed and friendly; not following strict rules of how to behave or do sth.）

句子大意：尽管已经退休，但他仍继续担任该公司的名义董事长。

11 C

A. ~ sth.（后面不能跟 sb.）给……加强力量（或装备）；使更强大（to send more people or equipment in order to make an army, etc.）

B. （后面不能跟 sb.）改善；加强（to improve sth. or make it stronger）

C. 准备对付；下决心应付 [to prepare yourself to deal with sth. unpleasant; to fill (oneself) with determination and courage]

D. ~ (sth.)（后面不能跟 sb.）使加强；使巩固（to make a position of power or success stronger so that it is more likely to continue）

句子大意：阿富汗过去四十年的境遇已经让阿富汗民众对命运的快速翻转做好了准备。

12 B

A. ~ sth. 解除（婚姻关系）；终止（商业协议）；解散（议会）（to officially end a marriage, business agreement or parliament）

B. 权力下放（to take power or responsibility from a central authority or government and give it to smaller and more local regions）

C. 放纵的；放荡的；道德沦丧的（enjoying immoral activities and not caring about behaving in a morally acceptable way）

D. [dɪˈbɔːtʃt] 道德败坏的；淫荡的；沉湎酒色的；嗜毒的（a debauched person is immoral in their sexual behaviour, drinks a lot of alcohol, takes drugs, etc.）

句子大意：在英国，（制定实施）健康政策的权力都下放给了地方政府，因此，北爱尔兰、苏格兰和威尔士在这方面步调并不一致。

13 C

A. 引用；引述；引证（the act of repeating sth. interesting or useful that another person has written or said）

B. 商（除法所得的结果）（a number which is the result when one number is divided by another）

C. （会议的）法定人数（the smallest number of people who must be at a meeting before it can begin or decisions can be made）

D. ~ (about sth.)（对自己行为的）顾虑，不安（a feeling of doubt or worry about whether what you are doing is right）

句子大意：必须有至少三分之一拥有流通股投票权的股东参与投票，表决结果才算有效。

14 C

A. 胜利的；获胜的；战胜的（having won a victory; that ends in victory）

B. 饭量大的；贪吃的；狼吞虎咽的（eating or wanting large amounts of food）

（对信息、知识）渴求的；求知欲强的（wanting a lot of new information and knowledge）

C. [ˌvælɪdɪkˈtɔːriən]（毕业典礼上）致告别辞的最优生（the student who has the highest marks/grades in a particular group of students and who gives the valedictory speech at a graduation ceremony）

D. （尤指正式演讲中的）告别，告别辞（the act of saying goodbye, especially in a formal speech）

句子大意：是不是有太多的家长让孩子参加课外数学班，导致如果你的孩子不报这些班，就无法学习荣誉课程（优等生课程）？又或者会导致我的孩子无法成为致告别辞的毕业代表？

15 C

A. take place 某事件发生（to happen）

B. take shape 成型；初具规模；逐渐成形（to become or begin to be clear, discernible, organized, or understandable）

C. take hold 固定下来；生根（to become strong; to be established）

D. 没有 take traction 的搭配；traction 的常见搭配：gain traction 取得进展，获得一定成功（to have a little bit of success）

句子大意：毒力更强的病毒变种正在全美蔓延开来。

16 D

A. ~ sb./sth. 宣布断绝与……的关系（to state publicly that you no longer wish to have a connection with sb./sth. because you disapprove of them）

B. 宣布，宣告（决定、计划等）（to tell people sth. officially, especially about a decision, plans, etc.）

C. 谴责；指责；斥责（to strongly criticize sb./sth. that you think is wrong, illegal, etc.）

D. (v.) 正式宣布（或公布、授予等）（to say or give sth. formally, officially or publicly）

pronounced (adj.) 显著的；很明显的；表达明确的（very noticeable, obvious or strongly expressed）

句子大意：这些国家在健康和福祉方面的长期进步最为显著。

17 C

A. ~ sb. 把（违法者或无居留权的人）驱逐出境；递解出境（to force sb. to leave a country, usually because they have broken the law or because they have no legal right to be there）

B. ['depəʊ]（大量物品的）贮藏处，仓库（a place where large amounts of food, goods or equipment are stored）

车库；修车厂（a place where buses or other vehicles are kept and repaired）

火车小站；公共汽车小站（a small station where trains or buses stop）

C. ['despɒt] 专制统治者；专制君主；暴君（a ruler with great power, especially one who uses it in a cruel way）

D. ~ about sth. or ~ over sth. 苦恼的；沮丧的；泄气的；失望的（sad, without much hope）

句子大意： 他们被指控支持这位专制者和叛乱分子。

18 C

A. 侵犯；违背；亵渎；妨害（an action that is in opposition to a law, agreement, principle, etc.; the action of entering an area or place without permission）

B. ~ (with sb.) 和谐；和睦；协调（peace and agreement）

没有 of one's own concord 的表达，正确表达为：of one's own accord 主动地；出于自愿（by one's own choice, without coercion; of one's own free will）

C. [və'lɪʃ(ə)n] 出于本人自己的意志；出于本人意愿，自愿（voluntarily, willingly）

D. 毒力；致病力（the quality of being extremely poisonous, infectious, or damaging, or the extent to which a disease or toxin possesses this quality）

句子大意： 罗斯福自愿将他的文件公之于众，但更多近来的总统在此问题上都别无选择。

19 A

A. 奋斗精神；毅力（the ability and determination to do sth. successfully despite difficult conditions）

on your mettle 奋发起来；准备尽最大努力（prepared to use all your skills, knowledge, etc. because you are being tested）

B.（烧水用的）壶，水壶（a container with a lid, handle and a spout, used for boiling water）

C. 荨麻（a wild plant with leaves that have pointed edges, are covered in fine hairs and sting if you touch them）

grasp the nettle 大胆处理棘手问题；迎难而上（to force yourself to be brave and do something that is difficult or unpleasant）

D. 状态（state or condition of health, fitness, wholeness, spirit, or form）

in fine/good fettle 健康；身心俱佳；状况良好（healthy; in good condition）

句子大意： 把繁重的工作负荷当成是推动自己向前、学习新技能、展示你奋发图强精神的好机会。

20 C

grinding 没完没了的；无休止的；无改进的（that never ends or improves）

prognosis（对病情的）预断，预后（an opinion, based on medical experience, of the likely development of a disease or an illness）

预测；预言；展望（a judgement about how sth. is likely to develop in the future）

A. ~ sth. 行使；运用（to use your power, rights or personal qualities in order to achieve sth.）

B. ~ sth. (from sb./sth.) 索取，设法得到（对方不愿提供的信息、钱财等）（to obtain information, money, etc., often by taking it from sb. who is unwilling to give it）

C. ~ sth. (from sb.) 要求；索取（to demand and get sth. from sb.）

常用搭配：exact a toll/price/cost 造成冲击，迫使……付出代价等（to create problems, loss, danger, etc. for someone or something）

D. 赞扬；颂扬（to praise sb./sth. very much）

句子大意：世界银行周二在一份报告中提出了这一严峻的预测。该报告警告，持续不断的乌克兰危机、供应链梗阻以及能源和食品价格飙升正对处在不同收入水平的各个经济体造成越来越大的冲击。

Practice 13

1 C

A. ~ sth. 组成或构成……（to be the parts that together form sth.）

B. be composed of 由……构成（to be formed from various things）（例句：Air is composed mainly of nitrogen and oxygen.）

~ sth. 构成……（to be the parts that something is made of）（例句：At that time, women composed only 1.6 percent of the US forces.）

C. ~ sth. 包括；包含；由……组成（to have sb./sth. as parts or members）（例句：The course comprises a class book, a practice book, and a CD.）

~ sth. 组成或构成……（to be the parts or members that form sth.）（例句：Italian students comprise 60 percent of the class.）

D. ~ of 由……组成；由……构成；包括（to be made of particular parts or things）

总结：在表达"构成……"的概念时，constitute/compose/comprise sth. 都可以。

句子大意：在俄罗斯工作的公民寄回国内的汇款是一些中亚国家经济的重要组成部分。

2 A

A. 不冷不热的；微温的（slightly warm, sometimes in a way that is not pleasant）

B. 胆小的，恐惧担心的（fearful or apprehensive, especially trembling from fear）

C.（液体、气体等）清澈的；清澄的；透明的；透光的 [(of a liquid, air, etc.) clear and transparent]

D. 表达清楚的；易懂的（clearly expressed; easy to understand）

句子大意：由于内需不温不火，进口增速呈现疲软的态势。

备注：

* 不瘟不火：只能用于表演领域，指戏曲不沉闷乏味，也不急促，恰到好处。

* 不温不火：不冷淡也不火爆，平淡适中。

* 不愠不火：指说话态度得当，做事有分寸。

3 B

A. 如果选用 mean，正确表达为：…mean further escalation of social unrest.

B. risk doing sth. 为常见表达，意为"可能会造成……"或"有……的风险"

C. 如果选用 cause，正确表达为：…might cause further escalation of social unrest.

D. 如果选用 trigger，正确表达为：…might trigger further escalation of social unrest.

句子大意：生活成本的攀升可能会进一步加剧社会动荡。

4 C

A. 发怒；怒斥（to show that you are very angry about sth. or with sb., especially by shouting）

~ (on) 猛烈地继续；激烈进行（to continue in a violent way）

B. ~ about sb./sth. 热烈谈论（或书写）；（热情洋溢地）奋笔疾书（to talk or write about sth. in a very enthusiastic way）

~ (at sb.) 咆哮；怒吼（to shout in a loud and emotional way at sb. because you are angry with them）

C. ~ sth. 毁坏；损坏；严重损害（to damage sth. badly）

D. ~ sth. 翻寻；乱翻；搜寻（to move things around carelessly while searching for sth.）

句子大意："二战"结束后不久成立的世界银行旨在帮助重建饱受蹂躏的经济，为中低收入国家提供财政支持。

5 A

industrial action 劳工行动；（尤指）罢工，怠工（action that workers take, especially stopping work, to protest to their employers about sth.）

A. ~ sb. 使残废；使跛；使成瘸子（to damage sb.'s body so that they are no longer able to walk or move normally）

~ sb./sth. 严重毁坏（或损害）（to seriously damage or harm sb./sth.）

B. （使）皱；成波纹（to crumple, wrinkle, or curl）

C. ~ (sth.) (up) (into sth.) 压皱；（使）变皱，起皱（to crush sth. into folds; to become crushed into folds）

~ (up)（脸）沮丧地皱起，哭丧着（If your face crumples, you look sad and disappointed, as if you might cry.）

D. （使）破碎，成碎屑（to break or break sth. into very small pieces）

（开始渐渐）衰退；崩溃；瓦解；消亡（to begin to fail or get weaker or to come to an end）

句子大意：本田通常会坚持至少保留两家零部件供应商，部分原因是防范任何可能的劳工行动对生产造成严重影响。

6 B

A. ~ sth. 炫耀；卖弄（to show sth. you are proud of to other people, in order to impress them）

~ yourself （性感地）招摇过市（to behave in a confident and sexual way to attract attention）

B. ~ sth. 使减弱；使降低效应（to make sth. weaker or less effective）

C. ~ sth. 损害；挫伤（信心、名誉等）（to damage sb.'s confidence, reputation, etc.）

D. 犯愚蠢的（或粗心的）错误（to make a stupid or careless mistake）

句子大意：政府保护包括减轻食品和能源价格上涨带来的影响，以及确保低收入国家获得足够的疫苗供应。

7 B

A. 预言；预告（to say that sth. will happen in the future）

B. ~ sth. on/upon sth. 使基于；使以……为依据（to base sth. on a particular belief, idea or principle）

C. 用预制构件制造（to manufacture sections of something, especially a building, that can be transported to a site and easily assembled there）

D. 给……开（药）（to tell sb. to take a particular medicine or have a particular treatment; to write a prescription for a particular medicine, etc.）

规定；命令；指示（to say what should be done or how sth. should be done）

句子大意：这部电影证明，基于好奇心、民主原则和人们可以为自己说话的理念来制作电影的方法是经久不衰的。

8 C

A. [ɔːˈrɔːrə] 极光；曙光（a phenomenon occurring in the night sky around the polar regions, caused by atmospheric gases interacting with solar particles to create streamers, folds, or arches of colored light）

B. 滑稽动作；古怪行径（amusing, frivolous, or eccentric behavior）

C. ~ (of sth.) 气氛；氛围；气质（a feeling or particular quality that is very noticeable and seems to surround a person or place）

D. 施舍物；救济金（money, clothes and food that are given to poor people）

句子大意：作为一位时尚教主和模特，她浑身散发着一种名流气息。

9 D

A. 磨光；擦亮；翻新或装修（房间、建筑等）（to make something, especially a room or building, look clean, new and in good condition）

B. ~ sth. 破坏……的完美；玷污（to spoil sth. that is beautiful or perfect in all other ways）

C. （动词原形：breed）~ sth. 孕育；导致（to be the cause of sth.）

D. 发芽，萌芽 [to send forth new growth (such as buds or branches)]

急速成长，迅猛发展（to grow and expand rapidly）

句子大意：正是在这对她成长产生巨大影响的三年时间里她萌生了对电影的兴趣。

10 D

A. 正确用法为：cause sth./cause sth. to do…

B. 表示原因时的用法为：drive sth.，没有 drive sth. doing 的表达

C. 表示原因时的用法为：trigger sth.，没有 trigger sth. doing 的表达

D. 表示原因时的用法为：send sth. doing

句子大意：俄罗斯对乌克兰港口的封锁使得全球粮价飙升，加剧了全球饥饿问题。

11 C

A. 逸事；趣闻（a short, interesting or amusing story about a real person or event）

B.（二者间的）对比，对照（a contrast between two things）

C. ~ (to sth.) 解毒药；解毒剂（a substance that controls the effects of a poison or disease）

　　~ (to sth.) 消除不快的事物；矫正方法（anything that takes away the effects of sth. unpleasant）

D. 防腐剂；抗菌剂（a substance that helps to prevent infection in wounds by killing bacteria）

句子大意：近年来，一些设计师走向了极繁主义，这一风格受到了许多人的欢迎，人们认为这种欢快热烈的风格能够抵消极简主义带来的紧张感。

12 D

固定搭配考查。

precious few/little of sth. 强调某事特别少（used for emphasizing how little there is of something）

A. 便宜地；廉价地（without spending or costing much money）

B. 昂贵地；仔细地；过分讲究地（in a way that is too formal and unnatural）

C. 罕有；不常（not very often）

D.（adj.）道貌岸然的；矫揉造作的（very formal, exaggerated and not natural in what you say and do）

句子大意：做公众演讲仍然是让大多数人最发怵的事情，多年来这种情况并未有多少改善。

13 D

A. ['detəneɪt] ~ (sth.)（使）爆炸；引爆（to explode, or to make a bomb or other device explode）

B. ~ sth. (in sth.) 以（某种货币）为单位，以……计价（to express an amount of money using a particular unit）

　　~ sb. or sth. (as) sth. 将……命名为（to give sb. or sth. a particular name or description）

C. ['diːmɑː(r)keɪt] ~ sth. 标出……的界线；给……划界（to mark or establish the limits of sth.）

　　常考近义词：delineate [dɪ'lɪnieɪt] ~ sth.（详细地）描述，描画，解释（to describe, draw or explain sth. in detail）

D. 标志，预示，象征（to be a sign of sth.）

　　表示，意指（to mean sth.）

句子大意："气候"是指宏观、长期的趋势，而"天气"则是指当下窗外天气的变化情况。

14 A

A. 方言；土语（the language spoken by a particular group or in a particular area, when it is different from the formal written language）

B. 模范；典型；范例（a person or thing that is a good or typical example of sth.）

C. ~ of sth. 表象；假象；外观（a situation in which sth. seems to exist although this may not, in fact, be the case）

D. 相似性（the fact of being or looking similar to sb./sth.）

常用搭配：bear resemblance to... 与……相似

句子大意：我相信，在接下来一两年，像共享办公空间、沙发客和时间银行等词语将会成为日常用语的一部分。

15 A

interlude（两事件之间的）间歇；插入事件（a period of time between two events during which sth. different happens）；（戏剧、电影等的）幕间休息（a short period of time between the parts of a play, film/movie, etc.）

A. 散布；散置；点缀（to intersperse with something as if by scattering）

be sprinkled with 等于 be interspersed with

B. ~ sb. with sth. 向某人抛撒……（to drop a lot of small things onto sb.）

大量地给某人……（to give sb. a lot of sth.）

C. 把（水、泥等）泼在……上；朝……上泼（或溅）（to make sb./sth. wet by making water, mud, etc. fall on them/it）

D. 热得难受（to be very hot in a way that makes you feel uncomfortable）

句子大意：这部电影穿插点缀有涉及"狂野西部"、驯兽、童星等方面的情节。

16 C

A. ~ sth. 防止蔓延（或恶化）（to prevent sth. harmful from spreading or getting worse）

B. ~ sth. 阻止蔓延（或恶化）（to stop sth. from spreading or getting worse）

C. ~ sth. 导致（不愉快的事）（to do sth. that might result in sth. unpleasant happening）

D. ~ sth. 控制，约束（尤指不好的事物）（to control or limit sth., especially sth. bad）

句子大意：为了在抑制通胀的同时不引发衰退，欧洲央行很可能会按照预发布的计划行事：将利率仅提高 0.25 个百分点。

17 C

A. ~ in... 比赛等获得第几名 [to finish a contest or competition in a particular position or place (as in first, second, third, etc.)]

B. ~ sth. (in sth.) 表明，清楚显示（尤指情感、态度或品质）（to show sth. clearly, especially a feeling, an attitude or a quality）（例句：The workers chose to manifest their dissatisfaction in a series of strikes.）

~ itself (in sth.) 显现；使人注意到（to appear or become noticeable）（例句：Lack of confidence in the company manifested itself in a fall in the share price.）

C. ~ (in/with sth.)（以某种结果）告终；（在某一点）结束（to end with a particular result, or at a particular point）

D. ~ sth. 部分捕杀，选择性宰杀（为防止动物种群量过多而杀掉其中一定数量）（to kill a particular number of animals of a group in order to prevent the group from getting too large）

句子大意：他试图窃取2020年选举的行为最终引发了暴乱。

18 D

A. ~ off（打折扣）销完；抛售（to sell something quickly and for a low price, usually because you need money）

B. ~ off 突然开始变得非常成功或受欢迎，腾飞（to begin suddenly to be very successful or popular）

C. ~ off 一走了之（to leave somewhere or someone suddenly）

（比赛）轻松得分（to win points easily in a competition）

打印（If you run off copies of something, you print them.）（例句：Please run me off five copies of this.）

D. ~ off（=hive off）分拆；剥离；衍生（to make part of a company into a new independent company）

句子大意：周一，葛兰素史克将会分拆消费者健康业务，成立新公司 Haleon。该业务部门主要销售牙膏和消炎药等药房骨干售卖品。

19 C

词组搭配考查。

A. make good 变得富有；获得成功（to become rich and successful; make sth. good or make good on sth.）

履行，执行（曾承诺或扬言要做的事）（to do sth. that you have promised, threatened, etc. to do）

B. 授予；册封（to give sb. a particular rank or title; to invest with an office or title）（例句：He was created a baron.）

C. ~ wonders 创造奇迹；产生奇效（to have a very good effect on someone or something）（例句1：Getting the job did wonders for her self-confidence. 例句2：This washing powder will work miracles on those difficult stains.）

D. ~ sth. 编造；捏造；虚构（to say or describe sth. that is not true, especially in order to trick people）

句子大意：在过去两年里，疫苗生产企业已经证明：只要有足够的资金支持，他们就可以创造奇迹。

20 C

A. 逐渐增强（to become gradually stronger）

B. ~ sth. (up) 使（价格）上浮；使（价格）维持于较高水平（to keep prices at a high or acceptable level）

C. ~ sth. 抵制；反抗（to resist or oppose sth.）

常见搭配：buck the trend 逆势而动（to be obviously different from the way that a situation is developing generally, especially in connection with financial matters）

D. ~ sb./sth. 帮助；支持（to give help or support to sb./sth.）

句子大意： 出乎意料的是，不断诞生独角兽私营企业（市值超过10亿美元）的地方正是欧洲，这与科技行业整体下滑的趋势形成鲜明对比。

Practice 14

1 C

A. energy-intensive 能源消耗量大的，能耗高的（using a lot of electricity, gas, etc.）

B. energy-efficient 节能的；高效节能；高能效的（using electrical or other energy in an economical way）

C. energy-dense 能量密度高的 [(of food) having a high calorie content in relation to its weight]

D. energy-conserving 节能的（relating to products, systems, etc. that use as little electricity, gas, etc. as possible）

句子大意： 调查发现，热量更高、能量密度更高的食品对手头紧张的人们而言是更好的购物选择。

2 C

A. 积极乐观的；自信的（thinking about what is good in a situation; feeling confident and sure that sth. good will happen）

表示赞同的；拥护的（expressing agreement or support）

B. 预兆；（尤指）恶兆，凶兆（a sign or warning of sth. that is going to happen in the future, especially when it is sth. unpleasant）

C. 对身心产生强烈影响的（having a strong effect on your body or mind）

强有力的（powerful）

D. 潜在的；可能的（that can develop into sth. or be developed in the future）

句子大意： 许多聚环丙烷化燃料的能源密度超过每升40兆焦耳，高于当前应用最为广泛的航空燃料的能源密度。

3 C

A. 多变的；易变的（often changing; likely to change）

可变的（able to be changed）

B. 可证实的；可考证的（able to be checked or proved）

C. 可实施的；切实可行的（that can be done; that will be successful）

可生存的；能独立发展的（capable of developing and surviving independently）

D. 十足的；名副其实的；不折不扣的（a word used to emphasize that sb./sth. can be compared to sb./sth. else that is more exciting, more impressive, etc.）（例句1：Pet stores stock a veritable arsenal of powders, soaps, collars, combs and ointments meant to curb flea infestations. 例句2：The hotel is a veritable landmark of Parisian hospitality.）

句子大意：必须以一种具有成本效益的方式对这种生物燃料进行规模化生产才能实现其商业化应用。

4 C

A. 优雅自信的；娴熟的（elegant, confident and/or highly skilled）

B. 虚华的；言辞浮夸的（showing that you think you are more important than other people, especially by using long and formal words）

C. (*adj.*) 视野不够开阔的（limited in outlook）

　　缺乏城市社会优雅品位的（lacking the polish of urban society）

　　(*n.*) 兴趣或观念地方化或受限的人（a person of local or restricted interests or outlook）

　　很土的人，土包子（a person lacking urban polish or refinement）

D. 谚语的；如谚语所说的（used to show that you are referring to a particular proverb or well-known phrase）

　　众所周知的；著名的（well known and talked about by a lot of people）

句子大意：他们将她描述成一个工作勤勉尽责的人，身上乡土气息太浓，没有城里人的优雅精致。

5 B

A. 报复；报复行动（a violent or aggressive act towards sb. because of sth. bad that they have done towards you）

B. 重复部分；（尤指乐曲的）反复（a repeated part of sth., especially a piece of music）

C. 刑罚终止令；（尤指）死刑缓刑令（an official order stopping a punishment, especially for a prisoner who is condemned to death）

　　延缓；缓解（a delay before sth. bad happens）

D. 重复乏味的（saying or doing the same thing many times, so that it becomes boring）

句子大意：更大的威胁是当年春季和夏季大宗商品价格暴涨的情况再次出现。

6 A

A. 常见搭配：in limbo 处于不确定、风雨飘摇、悬而未决的状态（in a state of uncertainty or of being kept waiting）

B. (*adj.*) 巨型的；特大的（very large; larger than usual）

　　(*n.*) 大型客机（尤指波音747）（a large plane that can carry several hundred passengers, especially a Boeing 747）

C. 肿块；隆起（a swelling under the skin, sometimes a sign of serious illness; have a lump in your throat）

　　（因愤怒或情绪激动而）喉咙哽住，哽咽（to feel pressure in the throat because you are very angry or emotional）

D. 惨败；可耻的失败（something that does not succeed, often in a way that causes embarrassment）

句子大意：工厂关停使得数千工人的生活没有了着落。

7 C

A. 重拳击打；用力地捶打 [a hard hit made with the fist (= closed hand)]

常考搭配：punch above your weight 超常发挥取胜；以小博大（to be or try to be more successful than others in doing sth. that normally requires more skill, experience, money, etc. than you have）

B. 一段（艰难）岁月；一段（痛苦）日子（a period of time of the type mentioned, usually a difficult or unhappy one）

常考搭配：a rough patch 一段艰难时期（a period of time in your life that is difficult or unpleasant）

C. fever pitch 高度兴奋；狂热（a very high level of excitement or activity）

D. 小袋子；荷包（a small bag, usually made of leather, and often carried in a pocket or attached to a belt）

邮袋（a large bag for carrying letters, especially official ones）

句子大意：硅谷的人才竞争现已达到白热化。

8 A

A. 将……加以考虑，重视，被迫应对（to consider something important when you are making plans and so be prepared for it; to be forced to deal with someone or something）

B. 使和解；调解（make friendly again, make peace between…）

C. ~ sb. (for sth.) 酬劳；付酬给某人（to pay sb. for work that they have done）

D. ~ sth. 收回（成本）；弥补（亏损）（to get back an amount of money that you have spent or lost）

句子大意：随着美国开始着手处理失控的消费习惯，我们作为一个国家也确实应该将教育成本问题考虑在内。

9 B

A. 规定；命令；指示（to say what should be done or how sth. should be done）

B. ~ sth. 宣布禁止（to say officially that sth. is banned）

C. (= circumscribe) 限制，限定（to constrict or limit）

　　(= conscript) 征召入伍；征兵（to force into military service）

D. ~ sth. 限制，约束（自由、权利、权力等）（to limit sb./sth.'s freedom, rights, power, etc.）

句子大意：有明文规定，在飞机降落过程中禁止使用电子设备。

10 C

A. 非法的，法律禁止的（forbidden by law or statute）

B. 非法的（not sanctioned by law）

C. 违背社会常规的；不正当的（not approved of by the normal rules of society）

D. 宣布……不合法；使……成为非法（to make something illegal）

句子大意：她与老板有不正当的关系。

11 A

A. ~ sth. (from sth.) 删除，去掉，辑除（不愿公之于众的信息）（to remove information from a document because you do not want the public to see it）

编辑；编写；拟订（to edit or revise something in preparation for publication）

B.（非法）篡改（后面通常加 with sth.）（to touch or make changes to something when you should not, especially when this is illegal）

C. ~ sth. 篡改；伪造（to change sth. in order to trick sb.）

D. 修正；整顿（to correct something that is wrong or damaged or to improve a bad situation）

句子大意：军方在公布这份文件前将会进行编辑，将涉密内容涂黑。

12 A

A. ~ sb./sth. 极大地打击；惩罚；使受到（严重经济损失）（to affect sb. badly or to punish them, especially by making them lose money）

~ sb./sth. 彻底战胜（或击败）（to defeat sb. completely）

B.（使）阻塞，堵塞（to block sth. or to become blocked）

C. 把……关在修道院里；使……与世隔绝（to make sb. spend time in a quiet or private place away from other people）

D. 腐蚀；生疮；腐败（to become a source of spreading corruption or evil, or cause sth. to decay as a result of spreading corruption or evil）

句子大意：这家国有金融集团受到了房地产和资本市场困境的严重冲击。

13 B

A.（防止栓塞等而植入的）血管支架（a small support that is put inside a blood vessel tube in the body, for example in order to stop sth. blocking it）

B. ~ (as sth.) 从事某项工作（或活动）的时间（a period of time that you spend working somewhere or doing a particular activity）

C.（尤指电影中的）特技表演（a dangerous and difficult action that sb. does to entertain people, especially as part of a film/movie）

意在引人注意的花招；噱头（something that is done in order to attract people's attention）

D. ~ (on sth.) 幽默短文，滑稽短剧，幽默讽刺小品（常用模仿手法）（a short piece of humorous writing or a performance that makes fun of sb./sth. by copying them）

句子大意：经过较为成功的 10 年任期后，该集团首席执行官在 6 月宣布辞职。他的继任者从他手里接管的将是一艘还未企稳的大船。

14 B

A.（同 hotchpotch）杂乱无章的一堆东西；大杂烩（a number of things mixed together without any particular order or reason）

B. 乏味的；单调的（boring and always the same）

C. 吊儿郎当的，闲混的，拖拖拉拉的（moving or proceeding at less than the normal, desirable, or required speed）

D. 咯噔咯噔动动摇摇的车；咯噔咯噔的摇动（a heavy coach or cart that moves with a deep rumbling sound）

句子大意：慢镜头中的现实世界总会显得更加精彩。即使是最乏味无聊的事件也像是动作片中最激动人心的镜头。

15 A

词组搭配考查。

do sth. with a vengeance 来势汹汹，猛烈地（used for emphasizing that something happens in an extreme way or with a lot of force）；程度更深地；出乎意料地（to a greater degree than is expected or usual）

A. 报复；报仇；复仇（the act of punishing or harming sb. in return for what they have done to you, your family or friends）

B. 报复；报仇（something that you do in order to make sb. suffer because they have made you suffer）

C. ~ sth.（只用做动词）报（某事）之仇；向（某人）报仇（to punish or hurt sb. in return for sth. bad or wrong that they have done to you, your family or friends）

D. [ˌretrɪˈbjuːʃ(ə)n] ~ (for sth.) 惩罚；报应（severe punishment for sth. seriously wrong that sb. has done）

句子大意：在疫情封锁结束后，旅客们强势回归航空旅行。

16 B

A. 常见搭配为 have a smell of...，而非用作动词构成 sth. smells of...

B. 固定搭配：smack of... 带有……的味道（负面）（to be a sign of something bad）

  常考近义词组：reek of.../stink of... 带有……的味道（负面）（to give off or have some strong, unpleasant odor; to be full of something distasteful or offensive）

C. 自鸣得意地笑；傻笑（to smile in a silly or unpleasant way that shows that you are pleased with yourself, know sth. that other people do not know, etc.）

D. 逃避（工作）；躲懒（to avoid doing sth. you should do, especially because you are too lazy）

句子大意：一些银行——特别是国际性大银行——不想涉足，这是因为他们担心赚穷人的钱多少带点剥削的味道。

17 A

exploit 英勇（或激动人心、引人注目）的行为（a brave, exciting or interesting act）

A. [prɪˈkoʊʃəs]（能力或行为）早熟的（having developed particular abilities and ways of behaving at a much younger age than usual）

B. ~ (with sth.) 专注；一门心思做某事（thinking and/or worrying continuously about sth. so that you do not pay attention to other things）

C. 大量的；充裕的（in large amounts）

D. [kə'prɪʃəs]（态度或行为）反复无常的；任性的（showing sudden changes in attitude or behaviour）

句子大意：在象棋领域，年少成名者大有人在，卡尔森本人就是一个天才少年。

18 C

A. 过去的；预先决定的；（结局）必不可免的

a foregone conclusion 预料中的必然结局（If you say that sth. is a foregone conclusion, you mean that it is a result that is certain to happen.）

B. 上述的；前述的（used to refer to sth. that has just been mentioned）

C. 现成的；随要随有的（ready or made available when needed）（例句 1：No explanation for his absence was forthcoming. 例句 2：Will financial support for the theatre project be forthcoming?）

D.（人）孤苦伶仃的，孤独凄凉的（alone and unhappy; left alone and not cared for）

（地方）凄凉的，荒芜的（A forlorn place feels empty and sad.）

不大可能成功的；难以实现的（unlikely to succeed, come true, etc.）（例句 1：Their only hope now is that the outside world will intervene but it is an increasingly forlorn hope. 例句 2：She appeared on daytime TV in a forlorn attempt to persuade the public of her innocence.）

句子大意：尽管东帝汶对此类项目一直雄心勃勃，但尚未获得国际融资。

19 A

A. ~ sth. 把（马或牛）赶入围栏（或关进畜栏）（to force horses or cows into a corral）

~ sb. 把（一群人）集中起来关在一起（to bring a group of people together and keep them in one place, especially in order to control them）

B. [kə'leɪt] ~ sth. 核对，校勘，对照（不同来源的信息）（to collect information together from different sources in order to examine and compare it）

~ sth. 整理（文件或书等）（to collect pieces of paper or the pages of a book, etc. and arrange them in the correct order）

C. 迷住；吸引住（to make you so interested or excited that you give it all your attention）

D. ~ (for sth.) 觅（食）（to search for food）

~ (for sth.)（尤指用手）搜寻（东西）（to search for sth., especially using the hands）

句子大意：警察将大部分示威者围拢到了靠近车站的一个狭小区域。

20 C

A. 枪管（the part of a gun like a tube through which the bullets are fired）

B.（动物的）洞穴，洞穴通道（a hole or tunnel in the ground made by animals such as rabbits for them to live in）

C. ['bærɑːʒ] 堰；拦河坝；火力网

~ (of sth.) 接二连三的一大堆（质问或指责等）（a large number of sth., such as questions or comments, that are directed at sb. very quickly, one after the other, often in an aggressive way）

D. 犁沟；车辙（a long narrow cut in the ground, especially one made by a plough for planting seeds in）

（脸上的）皱纹（a deep line in the skin of the face）

句子大意：面对一片质疑和批评声，这位年轻女孩表示自己"倍感压力"，但并不感到意外。

Practice 15

1 C

A. ['preljuːd] 为……作序；成为……的序曲/序幕（to serve as a prelude to sth.）

B. 作序言、绪论（to speak or write a preamble; to provide a preliminary statement or set of remarks）

C. 阻止；妨碍（to prevent sth. from happening or sb. from doing sth.）

D. 连续猛击；反复拳打；捶打（to keep hitting sb./sth. hard, especially with your fists）

句子大意：一位网站设计人员称，出于对婚姻的信仰，她不会设计有关非正统婚礼的网站。

2 B

A. ~ sth. 公开否认；拒绝承认（to state publicly that you have no knowledge of sth., or that you are not responsible for sth.）

~ sth. 放弃（财产、头衔等的）权利（to give up your right to sth., such as property or a title）

B. ~ sb. 诈骗；哄骗；欺骗（to trick or cheat sb.）

C. ~ sb./sth. 给……用兴奋剂（to give a drug to a person or an animal in order to affect their performance in a race or sport）

D. ~ sth. (from sth.) 开垦，利用，改造（荒地）（to make land that is naturally too wet or too dry suitable to be built on, farmed, etc.）

~ sth. (from sth.) 回收（废品中有用的东西）（to obtain materials from waste products so that they can be used again）

~ sb. (from sth.) 挽救；感化；使悔过自新（to rescue sb. from a bad or criminal way of life）

句子大意：检察官声称，博朗及其同谋通过篡改账户来欺骗银行和其他债权人。

3 B

A. 倒运的；不幸的（unlucky）

B. [hæp'hæzə(r)d] 随意的；无计划的；组织混乱的（with no particular order or plan; not organized well）

C. 小事故；晦气（a small accident or piece of bad luck that does not have serious results）

D. 或许；偶然地；侥幸地（used to express the possibility or hope that something is or will be the case）

句子大意：他们希望结束国美此前随意扩张的做法，关闭无法盈利的门店，通过更加精准的定位来开设新店。

4 B

A. 轴（旋转物体假想的中心线）（an imaginary line through the centre of an object, around which the object turns）

坐标轴（a fixed line against which the positions of points are measured, especially points on a graph）

B. 棱镜；三棱镜（a transparent glass or plastic object, often with ends in the shape of a triangle, which separates light that passes through it into the colours of the rainbow）

常考搭配：see/view...through the prism of... 透过……来看待……；从……角度来看待……

C. 血浆（the clear liquid part of blood, in which the blood cells, etc. float）

D. 像素（组成屏幕图像的最小独立元素）（any of the small individual areas on a computer screen, which together form the whole display）

句子大意：从"9·11"事件的角度来看，加强机场安保工作对威慑恐怖主义至关重要。

5 C

A.（后可连接 at/in/over/to do sth.）非常高兴；深感欣喜（to express great happiness about sth.）

B.（及物动词）享受；从……获得乐趣（to get great pleasure from sth.; to want very much to do or have sth.）

C. 退缩；畏缩（to move your body quickly away from sb./sth. because you find them or it frightening or unpleasant）

~ from sth. or from doing sth. or ~ at sth. 对……做出厌恶（或恐惧）的反应（to react to an idea or a situation with strong dislike or fear）

D. ~ sth. 收回（说过的话）（to say that sth. you have said earlier is not true or correct or that you did not mean it）

~ sth. 撤回，收回（协议、承诺等）（to refuse to keep an agreement, a promise, etc.）

句子大意：西方政策制定者一想到会在索马里陷入另一场血腥的反叛乱行动，就会退缩。

6 C

A. ~ sb./sth. from/against sth. 使免除（不愉快的经历）；使免受（不良影响）（to protect sb./sth. from unpleasant experiences or influences）

B. 暗示，旁敲侧击地指出（不快的事）（to suggest indirectly that sth. unpleasant is true）

C. ~ (sb. or sth.) 监（考）（to watch people while they are taking an exam to make sure that they have everything they need, that they keep to the rules, etc.）

美语常用同义词为：proctor（n.&v. 监考人员；监考……（如：to proctor an exam）

D. ~ sb. (with sth.) 使不胜负荷；使应接不暇（to give or send sb. so many things that they cannot deal with them all）

~ sth. 淹没；泛滥（to cover an area of land with a large amount of water）

句子大意：我将负责此次英语考试的监考。

7 C

A. 预兆；征兆（a sign of what is going to happen in the future）

B. ~ (on sth.) 征收额；（尤指）税款（an extra amount of money that has to be paid, especially as a tax to the government）

C. 职责；责任（the responsibility for sth.; if the onus is on someone to do something, it is their responsibility or duty to do it）

D. 谚语；格言（a well-known phrase expressing a general truth about people or the world）

句子大意：企业的产品自评不能被当作绝对真理。科学家、监管机构和公共健康部门有责任填补知识方面的空白。

8 B

A. [ɪˈpɪtəmi] the ~ of sth. 典型；典范（a perfect example of sth.）

B. [ˈepɪθet] 别称；绰号（an offensive word or phrase that is used about a person or group of people）

C. [ɪˈpɪfəni] 顿悟（a moment when you suddenly realize or understand something important）

D. [ˈepɪtɑːf] 悼文；祭文；（尤指）墓志铭，碑文（words that are written or said about a dead person, especially words on a gravestone）

~ (to sb./sth.) 遗物；遗存；遗迹（something which is left to remind people of a particular person, a period of time or an event）

句子大意："世界工厂"经常用来代指该国，但如今这一指称让一些企业紧张不安。

9 C

motif [məʊˈtiːf] 装饰图案（a design or a pattern used as a decoration）；（文学作品或音乐的）主题，主旨（a subject, an idea or a phrase that is repeated and developed in a work of literature or a piece of music）

A. ~ sb./sth. 扼要介绍；概述；写简介（to give or write a description of sb./sth. that gives the most important information）

B. ~ sb./sth. 描绘；描写（to show sb./sth. in a picture; to describe sb./sth. in a piece of writing）

C. 以……为特色；是……的特征（to include a particular person or thing as a special feature）

~ prominently (in sth.) 起重要作用；占重要地位（to have an important part in sth.）

D. ~ sth.（详细地）描述，描画，解释（to describe, draw or explain sth. in detail）

句子大意：澳大利亚央行称，国王查理三世的头像不会出现在该国的新版五澳元纸币上，取而代之的是彰显原住民文化的图案。

10 B

A.（尤指战争中）掠夺的财物（things that have been stolen, especially during a war, etc.）

B. 喝彩；称赞（an expression of praise or approval）

C. 行家；权威；专家（a person who knows a lot about a particular subject and who often talks about it in public）

D. 沉思；考虑；琢磨（to think about sth. carefully for a period of time）

句子大意：2月1日，该国安全部门突然搜查了一位著名寡头大亨的家，该委员会对此表示赞赏，称此举体现了对整治贿赂问题的重视。

11 C

A. 狡猾的；奸诈的（able to get what you want in a clever way, especially by tricking or cheating sb.）

灵巧的；精巧的（clever and skilful）

B.（尤指在商业或政治方面）精明谨慎的，老谋深算的（intelligent, careful and showing good judgement, especially in business or politics）

C. 可怕的，令人毛骨悚然的；不可思议的，神秘的（eerie, mysterious; strange or mysterious, often in a way that is slightly frightening）

D. 令人迷惑的难题；复杂难解的问题（a confusing problem or question that is very difficult to solve）

句子大意：她与最好的朋友有着惊人的相似之处。

12 C

homily [ˈhɒmɪli] 使人厌烦的说教 [a short speech advising someone how to behave (This word usually shows that you think the advice is boring.)]

A. earn ~ (for sth.) 因某事赢得称赞或认可（win praise or approval because you are responsible for sth. good that has happened）

do sb. ~ or do ~ to sb./sth. 使……值得赞扬（或表扬）（If sth. does credit to a person or an organization, they deserve to be praised for it.）

B. [krəˈdjuːləti] 轻信（willingness to believe that something is real or true, especially when this is unlikely）

C. 资格证书；证明书；证件（documents such as letters that prove that you are who you claim to be, and can therefore be trusted）

常考搭配：improve/burnish/tarnish one's...credentials，此处的 credentials 往往译为"形象或资质"

补充：green credentials 环保资质、理念或形象（the qualities that show you believe it is important to protect the natural environment）

* 例句1：The company has rebranded itself to promote its green credentials（提升环保形象）.

* 例句2：They are cutting down on air travel in an effort to improve their green credentials（改善环保形象）.

D. 信念；原则；宗教信仰（a set of principles or religious beliefs）

句子大意：南非人民对于一位玷污了自己改革家形象的总统所做的说教已经厌烦了。

13 C

A. [sesˈeɪʃən]（动词原形为 cease）结束或停止（ending or stopping）

B. [ˈseʃən]（动词原形为 cede）割让（an occasion when one person or country officially gives land or property to another, or the act of officially giving land or property away）

C. [sɪˈseʃ(ə)n]（动词原形为 secede [sɪˈsiːd] ~ from sth.）（从国家或大集团中正式地）脱离（the act of becoming independent and no longer part of a country, area, organization, etc.）

D. session（法庭的）开庭，开庭期；（议会等的）会议，会期（a formal meeting or series of meetings of a court, a parliament, etc.; a period of time when such meetings are held）

句子大意：当时，南苏丹脱离苏丹独立出来将造成混乱的局面。

14 B

A. 生性的，生就的（existing as part of a person's character and not likely to change）

（疾病）先天性的（born with a particular illness）

B. [kənˈdʒiːnɪəl]~ (to sb.) 合意的；适宜的（pleasant because it suits your character）

~ (to sth.) 适合的；适当的（suitable for sth.）

常考同根词：genial 友好的；亲切的；欢快的（friendly and kind）

C. 心平气和的，友善的（done or achieved in a polite or friendly way and without arguing）；前面为冠词"a"而非"an"，故不能选用 amicable

常考形近词：amiable（形容人）和蔼可亲的；亲切友好的（pleasant; friendly and easy to like）

D. [həˈredət(ə)ri] 遗传的；遗传性的（given to a child by its parents before it is born）

世袭的（that is legally given to sb.'s child, when that person dies）

句子大意：多年来，他与教练保持着融洽的关系。

15 C

A. ~ (with sth.)（在大小、重要性、质量等方面）相称的，相当的（matching sth. in size, importance, quality, etc.）

B. 可消耗的；会用尽的（intended to be bought, used and then replaced）

C. consummate [ˈkɒnsəmeɪt] 技艺高超的；完美的（extremely skilled; perfect）

D. [kənˈsəʊləbl] 可安慰的（able to be consoled）

句子大意：美国芯片设计商 Nvidia 是技艺高超的"淘金热里卖铲子"的一方。2016 年，人们对比特币和人工智能的关注催生出市场对其产品的新需求，该公司股价水涨船高。

备注：在投资界有一个很有名的说法：挖金矿的不一定赚钱，但是卖铲子的一定会赚到。

16 B

A. ~ sb.（用布等）蒙住……的眼睛（to cover sb.'s eyes with a piece of cloth or other covering so that they cannot see）

B. ~ sb. 攻其不备；出其不意地袭击（to attack sb. from the direction where they cannot see you coming; to catch or take unawares, especially with harmful or detrimental results）

C. ~ sb. 使……退出比赛，使……下场（尤指由于受伤）（to prevent sb. from playing in a team, especially because of an injury）

~ sb. 把……排除在核心之外；使……受排挤（to prevent sb. from having an important part in sth. that other people are doing）

D. ~ sth. 回避，规避（问题等）（to avoid answering a question or dealing with a problem）

句子大意：正当生活似乎一帆风顺的时候，她却突患重病。

17 B

A. （尤指以令人厌烦的方式）指使，强行规定（to tell sb. what to do, especially in an annoying way）

B. 使有必要；使正当（to make sth. necessary or appropriate in a particular situation; to serve as or give adequate ground or reason for）

C. ~ sth. 对……有影响（to have an influence on sth.）

D. 强调；突显（to emphasize or show that sth. is important or true）

句子大意：他过去曾照搬该委员会的说法，称该国袭击邻国的原因是北约扩张。

18 B

A. 仔细考虑（to think carefully about something over a period of time）

B. （为防止动物种群量过多而通常对最弱者的）选择性宰杀 [the act of killing some animals (usually the weakest ones) of a group in order to prevent the group from getting too large]

C. ~ (sth.) 减轻；（使）变麻木（to become or be made weaker or less severe）

~ sb. 使迟钝；使不活泼（to make a person slower or less lively）

D. 数字零（a zero）

空位，空白符号（a character which produces no effect or action but is used to fill up a space or to separate pieces of information）

句子大意：据报道，麦肯锡计划裁员2000人，这是该公司成立以来规模较大的一次裁员。

19 B

A. ['renɪgeɪd] n. 背叛者；变节者（a deserter from one faith, cause, or allegiance to another; an individual who rejects lawful or conventional behavior）；该词还可以作为动词和形容词使用（v. 变节，背教；adj. 变节的）

B. [rɪ'neɪg] ~ on sth. 违背（诺言）；背信弃义（to break a promise, an agreement, etc.）

C. ~ sth. 证明……错误；使站不住脚（to prove that an idea, a story, an argument, etc. is wrong）

~ sth. 使无效；使作废（If you invalidate a document, contract, election, etc., you make it no longer legally or officially valid or acceptable.）

D. ~ sth. 取消；使无效（to stop sth. from having any effect）

句子大意：对于一位国家领袖而言，为了避免冲突而背弃所有承诺是不可取的。

20 C

A. ~ (from sth.)（投票时）弃权（to choose not to use a vote, either in favour of or against sth.）

~ (from sth.) 戒；戒除（to decide not to do or have sth., especially sth. you like or enjoy, because it is bad for your health or considered morally wrong）

B. ~ (from sth.)（人）出生于；来自（to be from a particular place）

C. ~ (from somewhere) 逃走；逃遁（to escape from a place that you are not allowed to leave without permission）

~ (with sth.)（携款）潜逃（to leave secretly and take with you sth., especially money, that does not belong to you）

D. ~ (from sth.) 克制自己不去做某事（to make a considered, conscious effort not to do something）

句子大意：警方认为该嫌犯打算利用水路从香港潜逃。

Practice 16

1 C

A. ['pælətəb(ə)l] 可口的；味美的（having a pleasant or acceptable taste）

B. ~ (to sb.) 宜人的；可接受的（pleasant or acceptable to sb.）

可饮用的；适于饮用的（safe to drink）

C. 易于察觉的；明显的（that is easily noticed by the mind or the senses）

D. 易受影响的；容易摆布的（easy to influence or control）

句子大意：公职腐败是法治缺位的明显证据。

2 C

A. 缺点；缺陷；毛病（a fault in sth. or in the way it has been made which means that it is not perfect）

B. ~ sth. 给……消毒（to clean sth. using a substance that kills bacteria）

C. 已灭绝的；不再起作用的；不再使用的（no longer existing, operating or being used）

常考近义词：dysfunctional（身体系统或器官）功能失调的（impaired in function, especially of a bodily system or organ）；无法正常运转的，有故障的（not operating normally or properly）

D. 对……不满而不再忠诚的（no longer satisfied with your situation, organization, belief, etc. and therefore not loyal to it）

句子大意：这场危机已然相当严重，现有的解决机制已经失效。

3 D

A.（尤指对过错、罪行的）承认，招认，招供（a statement in which sb. admits that sth. is true, especially sth. wrong or bad that they have done）

B. 许可；批准（the act of allowing sb. to do sth., especially when this is done by sb. in a position of authority）

C. 提交；呈递；提交（或呈递）的文件、建议等（the act of giving a document, proposal, etc. to sb. in authority so that they can study or consider it; the document, etc. that you give）

D.（重病的）缓解期，减轻期（a period during which a serious illness improves for a time and the patient seems to get better）

句子大意：这位奥斯卡获奖作曲家在纽约居住了30多年，自去年11月以来一直在日本疗养，因为他在接受数年喉癌治疗、病情好转不久后，又被诊断出患有直肠癌。

4 B

A.（皮肤上摩擦或烫等引起的）水疱，疱（a swelling on the surface of the skin that is filled with liquid and is caused, for example, by rubbing or burning）

B. 咆哮，气势汹汹地说话，威吓（却通常作用不大）（loud, angry, or offended talk, usually with little effect）

C.（因难堪、羞愧）面部泛起的红晕（the red colour that spreads over your face when you are embarrassed or ashamed）

D. 斑点；疤痕；瑕疵（a mark on the skin or on an object that spoils it and makes it look less beautiful or perfect）

句子大意：在对社区的工作人员软硬兼施、又是威吓又是求情后，他们才送我妻子去医院做了产前检查。

5 C

A. ~ sth. (up) 煽动；激起（to make people feel sth. more strongly）

B. ~ sb./sth. 猛烈抨击（to criticize sb./sth. very strongly）

C. ~ sb./sth. 阻挠；妨碍（to prevent sb. from doing sth. that they have planned or want to do; to prevent sth. from happening）

D.（使）打旋，起旋涡（to move around quickly in a circle; to make sth. do this）

句子大意：由于票价较高和直飞航班不多，许多人甚至连张机票都很难订上。

6 C

A.（动词原形为find）（经寻找、研究或思考）发现，查明（to discover sth./sb. by searching, studying or thinking carefully）

B. ~ sth. 创建，创办（组织或机构，尤指提供资金）（to start sth., such as an organization or an institution, especially by providing money）

~ sth. 建立，兴建（城镇或国家）（to be the first to start building and living in a town or country）

C. ~ (on sth.) 失败；破产（to fail because of a particular problem or difficulty）

~ (on sth.) 沉没（to fill with water and sink）

D. 挣扎，踉跄前进（to move with great difficulty and in an uncontrolled way）

句子大意：本周出版的《瓦格纳》一书书名取自于1741年在巴塔哥尼亚沿岸沉没的同名小型护卫舰。

7 A

A. [ɪˈnɒkjuəs] 无恶意的；无意冒犯的（not intended to offend or upset anyone）

无害的；无危险的（not harmful or dangerous）

B. [nɒkˈtɜː(r)n(ə)l] 夜行的；夜出的（active at night）

夜间发生的（happening during the night）

C. [daɪˈɜː(r)n(ə)l] 日间活动的；昼行性的（active during the day）

D. [ɪˈmækjʊlət] 特别整洁的（extremely clean and tidy）

无误的；无过失的（containing no mistakes）

句子大意： 有些蘑菇貌似无毒，但实际上是有毒的。

8 C

A. ~ sth. 反驳；证明（言论等）错误（to say or prove that a statement or criticism is false）

B. ~ sb. (for sth./for doing sth.) 指责；批评（to speak severely to sb. because they have done sth. wrong）

C. 终于答应；不再拒绝（to finally agree to sth. after refusing）

变缓和；变温和（to become less determined, strong, etc.）

D. ~ from sth./doing sth. 克制自己不去做某事（to stop yourself from doing sth., especially sth. that you want to do）

常考同义词组：forbear from doing sth.（如：forbear from making a comment）

句子大意： 在分歧持续数周后，欧盟各国能源部长最终就天然气价格上限达成一致。原本持反对态度的德国最终同意这一上限。

9 B

A. ~ sth. (from sb.) 引出；探出；诱出（to get information or a reaction from sb., often with difficulty）

B. ~ sb./sth.（尤指机敏地）避开，逃避，躲避（to manage to avoid or escape from sb./sth., especially in a clever way）

~ sb. 使无法实现；使不记得；使不理解（If sth. eludes you, you are not able to achieve it, or not able to remember or understand it.）

常考同义表达：evade sb. 使达不到；未发生在（某人）身上（to not come or happen to sb.; to be elusive to sb.）

C. ~ sb./sth. (from sth.) 防止……进入；把……排斥在外（to prevent sb./sth. from entering a place or taking part in sth.）

D. ~ sb. (to sth.) 提拔，提升（有时指不该得到的职位）（to make sb. rise to a higher rank or position, sometimes to one that they do not deserve）

~ sb./sth. 高度赞扬（to praise sb./sth. very much）

句子大意： 利昂内尔·梅西多年来一直渴望在足球世界杯比赛中捧杯，此次比赛他终于得偿所愿。人们普遍认为梅西是近年来世界上最优秀的球员。

175

10 C

A. 掺杂；伪造；冒牌货（the act of making food or drugs worse in quality by adding something to them）

B. 改变；更改；改动（the act of making a change to sth.）

C. [ˌædjʊ'leɪʃ(ə)n] 奉承；吹捧（admiration and praise, especially when this is greater than is necessary）

D. [ˌæbə'reɪʃ(ə)n] 反常现象；异常行为（a fact, an action or a way of behaving that is not usual, and that may be unacceptable）

句子大意：他声称自己本无意欺世盗名，只是无法抗拒欢呼的人群给予他的赞誉与奉承。

11 B

A. ~ sb. 细心照顾；娇惯；纵容（to take care of sb. very well and make them feel as comfortable as possible）

B. ~ to sth. 迎合（to cater to the lower tastes and desires of others or exploit their weaknesses）

C. 沉思；考虑；琢磨（to think about sth. carefully for a period of time）

D. ~ sth. 预兆，预示（尤指坏事）（to be a sign or warning of sth. that is going to happen in the future, especially sth. bad or unpleasant）

句子大意：消费者往往会回报那些始终坚守原则而非仅仅迎合新潮的公司。

12 C

A. （尤指厌烦或心不在焉时）乱涂，胡写乱画（to draw lines, shapes, etc., especially when you are bored or thinking about sth. else）

B. ~ (over sb./sth.) 对……垂涎欲滴，过分痴迷（to show in a silly or exaggerated way that you want or admire sb./sth. very much）

C. 拖延；磨蹭；游荡（to take a long time to do sth. or go somewhere）

D. （逐渐）减少，缩小（to become gradually less or smaller）

句子大意：就股票表现而言，在该国入侵其邻国后不久即从该国撤离的企业要好于那些拖延不决或选择留下的企业。

13 B

A. 上帝；苍天；天佑（God, or a force that some people believe controls our lives and the things that happen to us, usually in a way that protects us）

B. 原产地；发源地；起源；出处（the place that sth. originally came from）

C. ~ (over sb./sth.) 优先；优先权（the condition of being more important than sb. else and therefore coming or being dealt with first）

D. 流行，普遍；患病率（the fact that something is very common or happens often）

句子大意：这里曾是全球最大的三家屠宰场之一，旨在为上海提供来源可信的肉类产品。

14 D

A. ~ sb./sth. 扼要介绍；概述；写简介（to give or write a description of sb./sth. that gives the most important information）

B. [prɪˈsɪpɪtət] ~ sth. 使……突然降临；加速（坏事的发生）（to make sth., especially sth. bad, happen suddenly or sooner than it should）

~ sb./sth. into sth. 使突然陷入（某种状态）（to suddenly force sb./sth. into a particular state or condition）

C. 阻止；妨碍；使……行不通；使……不可能（to prevent sth. from happening or sb. from doing sth.; to make sth. impossible）

D. [prəˈdʒekt] 预测；预计；推想（to estimate what the size, cost or amount of sth. will be in the future based on what is happening now）

展现；表现；确立（好印象）（to present sb./sth./yourself to other people in a particular way, especially one that gives a good impression）

句子大意：在掌管一个不断缩小的帝国期间，展示稳定性和连续性可以说就是她作为君主最为重要的工作。

15 C

A. ~ sth. 艰苦干成；努力加强（to put a lot of effort into making sth. successful or strong so that it will last）

~ sth. 伪造；假冒（to make an illegal copy of sth. in order to cheat people）

B. ~ (for sth.) 觅（食）（to search for food）

~ (for sth.)（尤指用手）搜寻（东西）（to search for sth., especially using the hands）

C. ~ sth. 涉过，驶过（浅水）（to walk or drive across a river or stream）

D. [ˈfiːɔː(r)d]（尤指挪威两岸峭壁间的）峡湾（a long narrow strip of sea between high cliffs, especially in Norway）

句子大意：这款四四方方的多用途车的四轮驱动和离地净高使得它可以爬上岩石，涉过溪流，与这位曾于"二战"尾声在领土辅助服务队接受驾驶和维修军车训练、不拘小节的君主相得益彰。

16 A

A. [prəʊˈdʒenɪtə(r)]（人或动、植物等的）祖先，祖代（a person or thing from the past that a person, animal or plant that is alive now is related to）

创始人；先驱（a person who starts an idea or a development）

B. [pɒˈsterəti] 后代；后裔（all the people who will live in the future）

C. 业主；所有人（the owner of a business, a hotel, etc.）

D. （行为方面的）倾向；习性（a tendency to a particular kind of behaviour）

句子大意：当伊丽莎白拥有第一只心爱的柯基犬苏珊时，她还是一位年方18岁的公主，苏珊孕育了女王后来所有的柯基（在一只腊肠混入这一血统后，它也诞下了混种犬）。

17 B

A. 可拆除装置，附加设备（如煤气灶、灯、搁架）（items in a house such as a cooker, lights or shelves that are usually fixed but that you can take with you when you move to a new house）

B. 固定设施（如房屋内安装的浴缸或抽水马桶）（a thing such as a bath/ bathtub or a toilet that is fixed in a house and that you do not take with you when you move house）

（定期定点举行的）体育活动，体育节（a sports event that has been arranged to take place on a particular date and at a particular place）

成为……的常客；长期置于某地的物品（a person or thing long established in the same place or position）（例句：He became a fixture/a regular feature on television in the 1980s.）

C. ~ sth. 研磨；刷新（to brighten something by polishing）

D. ~ sth. 磨光，擦亮（金属）（to polish metal until it is smooth and shiny）

句子大意：尽管胸针已不再流行，但数十年来她的衣柜里一直都少不了胸针的存在。

18 D

A. 疯狂地；狂暴地；狂乱地（done in a hurried way and in a state of excitement or confusion）

B. 狂热地；疯狂地（in a way that shows that you are extremely interested in something, to a degree that some people find unreasonable）

C. 很；极其（very; extremely）

D. 极其仔细地（in great detail）

句子大意：公主的穿戴没有任何地方存在失误。一切都是根据场合、职责、主人、宾客、习俗和礼节精心细致安排过的。

19 B

A. ~ sb./sth. 使眼花；使目眩（to make it difficult for sb. to see for a short time）

~ sb. (to sth.) 使思维混沌；使失去判断力（to make sb. no longer able to think clearly or behave in a sensible way）（例句：We shouldn't let our prejudices blind us to the facts of the situation.）

B. ~ sth. 损害；妨害；贻害（to spoil or damage sth., especially by causing a lot of problems）

C. ~ sth. 挑衅地挥舞，激动地挥舞（尤指武器）（to hold or wave sth., especially a weapon, in an aggressive or excited way）

D.（动词原形为 belie）~ sth. 掩饰；遮掩；给人以假象（to give a false impression of sb./sth.）

~ sth. 显示（某事）不正确；证明（某事）错误（to show that sth. cannot be true or correct）

句子大意：当地居民说，这些动辄二三十人的旅行团太吵，妨碍交通，还有人蹲在外面吃盒饭，有碍观瞻。

20 C

A. 机密的；保密的；秘密的（meant to be kept secret and not told to or shared with other people）

B. 蔑视的；鄙视的；表示轻蔑的（feeling or showing that you have no respect for sb./sth.）

C. 易见的；明显的；惹人注意的（easy to see or notice; likely to attract attention）

D. 表现出优越感的；居高临下的（behaving as though you are more important and more intelligent than other people）

句子大意： 有一段时间老一辈通常将大多数80后或90后看作是被宠坏的一代。这些人经常沉迷于社交网络、炫耀式消费和高度自我主义行为中。

第6章
词汇替换训练题库答案与译文

Practice 1

1 C

reverberate 有长久深刻的影响；产生广泛影响（to have a strong effect on people for a long time or over a large area）

A. ~ (with sb./sth.) 使产生联想；引起共鸣；和……的想法（或观念）类似（to remind sb. of sth.; to be similar to what sb. thinks or believes）

B. ~ (through sth.) 回响；回荡（to fill a place with sound）

C. 继续存留；缓慢消失（to continue to exist for longer than expected）

D. ~ sth. 充分利用（to get as much advantage or profit as possible from sth. that you have）

句子大意：疫情造成的打击仍在持续产生影响，新兴国家遭受的挫折将最为严重。

2 D

pointless 无意义的；无目标的；不值得做的（having no purpose; not worth doing）

A. 嬉戏的；欢闹的（playing in a lively happy way）

B. 活泼的；活蹦乱跳的；爱玩耍的（full of energy; wanting to play）

C. [fə'siːʃəs] 乱引人发笑的；不问场合耍聪明的（trying to appear amusing and intelligent at a time when other people do not think it is appropriate, and when it would be better to be serious）

D. 愚蠢的；可笑的（silly or amusing, especially when such behaviour is not suitable）

　　无聊的；不严肃的（having no useful or serious purpose）

句子大意：她称麻将是一种肤浅、无聊的游戏，听到自己29岁的女儿开始学打麻将的时候有点吃惊。

3 A

allegory ['æləg(ə)ri] 寓言；讽喻；寓言体；讽喻法（a story, play, picture, etc. in which each character or event is a symbol representing an idea or a quality, such as truth, evil, death, etc.; the use of such symbols）

常考近义词：parable（尤指《圣经》中的）寓言故事（a short story that teaches a moral or spiritual lesson, especially one of those told by Jesus as recorded in the Bible）

A. 寓言；寓言故事（a traditional short story that teaches a moral lesson, especially one with animals as characters; these stories considered as a group）

　　谎言；不实之词；无稽之谈（a statement, or an account of sth., that is not true）

181

B. 暗喻；隐喻（a word or phrase used to describe sb./sth. else, in a way that is different from its normal use, in order to show that the two things have the same qualities and to make the description more powerful）

C. [ˌæləˈgeɪʃ(ə)n]（无证据的）说法，指控（a public statement that is made without giving proof, accusing sb. of doing sth. that is wrong or illegal）

D. [priˈæmb(ə)l] 序言；绪论；开场白（an introduction to a book or a written document; an introduction to sth. you say）

句子大意： 这部电影与其说是一部寓言或奇幻电影，不如说是对一些基本人类问题带有诙谐意味的哲学思考。

4 A

ominous [ˈɒmɪnəs] 不祥的；恶兆的；不吉利的（suggesting that sth. bad is going to happen in the future）

A. 预示（坏事）的；先兆的（important as a sign or a warning of sth. that is going to happen in the future, especially when it is sth. unpleasant）

B. 煞有介事的；装腔作势的（very serious and intended to impress people）

炫耀的；自命不凡的（trying to appear important, intelligent, etc. in order to impress other people; trying to be sth. that you are not, in order to impress）

C. 荒唐的；极不合情理的（completely unreasonable, especially in a way that is shocking or annoying）

D. 很可能的；推断的（likely to be true, based on the facts that are available）

句子大意： 即使情节变得越来越不祥，电影导演仍保持一种轻盈感和视觉上的俏皮感，使影片安全地停留在爆米花电影的愉悦中。

5 D

reimagine 富有想象力地重新诠释；为了改进而重新构想，重塑（to think about again especially in order to change or improve）；开创或设想新的生活方式或身份 [to create or imagine a new lifestyle or identity for (oneself)]

A. ~ sth. 改变，修改（意见或计划）（to change your opinions or plans, for example because of sth. you have learned）

B. ~ (sth.) 更换，重新装配（机器设备）（to replace or change the machines or equipment in a factory so that it can produce new or better goods）

C. ~ sth. 对演讲、写作的修改（to change a speech or a piece of writing in order to improve it or make it more suitable for a particular purpose）

D. 改变……的本质（或界限）；重新定义；使重新考虑（to change the nature or limits of sth.; to make people consider sth. in a new way）

句子大意： 数十年来，华尔特·迪士尼都在努力将这个典型的游乐园按照主题公园的形式进行重塑，这既是对美国历史的致敬，也是对其未来发展的试验性愿景的致敬。

6 A

derelict ['derəlɪkt] 荒废的；被弃置的；破旧的（not used or cared for and in bad condition）；玩忽职守的（lacking a sense of duty; negligent）

A. 衰老的；老朽的；破旧的（very old and not in good condition or health）

B. 不光彩的；有损尊严的；丢脸的（bad and unacceptable; causing people to lose respect）

C.（言行）谨慎的，慎重的；考虑周到的（careful in what you say or do, in order to keep sth. secret or to avoid causing embarrassment or difficulty for sb.）

D. 特别整洁的（extremely clean and tidy）

无误的；无过失的（containing no mistakes）

句子大意：城市中一些破旧的地方已被清洁一新，变成了全新的公共空间。与南斯拉夫时期有关的野兽派建筑已被改用为展览场馆。

7 B

unpick sth. 拆去……的缝线；拆（编织物）的针脚（to take out stitches from a piece of sewing or knitting）；仔细剖析（If you unpick a difficult subject, you separate and examine its different parts carefully.）

常考同义词：unpack 分析；剖析 ~ (sth.)（to separate sth. into parts so that it is easier to understand）

A. 解去……的枷锁；释放（to release somebody from restrictions or constraints）

B. ~ (sth.) 阐释；说明；澄清；变得清楚易懂（to explain sth. that is difficult to understand or is mysterious）

C. ~ sth./sb. (on/onto sb.) 推卸（责任）；甩掉（包袱）（to pass the responsibility for sb./sth. to sb. else）

D. ~ sth. 打开；解开；拆开（to open sth. that is fastened, tied or wrapped）

~ sth. 消除，取消，废止（某事的影响）（to cancel the effect of sth.）

句子大意：他非常专业地剖析了每一幅画作的重要特点。

8 C

oblique 间接的；拐弯抹角的（not expressed or done in a direct way）；斜的；倾斜的（sloping at an angle）

A. 斜线的；对角线的（at an angle; joining two opposite sides of sth. at an angle）

B. 倾斜的；歪斜的（sloping in one direction）

C. 含蓄的；不直接言明的（suggested without being directly expressed）

怪诞的；荒唐的；荒谬的（strange in a way that is unpleasant or offensive）

D. 丑陋奇异的，奇形怪状的（extremely ugly in a strange way that is often frightening or amusing）

句子大意：他讲得转弯抹角，让我们难以摸透他的真正用意。

9 A

polished 优雅的，娴熟的（elegant, confident and/or highly skilled）

prickly 易怒的，爱生气的（easily annoyed or offended）；棘手的，难处理的，烫手的（difficult to deal with because people have very different ideas about it）

A. 动辄生气的，气量小的（easily annoyed or offended）

B. 困难重重的，麻烦的（abounding with difficulties, obstacles, or annoyances）

C. 棘手，麻烦的（a thorny issue, problem, subject, etc. is one that is difficult to deal with）

D. 瘦而结实的（thin but strong）

   硬而结实的，像金属丝的（stiff and strong; like wire）

句子大意：她并不是一个口若悬河的出色演说家，而他则优雅自信，尽管有时敏感易怒。

10 A

rambling 向四处延伸的；规划凌乱的（spreading in various directions with no particular pattern）；冗长而含糊的；不切题的（very long and confused）

A.（物）不清楚的；混乱的；难懂的（not clear or easy to understand）

   （人）糊涂的；迷惑的（unable to think clearly or to understand what is happening or what sb. is saying）

B. 吸引人的；引人入胜的（so interesting or exciting that it holds your attention completely）

C.（在式样、颜色或态度上）极不相同的，差异大的（very different in style, colour or attitude）

D.（非法带入或带出国境的）禁运品，走私货（goods that are illegally taken into or out of a country）

句子大意：总体而言，故事情节妙趣横生，不过有时冗长含糊。

11 C

nefarious [nɪˈfeərɪəs] 罪恶的；不道德的（criminal; immoral）

A. 模糊的；不清楚的（not clear）

B. 脆弱的；微弱的；缥缈的（so weak or uncertain that it hardly exists）

C. 不道德的；应受指责的；应受谴责的（morally wrong and deserving criticism）

D. 可了解的；可以理解的（capable of being understood）

   常考近义词：comprehensible (to sb.) 可理解的；能懂的（that can be understood by sb.）

句子大意：这种混乱可能会让人安心：主权财富基金似乎没有不可告人的计划。

12 A

hash out 仔细讨论；想办法解决；费力地去做（to have a long, drawn-out, and usually involved discussion of a matter or a problem）

A. 研究解决；通过反复研讨解决（to discuss something until you find a solution or reach an agreement）

B. 常用搭配：hammer out 经长时间讨论后达成协议或做出决定（to reach a decision or agreement after discussing it or arguing about it for a long time）

C. 粗制滥造；大量生产（to produce something in large quantities quickly and often carelessly）

D.（要某人安静）嘘（used to tell sb. to be quiet）

句子大意：相互争斗的欧洲领导人可能会在仔细讨论后敲定一项协议，在可持续的基础上推进单一货币和区域银行体系建设。

13 A

methodical 有条理的；有条不紊的（arranged, characterized by, or performed with method or order）

A.（修饰人时）有条理的；有效率的（able to plan your work, life, etc. well and in an efficient way）

B. 机械般的；呆头呆脑的；无思想的（done without thinking, like a machine）

C.（疾病、行为或某事产生的影响或结果）涉及全系统的；影响全身的（affecting or connected with the whole of sth., especially the human body）

常考形近 / 同义辨析词：systematic（做事的方式方法等）系统的；有条理的；有计划、有步骤的（done according to a system or plan, in a thorough, efficient or determined way）

由搭配看区别：

a systematic approach to sth./doing sth.

A systemic disease affects the entire body or organism.

Systemic changes to an organization impact the entire organization.

A systemic problem in a society pervades the entire society.

D. 有斑点的；有污点的（spotted, blotched, or stained; morally sullied or impure）

句子大意：她做事不紧不慢、有条不紊，从她的绘图可以看出她格外用心。

14 B

contour ['kɒntʊə(r)] 外形；轮廓（the outer edges of sth.; the outline of its shape or form）

A.（浅色背景衬托出的人或具体物体的）暗色轮廓（the dark outline or shape of a person or an object that you see against a light background）

（人的）体形；（事物的）形状（the shape of a person's body or of an object）

B. 概述；梗概（a description of the main facts or points involved in sth.）

轮廓线；略图（the line that goes around the edge of sth., showing its main shape but not the details）

C.（某个地区的）边缘；周围；外围（the outer edge of a particular area）

次要部分；次要活动；边缘（the less important part of sth., for example of a particular activity or of a social or political group）

D.（地区或群体的）边缘（the outer edge of an area or a group）

（指群体、事情或活动）次要部分，外围（groups of people, events and activities that are not part of the main group or activity）

句子大意：很显然，该委员会的目标一直都是要勾勒出可能对特朗普提起联邦诉讼的大致轮廓。

15 D

dissect sth. 仔细研究；详细评论；剖析（to study sth. closely and/or discuss it in great detail）

A. [daɪ'kɒtəmaɪz] 把……分成两叉，两分法（to divide something into two classes or groups, or become divided into two）

B. ['kɒnfekt] 制造，调制；泡制（to create something by combining different materials or items; to make candy by combining ingredients such as sugar, fruit, and nuts, or make preserves）

名词形式 confection（精美诱人的）甜点，甜食（a cake or other sweet food that looks very attractive）

C. ~ sth. 对半分；二等分（to divide sth. into two equal parts）

D. 剖析或认真思考以理解某事（to examine or think about something carefully in order to understand it）

句子大意：周四的听证会将就这位前总统在当天不作为的表现进行剖析。

16 D

a glut (of sth.) 供应过剩；供过于求（a situation in which there is more of sth. than is needed or can be used）；动词用法：glut sth. (with sth.) 超量供应；充斥（to supply or provide sth. with too much of sth.）

A. 贪吃者；吃得过多的人；饕餮（a person who eats too much）

~ for punishment/work 喜欢艰苦工作的人（a person who enjoys doing difficult or unpleasant tasks）

B. [vɪs'kɒsəti] 黏性；黏度（the thick and sticky quality of a liquid）

C. 谷蛋白；面筋（a sticky substance that is a mixture of two proteins and is left when starch is removed from flour, especially wheat flour）

D. 过剩；多余的量（a superfluous amount of something）

句子大意：由于在漫威电影宇宙（Marvel Cinematic Universe）中设定有关情节的电影数量过多，极客文化在过去三年里失去了一些魅力。

备注：漫威电影宇宙（Marvel Cinematic Universe，缩写为MCU），是由漫威影业基于漫威漫画角色制作的一系列电影组成的世界。

极客文化（geek culture）是一种起源于美国的新的反主流文化。极客一词，来自美国俚语"geek"的音译，一般理解为性格古怪的人。

17 A

cagey about sth. 守口如瓶的；讳莫如深的（not wanting to give sb. information）

A. 寡言少语；不愿与人交谈；有保留（unwilling to tell people about things）

B. [rɪ'neɪsnt] 新生的；复兴的（showing new life or activity）

C. 不守规章的；不服从指挥的；桀骜不驯的；难以控制的（unwilling to obey rules or follow instructions; difficult to control）

D. 难以驾驭的；行为乖戾的（difficult to control; behaving badly）

难以诊治的；难以治愈的（difficult to treat or cure）

句子大意：公司对其如何利用这些数据讳莫如深，并坚持称这不会侵犯到任何人的隐私。

18 A

indict sb. for sth. or ~ sb. on charges/on a charge of sth. 控告；起诉（to officially charge sb. with a crime）

A. ~ sb. (for sth.) 提讯；提审；控告（to bring sb. to court in order to formally accuse them of a crime）

B. ~ sth. 整理；排列；布置（to put sth. in a particular order; to make sth. neat or attractive）

C. （未提出证据）断言；指称（to state sth. as a fact but without giving proof）

D. 明确肯定（to state clearly and firmly that sth. is true）

~ yourself 坚持自己的主张；表现坚定（to behave in a confident and determined way so that other people pay attention to your opinions）

句子大意：该委员会将不得不就起诉特朗普的刑事归责是否充分一事做出决定。

19 A

upshot 最后结果；结局（the final result of a series of events）

A. 结果；效果（the result or effect of an action or event）

B. ~ (for sth.) 理由；动机；缘故（a reason for having particular feelings or behaving in a particular way）

C. 最好（或最精彩、最激动人心）的部分（the best, most interesting or most exciting part of sth.）

D. （通过体验或观察而学到或了解到的）要点、关键信息（a main point or key message to be learned or understood from something experienced or observed）

会议演讲或报告的要点总结（a main message or piece of information that you learn from something you hear or read）

句子大意：其结果是，亚洲从依赖外资转变为了依赖外需。

20 C

tank 彻底失败；破产；倒闭（to fail completely）

~ (sth.)（尤指故意）输掉比赛（to lose a game, especially deliberately）

A. ~ sth. 增加；加强；刺激（to increase sth.; to make sth. stronger）

B. ~ sb. (up) 鼓舞；鼓励（to make sb. feel cheerful or confident）

~ sth. (up) 使（价格）上浮；使（价格）维持于较高水平（to keep prices at a high or acceptable level）

C. 彻底失败，破产倒闭 [to fail completely (especially to go out of business)]

D. （使）逐渐展现；展示；透露（to be gradually made known; to gradually make sth. known to other people）

句子大意：科技股不断暴跌，不过，每天都有独角兽企业诞生。

Practice 2

1 D

smug 沾沾自喜的；自鸣得意的；自以为是的；自命不凡的（looking or feeling too pleased about sth. you have done or achieved）

A. 埋头苦干；坚持不懈地做（to work hard and steadily at sth., especially sth. that takes a long time and is boring or difficult）

n. 一段时间的艰苦工作（或努力）（a period of hard work or effort）

B. 势利小人；谄上欺下的人（a person who admires people in the higher social classes too much and has no respect for people in the lower social classes）

自以为优越的人；自命高雅的人（a person who thinks they are much better than other people because they are intelligent or like things that many people do not like）

C. ~ sb. 冷落；怠慢（to insult sb., especially by ignoring them when you meet）

~ sth. 拒不出席；拒不接受；抵制（to refuse to attend or accept sth., for example as a protest）

D. 自大的；妄自尊大的；自负的（thinking that you are more important than other people）

句子大意： 她那似有阴谋的评述和狡诈的眨眼示意给人自鸣得意的感觉，让人讨厌。

2 C

recapitulate [ˌriːkəˈpɪtʃəˌleɪt] (= recap) ~ on sth. or ~ sth. 重述；概括；回顾（to repeat the main points of an explanation or description）

A. ~ sth. 揭示（to show sth. that previously could not be seen）

B. ~ sth. (to sb.) 泄露，透露（秘密）（to give sb. information that is supposed to be secret）

C. ~ sth. 回顾；反思（to think about past events, for example to try to understand why they happened）

D. ~ sth. 披露（to allow sth. that was hidden to be seen）

句子大意： 这篇文章回顾了他在序言中给出的版本。

3 B

rapture 狂喜；欢天喜地；兴高采烈（the state of mind resulting from feelings of high emotion; joyous ecstasy; (often plural) an expression of ecstatic joy）

A. 猛禽；攫禽 [any bird of prey (= a bird that kills other creatures for food)]

B. 兴高采烈；欢欣鼓舞；喜气洋洋（a feeling of great happiness and excitement）

C. （关系的）破裂，决裂；绝交（the ending of agreement or of good relations between people, countries, etc.）

D. （水平或数量的）提高，升高，增加（an increase in the level or amount of sth.）

（建筑物的）外立面，立面图（one side of a building, or a drawing of this by an architect）

句子大意： 他的支持者兴高采烈地聆听了他的演讲。

4 A

penitence 忏悔；悔罪；愧疚（a feeling of being sorry because you have done sth. wrong）

A. ~ (for sth.) 后悔；懊悔；悔过；忏悔（the fact of showing that you are sorry for sth. wrong that you have done）

B. （战败国的）赔款（money that is paid by a country that has lost a war, for the damage, injuries, etc. that it has caused）

C. 沉默寡言；含蓄（an unwillingness to do something or talk about something）

D. [ˌretrɪˈbjuːʃ(ə)n] ~ for sth. 严惩；报应（severe punishment for sth. seriously wrong that sb. has done）

句子大意：在努力地保持耐心并进行忏悔后，这个月在乐观情绪中结束。

5 A

diatribe (against sb./sth.)（无休止的）指责；（长篇）抨击，谴责（a long and angry speech or piece of writing attacking and criticizing sb./sth.）

 A. [taɪ'reɪd] ~ (against sb./sth.)（批评或指责性的）长篇激烈讲话（a long angry speech criticizing sb./sth. or accusing sb. of sth.）

  常考近义词：harangue（~ sb.）呵斥；大声谴责；慷慨激昂地劝说（to speak loudly and angrily in a way that criticizes sb./sth. or tries to persuade people to do sth.）

 B. ~ (sth.) 气势汹汹地说话；威吓（但效果不大）（to talk in an aggressive or threatening way, but with little effect; angry or threatening talk or behavior from someone who wants to hide their fear or nervousness）

 C. [ʃə'rɑːd] 明显的伪装；做戏；装模作样（a situation in which people pretend that sth. is true when it clearly is not）

  打哑谜猜字游戏（a game in which one player acts out the syllables of a word or title and the other players try to guess what it is）

 D.（因尴尬或害羞）脸红，涨红了脸（to become red in the face because you are embarrassed or ashamed）

句子大意：周一，当这位领导人手握绿皮书出现在电视中时，他无休止的指责之词虽缺乏逻辑，但听起来又很熟悉。

6 A

heckle (sb.)（对演说者）责问，诘问，起哄（to interrupt a speaker at a public meeting by shouting out questions or rude remarks）

 A. ~ (sb.) 喝倒彩；起哄；发出嘘声（to shout criticism at players in a game, speakers at a meeting, performers, etc.）

  常考同义词 1：boo 发嘘声；喝倒彩（to show that you do not like a person, performance, idea, etc. by shouting boo）

  常考同义词 2：catcall 发嘘声反对；发出嘘声（make a noise or shout expressing anger at or disapproval of sb. who is speaking or performing in public）

  常考形近词：barrage ['bærɑːʒ] ~ (of sth.) 接二连三的一大堆（质问或指责等）（a large number of sth., such as questions or comments, that are directed at sb. very quickly, one after the other, often in an aggressive way）

 B. ~ sb. 呵斥；大声谴责；慷慨激昂地劝说（to speak loudly and angrily in a way that criticizes sb./sth. or tries to persuade people to do sth.）

 C. ~ sb./yourself 痛斥；严厉指责（to criticize or speak angrily to sb. because you do not approve of sth. they have done）

 D. ~ sth. (up) 笨拙地弄糟（某事物）（to spoil sth. by doing it badly）

句子大意：那天，我听到观众中有人大声吹口哨向我起哄。

189

7 C

pander 纵容某人的弱点或迎合值得怀疑的愿望和品位（to indulge somebody's weaknesses or questionable wishes and tastes）

pander to 为获得好感而迎合品位、观点粗俗低劣或不良的人（to cater to those with base, vulgar, or undesirable tastes or opinions, specifically with the intent of gaining their favor）

A. 沉思；考虑；琢磨（to think about sth. carefully for a period of time）

B. ~ after/for sth. 热切渴望；追求（to have a strong feeling of wanting something）

C. ~ to sth. 投合；满足某种需要或要求；满足……的需要（to provide people with something they want or need, especially something unusual or special）

D. 火山口（a large hole in the top of a volcano）

句子大意：在我决定成为竞选候选人时，我真不知道为获取支持需要迎合这么多的团体。

8 C

be beholden to sb. (for sth.)（因受恩惠而心存）感激；欠人情（owing sth. to sb. because of sth. that they have done for you）

A. 围攻；困扰；包围（to make somebody feel harassed, hemmed in, or under severe pressure）

B. ~ sb. 使迷惑；使糊涂（to confuse sb.）

C. ~ (to sb.) (for sth.) 感激的；蒙恩的（grateful to sb. for helping you）

负债的（owing money to other countries or organizations）

D. 显得彬彬有礼的；假斯文的；装出绅士派头的（quiet and polite, often in an exaggerated way; from, or pretending to be from, a high social class）

句子大意：随着各国中央政府伸出经济援手，银行也越来越心存感激。

9 B

impudent ['ɪmpjʊd(ə)nt] 粗鲁的；不恭的（rude; not showing respect for other people）

A. 不明智的；不谨慎的（not wise or sensible）

B. 盛气凌人的；性急的；仓促的；鲁莽的（confident in an aggressive way; done in haste without regard for consequences; heedless of the consequences）

常考近义词：rash 轻率的；鲁莽的（doing sth. that may not be sensible without first thinking about the possible results）

C. ['ɪndələnt] 懒散的；好逸恶劳的（not wanting to work）

D. ['breɪz(ə)n] 厚颜无耻的（open and without shame, usually about sth. that people find shocking）

句子大意：有些人举止得体，而其他人则鲁莽无礼。

10 A

chummy 非常友好的；亲切的（very friendly）

A. 意气相投的；志趣相投的；合得来的（pleasant to spend time with because their interests and character are similar to your own）

B. 先天的；天生的（existing since or before birth）

C. 狡猾的；奸诈的；诡诈的（able to get what you want in a clever way, especially by tricking or cheating sb.）
灵巧的；精巧的；巧妙的（clever and skilful）

D. 巧妙的；（尤指）狡诈的，诡计多端的（clever at getting what you want, especially by indirect or dishonest methods）

句子大意：实际上，真正的威胁来自某一个国家同该国跨国公司之间过分亲密的联系。

11 B

founder (on sth.) 失败；破产（to fail because of a particular problem or difficulty）

常考形近词 flounder，flounder 的意思是"挣扎"，摇摇欲坠但还没有倒下，founder 的意思是"崩溃，坍塌"，已经倒下了。

A. 困难重重；艰苦挣扎（to have a lot of problems and to be in danger of failing completely）

B. 砸锅；完全失败（to be a complete failure）

C. 阔步行走；神气地快速走动（to move quickly with exaggerated steps so that people will look at you）

D. ~ sth./sb. (from sth./sb.)（尤指强制地）分开，割裂（to split or break sth./sb. apart, especially by force）

句子大意：修建新机场的计划因为预算削减而落空。

12 D

be disinclined to do sth. 不情愿；不乐意；勉强（not willing to do sth.）

A. ~ sb./sth. or ~ doing sth. 极不喜欢；厌恶（to dislike sb./sth. very much）

B. [luːʃ] 名声不好却有吸引力的（not socially acceptable, but often still attractive despite this）

C.（对生产等）起阻碍作用的（acting as a deterrent）

D. be ~ to do sth. 不情愿；不乐意（not willing to do sth.）

句子大意：如果很多公司不愿离开，同样，当地政府也不愿失去这些公司和他们带来的税收。

13 A

inhabitable 适于居住或栖息的（If a place is inhabitable, people and animals can live there.）

A. 适合居住的（suitable for people to live in）

常考近义词：hospitable（作物生长条件）适宜的；（环境）舒适的（having good conditions that allow things to grow; having a pleasant environment）

B. 不适于居住的；（尤指）无遮蔽处的，荒凉的（difficult to stay or live in, especially because there is no shelter from the weather）

C. 不宜居住的；不舒适的（not fit for somebody to live in）

D. 不能成功的；不能继续存活的；无法发育成活的（not able to work as intended; not able to succeed; not able to continue to exist as, or develop into, a living being）

句子大意：尽管 WASP-96b 极不可能有任何生命存在，但使用同样的技术可以揭示围绕其他恒星运行的较小的岩石世界是否适合居住。

14 A

hackle（狗、猫等害怕或发怒时竖起的）后颈毛

make sb.'s hackles rise/raise sb.'s hackles 激怒某人（to make sb. angry）

A. ~ sb. 惹恼；激怒（to annoy sb. or make them angry）

   常考近义词：ruffle 激怒或让某人失望、紧张（to annoy or upset someone, or to make someone very nervous）

B. ~ sb. 使紧张；使恐惧（to make sb. nervous or frightened）

C. 轰鸣着缓慢行进（to move slowly and heavily, making a rumbling sound）

D. 漫步；闲逛（尤指在乡间）（to walk for pleasure, especially in the countryside）

   漫谈；闲聊；瞎扯（to talk about sb./sth. in a confused way, especially for a long time）

句子大意：他在会上的所作所为让他的老板大为光火。

15 A

obsequious 谄媚的；巴结逢迎的（trying too hard to please sb., especially sb. who is important）

A. 竭力讨好的；巴结的（trying too hard to please sb.）

   常考近义词1：servile 奴性的；逢迎的；恭顺的（wanting too much to please sb. and obey them）

   常考近义词2：sycophantic [sɪkəˈfæntɪk] 拍马的；说奉承话的；阿谀的 [(of a person or of behaviour) praising people in authority in a way that is not sincere, usually in order to get some advantage from them]

B. 非常尊敬的；深表崇敬的（showing great respect and admiration）

C. 恭敬的；恭顺的；尊敬的（showing that you respect someone and want to treat them politely）

D. 骄傲的；满足的（feeling pleased and satisfied about sth. that you own or have done, or are connected with）

   秀丽的；挺拔的；壮观的（beautiful, tall and impressive）

句子大意：他在20世纪70年代末回到华盛顿，成为一名谄媚逢迎的学者，被迫变得屈服顺从。

16 D

antithetical 对立的；对照的；正相反的（being in direct and unequivocal opposition; directly opposite or opposed）

A. 防腐的；抗菌的（able to prevent infection）

   无菌的；消过毒的（very clean and free from bacteria）

B. 表达明确的；毫不含糊的；斩钉截铁地（expressing your opinion or intention very clearly and firmly）

C. 公理的；不证自明的（true in such an obvious way that you do not need to prove it）

D. 相反的；迥然不同的（as different as possible from sth.）

句子大意：经过对量子力学的漫长探索后，突然之间出现了两种相互竞争且看起来完全对立的版本。

17 A

hackneyed 陈腐的（used too often and therefore boring）

A. 陈腐的；没有新意的；老掉牙的（something that is stale has been said or done too many times before and is no longer interesting or exciting）

　　常考同义词：banal [bəˈnɑːl] 平庸的；平淡乏味的；无关紧要的；陈腐的（very ordinary and containing nothing that is interesting or important）

B. 低劣的；蹩脚的；俗气的（cheap, badly made and/or lacking in taste）

C. 威吓的；吓唬的（threatening to do sth. evil or to hurt sb.）

D. 有害的；致死的；致祸的（bad or evil）

句子大意：尽管拜登和议员们将冰箱、恒温器和汽车等各种产品中的芯片描述为21世纪的"石油"，以求为该法案赢得支持，但这个表述在30年前就已经过时了。

18 A

unenviable 艰难的；讨厌的；不值得羡慕的（difficult or unpleasant; that you would not want to have）

A. 不想要的；不得人心的；易惹麻烦的（not wanted or approved of; likely to cause trouble or problems）

B. 平庸的；索然无味的（not impressing or exciting you at all）

C. 讨厌的；无礼的；声名狼藉的；不道德的（unpleasant or offensive; not considered morally acceptable）

D. 不爱出风头的；不爱炫耀的；谦逊的（not wanting to draw attention to yourself or to your abilities or status）

句子大意：非洲国家要就如何优先推动新冠疫苗接种而非破伤风和麻疹等常规疫苗接种做出艰难抉择。

19 D

finicky（对衣食等）过分讲究的，过分挑剔的（too worried about what you eat, wear, etc.; disliking many things）；需认真仔细对待的；需要注意细节的（needing great care and attention to detail）

A. 口味不寻常的；（尤指）挑食的，偏食的（liking some things and not others, especially food, in a way that other people think is unreasonable）

B. 迂腐的；学究气的（too worried about small details or rules）

C. 一丝不苟的；严谨的（being careful that every detail of sth. is correct）

　　讲究整洁的；有洁癖的（not liking things to be dirty or untidy）

D. 要求高的；需要高技能（或耐性等）的；费力的（needing a lot of skill, patience, effort, etc.）

句子大意：长期以来，园艺家用这种方法来繁殖植物，尤其是像兰花这种需要倍加呵护的植物。

20 A

exasperation 恼怒；愤慨（the feeling of being extremely annoyed and impatient because things are not happening in the way that you want them to happen）

  A. 烦恼；恼火；伤脑筋；心烦意乱（the state of feeling upset or annoyed）

  B.（对……的）异常依恋、执着（a very strong interest in sb./sth., that is not normal or natural）

  C. 恶化，加剧（the process of making something that is already bad even worse）

  D. 兴奋；兴高采烈（a feeling of very great joy or happiness）

   提高；晋升；提拔（an act of raising sth./sb. to a high position or rank）

句子大意： 聆听他在西点军校的演讲，我从他的声音中听出了恼怒之意和弦外之音——"已经够了"。

Practice 3

1 D

evince [ɪ'vɪns] ~ sth. 表明，表现，显示（感情或品质）（to show clearly that you have a feeling or quality）

laisssez-faire [ˌleɪseɪ 'feə(r)]（政府对私有企业的）自由放任政策（the policy of allowing private businesses to develop without government control）

  A. ~ sth. 引起，唤起（感情、记忆或形象）（to bring a feeling, a memory or an image into your mind）

  B. ~ sb. 使达不到；使不记得；使不理解（If sth. eludes you, you are not able to achieve it, or not able to remember or understand it.）

  C. ~ (doing) sth. 逃脱；躲开；躲避（to escape from sb./sth. or avoid meeting sb.）

  D. ~ sth. or ~ from sb. 流露，显露（感觉或品质）；（感觉或品质）显现（If you exude a particular feeling or quality, or it exudes from you, people can easily see that you have it.）

句子大意： 到目前为止，美国在人工智能监管方面表现出了比英国或欧盟更加自由放任的态度。

2 C

soirée ['swɑːreɪ]（尤指在家里举行的）社交晚会（a formal party in the evening, especially at sb.'s home）

ruckus ['rʌkəs] 喧闹；骚动；争吵（a situation in which there is a lot of noisy activity, confusion or argument）

  A.（由领导人或一般成员参加的为挑选候选人或制定政策的）政党会议；（政党的）全体成员，领导班子（a meeting of the members or leaders of a political party to choose candidates or to decide policy; the members or leaders of a political party as a group）

   （常指较大组织或政党内部志趣相投的）派别，小集团，小组（a group of people with similar interests, often within a larger organization or political party）

  B. 马戏团（a group of entertainers, sometimes with trained animals, who perform skilful or amusing acts in a show that travels around to different places）

   引人注意的人（或事）；热闹场面（a group of people or an event that attracts a lot of attention）

  C.（突然发生的）喧闹，骚乱，骚动（sudden noisy confusion or excitement）

  D.（古怪或少见的）混合物，调和物，调配品（尤指饮料或药物）（a strange or unusual mixture of things, especially drinks or medicines）

句子大意：奈飞将原定于周五晚上的社交晚会改为线上举行以避免出现骚动。

3 B

blasphemous ['blæsfəməs] 亵渎神明的；不敬神的；对神不敬的（offensive to God or someone's religious beliefs）

　　A. 多产的；创作丰富的（producing many works, etc.）

　　　富饶的；富庶的；肥沃的（able to produce enough food, etc. to keep many animals and plants alive）

　　B. [prə'feɪn] 亵渎神灵的；亵圣的（having or showing a lack of respect for God or holy things）

　　C. 有害的，恶性的（尤指潜移默化地）（having a very harmful effect on sb./sth., especially in a way that is gradual and not easily noticed）

　　D. 爱争执的；好斗的；爱滋事的（having a strong desire to argue or fight with other people）

句子大意：一名教会代表赞同这一起诉，并谴责这次展览，称其亵渎神明。

4 C

opprobrium [ə'proʊbriəm]（众人的）谴责，责难，抨击（severe criticism of a person, country, etc. by a large group of people）

　　A. 批准，通过，认可（计划、要求等）（agreement to, or permission for sth., especially a plan or request）

　　B. 压迫；压制；抑制；镇压（unfair and cruel treatment by a powerful person or government）

　　C. 严厉的批评；斥责；谴责（strong criticism）

　　D. [ˌæproʊ'beɪʃ(ə)n] 认可；批准（approval or agreement）

句子大意：朝鲜进行的第二次核试验使得亚洲紧张局势明显升级，招致国际社会的广泛谴责。

5 B

capitulate [kə'pɪtjʊleɪt] ~ (to sb./sth.) 屈服；屈从（to agree to do sth. that you have been refusing to do for a long time）

　　A. ~ sth. 变卖资产；变现（to sell possessions in order to change them into money）

　　　~ sth. 为……提供运营资本（或资金）（to provide a company etc. with the money it needs to function）

　　B. ~ to sb./sth. 屈服；屈从；抵挡不住（攻击、疾病、诱惑等）（to not be able to fight an attack, an illness, a temptation, etc.）

　　C. ~ sth.（船）翻，倾覆（If a boat capsizes or sth. capsizes it, it turns over in the water.）

　　D. ~ sth./sb. from sth./sb.（尤指强制地）分开，使分离，割裂（to split or break sth./sb. apart, especially by force）

句子大意：本轮反弹正迫使一些曾押注价格会因库存量大而下跌的逆市投资者投降。

6 B

studied 刻意的；精心安排的（deliberate and carefully planned）；知识渊博的，有学识的

（knowledgeable, learned）

A. 有学问的；知识渊博的；博学的（having a lot of knowledge because you have studied and read a lot）

通过训练（或经历）形成的；学到的；非天生的（developed by training or experience; not existing at birth）

B. 故意的；蓄意的；存心的（done on purpose rather than by accident）

C. ['stju:diəs] 勤奋的；好学的；用功的（spending a lot of time studying or reading）

D. 谨慎的；有保留的；不明确表态的（careful; not showing feelings or giving much information）

句子大意：他刻意冷淡地对待我们。

7 B

idle sb./sth.（尤指暂时地）关闭工厂，使（工人）闲着（to close a factory, etc. or stop providing work for the workers, especially temporarily）

A. ~ (doing) sth. 推迟；延缓；展期（to delay sth. until a later time）

B. ~ sth. 封存；搁置不用（to decide not to use or develop sth., for a period of time, especially a piece of equipment or a plan）

in mothballs（长期）封存；（长期）搁置（stored and not in use, often for a long time）

C. ~ sth. (from/against sth.) 使隔热；使隔音；使绝缘（to protect sth. with a material that prevents heat, sound, electricity, etc. from passing through）

D. 与外界隔绝的（having little contact with the outside world）

句子大意：这位德国副总理没有坚持"绿党"的理念，而是重启了长期搁置不用的火电站，此举进一步提高了他作风务实的声誉。

8 A

unprepossessing 不讨人喜欢的；不吸引人的；让人无良好（或深刻）印象的（not attractive; not making a good or strong impression）

A. 无吸引力的；不诱人的（not attractive or pleasant）

B. 可口的；味美的（having a pleasant or acceptable taste）

~ (to sb.) 宜人的；可意的；可接受的（pleasant or acceptable to sb.）

C. 荒唐的；极不合情理的（completely unreasonable, especially in a way that is shocking or annoying）

D. 谦虚谨慎的；不事张扬的；不爱炫耀的（not trying to appear more special, intelligent, important, etc. than you really are）

句子大意：阿什福德这个平凡无奇的小镇可能很快就会成为全球规模最大的"共享空间"项目所在地。

9 C

puerility [ˌpjʊəˈrɪlɪti] 幼稚；孩子气；幼稚的言行（the state of being immature, especially in being silly or trivial）

A. 纯洁；纯净（the state or quality of being pure）

B. 青春期（the period of a person's life during which their sexual organs develop and they become capable of having children）

C. 不成熟；幼稚（behaviour that is not as calm and wise as people expect from someone of your age）

D. 纯洁；无瑕（the quality or condition of being immaculate or spotless）

句子大意：她的谈吐非常奇特，总是鲁莽又幼稚。

10 D

nefarious [nɪˈfeərɪəs] 罪恶的；不道德的（criminal; immoral）

A. [ɪˈmɒlɪənt] 使平静的；使缓和的（making a person or situation calmer in the hope of keeping relations peaceful）

润肤的；护肤的（used for making your skin soft or less painful）

B. 自认为高人一等的；摆派头的（showing that you feel better, or more intelligent than sb. else）

C. [ˌsuːpə(r)ˈsɪlɪəs] 傲慢的；高傲的（behaving towards other people as if you think you are better than they are）

D. a hidden agenda 是固定搭配，意为：（言语或行为背后的）隐秘意图，秘密目的（the secret intention behind what sb. says or does）

句子大意：实际上，这种混乱局面可能会让人安心：该主权财富基金似乎没有不可告人的计划。

11 A

febrile [ˈfiːbraɪl] 紧张不安的，狂热的（nervous, excited and very active）；发热引起的（caused by fever）

A. 激动的；焦虑不安的（showing strong feelings of excitement or worry, often with a lot of activity or quick movements）

B. 精神错乱的，语无伦次的（常由发烧引起）（in an excited state and not able to think or speak clearly, usually because of fever）

极度兴奋的；特别愉快的（extremely excited and happy）

C. 淫秽的；色情的（encouraging sexual desire or containing too much sexual detail）

D. 婀娜多姿的；柔媚的（smooth and slow, often in a way that is sexually attractive）

句子大意：对通胀持续的同时经济增速放缓的预期使得市场上弥漫着一种焦虑不安的情绪。

12 A

nonchalance 冷淡，漫不经心，无动于衷（calm behaviour that suggests you are not interested or do not care）

A. 冷漠，无动于衷（a lack of emotion or emotional expressiveness）

B. [ˈæmpɑːs] 僵局；绝境（a difficult situation in which no progress can be made because the people involved cannot agree what to do）

C. 不耐烦；无耐心；急切（the annoyed feeling you get when something does not happen as quickly as you want it to or in the way you want it to）

D. 沉默寡言；含蓄；保留（an unwillingness to do something or talk about something, for example because you are nervous or being careful）

句子大意：我们继续交谈，一起用完了晚餐，但他的冷淡让我感到凄凉，有点绝望。

13 A

falsify sth. 篡改，伪造（文字记录、信息）（to change a written record or information so that it is no longer true）

A. 操纵或作弊 [to manipulate, exploit, or cheat in (a system, a situation, etc.) slyly or dishonestly for personal gain]（如：game the tax system 操纵税收体系）

B. ~ sth. 驯化；驯服；使易于控制（to make sth. tame or easy to control）

C. （不及物动词）~ with sth. 干扰；篡改（遗嘱、稿件等）（to render something harmful or dangerous by altering its structure or composition）

D. （使）逐渐变窄（to become gradually narrower; to make sth. become gradually narrower）

* 备注：报纸上经常出现的美国 tapering 措施就是"逐渐缩减"资产购买规模，意味着逐渐退出 QE——量化宽松政策，收回流动性。

句子大意：事实多次证明，基于未经验证的数据的评分系统存在造假的可能性，该媒体机构对此一再否认。

14 A

['daɪəˌtraɪb] diatribe (against sb./sth.)（无休止的）指责；（长篇）抨击，谴责（a long and angry speech or piece of writing attacking and criticizing sb./sth.）

A. [taɪ'reɪd] tirade (against sb./sth.)（批评或指责性的）长篇激烈讲话（a long angry speech criticizing sb./sth. or accusing sb. of sth.）

B. [ti'ɑːrə] tiara 冠状头饰（女子用，如公主在正式场合戴的镶有宝石的王冠式头饰）（a piece of jewellery like a small crown decorated with precious stones, worn by a woman, for example a princess, on formal occasions）

C. ['triːɑːʒ] triage 患者鉴别分类；伤员鉴别分类；治疗类选法（the process of deciding how seriously ill/sick or injured a person is, so that the most serious cases can be treated first）

D. 昏睡状态；催眠状态（a state in which sb. seems to be asleep but is aware of what is said to them, for example if they are hypnotized）

出神；发呆（a state in which you are thinking so much about sth. that you do not notice what is happening around you）

句子大意：特朗普最近反民主的长篇激烈言辞广受谴责，不过共和党的资深人士却对此缄默不言。

15 B

spurn sb./sth.（尤指傲慢地）拒绝（to reject or refuse sb./sth., especially in a proud way）

A. ~ sth. 促进，加速，刺激（某事发生）（to make sth. happen faster or sooner）

B. ~ sb./sth. 轻蔑；鄙视（to feel or show that you think sb./sth. is stupid and you do not respect them or it）

不屑于（接受或做）；轻蔑地拒绝（to refuse to have or do sth. because you are too proud）

常考同义词：slight（~ sb.）侮慢；冷落；轻视（to treat sb. rudely or without respect）

C. ~ (with sb.)（多指在友好气氛中）辩论，争论（to argue with sb., usually in a friendly way）

D. ~ sb. 给……留下精神创伤（to leave sb. with a feeling of sadness or mental pain）

~ sth. 损害……的外观（to spoil the appearance of sth.）

句子大意： 立法委员断然否决了一项由一位西弗吉尼亚州参议员支持的改革法案。

16 D

circumscribe ['sɜː(r)kəmˌskraɪb] ~ sth. 限制，约束（自由、权利、权力等）（to limit sb./sth.'s freedom, rights, power, etc.）

A. ~ sth. 设法回避；规避（to find a way of avoiding a difficulty or a rule）

B. ~ sth. 标出……的界线；给……划界（to mark or establish the limits of sth.）

C. ~ sth.（详细地）描述，描画，解释（to describe, draw or explain sth. in detail）

D. 限制，限定（数量、范围等）（to limit the size, amount or range of sth.）

句子大意： 随着供应链问题的消除，许多消费品的成本不断下降。同时，受利率上调的影响，房产价格也不断趋弱。但是任何通胀增速放缓给人们带来的宽慰都将是有限的。

17 B

suborn sb. 收买，买通（使作伪证等）；唆使（他人犯法）（to pay or persuade sb. to do sth. illegal, especially to tell lies in court）

A. ~ sb./sth. (to sb./sth.) 把……置于次要地位；使从属于（to treat sb./sth. as less important than sb./sth. else）

B. 向（某人）行贿；贿赂（to give sb. money or sth. valuable in order to persuade them to help you, especially by doing sth. dishonest）

C. ~ sth.（尤指作为惩罚）没收，把……充公（to officially take sth. away from sb., especially as a punishment）

D. ~ sb./sth. 给……服麻醉剂；在（食物、饮料）中掺麻醉剂（to give sb. a drug, often in their food or drink, in order to make them unconscious; to put a drug in food, etc.）

句子大意： 未具名消息人士向两家比利时媒体透露，卡塔尔买通了凯丽女士。

18 B

skimp on sth. 节省，吝惜（时间、钱等）（to try to spend less time, money, etc. on sth. than is really needed）

A. ~ sth. 不做（应做的事等）；不参加（to not do sth. that you usually do or should do）

B. 吝惜；限制（to get along on a scanty allowance）（例句1：Don't stint on the food. 例句2：They are not stinting with their praise.）

C. ~ sb./sth. 阻碍生长；妨碍发展；遏制（to prevent sb./sth. from growing or developing as much as they/it should）

D. ~ sth. 刷（磁卡）（to pass a plastic card, such as a credit card, through a special machine that is able to read the information that is stored on it）

句子大意： 朝鲜越来越明目张胆的导弹研发计划以及俄乌冲突都让日本确信，再也不能吝惜安全方面的开支了。

19 A

dilemma（进退两难的）窘境，困境（a situation which makes problems, often one in which you have to make a very difficult choice between things of equal importance）

A. ['kwɒndəri] 困惑；进退两难（the state of not being able to decide what to do in a difficult situation）

B. 采石场（a place where large amounts of stone, etc. are dug out of the ground）
被追猎的动物（或人）；追捕的对象；猎物（an animal or a person that is being hunted or followed）

C. 浪费，挥霍（金钱、时间等）（the act of wasting money, time, etc. in a stupid or careless way）

D. 壁球（a game for two players, played in a court surrounded by four walls, using rackets and a small rubber ball）
拥挤的环境（或处所）（If sth. is a squash, there is hardly enough room for everything or everyone to fit into a small space.）

句子大意： 由于该委员会一直未出面澄清此事，这令希望敲定奥运宣传计划的广告客户们陷入了两难境地。

20 D

frazzle ['fræzl]（使）疲倦；（使）变破烂，磨损（to put in a state of extreme physical or nervous fatigue）

A. ~ sth. 把……烫卷曲；把……烤焦（to heat sth. until it forms curls or until it burns）

B. ~ sb./sth. 压制，钳制（言论）；使缄默（to prevent sb. from expressing their opinions in public as they want to）

C. 困难重重；艰苦挣扎（to have a lot of problems and to be in danger of failing completely）

D. （使织物边沿）磨损，磨散（If cloth frays or sth. frays it, the threads in it start to come apart.）

句子大意： 那些想要保留《第42条法案》的人称，如果取消该法案，非法越境者只会更多，让早已疲于应对的美国庇护体系不堪重负。

备注：《第42条法案》是美国新冠大流行期间实施的移民政策。该政策下，政府可立即将边境移民驱逐，而不提供庇护听证会。

Practice 4

1 B

nefarious [nɪ'feəriəs] 罪恶的；不道德的（criminal; immoral）

A. 非铁的（not containing, including, or relating to iron）

B. 邪恶的；缺德的（morally bad）

C. 模糊的；不清楚的（not clear）

D. 滑稽可笑的；疯疯癫癫的（funny or amusing in a slightly crazy way）

句子大意：邪恶势力曾企图利用沮丧的年轻人来破坏该国的稳定。

2 B

fade 逐渐消逝；逐渐消失（to disappear gradually）；（运动员、运动队、演员等）走下坡路，衰落（If a sports player, team, actor, etc. fades, they stop playing or performing as well as they did before.）

A.（没有 sizzle out 的搭配）发出（油煎食物的）咝咝声（to make the sound of food frying in hot oil）

B. ~ out（令人失望地）逐渐终止，有始无终（to gradually end, often in a disappointing or weak way）

C.（没有 frazzle out 的搭配）使疲惫不堪（to completely exhaust somebody emotionally and physically）
使磨损破烂（to fray or become worn）

D.（没有 muzzle out 的搭配）~ sb./sth. 压制，钳制（言论）；使缄默（to prevent sb. from expressing their opinions in public as they want to）

句子大意：他们上的不是同一所大学，两人的关系也就逐渐淡了。

3 B

expire（因到期而）失效，终止；到期（to be no longer valid because the period of time for which it could be used has ended）

A. 衰弱；衰退；衰落（to become weaker or less effective）

B. 失效；期满终止（to be no longer valid because the period of time that it lasts has come to an end）
逐渐衰退；（逐渐）消失，结束（to gradually become weaker or come to an end）

C. ~ (into sth.) 退回原状；（好转后）再倒退（to go back into a previous condition or into a worse state after making an improvement）

D. ~ (on sth.) 失败；破产（to fail because of a particular problem or difficulty）

句子大意：官方预计非法越境人员数量将会出现激增。数千移民已经在路上；很多人已经在墨西哥北部等着《第42条法案》失效后再采取行动。

4 C

belie sth. 掩饰；遮掩；给人以假象（to give a false impression of sb./sth.）；显示（某事）不正确；证明（某事）错误（to show that sth. cannot be true or correct）

A. ~ sth. 背叛（原则或信仰）（to ignore your principles or beliefs in order to achieve sth. or gain an advantage for yourself）
（无意中）泄露信息，流露情感（to tell sb. or make them aware of a piece of information, a feeling, etc., usually without meaning to）

B. ~ sth. 构成……的基础；作为……的原因（to be the basis or cause of sth.）

C. ~ sth. 证明……是错误（或虚假）的（to show that sth. is wrong or false）

D. ~ belief, explanation, description, etc. 不可能，无法（相信、解释、描绘等）（to be impossible or almost impossible to believe, explain, describe, etc.）

句子大意： 研究结果证明那种认为细菌是简单、寂静独行者的观念是错误的。

5 C

A.（可以作介词和副词）虽然；尽管（without being affected by sth.; despite sth.）

B.（用于所言不包括的人或事物前）除……之外（used before you mention the only thing or person about which a statement is not true）

C.（作介词）缺乏，没有 in the absence of (something); without（例句：Absent any objections, the plan will proceed.）

D. ~ (from sth.)（投票时）弃权（to choose not to use a vote, either in favour of or against sth.）

　　~ (from sth.) 戒；戒除（to decide not to do or have sth., especially sth. you like or enjoy, because it is bad for your health or considered morally wrong）

句子大意： 由于缺乏可靠的信息流动，来自国外的企业和投资者只能猜测该国经济复苏需要的时间。

6 A

inscrutable [ɪn'skru:təb(ə)l] 难以捉摸的；难以理解的；神秘莫测的（If a person or their expression is inscrutable, it is hard to know what they are thinking or feeling, because they do not show any emotion.）

常考同义词：inconstruable 不能让人理解的，不能做出解释的（unable to be construed）

A. 难以理解的；高深莫测的（too strange or difficult to be understood）

　　（表情）难以琢磨的，微妙的（If sb. has an unfathomable expression, it is impossible to know what they are thinking.）

B. 难相处的；不爱交际的（unsociable）

C. 不能通行的（尤指因路况恶劣或被阻断）（impossible to travel on or through, especially because it is in bad condition or it has been blocked by sth.）

D. 未受伤的；毫发无损的（not hurt）

句子大意： 少报漏报新冠病毒死亡人数的不只是印度，但该国的数据尤其让人难以捉摸。

7 C

appreciable [ə'pri:ʃəb(ə)l]（大得）可以觉察到的，足以认为重要的；可观的（large enough to be noticed or thought important）

A. 担心的；恐惧的（worried or frightened that sth. unpleasant may happen）

B. 不道德的；应受指责的（morally wrong and deserving criticism）

C. 易于察觉的；可意识到的；明显的（that is easily noticed by the mind or the senses）

D. 好像有道理的，表面上讲得通的（reasonable and likely to be true）

　　巧言令色的；花言巧语的（good at sounding honest and sincere, especially when trying to trick people）

句子大意： 关税和出口管制都没有对我们的经济产生明显的负面影响。

8 C

amenable [əˈmiːnəb(ə)l] 顺从的；顺服的（easy to control; willing to be influenced by sb./sth.）

~ to sth. 可用某种方式处理的（that you can treat in a particular way）

A.（指事）心平气和的；友善的（done or achieved in a polite or friendly way and without arguing）

B.（指人）和蔼可亲的；亲切友好的（friendly and easy to like）

C. ~ (to sth.) 欣然同意（willing to do sth. or allow sth.）

~ (to sb.) 可以接受的；适合的（able to be accepted by sb.）

D.（主语是事物）获得大众认同的，认可的（agreed or approved of by most people in a society）可接受的；令人满意的；可容许的（that sb. agrees is of a good enough standard or allowed）

常考近义词：accepting

* 能够或愿意接受人或物的（able or willing to accept something or someone）

例句：I had become more accepting of death as an inevitable and natural part of life.

* 对不同类别的人和生活方式很有包容心的（tending to regard different types of people and ways of life with tolerance and acceptance）

例句：His parents are very accepting people.

句子大意：领导人——特别是美国的领导人——认为，大致程度的自由贸易将使世界更容易接受我们的政治价值观，也让我们的国家更加安全。

9 C

cede ~ sth. (to sb.) 割让；让给；转让（to give sb. control of sth. or give them power, a right, etc., especially unwillingly）

A.（使）结束，终止（to come to an end; to bring sth. to an end）

B. ~ sth. 推翻，撤销（判决等）（to officially decide that a legal decision, etc. is not correct, and to make it no longer valid）

C.（尤指勉强地）让与，让步；允许（to give sth. away, especially unwillingly; to allow sb. to have sth.）

D. ~ sth. (to sb.) 转让；让与（to officially arrange for sth. to belong to sb. else or for sb. else to control sth.）

句子大意：他向自己的人民承诺，如果这些国家要斡旋达成一项和平协议的话，他也不会向俄罗斯割让土地。

10 A

riveting 吸引人的；引人入胜的（so interesting or exciting that it holds your attention completely）

A. 使人神魂颠倒的；令人神魂颠倒的；使人入神的（someone or something that is entrancing is so beautiful or impressive that you give them all your attention）

常考同义词：absorbing 十分吸引人的；引人入胜的；精彩的（interesting and enjoyable and holding your attention completely）

B. 惊人的；让人震惊的（extremely unusual and surprising）

C. 酷热的；使人热得发昏的（extremely hot in an unpleasant or uncomfortable way）

D. 异想天开的；滑稽可笑的（unusual and not serious in a way that is either amusing or annoying）

句子大意：此书读来引人入胜，该副标题正是史密斯本人对自己生存技巧的描述。

11 C

sprightly 精力充沛的；精神矍铄的（full of life and energy）

venal [ˈviːn(ə)l] 贪赃枉法的；见利忘义的（prepared to do dishonest or immoral things in return for money）

sclerotic [skləˈrɒtɪk] 老朽僵化的（grown rigid or unresponsive especially with age）

  A. 谨慎的；细致的（done carefully and with a lot of attention to detail）

   严格的；严厉的（demanding that particular rules, processes, etc. are strictly followed）

  B. 公正的；正直的；正当的（morally right and good）

  C. 精神矍铄的（an old person who is spry is still very healthy and still has a lot of energy）

  D. （名词）传说中的小仙子，小精灵，小妖精（a small creature with magic powers, especially one that likes playing tricks）；（饮料品牌）雪碧

句子大意：年轻人将现年61岁的他视为一位撼动尼日利亚贪赃枉法、老朽僵化的政客的精力充沛的局外人。

12 A

disaffected（对组织或机构等）生厌的；不满的；不忠的（a disaffected member of a group or organization no longer feels any loyalty toward it）

  A. 不满的；不高兴的（annoyed or disappointed because sth. has happened to upset you）

  B. ~ (by sth.) 未受影响；未被损害；原封未动（not affected by sth., especially sth. bad or unpleasant; not damaged）

  C. 难以捍卫的；站不住脚的；不堪一击的（that cannot be defended against attack or criticism）

  D. 客观的；无私的；公正的（not influenced by personal feelings, or by the chance of getting some advantage for yourself）

   无兴趣的；不关心的；冷漠的（not interested）

句子大意：最后时刻还是对心怀不满的集团做了让步，以赢得他们的支持。

13 C

concession（尤指由政府或雇主给予的）特许权，优惠（a right or an advantage that is given to a group of people, an organization, etc., especially by a government or an employer）；（在某地的）特许经营权；（有时为大型建筑物或商场中的）销售场地，摊位（the right to sell sth. in a particular place; the place where you sell it, sometimes an area which is part of a larger building or store）

  A. 沉溺；放纵；纵容（the state or act of having or doing whatever you want; the state of allowing sb. to have or do whatever they want）

  B. ~ (from sth.) 免除；豁免（official permission not to do sth. or pay sth. that you would normally have to do or pay）

C.（公司授予的）特许经销权；（国家授予的）特别经营权，特许（formal permission given by a company to sb. who wants to sell its goods or services in a particular area; formal permission given by a government to sb. who wants to operate a public service as a business）

D. ['kɒmprəmaɪz] 妥协；折中；互让；和解（an agreement made between two people or groups in which each side gives up some of the things they want so that both sides are happy at the end）

句子大意：大约有十几家外国公司拥有开发锂矿的特许权，但是现在所有的开发合同都要重新审核。

14 A

insurrection 起义；暴动；叛乱（a situation in which a large group of people try to take political control of their own country with violence）

A. 起义；叛乱；造反（an attempt to take control of a country by force）

同义词：insurgence 起义，暴动，叛变行动（an organized rebellion aimed at overthrowing a constituted government through the use of subversion and armed conflict）

B. [ˌrɪsʌsɪ'teɪʃ(ə)n] 复活；复兴（the act of restoring to use, activity, vigor, or notice; reinvigoration）

C. [ˌrezə'rekʃ(ə)n] 复苏；复兴（a new beginning for sth. which is old or which had disappeared or become weak）

D. 旁敲侧击的话；影射；暗示（something that sb. insinuates）

句子大意：美国众议院国会山骚乱（备注：发生时间为 2021 年 1 月 6 日），调查委员会建议美国司法部以四项刑事罪名起诉前总统特朗普。四项罪名分别为：妨碍司法、密谋欺诈联邦政府、协助叛乱以及（串谋）向政府做虚假陈述。

15 B

inscrutable [ɪn'skru:təb(ə)l] 难以捉摸的；难以理解的；神秘莫测的（If a person or their expression is inscrutable, it is hard to know what they are thinking or feeling, because they do not show any emotion.）

A. 精力充沛的；精神矍铄的（full of life and energy）

B. [ˌenɪg'mætɪk] 神秘的；费解的；令人困惑的（mysterious and difficult to understand）

C. 无道德原则的；不诚实的；不公正的（without moral principles; not honest or fair）

D. [fə'si:ʃəs] 乱引人发笑的；不分场合耍聪明的（trying to appear amusing and intelligent at a time when other people do not think it is appropriate, and when it would be better to be serious）

句子大意：上一部俘获外国网播剧观众"芳心"的法国间谍是 Malotru，即法语惊悚剧《传奇办公室》中神秘莫测的主角。

16 B

A. [sə'tɪrɪk(ə)l] 讽刺的；讥讽的（using satire to criticize sb./sth.）

B. 服装的；（尤指）男装的；缝制的（relating to clothes, especially men's clothes, and the way they are made or worn）

C. 轻慢的；轻蔑的；嘲弄的（showing that you think that you are better than other people and do not take them seriously）

D. 讽刺的；嘲讽的；挖苦的（showing or expressing sarcasm）

句子大意： 牛仔裤可以有力传递主张平等的讯息，但对政客而言，牛仔裤极有可能成为穿搭陷阱。

17 A

surrender 投降（to admit that you have been defeated and want to stop fighting; to allow yourself to be caught, taken prisoner, etc.）

A. [kəˌpɪtʃʊˈleɪʃn] 投降（the act of surrendering or yielding）

投降条约（a document that sets out the agreed terms of surrender）

B. 总市值（the total value of a company's shares on a stock exchange）

常见表达：market capitalization or market cap

C. 斩首（the action of cutting off the head of a person or an animal）

D. 人头税；按人摊派的费用；按人付费制度（a tax or payment of an equal amount for each person; the system of payments of this kind）

句子大意： 粮食和弹药的缺乏迫使叛乱分子投降。

18 B

merge（使）合并，结合，并入（to combine or make two or more things combine to form a single thing）

A. ~ sb. (into sth./into doing sth.) or ~ sb. (to do sth.) 强迫；胁迫；迫使（to force sb. to do sth. by using threats）

B. ~ (into/with sth.) 合并；联合；结合（to come together to form one larger group, substance, etc.）

C. ~ (into sth.) 退回原状，（好转后）再倒退（to go back into a previous condition or into a worse state after making an improvement）

D. [kənˈdʒiːl] 变稠；凝结（to become thick or solid）

句子大意： 这场战争已经整合为一场同样针对该国的全球较量。

19 A

miscreant [ˈmɪskriənt] 歹人；邪教徒；不信教的人（someone who does something wrong or commits a crime）

A. 犯罪分子；作恶的人；道德败坏的人（a person who does wrong, illegal or immoral things）

B. [mɪsˈfiːzəns] 滥用职权（in law, the abuse of lawful authority in order to achieve a desired result）

不当履行（the act of engaging in an action or duty but failing to perform the duty correctly）

C. 懈怠；不作为；失职（in law, the omission of some act that is expected to have been performed）

D. 厌恶女人的男人（a man who hates women）

句子大意： 该城市许多人现在都觉得他制定的政策已经让坏人胡作非为而不会受任何处罚。

20 B

acquit sb. (of sth.) 宣判无罪（to decide and state officially in court that sb. is not guilty of a crime）

A. ~ sth.（尤指战时或紧急状态时）征用（to officially demand the use of a building, vehicle, etc., especially during a war or an emergency）

B. ~ sb. (of/from sth.) 宣告无罪；判定无责（to state formally that sb. is not guilty or responsible for sth.）

C. ~ sth. 征用，没收（私有财产）（to officially take away private property from its owner for public use）

D. 终于答应；不再拒绝（to finally agree to sth. after refusing）

变缓和；变温和；减弱（to become less determined, strong, etc.）

句子大意：陪审团宣告她无罪，但我依然认为她是有罪的。

Practice 5

1 B

put paid to sth. 使……结束或不再关注（to consider something finished or ended; to put something to rest or no longer give it any attention）

A. ~ sth. 废弃；抛弃；报废（to cancel or get rid of sth. that is no longer practical or useful）

B. ~ sth. 使泡汤；使成泡影（to cause sb./sth. to fail）

C. 擦坏；擦伤；刮坏；蹭破（to rub sth. by accident so that it gets damaged or hurt）

D. ~ sb./sth. 抢先报道（to publish a story before all the other newspapers, television companies, etc.）

句子大意：她上班总是醉醺醺的，让自己晋升的希望化为泡影。

2 C

depressing 令人抑郁的；令人沮丧的；令人消沉的（making you feel very sad and without enthusiasm）

A.（指人）气馁的；泄气的（feeling that it is useless to try to do something）

B.（指人）气馁的；垂头丧气的；心灰意懒的（having no hope or enthusiasm）

C.（指人）抑郁的；沮丧的；意志消沉的（very sad and without hope）

患抑郁症的（suffering from the medical condition of depression）

（指事物 = depressing）不景气的；萧条的；经济困难的（without enough economic activity or jobs for people）

D. ~ (with sb./sth.) 不再着迷的；不再抱幻想的（no longer feeling enthusiasm for sb./sth.; not believing sth. is good or worth doing）

句子大意：10月份的零售额下降，制造业和建筑业的景气度指标依然不高。

3 C

pithy ['pɪθi] 言简意赅的；精练的（short but expressed well and full of meaning）

A. 不完整的；参差不齐的（not complete; good in some parts, but not in others）

B. 易受影响的；可塑的；容易摆布的（easy to influence or control）

C. 简要的；简短生硬的（using few words and often not seeming polite or friendly）

D. 话多的；冗长的；啰唆的（using too many words, especially formal ones）

句子大意：当被一名记者问及为什么进行这次莽撞的飞行时，他胸有成竹，回答得十分精练："人不能无所事事。"

4 C

offbeat 另类的；不寻常的；不落俗套的；标新立异的（different from what most people expect）

A. 沉闷的；令人沮丧的；悲观的（dull or depressing; not having much hope for the future）

B. 过于拘谨的（not wanting to do sth. that might be considered dishonest or immoral）

神经质的；易呕吐的（easily upset, or made to feel sick by unpleasant sights or situations, especially when the sight of blood is involved）

C. 不因循守旧的；不因袭的；新奇的（not following what is done or considered normal or acceptable by most people; different and interesting）

D.（人或人的行为举止）古怪反常的；异乎寻常的（considered by other people to be strange or unusual）

句子大意：比赛项目既包括跑步和游泳等常规项目，也包括障碍赛和飞艇冲浪等较为另类的项目。

5 A

rife（坏事）盛行的，普遍的（If sth. bad or unpleasant is rife in a place, it is very common there.）

~(with sth.) 充斥，充满（坏事）（full of sth. bad or unpleasant）

A. 普遍的；盛行的；流行的（existing or most common at a particular time）

常考近义词：prevalent ~ (among sb.) or ~ (in sb./sth.) 流行的；普遍存在的；盛行的（that exists or is very common at a particular time or in a particular place）

B. 充满（移动着的人、动物等）的；拥挤的

常见搭配：be teeming with…

（某地）充满、充斥着……（containing or consisting of an extremely large number of people, animals, or objects that are all moving around）

C. 破坏性的；导致严重问题的（causing serious problems or damage）

D. 卓越的；杰出的；超群的（better or more important than everyone or everything else in a particular activity or subject）

句子大意：该公司拒绝接受采访，但一位前员工表示，在公司内部，歧视现象十分普遍。

6 A

ignominious 耻辱的；可耻的；不光彩的（that makes, or should make, you feel ashamed; characterized by or deserving shame or disgrace）

A. 不光彩的；有损尊严的；丢脸的（bad and unacceptable; causing people to lose respect）

B. 可解雇的；可免职的；可打发走的；可拒绝的（subject to dismissal）

C. 使觉醒的；使幻灭的（making someone disappointed by showing them that someone or something is not as good as they had believed）

D. 蔑视的；轻视的；轻蔑（meant to belittle the value or importance of someone or something）

句子大意：我相信，民众会为这艘伟大的战舰落得个如此不光彩的下场感到伤心。

7 A

intransigence 不妥协；拒绝调解；固执地不改变自己的想法或行为（an unreasonable refusal to change your ideas or behavior）

A. ~ on sth./on doing sth. or ~ that… 坚决要求；坚持；固执（an act of demanding or saying sth. firmly and refusing to accept any opposition or excuses）

B. 毅力；韧性；不屈不挠的精神（the quality of continuing to try to achieve a particular aim despite difficulties）

C. 沉溺；放纵；纵容（the state or act of having or doing whatever you want; the state of allowing sb. to have or do whatever they want）

D. 违规、违约行为（failure to do what is specified in a a rule, law, contract, etc.）

句子大意：对于德国的不妥协态度，法国有明显的挫败感，但高级官员把所有关于等级下调的言论均视为危言耸听。

8 A

manage to do sth. 完成（困难的事）；勉力完成（to succeed in doing sth., especially sth. difficult）

A. ~ to do sth. （不顾困难而）设法做到（to manage to do sth. despite difficulties）

B. ~ (over) sth. 深思熟虑（to think carefully about something over a period of time）

C. ~ sth. 策划，操纵，领导（复杂的事情）（to plan and direct a complicated project or activity）

D. ~ sth. (up) 找寻，聚集，激起（支持、勇气等）（to find as much support, courage, etc. as you can）
集合，召集，集结（尤指部队）（to come together, or bring people, especially soldiers, together for example for military action）

句子大意：这个枪手以某种方式设法避开了安保人员的注意。

9 B

surmise sth. or surmise that… 推测；猜测（to guess or suppose sth. using the evidence you have, without definitely knowing）

A. 理解；领会（to understand the meaning of a word, a sentence, or an action in a particular way）

B. 推论；推测；演绎（to form an opinion about sth. based on the information or evidence that is available）

C. ~ (doing) sth. 推迟；延缓；展期（to delay sth. until a later time）

D. ~ sth. 公开谴责；强烈反对（to strongly disapprove of sth. and criticize it, especially publicly）

句子大意：考古学家们仍然只能推测人类的起源。

10 A

coax 哄劝；劝诱（to persuade sb. to do sth. by talking to them in a kind and gentle way）

A. 温和地劝说（to encourage someone in a gentle way to do something）

B. ~ sb. 作弄；欺骗（to trick sb. by making them believe sth. that is not true, especially sth. unpleasant）

C. 表达"劝诱某人做某事"的正确搭配为：talk sb. into doing sth.

D. ~ sb. to do sth. 促使某人做某事（to make them decide to do it）

句子大意：地方当局继续利用温和诱导而非强迫的方式劝说老年人接种疫苗。

11　A

wrong-foot sb. 使措手不及；使窘态毕露（to put sb. in a difficult or embarrassing situation by doing sth. that they do not expect）

A. ~ sb. 使困惑惊讶；使惊疑（to confuse and surprise sb.）

~ sb./sth. 证明……有错（to prove sb./sth. wrong）

~ sb. 击败，战胜（敌人）（to defeat an enemy）

B. ~ sth. 使加重；使恶化（to make sth. bad become even worse by causing further damage or problems）

C. ~ sth. or ~ (sb.) doing sth. 容忍；纵容（to accept behaviour that is morally wrong or to treat it as if it were not serious）

D. ~ sth. or ~ sb. (in sth.) 使感觉更强烈；使确信（to make sb. feel or believe sth. even more strongly）

句子大意：本月英格兰银行未像人们预期的那样提高利率，让各大市场措手不及。

12　D

[əʊˈpaɪn] opine that... 表达，发表（意见）（to express a particular opinion）

A. 详述，仔细研究（to spend a lot of time thinking or talking about something unpleasant）

B. 集中注意力于……，瞄准（to go straight to the most important part of a situation or the part of a situation that you are most interested in）

C. 利用……以实现目标或获得优势（to use an event or a situation to help you to achieve something or to get an advantage）

D. 发表看法（to make a comment or observation on, usually in an editorial）

句子大意：我不喜欢对股市发表意见，我再次强调，我不知道股市短期内会有何表现。

13　A

necessitate [nəˈsesɪteɪt] 使成为必要（to make sth. necessary）

A. 使有必要；使正当；使恰当（to make sth. necessary or appropriate in a particular situation merit, deserve, necessitate, call for, demand）

B. 支配；摆布；决定（to control or influence how sth. happens）

C. 指示；意味着；代表（to be a feature that shows you what something is）

D. ~ sth. (in sth.) 以（某种货币）为单位（to express an amount of money using a particular unit）

~ sb. (as) sth. 将……命名为（to give sth. a particular name or description）

句子大意：面对当前席卷欧洲的一波疫情，或有必要重新采取严格的限制措施。

14 B

exaltation 褒扬；高度赞扬（great praise of someone or something）

recoil from sth./from doing sth. or ~ at sth. 对……做出厌恶（或恐惧）的反应（to react to an idea or a situation with strong dislike or fear）

A. 掺杂；伪造；冒牌货（the act of making a substance less pure by adding something else to it）

B. [ˌædjʊˈleɪʃ(ə)n] 称赞；吹捧；奉承（admiration and praise, especially when this is greater than is necessary）

C. 钦佩；赞赏；羡慕（a feeling of respect and liking for sb./sth.）

D. 改变；更改；改动（the act of making a change to sth.）

句子大意：许多观察人士非常反感这种过度吹捧一位领袖的做法。

15 A

untenable 难以捍卫的；站不住脚的；不堪一击的（that cannot be defended against attack or criticism）

A. 不稳固的；不牢靠的；摇晃的；不确切的（not firm or safe; not certain）

B. 粗略的；概略的；不完备的（not complete or detailed and therefore not very useful）

C. 难办的；棘手的；让人为难的（difficult or unpleasant）

用户黏着度高的；富有吸引力的（so interesting and well organized that the people who visit it stay there for a long time）

D. 粗制滥造的；劣质的（made or done badly and with not enough care）

奸诈的；卑鄙的（dishonest or unfair）

句子大意：如果新公布的数据并未显示通胀在减缓的话，鸽派的理由或将站不住脚，2022 年将有可能成为一个动荡不定的年份。

16 A

expletive（愤怒或痛苦时用的）秽语，咒骂语，感叹语（a word, especially a rude word, that you use when you are angry, or in pain）

tirade (against sb./sth.)（批评或指责性的）长篇激烈讲话（a long angry speech criticizing sb./sth. or accusing sb. of sth.）

A. 辱骂；咒骂（rude language and unpleasant remarks that sb. shouts when they are very angry）

B. ~ (against sb.) 不平的事；委屈；抱怨（something that you think is unfair and that you complain or protest about）

C. [ˈlaɪb(ə)l]（文字）诽谤，中伤（the act of printing a statement about sb. that is not true and that gives people a bad opinion of them）

D. 感叹；感叹语；感叹词（a short sound, word or phrase spoken suddenly to express an emotion）

句子大意：在纽约降落之后，他通过机场的公共广播激动地发表了一通满是咒骂的长篇大论。

17 B

bromide ['brəʊmaɪd] 溴化物（旧时尤用作镇静剂）（a chemical which contains bromine, used, especially in the past, to make people feel calm）；〈美俚〉平庸可厌的人，喜欢讲陈腔滥调的人；陈腔滥调（a commonplace or tiresome person; a commonplace or hackneyed statement or notion）

A. 真诚，诚意（an honest way of behaving that shows that you really mean what you say or do）

B. 平庸；平淡乏味；陈腐的事物；陈词滥调（the quality of being banal; things, remarks, etc. that are banal）

C. 义愤填膺地谴责；慷慨激昂地劝说（a long loud angry speech that criticizes sb./sth. or tries to persuade people to do sth.）

D. 甜言蜜语；情话；空洞的甜言蜜语（romantic words）

句子大意： 他的演讲满篇都是那些号召大家齐心协力之类的陈词滥调。

18 D

pontificate [pɒnˈtɪfɪkeɪt] (about/on sth.) 自以为是地谈论；目空一切地议论（to give your opinions about sth. in a way that shows that you think you are right）

A. ~ (sth.) 深思熟虑；沉思；苦思冥想（to think deeply about sth. for a long time）

B. ~ sth. or ~ on sth. 仔细考虑；深思熟虑；反复思考（to think very carefully about sth., usually before making a decision）

C. ~ to do sth. 屈尊；俯就（to do sth. that you think it is below your social or professional position to do）

~ to sb.（对某人）表现出优越感（to behave towards sb. as though you are more important and more intelligent than they are）

D. 宣传，宣扬，宣讲（教义、生活方式、体制等）（to tell people about a particular religion, way of life, system, etc. in order to persuade them to accept it）

说教（to give sb. advice on moral standards, behaviour, etc., especially in a way that they find annoying or boring）

句子大意： 世界经济论坛年会是一场对比研究，特别是汇聚在达沃斯的富有的局内人与数十亿局外人的对比。这些局内人在年会上自以为是地对这些局外人的命运高谈阔论。

19 C

pizzazz [pəˈzæz] 激情；活泼；风度（a lively and exciting quality or style）

A. ~ (of sth.) 疯狂；狂乱；狂暴（a state of great activity and strong emotion that is often violent or frightening and not under control）

B. [ˌpæpəˈrætsi] 狗仔队；狗仔（photographers who follow famous people in order to take photographs of them that newspapers and magazines will buy）

C. 耀眼；华丽；浮华（the quality of appearing very attractive, exciting and impressive, in a way that is not always genuine）

D. 集中力量的行动；闪击式行动（something which is done with a lot of energy）

句子大意：今年的年会参会人数可能比往年少了一半，各家公司也控制了派对数量和浮华程度。

20 D

damning 谴责的；诅咒的；清楚表明某人可以有错或有罪的（A damning report, judgment, remark, etc. is one that includes a lot of criticism or shows clearly that someone is wrong, guilty, or has behaved very badly.）

A. [pɪ'dʒɔrətɪv] 贬损的；轻蔑的（a word or remark that is pejorative expresses disapproval or criticism）

B. 贬低的；贬义的（showing a critical attitude towards sb.）

C. 爱挑剔的；吹毛求疵的（tending to criticize people or things a lot）

D. 证据充分的；有大量文件证明的（having a lot of written evidence to prove, support or explain it）

句子大意：由联合国指定的观察人员最近提交的一份证据确凿的报告勾勒出了一个和平协定，但由于该协定的谈判没有取得进展，联合国周四很可能会投票延长武器禁运和资产冻结的期限。

Practice 6

1 A

insistent 坚决要求的；坚持的；固执的（demanding sth. firmly and refusing to accept any opposition or excuses）

A. 坚决的；坚定不移的（determined not to change your belief or decision about something）

　　例句：She is adamant that the insights her team is providing into how the human brain works would simply not be possible any other way. 她坚持认为，她的小组为大脑工作原理提供的深刻阐释是其他途径根本无法做到的。

B. ~ sb. for/of sth. 为某事告诫某人（to tell someone that you do not approve of what they have done）

　　劝告某人做某事（to advise someone to do something）

C. [ˌæfɪ'deɪvɪt] 附誓书面证词；宣誓书（a written statement that you swear is true, and that can be used as evidence in court）

D. 敢于冒险的；大胆的（willing to take risks or to do sth. shocking）

句子大意：村民们坚持认为，扩大现有的采矿区不应超出已经划定的范围，因为他们不会从中获得任何好处。

2 C

prize 珍视；高度重视（to value sth. highly）

A. 较喜欢……（to like one thing or person better than another; to choose one thing rather than sth. else because you like it better）

B. ~ sb./sth. 宣传；宣扬；推广（to make a lot of people know about sth. and enjoy it）

　　~ sth. 使通俗化；使普及（to make a difficult subject easier to understand for ordinary people）

C. 重视；强调；高度评价（to place a high value on somebody or something）

D. 沉思；考虑；琢磨（to think about sth. carefully for a period of time）

句子大意：作为美联储主席，杰罗姆·鲍威尔高度重视可预见性，给投资者提供足够的指导，帮助他们为政策调整提前做好准备。

3 A

quiescent [kwi'es(ə)nt]（暂时）平静的，静止的 [(sb. or sth.) temporarily quiet and inactive]

A. [ˌækwi'es(ə)nt] 默许的，默认的，勉强顺从的（accepting or agreeing to something, although you do not want to）

B. ~ with sth. 熟悉；了解（familiar with sth., having read, seen or experienced it）

C. 习惯于（familiar with sth. and accepting it as normal or usual）

D. 乐于助人的；随和的；适应的（accommodating, friendly, indulgent, obliging）

句子大意：面对社会不公，刚正之人不会保持缄默。

4 B

take to sth. 喜欢；从事；喜爱（to begin to like someone or something）

A. 欺骗；吸收；接受（to include something; to understand and remember something that you hear or read; to trick someone into believing something that is not true）

B. 喜欢；爱上（to become fond of; cultivate a predilection for）

C. 纵情于；陶醉；酷爱（to enjoy something very much）

D.（relish 是及物动词）~ sth. or ~ doing sth. 享受；从……获得乐趣；渴望；喜欢（to get great pleasure from sth.; to want very much to do or have sth.）

常见搭配：relish the idea or thought of something 某事即将发生而让自己高兴

例句：She's relishing the prospect of studying in Bologna for six months.

句子大意：马里兰州一家苹果专卖店的员工将于周三就是否组建工会进行投票，但是苹果公司并不赞同员工组建工会的想法。

5 B

saccharine ['sækərɪn] 情感过分强烈而显夸张的；故作多情的（too emotional in a way that seems exaggerated; too pleasant or charming, with too much feeling to be believed）

A. 性欲的；性爱的；色情的（showing or involving sexual desire and pleasure; intended to make sb. feel sexual desire）

B.（失之过度或不恰当地）伤感的，充满柔情的；多愁善感的（producing emotions such as pity, romantic love or sadness, which may be too strong or not appropriate; feeling these emotions too much）

C. 肉体的；肉欲的；性欲的（connected with the body or with sex）

D. ~ about sth. 充满信心的；乐观的（cheerful and confident about the future）

句子大意：传统上，这个国家会用更煽情的描述对这些光辉的军事故事进行渲染，以博取公众的爱戴之情。

6 A

defy sb./sth. 违抗；反抗；蔑视（to refuse to obey or show respect for sb. in authority, a law, a rule, etc.; defy belief, explanation, description, etc.）；不可能，无法（相信、解释、描绘等）（to be impossible or almost impossible to believe, explain, describe, etc.）

subpoena [sə'pi:nə]（传唤证人出庭的）传票（a written order to attend court as a witness to give evidence）

A. ~ sth. 公然藐视，无视（法律等）（to show that you have no respect for a law, etc. by openly not obeying it）

B. 不知所措；挠头；支吾（to struggle to know what to say or do or how to continue with sth.）
   困难重重；艰苦挣扎（to have a lot of problems and to be in danger of failing completely）

C. ~ sth.（考试、测验等）失败，不及格（to fail an exam, a test or a course）
   ~ sb. 给（某人）不及格（to make sb. fail an exam, a test, or a course by giving them a low mark/grade）

D. ~ sth. or ~ that… 标志；预示；象征（to be a sign of sth.）

句子大意：他虽然不情愿作证，但有报道称，他并不想公然藐视出庭作证的传票。

7 A

taper（使）逐渐变窄（to become gradually narrower; to make sth. become gradually narrower）

备注：taper 是美联储政策术语，意为缩减购债规模。taper 与 QE 对应，QE 即量化宽松，通过购买债券、资产抵押证券等，为金融市场提供大规模的流动性支持。而 taper 就是"逐渐缩减"资产购买规模，意味着逐渐退出 QE，收回流动性，简而言之，就是收紧货币政策。

A. wind down（使）逐步收缩；（使）逐步结束（to end, or to finish something gradually; to gradually reduce work before stopping completely）

B. scale up 增加；扩大；提高（to make something larger in size, amount, extent etc. than it used to be）

C. buy back（动词）；buyback（名词）回购（A buyback, also known as a repurchase, is the purchase by a company of its outstanding shares that reduces the number of its shares on the open market.）

D. cut back 缩减（to reduce the amount of something, especially money that you spend）

句子大意：美联储官员周三表示，准备开始"缩减购债规模"，也就是慢慢取消疫情期间推出的经济刺激措施。

8 D

parse sth.（对句子）作语法分析；作句法分析（to divide a sentence into parts and describe the grammar of each word or part）

A. ~ sth. 减轻，缓和（疾病或不适）（to make a disease or an illness less painful or unpleasant without curing it）

B. ~ over sth. 用心阅读；细心研究（to read or study attentively —usually used with over）

C. ~ from sth.（对官方意见）不同意，持异议（to have or express opinions that are different from those that are officially accepted）

D. ~ sth. 仔细研究；详细评论；剖析（to study sth. closely and/or discuss it in great detail）

句子大意：周三，美联储将发布最新经济预测，投资者可能会对此进行仔细解析。如果央行预测的加息路径比预期的更为温和，他们可能会放心一些。

9 D

denigrate ['denɪˌɡreɪt] ~ sb./sth. 诋毁；诽谤；贬低（to criticize sb./sth. unfairly; to say sb./sth. does not have any value or is not important）

A. ~ sth. 取消；使无效（to stop sth. from having any effect）

~ sth. 否定；否认（to state that sth. does not exist）

B. [rɪ'neɪɡ] ~ on sth. 违背（诺言）；背信弃义；食言（to break a promise, an agreement, etc.）

C. ['desɪˌmeɪt] ~ sth. 大量毁灭，大批杀死（某地区的动物、植物或人）（to kill large numbers of animals, plants or people in a particular area）

~ sth. 严重破坏；大大削弱（to severely damage sth. or make sth. weaker）

D. ~ sb./sth. 诽谤；诋毁；污辱（to harm sb.'s reputation by making unfair or false statements about them）

句子大意：我们必须公平竞争，绝不诋毁其他公司。

10 A

schism ['skɪz(ə)m; 'sɪz(ə)m] 分裂；宗派活动；（尤指）教会分裂（strong disagreement within an organization, especially a religious one, that makes its members divide into separate groups）

A.（关系的）破裂，决裂；绝交（an end to a friendly relationship or to a peaceful situation）

B. 怀疑态度；怀疑主义（an attitude of doubting that claims or statements are true or that sth. will happen）

C. 犬儒主义；愤世嫉俗；冷嘲热讽（the belief that people are only interested in themselves and are not sincere; the fact of using someone's feelings or emotions to your own advantage; an attitude of scornful or jaded negativity, especially a general distrust of the integrity or professed motives of others）

D. 狂喜；欢天喜地；兴高采烈（a feeling of extreme pleasure and happiness）

句子大意：无神论内部或许有流派之分，无神论者相互也会争论，但说成分裂是不对的。

11 A

mundane 单调的；平凡的（not interesting or exciting）

A. 一般的；平常的；平凡的；平庸的（ordinary; not special or remarkable in any way）

B. 病态的；不正常的（having or expressing a strong interest in sad or unpleasant things, especially disease or death）

C. 受虐狂式；受虐狂的（relating to or experiencing the desire to be humiliated and abused by others in order to feel sexually fulfilled）

D. 不爱出风头的；不爱炫耀的；谦逊的（not wanting to draw attention to yourself or to your abilities or status）

句子大意：你有多少时间是浪费在世俗琐事上，而不是用来完成你所热爱的挑战或者你上司所欣赏的工作上呢？

12 A

derogatory 贬低的；贬义的（showing a critical attitude towards sb.）

　A. 蔑视的；轻视的（showing that you have no respect for someone or something）

　B. 自认为高人一等的；摆派头的（showing that you feel better, or more intelligent than sb. else）

　C. 傲慢的；高傲的（behaving towards other people as if you think you are better than they are）

　D. 虚华的；言辞浮夸的；自负傲慢的（showing that you think you are more important than other people, especially by using long and formal words）

句子大意：研究发现，使用负面、贬损的语言——即使是对自己说——也会使你的心情变糟。

13 C

pomp 排场；气派；盛况（the impressive clothes, decorations, music, etc. and traditional customs that are part of an official occasion or ceremony）

pomp and ceremony 正式庄重的仪式（the performance of some solemn act according to prescribed form）

　A. 庆典；庆祝活动（a special event that people organize in order to celebrate sth.）

　B. 兴奋；兴高采烈（a feeling of very great joy or happiness）

　　提高；晋升；提拔（an act of raising sth./sb. to a high position or rank）

　C. 〈古〉形式，仪式；（仪式的）隆重（formal and impressive ceremony）

　　常考习语：pomp and circumstance 盛大庄重的仪式（the ceremonial formality surrounding a public event）

　D. （对法律、习俗的）遵守，奉行；（节日的）庆祝（the practice of obeying a law, celebrating a festival or behaving according to a particular custom）

　　宗教（或传统节日）的仪式（an act performed as part of a religious or traditional ceremony）

句子大意：今天她的葬礼不会有军队护送，街道两边没有拥挤的人群，也不会有隆重的仪式。

14 A

freewheeling 随心所欲的；无拘无束的（not concerned about rules or the possible results of what you do）

esoteric [ˌesəʊˈterɪk] 只有内行才懂的；难领略的（likely to be understood or enjoyed by only a few people with a special knowledge or interest）

　A. 无限制的；不受约束的；自由的（not controlled or restricted）

　B. 不受法规约束的；不受管制的（not controlled by laws or regulations）

　C. 不加约束的；不受限制的；放任的（If sth. harmful is unchecked, it is not controlled or stopped from getting worse.）

　D. 未受损害的；未被污染的；未被玷污的（not damaged or spoiled by sth. unpleasant）

句子大意：这个乐团恣意洒脱、不拘一格，涉猎的音乐风格如同其成员构成一样多元。乐团早期曾采用电子乐器，后来又融入了自由爵士乐、蓝调、摇摆乐和节奏布鲁斯，这种杂糅的音乐风格非常前卫，只有内行人才能领略其中玄妙。

15 B

polemical [pəˈlemɪk(ə)l] 争论的；挑起辩论的 [involving strong arguments for or against sth., often in opposition to the opinion of others; (of a piece of writing or a speech) strongly attacking or defending a particular opinion]

A. 善于表达的（good at expressing ideas or feelings clearly in words）

B. 辩证的（able to discover the truth of ideas by discussion and logical argument and by considering ideas that are opposed to each other）

C. 讽刺的；讥讽的（using satire to criticize sb./sth.）

D. 护身符，驱邪物（为祛邪防病等佩戴的珠宝）（a piece of jewellery that some people wear because they think it protects them from bad luck, illness, etc.）

常考同义词：talisman [ˈtælɪzmən] 护身符；驱邪物（an object that is thought to have magic powers and to bring good luck）

句子大意： 弗里德曼用自己的辩才说服委员会接受了自己坚持的自愿兵役制度。

16 A

cacophony [kəˈkɒfəni] 刺耳的嘈杂声（a mixture of loud unpleasant sounds）

A. 不和谐；不协调；不一致（lack of agreement）

B. 交响乐；交响曲 [a long complicated piece of music for a large orchestra, in three or four main parts (called movements)]

C. 管弦乐队（a large group of people who play various musical instruments together, led by a conductor）

D. 小瀑布（尤指一连串瀑布中的一支）（a small waterfall, especially one of several falling down a steep slope with rocks）

倾泻（或涌出）的东西（a large number of things falling or coming quickly at the same time）

句子大意： 在印度，国家大事几乎全被地方政治的嘈杂声音所淹没，要得出合理的结论难上加难。

17 A

parochial [pəˈrəʊkiəl] 只关心本地区的；地方观念的（only concerned with small issues that happen in your local area and not interested in more important things）

A. 只关心本国利益的；思想褊狭的；保守的（only interested in your own country, ideas, etc. and not in those from outside）

B. [prəˈvɜː(r)biəl] 谚语的；谚语表达的；如谚语所说的（used to show that you are referring to a particular proverb or well-known phrase）

（不能用在名词前）众所周知的，著名的（well known and talked about by a lot of people）

C. [ˌpærəˈbɒlɪkəl] 比喻的；寓言似的；抛物线的（relating to or resembling a parable; relating to, resembling, or having the form of a parabola）

D. [ˈpæriə] 被社会遗弃者；贱民（a person who is not acceptable to society and is avoided by everyone）

句子大意：英国脱欧后欧盟的地方观念会更强、自由度会减弱，但失去了欧元的欧盟根本就不可能继续存在下去。

18 A

acerbity [ə'sɜ:bəti] 苦酸；（语言等的）尖酸刻薄（bitterness or sharpness in tone, taste, or manner）

A.（书面或口头表达）不友好、残忍冷酷（an unfriendly and cruel quality in written or spoken words）

B. 禁欲；独身（a state of not having sex for a period of time, or never having sex）

C. [krə'dju:ləti] 轻信（the quality of being too ready to believe things and therefore easy to trick）

D. 易受欺骗（the quality of being easily deceived or tricked, and too willing to believe everything that other people say）

句子大意：我希望我们的会议能够在友好而激烈的氛围中进行。

19 A

impersonal 缺乏人情味的；冷淡的（lacking friendly human feelings or atmosphere; making you feel unimportant）

brusque [brʊsk] 寡言而无礼的；粗暴的，唐突的（using very few words and sounding rude）

A. 简短而失礼的；唐突无礼的（appearing rude because very few words are used, or because sth. is done in a very quick way）

B. 敏捷的，忙碌的（quick or busy）

   务实自信的（practical and confident）

C. 怪诞的；荒谬的；丑陋奇异的（strange in a way that is unpleasant or offensive; extremely ugly in a strange way that is often frightening or amusing）

D. 冒犯的，粗俗的，粗鲁的（尤其有关性的）（offensive or rude, especially about sex）

句子大意：他那双锐利的灰色眼睛半带厌烦地扫了她一眼，显得不近人情且粗暴无礼。

20 A

sobriquet ['səʊbrɪkeɪ] 绰号；外号（an informal name or title that you give sb./sth.）

A. ['epɪθet] 别称；绰号；诨名（an offensive word or phrase that is used about a person or group of people）

   常考同义词：moniker 名字；绰号（a name, or a nickname）

B.（尤指罪犯所用的）化名，别名（a false or different name, especially one that is used by a criminal）

   （档案、互联网地址等用的）别名，假名（a name that can be used instead of the actual name for a file, Internet address, etc.）

C.（尤指作者使用的）假名；化名；笔名（a name used by sb., especially a writer, instead of their real name）

D. [sə'lɪləkwi] 独白（的台词）；独白（a speech in a play in which a character, who is alone on the stage, speaks his or her thoughts; the act of speaking thoughts in this way）

句子大意：这条高速路上车流量很大，对那些为旅客提供服务的企业而言极具吸引力，最终获得了"热狗高速路"的绰号。

Practice 7

1 C

dicey ['daɪsi] 前途未卜的；冒险的；危险的（uncertain and dangerous）

A. 紧贴的；黏人的（wanting to be with another person all the time in a way that is annoying）

B. 又黑又脏的；昏暗的；肮脏的（dark and dirty）

C. 冒险的；危险的；困难的（involving risk, danger or difficulty）

D. 低劣的；蹩脚的；俗气的；乏味的（cheap, badly made and/or lacking in taste）

句子大意： 股市似乎没有受到影响，但形势很不稳定。

2 C

delineate sth. （详细地）描述，描画，解释（to describe, draw or explain sth. in detail）；确定……的界限（to decide or show the exact limits of something）

A. ~ sth. 定……的界限；限定；界定（to decide what the limits of sth. are）

B. ['diːmɑː(r)keɪt] ~ sth. 标出……的界线；给……划界（to mark or establish the limits of sth.）

C. 描写；描述；刻画（to describe sth. in words, or give an impression of sth. in words or with a picture）

D. 征募；征召（to make sb. join the armed forces; to pick especially for required military service）

常考同义词：conscript（常用表达 conscript sb. into sth.）征募；征召（to make sb. join the armed forces）

句子大意： 他在书中描述了美国特工为了获取科技或制造技术以加速美国发展的秘密行动。

3 A

stolid 不动感情的；不关心的；淡漠的；无动于衷的（not showing much emotion or interest; remaining always the same and not reacting or changing）

pan（移动摄像机）追拍（If a camera pans, or if you pan it, it moves sideways slowly to film something else or to follow something that is moving.）

A. 无表情的；无动于衷的；不动声色的（not showing any feeling or emotion）

B. （强烈得）难以言传的，无法形容的（too strong to be put into words）

C. （美好得）难以形容的，不可言喻的（too great or beautiful to describe in words）

D. 不能通行的（尤指因路况恶劣或被阻断）（impossible to travel on or through, especially because it is in bad condition or it has been blocked by sth.）

句子大意： 有时，摄像机会从总统不动声色的言谈举止上移开，转向穿着灰色制服的军校学生脸上。

4 C

augury ['ɔːgjʊri] 预兆；征兆（a sign of what will happen in the future）；占卜，占卜术（the skill or practice of telling what may happen in the future）

A. 占卜；预测；预言（the act of finding out and saying what will happen in the future）

B. 预言（a statement that sth. will happen in the future, especially one made by sb. with religious or magic powers）

预言能力（the power of being able to say what will happen in the future）

C. 预兆；征兆；（尤指）恶兆，凶兆（a sign or warning of sth. that is going to happen in the future, especially when it is sth. unpleasant）

常考同义词：presage ['presɪdʒ]（尤指）恶兆，凶兆（to be a sign that something is going to happen, especially something bad）

D. ['priːˌsɪŋkt] 步行商业区（a commercial area in a town where cars cannot go）

选区（one of the parts into which a town or city is divided in order to organize elections）

句子大意：有些人认为，镜子破碎预示着未来七年会走霉运。

5 B

machination [ˌmækəˈneɪʃn] 阴谋；诡计（a scheming or crafty action or artful design intended to accomplish some usually evil end）

A. ['mekəˌnɪz(ə)m] 方法；机制（a method or a system for achieving sth.）

B. (=maneuvering) 手段；伎俩；花招（clever, skilful, and often dishonest ways of achieving your aims）

C. （统称）机器；（尤指）大型机器（machines as a group, especially large ones）

组织，机构；系统，体制（the organization or structure of sth.; the system for doing sth.）

D. 运作方式，工作原理（the workings of something such as a system, organization, or piece of equipment are the parts that control it or make it work）

句子大意：尽管此前内阁承诺要建设一个更加开放透明的政府，但是公众对于内阁内部的各种图谋仍不得而知。

6 A

foible （性格上无伤大雅的）怪癖，弱点，小缺点（a silly habit or a strange or weak aspect of a person's character, that is considered harmless by other people）

A. 弱点；缺点（a bad or weak aspect of sb.'s character）

B. 瑕疵；斑点；疤痕；污点（a mark or spot that spoils the appearance of something; a mark on someone's skin, such as a pimple or a scar; a mistake or dishonest action that spoils someone's reputation or career）

C. 愚蠢（或粗心）的错误（a stupid or careless mistake）

D. 开花植物（a plant that flowers, esp. in a specified way）（形容人：a late bloomer 大器晚成的人）

愚蠢的小错误；出丑（a silly or embarrassing mistake that does not have serious results）

句子大意：新闻媒体都在无情剖析他的那些小缺点与挫折经历。

7 A

lurid 俗艳的；花哨的（too bright in colour, in a way that is not attractive）；（故意地）耸人听闻的，令人毛骨悚然的（shocking and violent in a way that is deliberate）

A. 情节剧式的；夸大的；耸人听闻的（full of exciting and extreme emotions or events; behaving or reacting to sth. in an exaggerated way）

B. 表达清楚的；易懂的（clearly expressed; easy to understand）

（尤指生病期间或病愈后，糊涂状态中或过后）头脑清晰的，清醒的（able to think clearly, especially during or after a period of illness or confusion）

C. 不合理的；不能当真的（unreasonable; that you cannot take seriously）

D. 淫秽的；色情的（encouraging sexual desire or containing too much sexual detail）

句子大意： 他与威尔士王妃戴安娜的婚姻在耸人听闻的小报头条和对彼此不忠的指控中破裂，在许多人眼中，这依然是他公共生活的决定性事件。

8 A

misbegotten 设计（或规划）拙劣的（badly designed or planned）

A. 计划不完善的；考虑不周的（not well planned or considered）

常考同义词：ill-conceived 考虑不周的；构想拙劣的（badly planned or designed）

B. 鲁莽的；冲动的；轻率的（acting or done quickly and without thinking carefully about the results）

C. 言行不得体的；不圆通的；没策略的（saying or doing things that are likely to annoy or to upset other people）

D. 缺乏技巧的；无能的；笨拙的（acting or done with no skill）

句子大意： 农业贸易是一项古老的人类活动，仅占世界商品贸易额的8%，但受不合理政策的影响却最严重。

9 C

deplore sth. 公开谴责；强烈反对（to strongly disapprove of sth. and criticize it, especially publicly）；哀叹；哀悼；痛惜（to feel or express grief for）

A. ['deprɪkeɪt] ~ sth. 对……表示极不赞成；强烈反对（to feel and express strong disapproval of sth.）

B. ~ sb./sth. (as sth.)（公开）谴责；（强烈）批评（to strongly criticize sb./sth., especially publicly）

C. ~ sth. 哀怨；悲叹（to complain or say that you are not happy about sth.）

常考同义词：bewail (~ sth.) 悲悼；哀叹；为……感到悲恸（to express great sadness about sth.）

D. ~ sb./sth. 长期搅扰（to cause a lot of problems for sb./sth. over a long period of time）

句子大意： 环顾周围，多数现代剧中都缺乏风格与高雅，令人痛惜。

10 D

backtrack 原路返回；（屈于压力而）改变声明（或主张）；出尔反尔；退缩（to change an earlier statement, opinion or promise because of pressure from sb./sth.）

常考同义词：back down 打退堂鼓，让步，放弃原主张（to stop asking for something, or to stop saying that you will do something, because a lot of people oppose you）

A. 坚守信念，坚守阵地（to refuse to change your opinions, beliefs, or decisions despite pressure to change them; to hold to one's position）

B. ~ (on sb.) 产生事与愿违的不良（或危险）后果；适得其反（to have the opposite effect to the one intended, with bad or dangerous results）

C. ~ sth. 重提；再次讨论（to return to an idea or a subject and discuss it again）

D. 变卦，收回意见、立场、主张（to show that you are no longer certain about a previous opinion, intention, or promise）

句子大意：在美国参议院就大麻合法化法案屈于压力而改变主张之际，德国则在考虑将大麻合法化。德国的潜在大麻市场预计可达 166 亿美元。

11 A

aberrant [æˈberənt] 违反常规的；反常的；异常的（not usual or not socially acceptable）

常考同义词：anomalous [əˈnɒmələs] 异常的；反常的（different from what is normal or expected）

A. [ˈdiːviənt] 不正常的；异常的；偏离常规的（different from what most people consider to be normal and acceptable）

B. 公然违抗的；反抗的；挑衅的（openly refusing to obey sb./sth., sometimes in an aggressive way）

C. ~ (to sb.)（尤指因道德原因）令人憎恨的，令人厌恶的（causing hatred, especially for moral reasons）

D. [ˈɒpjulənt] 豪华的；富丽堂皇的；华丽的（made or decorated using expensive materials）

句子大意：在一个餐馆（普遍）供应蜗牛的国度，快餐明显属于文化上的异类。

12 C

personify sth. 是……的典型；集中表现（to be an example of a quality or characteristic, or to have a lot of it）

~ sth. (as sb.) 拟人化；把……比拟成某人（to show or think of an object, quality, etc. as a person）

A. ~ sth. 是……的典型（或典范、榜样）（to be a typical example of sth.）

用法提示：A exemplifies B（A 是 B 的典范）或者 B is exemplified by A（B 体现在 A 上）

B. ~ sth. 作为……的典型；是……的典范（to be a typical example of sth.）

C.（v.）~ sth. 将（概念或品质）具体化；拟人化 [to give a definite or human form to a particular idea or quality = put a human face on sth. (to make sth. more appealing, easier to understand, or easier to care about by connecting it to an actual person)]

（adj.）化身的；拟人化的（in human form）

* 特殊用法：incarnate 作为形容词使用，置于名词后。例句如下：

例句 1：The Toyota Camry has long been hailed as reliability incarnate. 丰田凯美瑞汽车长期以来一直被称作稳定性的化身 / 代表。

223

例句2：He is devil incarnate. 他是魔鬼的化身。

D. ~ sth. 成为……的典范（或典型）（to be a perfect example of sth.）

句子大意：人们将正义化身成一个蒙着双眼的女神。

13 D

allow 接受；承认；同意（某事属实或正确）（to accept or admit sth.; to agree that sth. is true or correct）

A. 允许；准许（to allow sb. to do sth. or to allow sth. to happen）

B. ~ sth. 设定；设想；假设（to accept sth. as true or existing and to act on that basis）

~ to do sth. 妄行；越权行事（to behave in a way that shows a lack of respect by doing sth. that you have no right to do）

C. ~ sth. 装出；假装（to pretend to have a particular feeling or quality）（如：assume an air of confidence in spite of her nervousness）

D. 承认（属实）（to accept that sth. is true）

~ sb./sth.（微笑、挥手等）致意（to show that you have noticed sb./sth. by smiling, waving, etc.）

句子大意：拜登确实承认"我们仍然有新冠的问题"。

14 B

incendiary 放火的；纵火的；能引起燃烧的（designed to cause fires）；煽动的（causing strong feelings or violence）

A. 易燃的；可燃的（likely to burn very quickly and easily）（只有本义）

B. 易燃的（something that is inflammable burns easily）

易激动的；易激怒的（full of strong emotions or violence）（与 flammable 相比，inflammable 还有这一比喻义）

常考同义词：inflammatory 煽动性的；使人发怒的（intended to cause very strong feelings of anger）

C. 狂热的（nervous, excited and very active）

发热引起的（caused by fever）

D. 模糊的；不清楚的（not clear）

句子大意：人们很容易将具有如此煽动性的声明当成是一个心存积怨的男人发出的大声抱怨。

15 A

pomp and pageantry 壮观的场面、仪式（spectacular display）

A.（习惯表达）pomp and circumstance 隆重、宏大的排场（celebration accompanied by traditional formalities and ceremony）

常考同义表达：pomp and ceremony 盛典，壮观的仪式（the performance of some solemn act according to prescribed form）

B.（社会或行业中的）礼节，礼仪，规矩（the formal rules of correct or polite behaviour in society or among members of a particular profession）

C. 行为；风度；举止（the way you look and behave）

D. 风度；仪态；举止（the way in which a person stands and moves）

句子大意：周六，一条1.3公里长、连接该湖与波罗的海的人工航道将会在盛大的仪式中亮相。

16 C

strident ['straɪd(ə)nt] 强硬的；咄咄逼人的（aggressive and determined）

A. 费力的；繁重的；艰苦的（needing great effort and energy）

   劲头十足的；顽强的（showing great energy and determination）

B. 严格的；严厉的（very strict and that must be obeyed）

C. 好斗的；挑衅的；富于攻击性的（behaving in an angry or rude way that shows you want to fight, attack, or argue with someone）

D. 粗鲁的；不恭的（rude; not showing respect for other people）

   常考形近词：imprudent 不明智的；不谨慎的（not wise or sensible）

句子大意：印度在与邻国的关系上显然正日趋强硬。

17 C

wayward 难以控制的；任性的；倔强的（difficult to control; unruly）

A. 热闹的；充满活力的；活蹦乱跳的（noisy and full of life and energy）

B. 吵闹的；惹是生非的；捣乱的（making a lot of noise or likely to cause trouble）

C. (= wilful) 故意的；有意的；成心的（done deliberately, although the person doing it knows that it is wrong）

   任性的；固执的；倔强的（determined to do what you want; not caring about what other people want）

D. 怀着渴望的，一厢情愿的（wishing for something, or expressing a wish or longing）

   常见表达：wishful thinking 一厢情愿的想法，如意算盘，痴心妄想

句子大意：查尔斯继承执掌的王室已经受到了一系列动荡的冲击，他始终难以控制家族成员的任性妄为。

18 A

prerogative [prɪ'rɒɡətɪv] (n.) 特权；优先权（a right or advantage belonging to a particular person or group because of their importance or social position）；(adj.)（有）特权的；依照特权享有的

A. （有钱有势者的）特权，特殊待遇（the rights and advantages that rich and powerful people in a society have）

B. 过度或不适当的自由（excessive or undue freedom or liberty）

   ~ to do sth. 放肆，放纵（freedom to do or say whatever you want, often sth. bad or unacceptable）

   放荡，纵欲，淫乱 [freedom to behave in a way that is considered sexually immoral (= licentiousness)]

C. 贬低的；贬义的（showing a critical attitude towards sb.）

D. ['pɜ:(r)ɡət(ə)ri] 炼狱；受难的处所（或状态），折磨，磨难（any place or state of suffering）

句子大意：他将会是一位积极进取的国王，可能会把自己的王室特权利用到极致，但又不会逾矩。

19 A

inscrutable [ɪnˈskruːtəb(ə)l] 难以捉摸的；难以理解的；神秘莫测的（If a person or their expression is inscrutable, it is hard to know what they are thinking or feeling, because they do not show any emotion.）

A. 不可理解的；高深莫测的（impossible to understand）

B. ~ to sth. 不可渗透的；不透气的；不透水的（not allowing a liquid or gas to pass through）

C. ~ to sth. 不受影响的（not affected or influenced by sth.）

不能渗透的；不透气的；不透水的（not allowing a liquid or gas to pass through）

D. 不能通行的（尤指因路况恶劣或被阻断）（impossible to travel on or through, especially because it is in bad condition or it has been blocked by sth.）

句子大意：2007年，当金融工具变得越来越让人难以捉摸之时，琼斯开始看空整个行业。

20 C

palatable [ˈpælətəb(ə)l] 可口的；味美的（having a pleasant or acceptable taste）

~ (to sb.) 宜人的；可意的；可接受的（pleasant or acceptable to sb.）

A. 开胃的；引起食欲的；使渴的（that smells or looks attractive; making you feel hungry or thirsty）

B. 吸引人的；诱人的；有吸引力的（something that is tempting is attractive, and makes people want to have it, do it, etc.）

C. 可接受的；令人满意的；可容许的（that sb. agrees is of a good enough standard or allowed）

D. 可憎的；可恨的；令人讨厌的（that deserves to be hated）

句子大意：即使是最恶心的香烟盒警戒图片长期下去也可能会让人们感到麻木，加拿大似乎就是一个例子。

Practice 8

1 A

A.（尤指从事研究工作的）科学家，研究员（a scientist, especially one doing research）

B. 藏红花；番红花粉（用作食用色素）（a bright yellow powder made from crocus flowers, used in cooking to give colour to food）

C. 爱好者；行家里手（a person who is very interested in a particular subject or activity and knows a lot about it）

备注：日常生活中常常听到人们说叠 buff，意思是增加一个增益效果（对自己而言）或者减益效果（对对手而言）。buff 是一个游戏用语，原意为：使外形更健壮、更健美。在游戏中 buff 是指为角色添加了额外的增强效果或减弱效果。增强 buff 常用于己方队友，以达到增强队友攻击力的目的。

D. 抢劫犯；拦路抢劫者（a person who threatens or attacks sb. in order to steal their money, especially in a public place）

句子大意：研究人员想要以开放的态度研究这些数据，认为任何研究结果最终都可能有用。

2 C

drive (one) batty 激怒某人，让某人沮丧不已（to annoy or frustrate one to the point of exasperation）

cacophonous [kəˈkɒfənəs] 发音不和谐的；刺耳的；声音刺耳的（having an unpleasant mixture of sounds）

A. （对人命、财产等）引起灾难的，灾难性的（causing great damage to people's lives, property, etc.）

B. 令人迷惑的难题；复杂难解的问题（a confusing problem or question that is very difficult to solve）

C. 不协和的；刺耳的；不调和的；不一致的（making or involving a combination of sounds that is unpleasant to listen to）

D. 堕落的；颓废的；贪图享乐的（having or showing low standards, especially moral ones, and an interest only in pleasure and enjoyment rather than serious things）

句子大意：自骑马人把鞭子甩得啪啪响而让这位德国哲学家抓狂以来，人们就在想如果他当时生活在声音嘈杂的现代城市又会怎么样。

3 C

banality 平庸；平淡乏味；陈腐的事物；陈词滥调（the quality of being banal; things, remarks, etc. that are banal）

A. 选择（做什么事或做事方式）的自由（freedom to choose what you do or the way that you do it）

B. 海拔；高程（the height above sea level）

C. 陈词滥调；老生常谈（a comment or statement that has been made very often before and is therefore not interesting）

D. 独处；独居（the state of being alone, especially when you find this pleasant）

句子大意：他们对所有（鼓励人们）为了更加美好的明天而在今天做出牺牲的老生常谈都点头表示认可。

4 D

interminable 冗长的；没完没了的（lasting a very long time and therefore boring or annoying）

A. 断断续续的；间歇的（stopping and starting often over a period of time, but not regularly）

B. 不适当的；不恰当的（not pertinent; irrelevant）

C. 粗鲁无礼的；不敬的（rude and not showing respect for sb. who is older or more important）

D. 不停的；持续不断的（never stopping）

句子大意：《里斯本条约》获得广泛支持，倒不是因为它能带来什么实际利益，而是因为条约的失败也许会导致欧盟又一次陷入马拉松式的内部争论。

5 C

self-defeating 事与愿违的；适得其反的；弄巧成拙的（causing more problems and difficulties instead of solving them; not achieving what you wanted to achieve but having an opposite effect）

A. 只为个人打算的；一心谋私利的（interested only in gaining an advantage for yourself）

B. 谦逊的；不求闻达的（not wanting to attract attention to yourself or your abilities）

C. 产生相反效果的；事与愿违的（having the opposite effect to the one which was intended）

D. 起到平衡、制衡或抵消作用的（having an effect that is equal and opposite to something else）

句子大意：该教育政策可能适得其反，而且不切实际。

6 D

unobtrusive 不张扬的；不招摇的；不引人注目的（not attracting unnecessary attention）

A. 不具建设性的（not serving to promote improvement or advancement）

B. 似乎不真实的；不令人信服的（not seeming true or real; not making you believe that sth. is true）

C. 毫不怀疑的；无危险意识的；无戒备心的（feeling no suspicion; not aware of danger or of sth. bad）

D. 不引人注目的；不起眼的（not attracting attention; not easy to notice）

句子大意：在任何一部谋杀悬疑电影中，我们都应留心关注角落里那个无趣阴郁的男人（或女人）；安静、不起眼的人物有可能是致命的。

7 C

extraneous 没有直接联系的；无关的；外来的，外部的（not directly connected with the particular situation you are in or the subject you are dealing with）

A. 有关的；恰当的；相宜的（appropriate to a particular situation）

B. 无法分开的；分不开的（too closely linked to be separated）

C. 无关紧要的；不相关的（not important to or connected with a situation）

D. 不可阻挡的；无法改变的（that cannot be stopped or changed）

句子大意：欧洲新教和英语区已经远离世界其他文化，它们现在就像局外的文化半岛一样突兀。

8 A

bungle sth. 笨拙地做；失败 [to make or do (something) in a clumsy or unskillful way; to fail at sth.]

recrimination [rɪˌkrɪmɪˈneɪʃ(ə)n] 相互责难，反责，反控（a situation in which people are accusing or criticizing each other; a statement accusing or criticizing someone who has accused or criticized you）

A. ~ sth. up 笨拙地弄糟（某事物）（to spoil sth. by doing it badly）

常考同义词：fumble 笨手笨脚地做（某事）；笨拙地摸找（某物）（to use your hands in an awkward way when you are doing sth. or looking for sth.）

B. ~ at sth. （因吃惊而）不知所措，犹豫不决（to be slow to do or accept sth. because you are surprised or shocked by it）

C. ~ sb. 匆匆送走；推搡；赶（to push or send sb. somewhere quickly and not carefully）

~ sth. with sth. 额外免费提供（设备等）；（尤指出售计算机时）赠送软件（to supply extra equipment, especially software when selling a new computer, at no extra cost）

D. 打斗；闹事（to take part in a noisy and violent fight, usually in a public place）

句子大意：在贸然推出迷你预算吓到投资者后，英国首相被吞没在一阵指责声中。

9 C

acrimonious 尖刻的；讥讽的；激烈的（angry and full of strong bitter feelings and words）

A. 恶意的；居心不良的；故意使人苦恼的（behaving in an unkind way in order to hurt or upset sb.）

B. 有同情心的；表示怜悯的（feeling or showing sympathy for people who are suffering）

C. 充满激情的，（尤指）怒气冲冲的（showing strong emotions, especially anger）

D. 极度亢奋的，精神错乱的，语无伦次的（常由发烧引起）（in an excited state and not able to think or speak clearly, usually because of fever）

极度兴奋的；特别愉快的（extremely excited and happy）

句子大意：在政治会议中，敌对阵营之间的辩论往往是尖刻激烈的。

10 A

vitriol ['vɪtrɪəl] 尖刻无情的话（或批评）（very cruel and bitter comments or criticism）

A.（态度、言辞）尖刻，讥讽（angry bitter feelings or words）

B. 仇恨；愤怒；敌意；憎恶（a strong feeling of opposition, anger or hatred）

C. 和睦；友好（a friendly relationship between people or countries）

D. 敌意；敌对；仇恨（feelings of hatred towards sb.）

句子大意：所到之处，人们都会对他说些尖刻无情的话，摆出居高临下的架势。

11 B

clinical（分析等）冷静客观的（objective and devoid of emotion; coolly analytical）（例句：All this questioning is so analytical and clinical–it kills romance.）；冷漠无情的（expressing no emotion or feelings）（例句：She seems to have a very clinical attitude towards her children.）；简陋的；无装饰的（very plain; without decoration）（例句：We were going to paint our kitchen white, but we decided that would look too clinical.）

A. 十分准确、精准的 [extremely accurate; precise (surgical airstrikes against enemy compounds)]

B. 客观的；就事论事的；不带个人感情的（not influenced by personal feelings or opinions; considering only facts）

C. 批评的；批判性的；挑剔的（expressing disapproval of sb./sth. and saying what you think is bad about them）

D. 主观的（非客观的）（based on your own ideas or opinions rather than facts and therefore sometimes unfair）

句子大意：对这一问题冷静客观的分析取得了意想不到的结果。

12 A

preponderance 优势；多数；主体（If there is a preponderance of one type of people or things in a group, there are more of them than others; a superiority in weight, power, importance, or strength）

A. 数量占优；普遍（a superiority in numbers or amount; the quality of prevailing generally; being widespread）

B. 荒谬，愚蠢的行为（foolish behavior, absurdity, insanity, senselessness）

C. 重量，重要性（weight or significance）

D. 原产地；发源地；起源；出处（the place that sth. originally came from）

句子大意：东方口味的食物在数量上似乎占优势，因为很多客人来自远东地区，这一点也就可以理解了。

13 B

injunction（法院的）强制令，禁制令（an official order given by a court which demands that sth. must or must not be done）

A.（引起某种结果的事物等的）结合，同时发生（a combination of events, etc., that causes a particular result）

B.（法庭的）禁令（an official order from a court that orders you not to do sth.）

常考同义词：restraining order (against sb.) 限制令（an official order given by a judge which demands that sth. must or must not be done）

C. 十字路口；交点（a place where two or more roads, lines, etc. meet or cross each other）

D. ['ædʒʌŋkt] 附属物；附件（a thing that is added or attached to sth. larger or more important）

句子大意：法院将于周五就该禁令举行另一场听证会。

14 A

fudge sth. or fudge on sth. 含糊其词；回避（to avoid giving clear and accurate information, or a clear answer）

A. ~ sth.（尤指不诚实地）逃避（to avoid doing sth., especially in a dishonest way）

B.（作不及物动词使用，常见表达为 hedge on the issue）避免正面回答；不直接许诺；拐弯抹角（to avoid giving a direct answer to a question or promising to support a particular idea, etc.）

C. 笨嘴拙舌地说话；支支吾吾地说（to have difficulty speaking clearly or finding the right words to say）

D. 不知所措；支吾（to struggle to know what to say or do or how to continue with sth.）

困难重重（to experience difficulties and be likely to fail）

句子大意：政府通过拒绝提供确切数字来回避这一问题。

15 B

pugnacious 爱争吵的；粗暴的；好斗的；寻衅的（tending to argue or be bad-tempered; slightly aggressive）（本句句意突出的是"好斗性"而非"易怒的、脾气不好的"）

petulant 闹脾气的；爱耍性子的；赌气的；任性的（bad-tempered and unreasonable, especially because you cannot do or have what you want）

A. ['pɔɪnjənt] 让人深感痛苦、遗憾的；深刻的；辛辣贴切的（causing a sharp sense of sadness, pity, or regret; particularly penetrating and effective or relevant）

B. 爱争执的；好斗的；爱滋事的（having a strong desire to argue or fight with other people）

C. 爱生气的；易怒的；脾气坏的（easily annoyed by unimportant things; bad-tempered）

D. 脾气乖戾的；易怒的（bad-tempered and unpleasant）

句子大意：该国将有一位新总统产生，但任性好斗的现任总统无意告别权力。

16 C

bankroll sb./sth. 资助；提供资金给（to support sb./sth. by giving money）

A. ~ sth. 趁机利用……赚钱 [to exploit a situation in order to get personal benefit, especially money; to take advantage of (something) in order to make money]

B. ~ sth. 利用……以获得优势或好处（to use an event or a situation to help you to achieve something or to get an advantage）

C. ~ sth. or sb. 为某事或某人提供必要的资金（to furnish with necessary funds）

D. 指望；依赖；依靠 [to depend on something happening or on someone doing something; to rely on a future occurrence (even though it might not happen)]

该词组使用语境示例如下：

*Can I bank on your support?

*I wouldn't bank on him being there.

*"Do you think she'll come?" "I wouldn't bank on it."

*I'd banked on getting a pay rise this year.

句子大意：卡布贾曾是卢旺达最富有的人之一，被指控在种族屠杀中为胡图族极端分子提供资金支持。

17 A

ignominious [ˌɪɡnəˈmɪniəs] 耻辱的；可耻的；不光彩的（that makes, or should make, you feel ashamed）

A. 可耻的；丢脸的（that should make you feel ashamed）

B. 虚假的；假装的（not genuine but intended to seem real）

C. 欺诈；诈财骗局（a clever and dishonest plan for making money）

D. 浮沫；浮垢；浮渣（a layer of bubbles or an unpleasant substance that forms on the surface of a liquid）

（骂人的话）渣滓，败类（an insulting word for people that you strongly disapprove of）

句子大意：他们或许会认为，昨天，雷曼兄弟的大厦轰然倒塌，今天，国际货币基金组织的总裁就会以一种不光彩且震惊世人的方式屈服。

18 A

largesse[lɑː(r)ˈdʒes]（复数：largesses）慷慨解囊；施舍；（给穷人的）钱，赠款（the act or quality of being generous with money; money that you give to people who have less than you）

A. [mjuːˈnɪfɪsəns] 慷慨 generosity（常使用其形容词形式 munificent，指人，如：a munificent benefactor 慷慨的捐款人、施主；指物，如：a munificent gift 一件颇显大方的礼物）

B. ['æmpɑːs] 僵局；绝境（a difficult situation in which no progress can be made because the people involved cannot agree what to do）

C. [deɪ'mɑːʃ] 行动方针；外交照会、抗议或交涉（a course of action; a petition or protest presented through diplomatic channels）

D. 巨大；重大；重要性（the great size or importance of sth.; the degree to which sth. is large or important）

句子大意：仍然有人抱有理所应得和懒惰的思想，尤其是那些习惯了从国家的慷慨中获益的人。

19 B

discredit sb./sth. 败坏……的名声；使丧失信誉；使丢脸（to make people stop respecting sb./sth.）

discredit sth. 使不相信；使怀疑；使不可置信（to make people stop believing that sth. is true; to make sth. appear unlikely to be true）

A. 使丢脸；使蒙受耻辱（to behave badly in a way that makes you or other people feel ashamed）

使名誉扫地；使失势；使失去地位（to lose the respect of people, usually so that you lose a position of power）

B. ~ sth. 批判；驳斥；揭穿……的真相（to show that an idea, a belief, etc. is false; to show that sth. is not as good as people think it is）

C. 不予考虑；摒弃；对……不屑一提（to decide that sb./sth. is not important and not worth thinking or talking about）

D. ~ sth. 定……的界限；限定；界定（to decide what the limits of sth. are）

句子大意：戳穿谣言并纠正错误信息的有效策略是什么？

20 B

effusive 感情过分流露的；太动感情的；奔放的（showing much or too much emotion）

A. [vəʊ'sɪfərəs] 大声疾呼的；喧嚣的；大叫大嚷的（expressing your opinions or feelings in a loud and confident way）

B. 充满自信的；精力充沛的；热情洋溢的（full of confidence, energy and good humour; overflowing with enthusiasm or excitement）

常考同义词：exuberant 精力充沛的；热情洋溢的；兴高采烈的（full of energy, excitement and happiness）

C. ['lʌʃəs] 美味的；甘美的；可口的（having a strong pleasant taste）

柔软的；柔和的；绚丽的；悦耳的（soft and deep or heavy in a way that is pleasing to feel, look at or hear）

D. 汁多味美的（containing a lot of juice and tasting good）

肉质的；多汁的（having leaves and stems that are thick and contain a lot of water）

句子大意：除了最热情洋溢的赞美，对该活动的所有情绪都必须克制——因此，桥梁上、广告牌上、18米高的花篮装饰上满是宣传标语。

Practice 9

1 A

take away from 削弱、减损（价值、积极影响等）（to reduce the positive effect or success of something）

straggly 蔓生的；杂乱地蔓延的（growing or hanging in a way that does not look tidy or attractive）

 A. ~ sb./sth. (from sth.) 降低，减损（价值、名誉等）（to reduce the quality, value, or importance of something by taking something away from it）

 B. 转移（注意力）；分散（思想）；使分心（to take sb.'s attention away from what they are trying to do）

 C. ~ sth. from... （从总量中）扣除，减去……（to take away money, points, etc. from a total amount）

 D. ~ sb./sth. 败坏……的名声；使丧失信誉；使丢脸（to make people stop respecting sb./sth.）

句子大意：她头发凌乱，让她本来清秀的外表减分了。

2 A

mendacity [menˈdæsəti] 撒谎；捏造；说瞎话（the act of not telling the truth）

deplorable 糟透的；令人震惊的；令人愤慨的（very bad and unacceptable, often in a way that shocks people）

 A. [ˈsʌbtə(r)ˌfjuːdʒ]（通常指欺骗性）秘密手段；诡计（a secret, usually dishonest, way of behaving）

 B. 离心机（a machine with a part that spins around to separate substances, for example liquids from solids, by forcing the heavier substance to the outer edge）

 C. 庇护；避难（shelter or protection from danger, trouble, etc.）

 D. [ˈdeljuːdʒ] 暴雨；大雨；洪水（a sudden very heavy fall of rain）

  涌现的事物，蜂拥而至的事物（a large number of things that happen or arrive at the same time）

句子大意：你需要克服这种糟糕透顶的说谎的恶习，否则不管你说什么都不会有人信了。

3 B

import 重要性（importance）

[sing] the ~ (of sth.) 意思；含意（the meaning of sth., especially when it is not immediately clear）

 A. ~ sb. or sth. （通常见于科幻作品）（被）远距离传送 [(usually in science fiction) to move sb./sth. immediately from one place to another a distance away, using special equipment; to be moved in this way]

 B. 重要性；重要；重大（the quality of being important）

 C. （旧时的）流放 [(in the past) the act of sending criminals to a place that is far away as a form of punishment]（例句：In the past, British convicts could be sentenced to transportation to Australia. 过去，英国的犯人可被判处流放至澳大利亚。）

 D. 优势；优越的地位（the variant of a point of vantage）

句子大意：这部电影既有历史意义又有艺术价值，值得一看。

4 A

plaintive（声音）悲伤的，哀怨的（sounding sad, especially in a weak complaining way）

A. [ˌmelən'kɑlɪk] 忧郁的；忧郁症的（feeling or expressing sadness, especially when the sadness is like an illness）

   常考同义词：dejected 沮丧的；情绪低落的；垂头丧气的（unhappy and disappointed）

B. 重复乏味的（saying or doing the same thing many times, so that it becomes boring）

C. 坦率的；坦诚的；直言不讳的（saying what you think openly and honestly; not hiding your thoughts）

   （照片）偷拍的（a candid photograph is one that is taken without the person in it knowing that they are being photographed）

D. 冷酷无情的；无同情心的；冷漠的（not caring about other people's feelings or suffering）

句子大意： 他为其现行的政策致歉时几乎透着悲伤哀怨的语气。

5 A

stricture 通常用复数形式：strictures (on sb./sth.) 严厉批评（a severe criticism, especially of sb.'s behaviour; strictures against/on sth.）；限制；约束；束缚（a severe moral or physical limit）

A. 限制；限定；约束（a thing that limits or restricts sth., or your freedom to do sth.）

B. ['stætʃə(r)] 声望；名望（the importance and respect that a person has because of their ability and achievements）

C.（某宗教的）圣典，经文，经典（the holy books of a particular religion）

D. ['kærɪkətʃʊə(r)] 人物漫画（a funny drawing or picture of sb. that exaggerates some of their features）

   夸张的描述（a description of a person or thing that makes them seem ridiculous by exaggerating some of their characteristics）

句子大意： 如果当初他们厉行自己宣扬的道德约束的话，他们如今实施的严打行动或许能让人们更容易接受一些。

6 C

unfazed 未受干扰的；不担忧的；泰然自若的（not worried or surprised by sth. unexpected that happens）

legal jeopardy 在刑事审判中可能被发现有罪并被判刑的风险

A. 公正的；不偏不倚的；无偏见的（fair and not influenced by your own or sb. else's opinions, desires, etc.）

B. 无节制的；奔放的；极端的（not controlled and therefore extreme）

C. 平静的；镇定的；沉着的（calm）

D. 野性的；未驯服的；未受抑制的；未调教的（allowed to remain in a wild state; not changed, controlled or influenced by anyone; not tamed）

句子大意： 在审判过程中被定罪和判刑的风险对于史密斯先生而言并不陌生，因此，他看上去泰然自若，并不怎么担心。

7 A

parlous ['pɑːləs] 恶劣的；极不确定的；危险的（very bad and very uncertain; dangerous）

A. 不确定的；不保险的；危险的（not safe or certain; dangerous）

B. 闹脾气的；爱耍性子的；赌气的；任性的（bad-tempered and unreasonable, especially because you cannot do or have what you want）

C. 荒唐的；极不合情理的（completely unreasonable, especially in a way that is shocking or annoying）

D. 慢条斯理的；沉闷乏味的（too slow and careful; serious and boring）

　缓慢的；笨拙的；笨重的（moving slowly and heavily; able to move only slowly）

句子大意： 现在已经暴露无遗的一点就是，如果没有亿万富翁金主的慷慨援助，切尔西球队按照现在的竞技状态是难以为继的，这体现出如果该项体育运动的财务状况糟糕透顶的话，那么几乎其他任何产业都会随之沉沦。

8 C

shambolic [ʃæm'bɒlɪk] 混乱的；没有次序的；乱七八糟的（lacking order or organization）

A. 虚假的；假装的（not genuine but intended to seem real）

B. ~ of sth. 使用象征的；作为象征的；象征性的（containing symbols, or being used as a symbol）

C. 无秩序的；无计划的；组织混乱的（with no particular order or plan; not organized well）

D. 倒运的；不幸的（not lucky; unfortunate）

句子大意： 从阿富汗混乱不堪地撤出一年之后，美国政府应该加大力度为其犯下的错误赎罪。

9 B

irritated at/by/with sth. 烦恼；恼怒（annoyed or angry）

A. v. ['ɪtəreɪt] 迭代（数学或计算过程，或一系列指令）（to repeat a mathematical or computing process or set of instructions again and again, each time applying it to the result of the previous stage）

B. adj. [aɪ'reɪt] 极其愤怒的；暴怒的（very angry）

C. n. ['aɪə(r)] 愤怒（anger）

D. n. [taɪ'reɪd] ~ against sb./sth.（批评或指责性的）长篇激烈讲话（a long angry speech criticizing sb./sth. or accusing sb. of sth.）

句子大意： 由于内阁席位分配对其构成阻力，这位前总理一怒之下发威，造成了巨大破坏。

10 B

massage ['mæsɑːʒ] 按摩；推拿；美化（事实），窜改（数据）（to change numbers or information in order to make a situation seem better than it really is）

常考同义表达： cook the books 篡改；杜撰；捏造（to change facts or figures dishonestly or illegally）

A. ~ sth. 揉捏，按摩，推拿（肌肉等）（to rub and squeeze muscles, etc. especially to relax them or to make them less painful）

B. ~ sth. 篡改；伪造（to change sth. in order to trick sb.）

C. ~ sth. 怀抱；怀有；心藏（to have a strong feeling or idea in your mind for a long time）

D. ~ sb. with sth. 帮忙；给……提供方便（to help sb. by doing what they want）

~ sth./yourself to sth. 顺应，适应（新情况）（to change your behaviour so that you can deal with a new situation better）

句子大意：我不知道他们是不是在美化数据，即使他们需要美化数据，最好的办法也应该是在正常时间范围内做完。

11 B

dither 犹豫不决；踌躇（to hesitate about what to do because you are unable to decide）

A.（代替某一词语以免重复）同样，也一样（used instead of a particular word or phrase, to avoid repeating it）

B. ['væsɪleɪt] 观点（或立场等）摇摆；动摇（to keep changing your opinion or thoughts about sth., especially in a way that annoys other people）

常考同义词：oscillate (between A and B)（情感或行为）摇摆，波动，变化（to keep changing from one extreme of feeling or behaviour to another, and back again）

C. ~ sth./sb. 摆脱；抛弃；丢弃（to get rid of sth./sb. because you no longer want or need it/them）

D. ~ sth. (to sth.) 拴（牲畜）（to tie an animal to a post so that it cannot move very far）

句子大意：如果世界三大经济体的政客们继续踌躇不决，将可能发生又一轮全球性经济衰退。

12 B

remit of sb./sth. or remit to do sth. 职权范围；控制范围；影响范围（the area of activity over which a particular person or group has authority, control or influence）

A. 许可证，特许证（尤指限期的）（an official document that gives sb. the right to do sth., especially for a limited period of time）

B. within/outside the purview of sth. 在（个人或组织等的）权限之内／之外；在（文件、法律等的）范围内／外 [within/outside the limits of what a person, an organization, etc. is responsible for; (not) dealt with by a document, law, etc.]

常考近义词：province 知识（或兴趣、职责）范围；领域（a person's particular area of knowledge, interest or responsibility）

C. 代理权；代表权（the authority that you give to sb. to do sth. for you, when you cannot do it yourself）

D. ['pri:ˌsɪŋkt] 步行商业区（a commercial area in a town where cars cannot go）

警区；分区警察局；派出所（a part of a city that has its own police station; the police station in this area）

句子大意：法官称，该人道主义组织在其地域职责范围之外运作，违反了相关法律要求。

13 C

convoluted 错综复杂的；晦涩难懂的（extremely complicated and difficult to follow）

名词形式：convolution 错综复杂的东西；晦涩费解的事（a thing that is very complicated and difficult to follow）

A. 合流的；汇合的（flowing together; blended into one）

B. 流入的；能流动的（flowing in or into）

C. 复杂的；详尽的；精心制作的（very complicated and detailed; carefully prepared and organized）

D. ~ sth. 使发生；实现（to make sth. happen）

句子大意：去年，新冠疫情引发了芯片短缺，这一复杂流程的脆弱性变得显而易见。

14 B

gibberish 胡说八道，无稽之谈；莫名其妙的话，令人费解的话（words that have no meaning or are impossible to understand）

A.（尤指许多人同时说话时）急促不清的话（fast speech that is difficult to understand, especially when a lot of people are talking at the same time）

B. 含混不清的话；胡言乱语（talking that is confused or silly and is difficult to understand）

C.（很可能持续不长的）好景，好运；泡沫（a good or lucky situation that is unlikely to last long）

D. 失礼；失态；失言（a mistake that a person makes in public or in a social situation, especially sth. embarrassing）

句子大意：他走出酒馆后，突然在人行道上开始大声喊着让人不知所云的醉话。

15 A

wriggle 扭动；蠕动；蜿蜒行进（an act of wriggling）

A.（轻微的）摆动，扭动，摇动，起伏（a small movement from side to side or up and down）
wiggle room = wriggle room，前者更为常见，意为"（为……留有）余地"

B. 咯咯笑；傻笑（a slight silly repeated laugh）

C.（海滨或河边的）卵石滩（a mass of small smooth stones on a beach or at the side of a river）
（诊所或律师事务所挂的）招牌（a board with a sign on it, in front of a doctor's or lawyer's office）；注意其复数形式 shingles：带状疱疹（a disease that affects the nerves and produces a band of painful spots on the skin）

D. 诈骗；骗取（a situation in which sb. uses dishonest or illegal methods in order to get money from a company, another person, etc.）

句子大意：他的表态为美联储在通胀居高不下时再一次大幅加息留有余地。

16 B

rambunctious [ræmˈbʌŋkʃəs] 难以控制或管教的（difficult to control or handle, unruly）；喧闹的（turbulently active and noisy）

A.（描述体育动作）迅速的，劲头十足的 [(describing actions in sport) done very fast or with great energy]
言辞激烈的；尖刻的（very critical）

B. 热闹的；充满活力的；活蹦乱跳的（noisy and full of life and energy）

C. 让人非常费解的（extremely confusing or difficult to understand）

D. 令人困惑的；使人糊涂的（making you feel confused because there are too many things to choose from or because sth. is difficult to understand）

句子大意：这次社交聚会变得喧闹不堪，场面失控。

17 C

tangential [tæn'dʒenʃəl]（= tangental）稍微沾边的；离题的；不相干的（having only a slight or indirect connection with sth.）

A. 紧密相关的；切题的（closely connected with the subject you are discussing or the situation you are thinking about）

~ (to sth./sb.) 有价值的；有意义的（having ideas that are valuable and useful to people in their lives and work）

B. 有形的；实际的；真实的（that can be clearly seen to exist）

C. 无关紧要的；不相关的（not important to or connected with a situation）

D. 难以形容（或理解）的；不易度量的（that exists but that is difficult to describe, understand or measure）

无形的（指不以实体存在的公司资产）（that does not exist as a physical thing but is still valuable to a company）

句子大意：这个环保组织通过破坏艺术品进行的抗议行为与封锁道路等以往更为传统的抗议活动相比给公众带来的不便没有那么直接，不过这种抗议行为让人感觉与气候问题更不沾边了。

18 B

anodyne ['ænəˌdaɪn] 不得罪人的；温和的（unlikely to cause disagreement or offend anyone; not expressing strong opinions）

A. 无味道的；淡而无味的（having almost no taste or flavour）

没有趣味的；枯燥乏味的（not interesting or exciting）

B. 中立的；持平的；无倾向性的（not supporting or helping either side in a disagreement, competition, etc.）

C.（液体、气体等）清澈的；清澄的；透明的；透光的 [(of a liquid, air, etc.) clear and transparent]

D. 阴险的，狡猾的，暗中为害的（something that is insidious is dangerous because it seems to be harmless or not important but in fact causes harm or damage）

句子大意：教育多元化是一个晦涩且具有争议的概念，这一有意含糊其辞的概念也是应对种族这一敏感话题的一种温和方式。

19 A

spurious ['spjʊəriəs] 虚假的；伪造的（false, although seeming to be genuine; outwardly similar or corresponding to something without having its genuine qualities）；建立在错误的观念（或思想方法）之上的；谬误的（based on false ideas or ways of thinking）

A. 假的；伪造的（pretending to be real or genuine）

B. 大而空的；又黑又深的；像洞穴的（very large and often empty and/or dark; like a cave）

C. [səˈleɪʃəs] 淫秽的；色情的（encouraging sexual desire or containing too much sexual detail）

D. 多孔的；透水的；透气的（having many small holes that allow water or air to pass through slowly）

   漏洞多的，能被渗透的（capable of being penetrated）

句子大意：支持关停这家工厂的观点中有些还算值得商榷，其他的则就纯属谬论了。

20 C

iconoclastic [aɪˌkɒnəˈklæstɪk] 批评传统信仰（或习俗思想）的（criticizing popular beliefs or established customs and ideas; attacking the beliefs, customs, and opinions that most people in a society accept）

A. 符号的；图标的；图符的；偶像的（acting as a sign or symbol of sth.）

B. 反语的；讽刺的（showing that you really mean the opposite of what you are saying; expressing irony）

C. 非正统的；非传统的；不正规的（different from what is usual or accepted; breaking with convention or tradition）

   常考同义词：nonconformist 不遵循传统规范的（different from the way that most people usually think or behave）

D. 铁定的；不容置疑的（so strong that it cannot be challenged or changed）

句子大意：他这种反传统的倾向会让他惹上麻烦。

Practice 10

1 A

obnoxious 极讨厌的；可憎的；令人作呕的（extremely unpleasant, especially in a way that offends people）

A. [ʌnˈpælətəb(ə)l] 令人不快的；难以接受的（unpleasant and not easy to accept）

   难吃的；不可口的（not pleasant to taste）

   常考同义词 1：unsavoury 讨厌的；无礼的；声名狼藉的；不道德的（unpleasant or offensive; not considered morally acceptable）

   常考同义词 2：revolting 令人作呕的；极其讨厌的（extremely unpleasant）

B. 夜行的；夜出的（active at night）

   夜间发生的（happening during the night）

C. 反叛的；叛逆的；桀骜不驯的（unwilling to obey rules or accept normal standards of behaviour, dress, etc.）

   叛乱的；造反的；反对权威的（opposed to the government of a country; opposed to those in authority within an organization）

D. 不可信任的；背叛的；奸诈的（that cannot be trusted; intending to harm you）

   有潜在危险的（dangerous, especially when seeming safe）

句子大意：一位客户前来缴纳高额取暖费，随手将数千便士的硬币直接倒在了柜台上，出纳员见此情景不由睁大了眼睛，客户这一让人反感的举动也是有意为之。

2 A

A. *adj.* 不顾；不加理会 [having or showing no regard; heedless; unmindful (often fol. by of)]

   adv. 对建议、警告、困难等不关心，不顾（without concern as to advice, warning, hardship, etc.）

B. ~ sth.（= in spite of sth.）即使；尽管（used to show that sth. happened or is true although sth. else might have happened to prevent it）

C. ~ of sth. 不顾、不考虑、不管……（despite a particular fact, situation, or quality）

D. 分别；各自；顺序为；依次为（in the same order as the people or things already mentioned）

句子大意： 警察设置了路障以阻止人们前往其墓地。当数千人不顾危险依然试图前往该公墓时，警方做出了暴力反应。

3 A

spoof sth. 滑稽地模仿（电影、电视节目等）（to copy a film/movie, television programme, etc. in an amusing way by exaggerating its main features; to make good-natured fun of）；*n.* 滑稽的模仿（a light-hearted imitation of someone or something）

A. *v.* ~ sb./sth. 滑稽地模仿；夸张地演绎（to copy the style of sb./sth. in an exaggerated way, especially in order to make people laugh）

   n. 滑稽模仿作品（文章、音乐作品或表演等的滑稽模仿）（a piece of writing, music, acting, etc. that deliberately copies the style of sb./sth. in order to be amusing）

B. ~ sb./sth. 吓；惊吓；受惊（to frighten a person or an animal; to become frightened）

C. ~ about sth. 杂乱无章地瞎扯（to speak or write at length and with many digressions）

D. 痛饮狂欢；狂饮作乐（to spend time drinking alcohol, laughing and enjoying yourself in a noisy way with other people）

句子大意： 这个学生因为滑稽地模仿老师而成为网红。

4 C

stutter 突突地吃力行驶（或艰难启动、艰难运转）（to move or start with difficulty, making short sharp noises or movements）

A. 闷闷不乐；自怨自艾（to spend your time doing nothing and feeling sorry for yourself; to be full of self-pity or sulky unhappiness and lose interest in everything else）

B. ~ (sth.)（鸟或昆虫）拍（翅），振（翅），鼓（翼）（When a bird or an insect flutters its wings, or its wings flutter, the wings move lightly and quickly up and down.）

C. 衰弱；衰退；衰落（to become weaker or less effective）

   蹒跚；摇晃；犹豫；畏缩（to walk or behave in a way that shows that you are not confident）

D.（成功地）对付，处理（to deal successfully with sth. difficult）

句子大意： 现在全球经济运行艰难，孟加拉国的经济也将如此。

5 B

inexorable 不可阻挡的；无法改变的（that cannot be stopped or changed）；不为所动的，冷酷无情的（not capable of being persuaded by entreaty; relentless）

A. 无法分开的；分不开的（too closely linked to be separated）

B. 不可避免的；不能防止的（that you cannot avoid or prevent）

C. 特别整洁的（extremely clean and tidy）

   无误的；无过失的（containing no mistakes）

D. 难以理解的；高深莫测的（too strange or difficult to be understood）

句子大意： 也是在这一时期，犯罪案件数量开始呈现势不可当的上升势头，让警方面临巨大的压力。

6 A

loyalty to/towards sb./sth. 忠诚；忠实；忠心耿耿（the quality of being faithful in your support of sb./sth.）

proffer sth. to sb. or proffer sb. sth. 端着（给……）；递上（to offer sth. to sb., by holding it out to them）；提出，提供（建议、解释等）（to offer sth. such as advice or an explanation）

A. （尤指对君主的）效忠宣誓（a promise to be loyal to sb., especially a king or queen）

B. 不动产；房产（real estate）

C. ~ of/for (doing) sth. 才能；能力（a particular ability for doing sth.）

D. 虚弱；衰弱（weakness and poor health）

   （性格或道德上的）弱点，懦弱，软弱（weakness in a person's character or moral standards）

句子大意： 在关键的参议院和州长竞选中，这位前总统基于忠诚度而非候选人的胜任资格提供支持。

7 A

gratuitous 免费的（complimentary; not costing or charging anything）；无正当理由（或目的）的；无谓的（done without any good reason or purpose and often having harmful effects）

A. 不合理的；不必要的；无正当理由的；不适当的（not reasonable or necessary; not appropriate）

   常考同义词：uncalled-for、unjustified

B. 有益健康的（good for your health）

   有道德的；有良好道德影响的（morally good; having a good moral influence）

C. [ˈɡrætɪs] 免费的；无偿的（done or given without having to be paid for）

D. [ˌɡlædiəˈtɔːriəl] 格斗（者）的；争论（者）的（like a gladiator, or relating to gladiators）

句子大意： 很多观众抱怨说影片中有太多无谓的色情和暴力镜头。

8 C

inexpedient 不适宜的；不明智的；不适当的（not fair or right）

常考反义词：expedient *n.* 权宜之计；应急办法（an action that is useful or necessary for a particular purpose, but not always fair or right）；*adj.* 得当的；可取的；权宜之计的（useful or necessary for a particular purpose, but not always fair or right）

A. [ˌekspəˈdɪʃəs] 迅速而有效的；迅速完成的（that works well without wasting time, money, etc.）

B. 可牺牲的；可消耗的；可毁灭的（If you consider people or things to be expendable, you think that you can get rid of them when they are no longer needed, or think it is acceptable if they are killed or destroyed.）

C. ~ (for sb.) (to do sth.) 不明智；不可取（not sensible or wise; that you would advise against）

常考同义词：injudicious 不明智的；不当的（not sensible or wise; not appropriate in a particular situation）

D. 不可或缺的；必不可少的（too important to be without）

句子大意：事实证明，从营养角度而言，这是一个值得怀疑的不适当的减肥方式。

9 C

invoke sb./sth. 提及，援引（某人、某理论、实例等作为支持）（to mention a person, a theory, an example, etc. to support your opinions or ideas, or as a reason for sth.）

invoke sth. 使产生，唤起，引起（感情或想象）（to make sb. have a particular feeling or imagine a particular scene）

A. ~ sth. 重复，附和（想法或看法）（to repeat an idea or opinion because you agree with it; echo sth.）；（尤因感到意外而）重复……的话，模仿（to repeat what sb. else has just said, especially because you find it surprising）

~ sth. 引起，唤起（感情、记忆或形象）（to bring a feeling, a memory or an image into your mind）（选择该词义时 invoke 是同义词）

B. ~ sb. (into sth./into doing sth.) or ~ sb. to do sth. 挑衅；激怒；刺激（to say or do sth. that you know will annoy sb. so that they react in an angry way）

C. ~ sth. (as sth.) 提及（原因）；举出（示例）（to mention sth. as a reason or an example, or in order to support what you are saying）

~ sth. 引用；引述；援引（to speak or write the exact words from a book, an author, etc.）

D. 煽动；鼓动（to encourage sb. to do sth. violent, illegal or unpleasant, especially by making them angry or excited）

句子大意：在对英国议会所做的演讲中，他援引了温斯顿·丘吉尔的话，而在对德国联邦议院所做的演讲中，他则提及了柏林墙。

10 D

quotidian [kwoʊˈtɪdiən] 寻常的；普通的；司空见惯的（ordinary; typical of what happens every day）

A. 商（除法所得的结果）（a number which is the result when one number is divided by another）

B. 表达方式地道的；符合（某一）语言习惯的（containing expressions that are natural to a native speaker of a language）

C. 监护人；看守人；保管人（a person who takes responsibility for taking care of or protecting sth.）

（建筑物的）管理员，看管人，看门人（a person whose job is to take care of a building such as a school or a block of flats or an apartment building）

D. 平凡的；普通的；普遍的（done very often, or existing in many places, and therefore not unusual）

句子大意： 人们在寻常现实中很难想象他的成长环境。

11 D

dawdle 拖延；磨蹭；游荡（to take a long time to do sth. or go somewhere）；闲站着；闲荡；徘徊（to stand or wait somewhere especially with no obvious reason）

flurry 一阵忙乱（或激动、兴奋等）（an occasion when there is a lot of activity, interest, excitement, etc. within a short period of time）

A. （逐渐）减少，变小，缩小（to become gradually less or smaller）

B. （尤指厌烦或心不在焉时）乱涂，胡写乱画（to draw lines, shapes, etc., especially when you are bored or thinking about sth. else）

C. 拖脏（衣服等）；拖泥溅水地走 [to wet and soil (as a garment) by dragging in mire]

D. 蹉跎（时光）；延误；拖拉（to do sth. too slowly; to take too much time making a decision）

句子大意： 在 2017 年首次币发行（ICOs）热潮正酣之际，其他的加密货币交易所都拖拖拉拉、行动迟缓，而币安则抓紧时间行动起来，让短时间内冒出的一批新加密货币上市发行。

12 C

obliterate sth. 毁掉；覆盖；清除（to remove all signs of sth., either by destroying or covering it completely）

A. （只有名词形式）被遗忘；被忘却；湮没（the state in which sb./sth. has been forgotten and is no longer famous or important）

被摧毁；被毁灭；被夷平（a state in which sth. has been completely destroyed）

B. 押头韵；用头韵体作诗；使成头韵体（to begin consecutive or neighboring words with the same consonant sound, or contain such sound matches）

C. 排除；清除；消除（to remove or get rid of sth./sb.）

D. [dɪˈlɪnieɪt] ~ sth. （详细地）描述，描画，解释（to describe, draw or explain sth. in detail）

句子大意： 加密货币领域如果彻底崩盘，他的财富大概率也会灰飞烟灭，因为他的大部分财富是以数字资产的方式持有。

13 A

overwhelm sb. 压垮；使应接不暇（to be so bad or so great that a person cannot deal with it; to give too much of a thing to a person）

A. 使不堪承受；使疲于应对；使应接不暇（to make sb. have more of sth. than they can deal with）

B. 成群地来回移动（to move around in a large group）

成群地飞来飞去（to move around together in a large group, looking for a place to live）

常用搭配：swarm with sb. or sth./be swarming with sb. or sth.

C. 热得难受（to be very hot in a way that makes you feel uncomfortable）

D. ~ sth. 弄脏；留下污迹（to make a dirty mark on a surface）

句子大意：随着新冠疫情旅行限制的取消，（游客的涌入）已经让许多旅游景点不堪重负了。

14 A

lurid ['ljʊərɪd]（故意地）骇人听闻的，令人毛骨悚然的（shocking and violent in a way that is deliberate）

A. 哗众取宠的；耸人听闻的（trying to get your interest by presenting facts or events as worse or more shocking than they really are）

B. 喜欢感官享受的；耽于肉欲的（suggesting an interest in physical pleasure, especially sexual pleasure）

C. ~ (about sth.) 充满信心的；乐观的（cheerful and confident about the future）

D. 表达清楚的；易懂的（clearly expressed; easy to understand）

（尤指生病期间或病愈后，糊涂状态中或过后）头脑清晰的，清醒的（able to think clearly, especially during or after a period of illness or confusion）

句子大意：他们依然在向人们灌输对这种病毒的恐惧，对该国的大量死亡病例进行耸人听闻的报道。

15 A

surmise sth. or surmise that... 推测；猜测（to guess or suppose sth. using the evidence you have, without definitely knowing）

A. 认为；猜想；推断；理解（to believe or understand that sth. is true because of information or evidence you have）

B. ~ about/over sth. or ~ that... 苦恼；烦躁；焦虑不安（to be worried or unhappy and not able to relax）

C. ~ that... 想；希望；期望（to hope and expect that sth. is true）

D. 明确肯定；断言（to state clearly and firmly that sth. is true）

句子大意：从历史上看，女性受教育程度不及男性，专家推测这可能是过去女性患上阿尔茨海默病的风险增加的原因。

16 A

placate [plə'keɪt] ~ sb. 安抚；平息（怒气）（to make sb. feel less angry about sth.）

A. ~ sb. 使平静；抚慰（to make sb. feel less angry or upset）

常考同义词：pacify sb. 使平静；平息；抚慰（to make sb. who is angry or upset become calm and quiet）；pacify sth. 平息战争；使实现和平（to bring peace to an area where there is fighting or a war）

B. ~ sth. 使失去法律效力；废止（to make sth. such as an agreement or order lose its legal force）

C. ~ sth. 设路障防护；阻挡（to defend or block sth. by building a barricade）

D. 倾泻；流注（to flow downwards in large amounts）

句子大意：为了安抚抗议者，他同意 2022 年卸任。

17 A

take sb. to task (for sth.) 因某人犯错而对其严厉批评或指责（reprimand or criticize someone severely for a fault or mistake; to scold, reprimand, lecture, or hold one accountable for some wrong or error they committed.）

patriarchal [ˌpeɪtri'ɑː(r)k(ə)l] 男人统治的；男性主宰的（ruled or controlled by men; giving power and importance only to men）；族长的；家长的（connected with a patriarch）

pomposity [pɒm'pɒsɪti] 自大；夸大；傲慢；自负（an excessive sense of self-importance, usually displayed through exaggerated seriousness or stateliness in speech and manner）

A. 傲慢（unfriendly behaviour that shows you consider yourself better than other people）

B. [prə'pensəti]（行为方面的）倾向；习性（a tendency to a particular kind of behaviour）

C. [ɪ'pɪfəni] 顿悟（a moment when you suddenly realize or understand something important）

D. [ˌserən'dɪpəti] 机缘巧合，缘分天定（the fact of sth. interesting or pleasant happening by chance）

句子大意：这位电影导演此前曾厉声斥责劳伦斯所持的男性主宰一切的傲慢态度。

18 B

austere [ɔː'stɪə(r)] 朴素的；简陋的；无华饰的（simple and plain; without any decorations）；严肃的；严厉的（strict and serious in appearance and behaviour）；苦行的；禁欲的（allowing nothing that gives pleasure; not comfortable）

A. ['ɔːgə(r)] 预示；占卜；预言（to be a sign that sth. will be successful or not successful in the future）

B. [ɔː'gʌst] 威严的；庄严的（old, serious, and respected）

C. ~ sth. 增加；提高；扩大（to increase the amount, value, size, etc. of sth.）

D. ['ækjʊmən] 精明；敏锐（the ability to understand and decide things quickly and well）

句子大意：他个子高高的，外表冷峻严肃，令人生畏。

19 A

irk sb. (to do sth.) or it irks sb. that... 使烦恼；激怒（to annoy or irritate sb.）

showboating ['ʃəʊˌbəʊtɪŋ] 卖弄；炫耀（behavior that is intended to make people notice and admire you）

A. ~ sb. or it riles sb. that... 惹恼；激怒（to annoy sb. or make them angry）

B. 挫败；制止（非法活动等）（to stop sth. from happening, especially sth. illegal; to prevent sb. from doing sth.）

C.（只有名词形式）愤怒；憎恨（anger or hatred）

D. ~ sb. (into doing sth.) 哄骗（某人做某事）；诱骗（to trick sb. into doing sth., especially by being nice to them）

~ sb. 吸引（某人）；使感兴趣（to attract or interest sb.）

句子大意：美国作出的承诺让该国大为光火，因此，该国可能会寻找办法来表达对哈里斯炫耀行为的不满。

245

20 C

consummate ['kɒnsə,meɪt] 技艺高超的；完美的（extremely skilled; perfect）

tinge sth. (with sth.)（轻微地）给……着色（to add a small amount of colour to sth.）；使略带……感情（或性质）（to add a small amount of a particular emotion or quality to sth.）

showman 善于引起公众注意的人；喜欢出风头的人（a person who does things in an entertaining way and is good at getting people's attention）

A. 平凡的；普通的；普遍的（done very often, or existing in many places, and therefore not unusual）

B. [kə'menʃərət] ~ with sth.（在大小、重要性、质量等方面）相称的，相当的（matching sth. in size, importance, quality, etc.）

C.（尤指待人接物）精明的，八面玲珑的，左右逢源的，长袖善舞的（skilful and clever, especially in dealing with people）

D. [prə'fjuːs] 大量的；众多的；丰富的（produced in large amounts）

句子大意：斯皮尔伯格对自己战后居住在郊区的犹太家庭进行了详尽而又充满情感和智慧的描述，不过，他避开了婴儿潮时代传记中常见的那种泛黄的恋旧情怀。这部电影风趣又睿智，这位电影创作者技艺高超，善于博取公众眼球，现如今的他开始放慢脚步反思过往。

Practice 11

1 C

deign [deɪn] 降低身份；屈尊做某事（to condescend to do something; to do something that one considers below one's status）

A. ~ sth. or ~ to do sth. 假装，佯装（有某种感觉或生病、疲倦等）（to pretend that you have a particular feeling or that you are ill/sick, tired, etc.）

B. ~ over sb./sth. 成为最佳；成为……中最重要的（to be the best or most important in a particular situation or area of skill）

C. ~ to do sth. 屈尊；俯就（to do sth. that you think it is below your social or professional position to do）

~ to sb.（对某人）表现出优越感（to behave towards sb. as though you are more important and more intelligent than they are）

D. ~ sb./sth. 诋毁；诽谤；贬低（to criticize sb./sth. unfairly; to say sb./sth. does not have any value or is not important）

句子大意：现在比利已经出名了，我觉得他可能都不会降低身份打电话给自己的母亲。

2 A

sag（物价等）下跌；萎顿，消衰（to become weaker or fewer）

A. 疲乏；变弱；热情衰减（to become tired, weaker or less enthusiastic）

B. ~ sb./sth. as sth. 把……称作；给……起诨名（to give sb./sth. a name that describes what they are or do）

~ along 跟随；尾随（to accompany or follow somebody, often when your presence is unwanted）

C. ~ behind sb./sth. or ~ behind 缓慢移动；发展缓慢；滞后；落后于（to move or develop slowly or more slowly than other people, organizations, etc.）

D. ~ sb./sth. 压制……的言论自由；使缄默（to prevent sb. from speaking freely or expressing their opinion）

句子大意： 石油输出国组织与包括俄罗斯在内的盟国就通过减少石油产量来提振不断下滑的油价达成共识。

3 D

strident ['straɪd(ə)nt] 刺耳的（having a loud, rough and unpleasant sound）；措辞强硬的；咄咄逼人的，态度坚定的（aggressive and determined）

A. 严格的；严厉的（very strict and that must be obeyed）

紧缩的；短缺的；银根紧的（difficult and very strictly controlled because there is not much money）

B. 刺耳的；尖厉的（sounding loud and rough）

C. 热闹的；充满活力的；活蹦乱跳的（noisy and full of life and energy）

D. 尽心尽力的；坚信；坚定的（willing to work hard and give your time and energy to sth.; believing strongly in sth.）

句子大意： 尽管环保组织依然持乐观态度，但是就连那些最坚定支持改变规则的人也承认，此次能源危机已经让政局充满挑战。

4 A

gripe about sb./sth. 抱怨；发牢骚（to complain about sb./sth. in an annoying way）

A. ~ about sb./sth. 抱怨；发牢骚（to complain about sb./sth. in a way that other people find annoying）

常考同义词：grumble 咕哝；嘟囔；发牢骚（to complain about sb./sth. in a bad-tempered way）

B. 使活跃起来；使产生兴趣（to make sb. want to start doing sth. when they were not active or interested in doing it）

~ sth. 激起（某种情感）（to make sb. feel a particular emotion）

~ sb. 激怒；使激动（to make sb. angry, excited or full of emotion）

C. ~ at sb./sth. 狙击；打冷枪（to shoot at sb. from a hiding place, usually from a distance）

冷言冷语地指摘；抨击（to criticize sb. in an unpleasant way）

D. 痛饮狂欢；狂饮作乐（to spend time drinking alcohol, laughing and enjoying yourself in a noisy way with other people）

句子大意： 人们对经济状况、利率和房价抱怨连连。

5 A

balm 镇痛软膏；护肤膏；令人感到安慰（或镇定）的事物（something that makes you feel calm or relaxed）

A. [sælv] 药膏，软膏；缓和物，安慰物（an ointment for wounds, sores, etc; anything that heals or soothes）

B.（危险、灾难、损失等的）避免方式，解救途径（a way of protecting sb. from danger, disaster, loss, etc.）

C. [sɪˈdɪʃ(ə)n] 煽动叛乱的言论（或行动）（the use of words or actions that are intended to encourage people to oppose a government）

D. [sɪˈdeɪʃ(ə)n] 药物镇静；镇静状态（专指使用药物镇静）（the use of drugs to make someone calmer, or to make them sleep）

句子大意：最近几周，该国经历了抗议、食品和油价飙升以及总理更迭，即将举行的这些赛事将会为人们带来快乐以及该国迫切需要的经济"镇痛剂"。

6 C

conspicuous 易见的；明显的；惹人注意的（easy to see or notice; likely to attract attention）

A. 显而易见；明白易懂；显然（easy to see or understand）

  貌似的；表面上的；未必真实的（that seems to be real or true but may not be）

B. 清楚的；显而易见的；显然的（clear; easily seen）

C. 炫耀的；卖弄的（different, confident and exciting in a way that attracts attention）

D. 清楚明白的；易于理解的（clear and easy to understand）

  直截了当的；不隐晦的；不含糊的（said, done or shown in an open or direct way, so that you have no doubt about what is happening）

句子大意：有一段时间老一辈人通常将大多数80后或90后看作是被宠坏的一代，认为他们经常沉迷于社交网络、炫耀式消费和高度自我主义行为中。

7 C

spike sth. (with sth.) 在……中偷偷掺入（烈酒、毒药或毒品）（to add alcohol, poison or a drug to sb.'s drink or food without them knowing）

A. ~ sth. 编造；捏造（to invent false information in order to trick people）

  ~ sth. 制造；装配；组装（to make or produce goods, equipment, etc. from various different materials）

B. ~ sth. 挨户销售；巡回销售（to try to sell goods by going from house to house or from place to place）

  兜售，宣传，传播（思想、消息）（to spread an idea or story in order to get people to accept it）

C. ~ sb./yourself (with sth.) 毒死；毒害（to harm or kill a person or an animal by giving them poison）

  ~ sth. 下毒；在……中放毒（to put poison in or on sth.）

  ~ sth. 毒化；败坏；使恶化（to have a bad effect on sth.）

D. ~ sth. 预备（饭菜）；做（饭）（to make food ready to be eaten）

  ~ sth. (from sth.) 调制，配制（药品等）（to make a medicine or chemical substance, for example by mixing other substances together）

句子大意：据称有8名俄军士兵因吃了一位看起来很友好的老太太下过毒的馅饼而死亡。

8 A

demystify sth. 使明白易懂；深入浅出地解释（to make sth. easier to understand and less complicated by explaining it in a clear and simple way）

A. (= give something a human face) 通过具象化的阐述让普通人理解或明白（to make an important event or principle understandable to ordinary people by directing their attention to the way it affects a particular person）

　　B. 对……做正面倾向性解释，朝着好的方向说，用言辞美化某种情况（to report or relay information to someone else in a way that makes their interpretation or understanding of it more palatable, acceptable, or favorable; make your own version of something）

　　C. 重视；强调；高度评价（to place a high value on somebody or something）

　　D. 泼冷水；扫……的兴；抑制 [to make (something) less strong, active, or exciting]

句子大意：数十年来，尼克·凯夫以其饱满、低沉的嗓音和让人百听不厌的歌曲收获了大量歌迷。最近他开始深入浅出地解释他的创作过程。

9　A

sporadic 偶尔发生的；间或出现的；阵发性的；断断续续的（happening only occasionally or at intervals that are not regular）

　　A. [ˌepɪˈsɒdɪk] 偶尔发生的；不定期的（happening occasionally and not at regular intervals）

　　B. 只有内行才懂的；难领略的（likely to be understood or enjoyed by only a few people with a special knowledge or interest）

　　C. 有弹性的；有弹力的（able to stretch and return to its original size and shape）
　　　灵活的；可改变的；可伸缩的（that can change or be changed）

　　D. 复杂的；详尽的；精心制作的（very complicated and detailed; carefully prepared and organized）

句子大意：女王正经历"偶发的行动不便问题"。

10　B

demonstrative [dɪˈmɒnstrətɪv] n. 指示代词；限定词　adj. 公开表露感情（尤指爱慕之情）的；感情外露的

　　A. 挚爱的；充满深情的；深情款款的（showing that you love or care about someone or something）

　　B. 激起感情的；有感染力的；激动人心的（causing people to feel strong emotions）
　　　情绪激动的；感情冲动的（showing strong emotions, sometimes in a way that other people think is unnecessary）

　　C. 假装的；做作的（not natural or sincere）

　　D. 激起感情的；有感染力的；激动人心的（arousing or able to arouse intense feeling）

注意：emotional 可以指人（an emotional person），但 emotive 只能指事物（an emotive speech/language），不能指人。在指事物时，emotive 和 emotional 也有区别：Emotive is used with regard to something that makes you have intense feelings rather than just having intense feelings. For example, an emotive conversation（有感染力的对话）will result in getting people's emotions riled up, while an emotional conversation（带着情绪进行的对话）is one in which people go into it with a lot of intense feelings already.

句子大意：在辩论中，他经常会感情外露，挥舞着胳膊以示强调。

11 A

plethora 过多；过量；过剩（an amount that is greater than is needed or can be used）

A. [ˈsɜː(r)fɪt] ~ (of sth.) 过量（an amount that is too large）

B. ~ (of sth.) 足量；充足（an amount of sth. that is enough for a particular purpose）

C. ~ (of sth.) 大量；许多（a large number or amount of sth.）

D. ~ (of sth.) 一系列；一连串；一批（a series of things or people that come closely one after another）

句子大意：任何新标准都将与过多的现行标准进行竞争，可能会放大该产业业已存在的（标准）互不兼容问题。

12 B

nebulous 形体不明的，朦胧的，模糊的（not developed or clear enough to describe）

A. 星云的；星云状的；云状的（any of numerous clouds of gas or dust in interstellar space）

B. 记不清的；模糊的（not clear because of a lack of memory, understanding or detail）

主意不定的；困惑的（uncertain or confused about sth.）

C. 汁多味美的（containing a lot of juice and tasting good）

肉质的；多汁的（having leaves and stems that are thick and contain a lot of water）

D. 简明的；言简意赅的（expressed clearly and in a few words）

句子大意：该公司对他们将要制造的下一种车型只有模糊的概念。

13 A

reveller（醉酒）狂欢者（a person who is having fun in a noisy way, usually with a group of other people and often after drinking alcohol）

shell out 支付（特别是成本出乎意料或不情愿支付的钱）（pay money for something, especially when the cost is unexpected and not wanted）；常考近义表达：cough up 不情愿地拿出钱（通常是经过一段时间的躲避后）（to produce or present something, such as an amount of money, often after a period of evasion）

A. 喜欢社交活动的人；喜欢寻欢作乐的人（a person who likes going out and who has an exciting social life）

参加狂欢聚会的人（a person who goes to raves）

B.（一段时间）狂饮作乐，大量吸毒（a period of drinking a lot of alcohol or taking a lot of drugs）

C.（善意的）玩笑，打趣（friendly remarks and jokes）

D. 园林管理员；护林人（a person whose job is to take care of a park, a forest or an area of countryside）

句子大意：政府在4月份停止了有关节日门票增值税减税的优惠政策。参加格拉斯顿伯里摇滚音乐节的人们必须花280英镑购买门票。

14 B

push through 强行或使得某个提议特别是法案获得通过（to force or enable the passage of some proposal, especially a legislative bill）

备注：In this usage, a noun or pronoun can be used before or after "through".

A. ~ through… 穿入；穿进；刺入（to penetrate, perforate, or cut through someone or something）

B. ~ through 使……获得通过、顺利完成（to cause someone or something to complete a process, especially a process of approval）

C. ~ through 恢复健康；痊愈；渡过难关（to manage to stay alive after you have been very sick or very badly injured; to succeed in a very difficult situation, or to help someone to do this）

D.（没有 pitch through 的搭配）推销；争取支持（或生意等）（to try to persuade sb. to buy sth., to give you sth. or to make a business deal with you）

句子大意：数月来，他们一直尽力想要通过一项员工减薪计划，但该计划屡屡被工会推翻。

15 A

gag sb. 捂住，塞住（某人的嘴）（to put a piece of cloth in or over sb.'s mouth to prevent them from speaking or shouting）

~ sb./sth. 压制……的言论自由；使缄默（to prevent sb. from speaking freely or expressing their opinion）

A. ~ sth. 压抑（声音）；使（声音）降低；使听不清（to make a sound quieter or less clear）；压制；扼杀；阻止；抑制（to repress; stifle）

~ sb./sth. (up) in sth. 裹住，覆盖，蒙住（以保暖）（to wrap or cover sb./sth. in order to keep them/it warm）

B. 拖着脚走（to walk slowly without lifting your feet completely off the ground）

~ (sth.) 洗（牌）（to mix cards up in a pack/deck of playing cards before playing a game）

C. ~ sb.（尤指通过"嘘"声或把手指竖在嘴唇上）要某人安静，嘘（to tell sb. to be quiet, especially by saying shush, or by putting your finger against your lips）

D.（因尴尬或害羞）脸红，涨红了脸（to become red in the face because you are embarrassed or ashamed）

~ to do sth.（因某事）羞愧，尴尬（to be ashamed or embarrassed about sth.）

句子大意：辩论只能通过政府电视频道播放，这样就可以让他压制异议人士的声音。

16 A

callous 冷酷无情的，无同情心的，冷漠的（not caring about other people's feelings or suffering）

A. 冷漠的；无同情心的（not sympathetic about the problems or suffering of other people）

常考同义词：unfeeling 漠不关心的；无情的；无怜悯心的（not showing care or sympathy for other people）

B. ['pæliətɪv] n. 治标药物；缓解剂；治标措施；保守疗法（a medicine or medical treatment that reduces pain without curing its cause）

adj. 减轻疼痛的，缓和的（reducing the pain or other bad effects of a terminal illness that cannot be cured）

C.（态度或行为）反复无常的；任性的（showing sudden changes in attitude or behaviour）

变化无常的；变幻莫测的；多变的（changing suddenly and quickly）

D. 异常的；难以解释的（strange and difficult to explain）

句子大意：哈里和梅根指责王室对待他们冷漠无情且带有种族主义倾向。

17 A

prissy 大惊小怪的；拘泥谨慎的；过于讲究的（very easily offended or upset by unpleasant behavior, in a way that you think is silly）；服装过于讲究整洁、古板的（prissy clothes or designs look silly because they are too neat and traditional）

A. 一本正经的；循规蹈矩的；古板的（always behaving in a careful and formal way, and easily shocked by anything that is rude）

正式的；端庄的（formal and neat）

B. 优质的；上乘的；优异的（of the best quality; excellent）

典型的；有代表性的（a prime example of sth. is one that is typical of it）

最可能的；首选的；最适宜的（most likely to be chosen for sth.; most suitable）

C. [praɪˈmɔː(r)diəl] 原生的；原始的（existing at or from the beginning of the world）

基本的（very basic）

D. [ˈprɪstiːn] 崭新的；清新的（fresh and clean, as if new）

未开发的；处于原始状态的（not developed or changed in any way; left in its original condition）

句子大意：如果上周我开始骂人时，就有人开始给我做谨小慎微的手势的话，那么我愤怒的攻击言语会比当时难听得多。

18 A

contagion（思想、风气等）传播，蔓延，流行；（传播中的）不良影响，歪风邪气（the tendency to spread, as of a doctrine, influence, or emotional state; a harmful, corrupting influence）

例句：Experts feared that violence on television was a contagion affecting young viewers. 专家们担心，电视上播放的暴力画面会对年轻观众产生不良影响。

A. 污染，玷污，腐化思想或道德（something that physically contaminates a substance or that corrupts a person morally）

B. ~ (of sb./sth.) 谴责；指责（an expression of very strong disapproval）

C. 屈尊；恩赐（高高在上的）态度（the behavior of someone that shows they think they are more important or more intelligent than other people）

D. 痉挛；抽搐（a sudden shaking movement of the body that cannot be controlled）

动乱；骚动（a sudden important change that happens to a country or an organization）

句子大意：他继续努力让自己的国家免受外来思想的侵害。

19 A

impending 即将发生的；迫在眉睫的（that is going to happen very soon）

A. 即将发生的；临近的（likely to happen very soon）

B. 壮观的；令人印象深刻的（impressive to look at; making a strong impression）

C. 不明智的；不谨慎的（not wise or sensible）

D. 特别整洁的（extremely clean and tidy）

　　无误的；无过失的（containing no mistakes）

句子大意：他不知道为什么，可他隐约觉得灾难即将来临，这让他倍感压抑。

20 D

uncanny 异常的；难以解释的；不可思议的（strange and difficult to explain）

A. 狡猾的；奸诈的；诡诈的（able to get what you want in a clever way, especially by tricking or cheating sb.）

　　灵巧的；精巧的；巧妙的（clever and skilful）

B. 不整洁的；凌乱的；不修边幅的（not well cared for; not neat or tidy）

C. 不适当的；过分的；过度的（more than you think is reasonable or necessary）

D. 怪异的；神秘的；恐怖的（strange and mysterious, and sometimes frightening）

句子大意：尽管该国成为"国际弃儿"，但是该国消费者和企业似乎拥有一种不可思议的保持一切如常的能力。

Practice 12

1 C

hubris ['hju:brɪs] 狂妄自大（excessive pride or self-confidence; arrogance）

A. 残骸；碎片；破片（pieces of wood, metal, brick, etc. that are left after sth. has been destroyed）

　　残渣；垃圾；废弃物（pieces of material that are not wanted and rubbish/garbage that are left somewhere）

B. 手段；策略；方法；技巧（a method of doing sth. that produces a particular result or effect）

　　花招；计谋；诡计（a plan or trick that is used to get sth. that sb. wants）

C. 自负；骄傲自大（too much pride in yourself and what you do）

　　巧妙的言辞；别出心裁的比喻（a clever expression in writing or speech that involves a comparison between two things）

D. 欺骗，欺诈（行为）；诡计（dishonest behaviour that is intended to make sb. believe sth. that is not true; an example of this behaviour）

句子大意：在技术上无限狂妄自大是很危险的。

2 C

incontinent 大小便失禁的（unable to control your bladder or bowels）；无节制的，不能抑制的（incontinent behavior or emotion is not controlled well）

A. ~ with sth. 不一致；相矛盾（If two statements, etc. are inconsistent, or one is inconsistent with the other, they cannot both be true because they give the facts in a different way.）

　　~ with sth. 不符合（某套标准、思想等）（not matching a set of standards, ideas, etc.）；反复无常的；没有常性的（tending to change too often; not staying the same）

B. ~ with sth.（与某事物）不一致，不相配（Two actions, ideas, etc. that are incompatible are not acceptable or possible together because of basic differences.）

~ with sb.（与某人）合不来，不能和睦相处（Two people who are incompatible are very different from each other and so are not able to live or work happily together.）

C. 无节制的；奔放的；极端的（not controlled and therefore extreme）

D. 异常的；难以解释的（strange and difficult to explain）

句子大意： 与特朗普毫无禁忌的大国沙文主义相比，他的核心理念似乎更接近于罗纳德·里根的小国意识形态。

3 D

grubby 肮脏的；邋遢的；污秽的（rather dirty, usually because it has not been washed or cleaned）；卑鄙的；可鄙的 [unpleasant because it involves activities that are dishonest or immoral (If you describe an activity or someone's behaviour as grubby, you do not think that it is honest, fair, or acceptable.)]

A. 破旧的；破败的；破烂的（in poor condition because they have been used a lot）

不公正的；不讲理的（unfair or unreasonable）

B. 脾气乖戾的；易怒的（bad-tempered and unpleasant）

C. 像灌木的；灌木状的（like a shrub）

D. 肮脏的；污秽的（dirty）

淫秽的；下流的（sexually offensive）

句子大意： 他不想让这个故事落入卑鄙的通俗小报手里。

4 A

bailiff 法警（an official who keeps order in court, takes people to their seats, watches prisoners, etc.）

frantic 紧张忙乱的；手忙脚乱的（done quickly and with a lot of activity, but in a way that is not very well organized）；（由于恐惧或担心）无法控制感情的，发狂似的（unable to control your emotions because you are extremely frightened or worried about sth.）

A. 歇斯底里的；情绪狂暴不可抑止的（in a state of extreme excitement, and crying, laughing, etc. in an uncontrolled way）

B. ~ with sth. 充满（不愉快事物）的（filled with sth. unpleasant）

焦虑的；忧虑的；担心的（causing or feeling worry and anxiety）

C. (= fanatical) 狂信的，狂热的，入迷的（very enthusiastic about a sport or activity）

D. 忙碌的；繁忙的（very busy; full of activity）

句子大意： 这两名法警使劲地挟他出门，而他那疯狂的喊叫声还久久回荡在法庭中，似乎永无止息。

5 A

feel the pinch 感到手头拮据（to have financial problems; to have less money than you need）

A. 由于缺少资金或资源而面临经济压力（to be under strain from a lack of money or resources）

常考近义词组1：feel the squeeze 应对高度紧张或压力较大的局面（to be dealing with an intensely stressful or high-pressure situation）

常考近义词组2：feel the draught 承受由于周边的经济、社会或政治变革而造成的经济困难（suffer financially as a result of economic, social or political changes around you）

B. 应对或面对强烈的压力（非经济方面）或敌意（to deal with or come up against intense pressure or hostility）

C. 感觉格格不入，难以融入（not in the proper situation, not belonging; inappropriate for the circumstances or location）

D. 感到开心放松（to feel happy and calm）

句子大意：他知道，到10月份竞选连任时，处在水深火热中的巴西人民可能会对他进行惩罚。

6 A

like gold dust 难以找到；很难得到（difficult to find or obtain; very valuable or difficult to get because a lot of people want it）

A. 容易出售的；畅销的；有销路的（easy to sell; attractive to customers or employers）

B. 可获得的；可购得的；可找到的（that you can get, buy or find）

C. 可达到的；可获得的（that you can achieve）

D. 可到达的；可接近的；可进入的；可使用的；可见到的（that can be reached, entered, used, seen, etc.）

容易理解的；易懂（easy to understand）

易接近的；易相处的；易打交道的（easy to talk to and to get to know）

句子大意：在一个各种节日大量涌现的时代，这个音乐节经久不衰，由此可见，他们有一点做得很好：音乐节的门票一票难求。

7 A

space out 走神，迷迷糊糊（to be or become distracted, preoccupied, or unfocused from the present moment or the task at hand; to be or become confused, disoriented, or stupefied, from or as from drug use）

A. 使不辨方向，使迷失方位；使精神混乱（to make someone confused about where they are or what direction they are moving in; to make someone unable to think clearly or make sensible decisions）

B. 使气馁，使沮丧（to discourage or dishearten somebody）

C. （使）消散，消失；驱散（to gradually become or make sth. become weaker until it disappears）

~ sth. 挥霍，浪费，消磨（时间、金钱等）（to waste sth., such as time or money, especially by not planning the best way of using it）

D. 切断（电话服务）；停止供应（水、电或燃气）（to officially stop the supply of telephone lines, water, electricity or gas to a building）

句子大意：在演讲过程中，他突然开始迷糊，声音渐渐变小，用他人难以听懂的话低语起来。

8 A

be raring to do sth. 渴望做某事（very enthusiastic about starting to do sth.）

A. 热切的；渴望的；渴求的（very interested and excited by sth. that is going to happen or about sth. that you want to do）

B. 犹豫的；踌躇的；不情愿的（slow to speak or act because you feel uncertain, embarrassed or unwilling）

C. 勇敢的；敢于冒险的（brave; willing to do dangerous or unusual things; involving danger or taking risks）

D. 热衷的；酷爱的 [very enthusiastic about sth. (often a hobby)]

~ for sth. 渴望的；渴求的（wanting to get sth. very much）

句子大意：他迫不及待地要重返政坛。

9 A

squeamish 易心烦意乱的；易恶心的；神经脆弱的（easily nauseated or sickened; easily shocked or disgusted）；过于拘谨的；神经质的（excessively fastidious or scrupulous）

A. 恶心的；欲吐的（feeling sick; wanting to vomit）

稍感紧张的；略有不安的；心神不定的（slightly nervous or worried about sth.）

B. 软而易压坏（或压扁）的（soft and easy to crush or squeeze）

C. 低劣的；蹩脚的；俗气的；乏味的（cheap, badly made and/or lacking in taste）

未干透的；发黏的（not dry and therefore slightly sticky）

D. 易惊而难以驾驭的（easily excited or frightened and therefore difficult to control）

轻浮的；易变的；反复无常的（not very serious and with ideas and feelings that keep changing）

句子大意：我见血就觉得恶心／晕血。

10 C

qualms [kwɑːmz] ~ about sth.（对自己行为的）顾虑，不安（a feeling of doubt or worry about whether what you are doing is right）

A.（鸭子的）呱呱声，嘎嘎声（the sound that a duck makes）

江湖郎中；冒牌医生；庸医（a person who dishonestly claims to have medical knowledge or skills）

B. 新奇有趣的；古色古香的（attractive in an unusual or old-fashioned way）

C. 疑惑，忧虑，担心，不安（a feeling of fear or doubt about whether something is right or will have a good result）

D. 歪曲；误传；曲解；错报；（法律）旨在欺骗或诱导他人的虚假陈述（an intentionally or sometimes negligently false representation made verbally, by conduct, or sometimes by nondisclosure or concealment and often for the purpose of deceiving, defrauding, or causing another to rely on it detrimentally）

句子大意：缅甸的将军们对流不流血毫无顾忌。

11 B

machination[ˌmæʃɪˈneɪʃn] 阴谋；诡计（a secret and complicated plan）

A. 机械化；机械化作业（using machines to do something that was previously done by people or animals）

B. 密谋；勾结；串通（secret agreement especially in order to do sth. dishonest or to trick people）

C. 估计；估算；计算（the act of calculating sth., especially in a way that is not very exact）

最后审判日；算总账（a time when sb.'s actions will be judged to be right or wrong and they may be punished）

D.（极具才智的）决策者；主谋；出谋划策者 [an intelligent person who plans and directs a complicated project or activity (often one that involves a crime)]

句子大意： 人们越来越难将不断飙升的汽油价格归咎于石油输出国组织的阴谋了。

12 A

down tools 罢工（to stop working, especially as a protest）

A. 出去；罢工（to suddenly leave a person who needs you or a situation that depends on you; to stop working as a way of protesting about something）

B. 正确搭配：take to the streets 走上街头抗议（to go outside on the streets）

C. 继续行走（to continue walking in your intended direction）

D. 固定下来；生根；扛着（to become stronger and difficult to stop）

句子大意： 一些航空运输管控人员也可能会举行罢工。

13 D

vindicate sth. 证实；证明有理（to prove that sth. is true or that you were right to do sth., especially when other people had a different opinion）

vindicate sb. 澄清（责难或嫌疑）；证明（某人）无罪（责）（to prove that sb. is not guilty when they have been accused of doing sth. wrong or illegal）

A. 展览，展示（to show someone or something in a way that attracts attention and emphasizes their good qualities）

B. ~ on sth.（尤指靠有限的食物或钱）维持生活，度日（to manage to stay alive, especially with limited food or money）

存在；有效（to exist; to be valid）

C. ~ sb./sth. 征服；制伏；使屈服；使服从（to defeat sb./sth.; to gain control over sb./sth.）

D. ~ sth. 证实；确认；确证（to prove that sth. is true）

~ sth. 使生效；使有法律效力（to make sth. legally valid）

~ sth. 批准；确认……有效；认可（to state officially that sth. is useful and of an acceptable standard）

句子大意： 他们解决该问题的办法已经通过取得的积极成效得到了印证。

14 B

trounce sb. 彻底打败；击溃（to defeat sb. completely）

A.（在比赛或其他竞赛中）落后，失利，失败（to be losing a game or other contest）

B. ~ sth./sb. 赢；胜过；打败（to beat sth. that sb. says or does by saying or doing sth. even better）

C. ~ (on/over) sb./sth. 践踏，摧残（人权、心灵等）（to ignore sb.'s feelings or rights and treat them as if they are not important）

D. ~ sth. 超出，超越（通常的界限）（to be or go beyond the usual limits of sth.）

句子大意：5月9日，他在总统竞选中击败了劲敌。

15 A

complicity in sth. 同谋；共犯；勾结（the act of taking part with another person in a crime）

A. ~ (of sb.) (in sth.)（被）牵连，牵涉（the fact of being involved, or of involving sb., in sth., especially a crime）

B.（众多复杂而又难以预料的）结果，后果（one of the large number of complicated and unexpected results that follow an action or a decision）

C. 帮凶；共犯；同谋（a person who helps another to commit a crime or to do sth. wrong）

D. 证实；加强（evidence or information that supports what someone has said）

句子大意：6月24日，最高法院维持有关莫迪没有参与2002年动乱的判决。

16 A

deferential 恭敬的；恭顺的；尊敬的（showing that you respect someone and want to treat them politely）

A. 非常尊敬的；深表崇敬的 [(= reverential) showing great respect and admiration]

B. ~ (to sb./sth.) 漠不关心；不感兴趣（having or showing no interest in sb./sth.）

C. ~ (to sb./sth.) 威慑 [a thing that makes sb. less likely to do sth. (= that deters them)]

D. 能延期的；能缓役的（capable of or suitable or eligible for being deferred）

句子大意：印度法庭比以往更加听命于政府。

17 B

coastal 沿海的；靠近海岸的（of or near a coast）

A. [pəˈlædʒɪk] 远海的；远洋的（connected with, or living in, the parts of the sea that are far from land）
浮游鱼类（反义词：benthic 底栖的；海底生物）

B. [ˈlɪtərəl] 海滨的；沿岸的；沿海的（relating to or near the coast）
沿海地区（the part of a country that is near the coast）

C. [ˌɑːrkɪˈpelædʒɪk] 群岛的（of, relating to, or located in an archipelago）

D. 半岛上的；与半岛有关的（on or connected with a peninsula）

句子大意：他将参加里海五个沿海国家的峰会。这五个国家是：俄罗斯、阿塞拜疆、伊朗、哈萨克斯坦和土库曼斯坦。

18 D

spotty（质量）参差不齐的，不规则的，时有时无的（only good, successful, or effective on some occasions or in some situations）

　　A. 布满斑点的；有色斑的（covered with small marks or spots）

　　B. 有斑点的；花斑的；斑驳的（marked with spots of colour, or shade）

　　C. 明显的；显然的；易理解的（easy to see or understand）

　　D. 低劣的；未必是真的；靠不住的（of low value; probably not genuine or of a quality that you can rely on）

句子大意： 针对家庭暴力和性骚扰的保护措施仍然不足。

19 A

disavow sth. 不承认；否认；拒绝对……承担责任（to state publicly that you have no knowledge of sth. or that you are not responsible for sth./sb.）

　　A. ~ sb./sth. 与……断绝关系；否认对……的责任（to decide that you no longer want to be connected with or responsible for sb./sth.）

　　B. 谴责；指责；斥责（to strongly criticize sb./sth. that you think is wrong, illegal, etc.）

　　C. ~ sth. 公开宣布放弃（原先的信仰、观点等）（to say, often publicly, that you no longer have the same belief or opinion that you had before）

　　D. ~ on sth. 未能兑现承诺；背信弃义（to not do what you previously agreed to do; to fail to keep a promise or agreement）

句子大意： 政客们以和解为名拒绝承认国民卫队曾经代表自己进行过杀戮行为。

20 B

seethe 强压怒火；生闷气（to be extremely angry about sth. but try not to show other people how angry you are）

~ (with sth.) 充满，遍布，到处都是（人、动物）（to be full of a lot of people or animals, especially when they are all moving around）

　　A. ~ sb. 激怒；使不安；使烦乱（to make sb. feel angry, anxious or nervous）

　　B. ~ at sb./sth. 对……大为生气，十分恼火（to be very angry, sometimes without expressing it）

　　C. ['fʊlmɪneɪt] ~ against sb./sth. 愤怒谴责；怒斥（to criticize sb./sth. angrily）

　　D. ~ (in/with sth.)（以某种结果）告终；（在某一点）结束（to end with a particular result, or at a particular point）

句子大意： 许多人对领导人的腐败无能怒火中烧，尽管很多不满是针对具体的地方官员，而非政府本身。

Practice 13

1 C

sweeping 影响广泛的；大范围的；根本性的（having an important effect on a large part of sth.）

A. 涉及各种各样的人（或事物）的；广泛的（including a great variety of people or things）

音重的；乡音浓的（If sb. has a broad accent, you can hear very easily which area they come from.）

B.（尤指割了庄稼的）一长条田地（a long strip of land, especially one on which the plants or crops have been cut）

一长条；一长片（a large strip or area of sth.）

常用搭配：a large/vast swathe of 一大片……

C. 常见于"A is part of a broader/wider B"，A 是 B 的一部分，如：part of a broader reorganization/program/movement 等，此时用比较级 broader 或 wider，即 B 包括了 A

D. 大量的；广泛的；范围大的（including a large number or variety of different people or things; covering a large area）

习语：give sb./sth. a wide berth 对……避而远之；退避三舍（to not go too near sb./sth.; to avoid sb./sth.）；wide of the mark 不准确；离谱（not accurate）

句子大意： 随着先进驾驶系统的日益普及，美国国家公路交通安全管理局（简称 NHTSA）对这些系统的安全性进行了大范围调研，这些发现即是其中一部分调研结果。

2 A

redact [rɪ'dækt] ~ sth. (from sth.) 删除，去掉，辑除（不愿公之于众的信息）（to remove information from a document because you do not want the public to see it）

A. ~ sth. 编辑，编纂，校订（文章、书籍等）（to prepare a piece of writing, a book, etc. to be published by correcting the mistakes, making improvements to it, etc.）

B. ['erʊdaɪt] 博学的；有学问的（having or showing great knowledge that is gained from academic study）

C. 诡计；骗术（a way of doing sth. or of getting sth. by cheating sb.）

D. ~ (into/with sth.) 合并；联合；结合（to come together to form one larger group, substance, etc.）

句子大意： 汽车制造商被允许编辑对事故发生过程的描述，这是特斯拉以及福特等汽车制造企业经常使用的做法，使得数据解释更加困难。

3 A

enamor 使迷恋；迷住（to cause someone to like or love something or someone）

A. be smitten (with/by sb./sth.) 突然爱上；一下子爱上（suddenly feeling that you are in love with sb.）

~ with/by sth. 痛感；备受……的煎熬（severely affected by a feeling, disease, etc.）

B. ~ sth. 使具活力；使生气勃勃（to make sth. more lively or full of energy）

C.（没有 be enchanted with... 的搭配）be enchanted by... 使着迷；使陶醉（to attract sb. strongly and make them feel very interested, excited, etc.）

D.（尤指慢舞时）接吻拥抱；卿卿我我（to kiss and hold sb. closely, especially when you are dancing slowly）

句子大意： 我们太执迷于大型科技公司了，这掩盖了其他方面存在的巨大弱点。

4 A

be loth to do sth.（= be loath to do sth.）不情愿；不乐意；勉强（not willing to do sth.）

[kəˌpɪtʃʊˈleɪʃn]（有条件的）投降；投降条约（surrender or a giving up of resistance; a document that sets out the agreed terms of surrender）

A. 屈服；投降；归顺（the act of accepting that sb. has defeated you and that you must obey them）

B.（对麻醉品等的）适应；毒瘾；成为习惯（a decline or diminishing response to a repeated stimulus）

C. 旁敲侧击的话；影射；暗示（something that sb. insinuates）

D. 减弱；稀释；衰减；变细（the act of reducing the strength, amount, or size of something）

句子大意：拜登扬言要对该国强硬，不愿意做可能会被共和党人描述为投降的事情。

5 A

aberration [ˌæbəˈreɪʃ(ə)n] 脱离常规；反常现象；异常行为（a fact, an action or a way of behaving that is not usual, and that may be unacceptable）

A. ~(in sth.) 异常事物；反常现象（a thing, situation, etc. that is different from what is normal or expected）

B. 痛恨；极其讨厌的人或物（the feeling that you have when you dislike something very much, usually because you think it is immoral）

C. [ˈæbstɪnəns] ~ (from sth.)（因道德、宗教或健康原因对饮食、酒、色等的）节制；禁欲（the practice of not allowing yourself sth., especially food, alcoholic drinks or sex, for moral, religious or health reasons）

D. 党羽；拥护者；遗民（a supporter of a set of ideas, an organization, or a person）

句子大意：他们会分析社交媒体上的帖子，收集生物特征数据，追踪手机，用警方摄像头录制视频，并对所获得的信息进行筛选，从中找到模式和异常情况。

6 A

clique 派系；私党；小集团；小圈子（a small group of people who spend their time together and do not allow others to join them）

A. [ˈkoʊtəri]（志趣相同、合伙做事而排外的）小圈子，小集团（a small group of people who have the same interests and do things together but do not like to include others）

B. 团体；社团；界（a group of people who share the same religion, race, job, etc.）

C. 秘密会议；秘密会议与会者（a meeting to discuss sth. in private; the people at this meeting）

D. 暗中从事的；保密的；秘密的（done secretly or kept secret）

句子大意：该高尔夫俱乐部由一个非常不友好的排外小圈子运营。

7 D

aroma（通常指食物、饮料的）香味，香气，芳香（a strong, pleasant smell, usually from food or drink）（例如：the aroma of freshly baked bread 新出炉的面包的香味）

A.（植物本身散发的自然的）香味（a pleasant natural smell）（例如：the scent of roses 玫瑰的香味）
（动物本身散发的）气味（例句：The dogs must have lost her scent. 狗准是闻不到她的气味了。）

B. 芳香，淡淡的香气 [a sweet or delicate odor (as of fresh flowers, pine trees, or perfume)]（通常指鲜花、松树或香水的味道）

香水（a liquid that you put on your skin in order to make yourself smell nice）（例如：a brand new fragrance for men 新款男士香水）

备注：

*fragrance 比 perfume 更加正式，更适用于书面语或较为专业的语境。

*fragrance 和 scent、aroma 以及 odor 的关系：Fragrance is especially associated with flowers. The scent（气味，中性词，本身没有好坏之分）of something that smells good is typically called a fragrance or an aroma（好闻），while the scent of something that smells bad is typically called an odor（不好闻）。

C. 特别的气味，尤指臭气、臭味（a particular smell, esp. a bad one）

D. 固定表达：the nose of wine 葡萄酒中酒香和果香的统称，即葡萄酒香气（a term used to describe the scents and aromas that a glass of wine gives off）

句子大意： 全面分析葡萄酒香极为复杂，成本高昂。

8 A

acquittal 宣告无罪；无罪的判决（an official decision in court that a person is not guilty of a crime）

A. [ˌɪɡˌzɒnəˈreɪʃ(ə)n] 免罪，声明……无罪（the act of showing or stating that someone or something is not guilty of something）

B. 赦罪；赦免（a formal statement that a person is forgiven for what he or she has done wrong）（注意含义：有罪但被赦免）

C. ~ (from sth.) 获准离开，免职；出院；退伍（the act of officially allowing sb., or of telling sb., to leave somewhere, especially sb. in a hospital or the army）

D. 默然接受；默认；默许（the fact of being willing to do what sb. wants and to accept their opinions, even if you are not sure that they are right）

句子大意： 虽然一些案件最终定罪，但另一些案件则以无罪释放或不予受理告终。

9 B

heist（对商店、银行贵重物、钱的）盗窃（an act of stealing sth. valuable from a shop/store or bank）

A. 黑客（秘密窥视或改变他人计算机系统信息）（a person who secretly finds a way of looking at and/or changing information on sb. else's computer system without permission）

B. ~ (of sth.) 偷；偷窃；盗窃罪（the crime of stealing sth. from a person or place）

C. [ˈdiːɪst] 自然神论者（否认三位一体、圣经的启示、神迹以及任何救赎或拯救的超自然行为，认为上帝是冷漠无情且不参与人类事务的）（those who hold that God created the universe and established rationally comprehensible moral and natural laws but does not intervene in human affairs through miracles or supernatural revelation）

D. [ˈælkəmɪst] 炼金术士（a person who studied alchemy）

句子大意： 在疫情期间，该国通过盗窃加密货币这种获利丰厚且相对没有风险的途径筹集资金以维持统治。

10 A

compunction about doing sth. 对做某事感到内疚、愧疚（a guilty feeling about doing sth.）

A. ~ (about sth.)（对自己行为的）顾虑，不安（a feeling of doubt or worry about whether what you are doing is right）

B.（引起某种结果的事物等的）结合，同时发生（a combination of events, etc., that causes a particular result）

常见搭配：in conjunction with 与……结合、配合

C.（法院的）强制令，禁制令（an official order given by a court which demands that sth. must or must not be done）

D. 罗盘；罗经；指南针；罗盘仪（an instrument for finding direction, with a needle that always points to the north）

常考搭配：moral compass 道德准则（the person's ability to judge what is right and wrong and act accordingly）

句子大意：如果你认为他们攻击别人的网络时会有道德上的内疚感，那你可就错了。

11 C

bristle with sth. or at sth.（对某人的言行）大为恼怒；被激怒（to suddenly become very annoyed or offended at what sb. says or does）；（背部或颈部的毛因惊吓或发怒）竖起，耸起（to stand up on the back and neck because the animal is frightened or angry）

A. ~ from sth./from doing sth. or ~ at sth. 对……做出厌恶（或恐惧）的反应（to react to an idea or a situation with strong dislike or fear）

B. ~ at sth.（因痛苦或尴尬）龇牙咧嘴，皱眉蹙额（to suddenly make an expression with your face that shows that you are feeling pain or embarrassment）

C. ~ at sb. or sth. 对……感到不悦或愤怒（to look at someone or something with displeasure）

D. the ~ of sth.（难题或问题的）关键，最难点，症结（the most important or difficult part of a problem or an issue）

句子大意：他们对这类言论感到愤慨，因为他们明白当华尔街为一位新"皇帝"加冕时，也注定要让其垮台。

12 A

privation [praɪˈveɪʃ(ə)n] 贫困；匮乏；艰难（a lack of the basic things that people need for living）

A. 贫困；丧失；剥夺（the fact of not having sth. that you need, like enough food, money or a home; the process that causes this）

B. 私有化；非国营化（the sale of a business or industry that was owned and managed by the government）

C. 大火灾；大火（a very large fire that destroys a lot of land or buildings）

D.（老鼠、害虫、盗贼）大批出没；（昆虫）传染（a situation in which a lot of insects or animals are in a place and are causing damage or disease）

句子大意：在战争期间，有几个村庄因长期孤立而面临严重匮乏的局面。

13 A

purgatory ['pɜ:(r)gət(ə)ri] 炼狱（a place or state in which the souls of dead people suffer for the bad things they did when they were living, so that they can become pure enough to go to heaven）；受难的处所（或状态）；惩戒所；折磨；磨难（any place or state of suffering）

- A. 在地狱边缘；心神不定；处于不知所措的境地（an imaginary place for lost, forgotten, or unwanted persons or things; an unknown intermediate place or condition between two extremes: in limbo）
- B. [lɪ'bi:dəʊ] 力比多；性欲；性冲动（sexual desire）
- C. 避难所；庇护所（a safe place, especially one where people who are being chased or attacked can stay and be protected）
- D. 净化；（吃泻药）通便（the act of purging the body by the use of a cathartic to stimulate evacuation of the bowels）；涤罪；证明无罪（the act of purging or being purged, especially from guilt or sin）

句子大意： 现在，距离 2050 年的限期还有一半，该城市已经进入了一个充满不确定性的"炼狱"。以前就曾有人宣告过它的灭亡。

14 A

transience ['trænziəns] 短暂，转瞬之间 [the quality of being transient (= temporary)]

- A. 短暂，瞬息，暂时（the state or quality of lasting only for a short time）
- B. 超越，超绝，卓绝；超验（a state of being or existence above and beyond the limits of material experience; the state of excelling or surpassing or going beyond usual limits）
- C. 变形（the act or process of changing or being changed completely）
- D. 半透明 [the quality of being translucent (= almost transparent, in an attractive way)]

句子大意： 由于没有实现理想，他们发出了人生短暂的哀叹。

15 D

poignant ['pɔɪnjənt] 令人沉痛的；悲惨的；酸楚的（having a strong effect on your feelings, especially in a way that makes you feel sad）

- A. 爱争执的；好斗的；爱滋事的（having a strong desire to argue or fight with other people）
- B. 虚华的；言辞浮夸的（showing that you think you are more important than other people, especially by using long and formal words）
- C. 预谋的；事先策划的（planned in advance）
- D. 使人痛苦的；令人苦恼的（making you feel extremely upset, especially because of sb.'s suffering）

句子大意： 这部影片讲述了一位中年父亲寻找未曾谋面的儿子的故事，既具喜感又令人沉痛。

16 B

unwittingly 糊里糊涂地；茫然；无意地（without being aware of what you are doing or the situation that you are involved in）；近义词：unknowingly/unawares/unconsciously

- A. 意料之中的；不令人吃惊地；自然地（in a way that you expected）

B. 不留神地；未注意到；不知不觉地（without noticing or realizing）

C. 会意地；心照不宣地；知情地（in a way that shows that you know or understand about sth. that is supposed to be secret）

D. 故意；蓄意；存心（done in a way that was planned, not by chance）

句子大意： 她最终进了温哥华的一所大学学习计算机。她无意间和许多因害怕地方冲突而移民的叙利亚人走了一样的路。

17 D

paroxysm ['pærək‚sɪz(ə)m] 突然发作（a sudden strong feeling or expression of an emotion that cannot be controlled）；突发症征（a sudden short attack of pain, causing physical shaking that cannot be controlled）

A. ['pætwɑ:] 方言；土语；土话方言；土话（a form of a language, spoken by people in a particular area, that is different from the standard language of the country）

B. 矛盾的人（或事物、情况）（a person, thing or situation that has two opposite features and therefore seems strange）

似非而是的隽语；悖论；悖论修辞（a statement containing two opposite ideas that make it seem impossible or unlikely, although it is probably true; the use of this in writing）

C. （房屋外面或后面的）露台，平台（a flat hard area outside, and usually behind, a house where people can sit）

D. （感情的）爆发，迸发（a sudden strong expression of an emotion）

（活动的）激增；（态度的）激化（a sudden increase in a particular activity or attitude）

句子大意： 在邻国每一次动荡之后，该国人口都会因为难民涌入而激增。

18 C

exemplify sth. 是……的典型（或典范、榜样）（to be a typical example of sth.）；举例说明；例证；例示（to give an example in order to make sth. clearer）

A. ~ sth. 使死皮剥脱（to remove dead cells from the surface of skin in order to make it smoother）

B. ~ sb. 使烦恼；使恼怒；激怒（to annoy or irritate sb. very much）

C. ~ sth. 成为……的典范（或典型）（to be a perfect example of sth.）

D. ~ sb. 使高兴；使兴奋；使激动（to make sb. feel very happy and excited）

句子大意： 正在建设中的多座高楼大厦体现了这座城市的经济发展状况。

19 A

scrawl 马马虎虎（或潦草）地写（to write sth. in a careless untidy way, making it difficult to read）

A. 草草记下，匆匆书写（尤指因时间仓促）（to write sth. quickly and carelessly, especially because you do not have much time）

胡写；乱画（to draw marks that do not mean anything）

B. 争抢；抢占；争夺（to push, fight or compete with others in order to get or to reach sth.）

常见搭配：scramble for sth./scramble to do sth.

C. ~ (around/about) (for sth.) 忙乱地找；翻找（to try to find or to do sth. in a hurry or with difficulty, often by moving your hands or feet about quickly, without much control）

D. 擦坏；擦伤；刮坏；蹭破（to rub sth. by accident so that it gets damaged or hurt）
勉强获得；费尽千辛万苦获得（to succeed in getting or achieving something, but with difficulty or by a very small amount）（例句：Her grades weren't great, but she scraped into university. 她的分数不高，但是勉强进入了大学。）

句子大意：他们围攻了这栋大楼，打碎玻璃，将金属门砸到变形，四处涂鸦反战标语。

20 A

demean sb./sth. 贬低；贬损；使失尊严（to make people have less respect for sb./sth.）

A. ~ sb./sth. 贬低；轻视（to suggest that sb./sth. is not important or valuable）

B. ~ sb. (from sth.) (to sth.) 使降级，使降职，使降低地位（常作为惩罚）（to move sb. to a lower position or rank, often as a punishment）

C. 使清醒，醒悟（to make somebody stop believing that something or somebody is worthwhile, right, or deserving of support）

D. ~ sth. 哀怨；悲叹（to complain or say that you are not happy about sth.）

句子大意：她对贬低该已故越南领袖的社论予以谴责。

Practice 14

1 C

ostensibly 表面上（而实际上……）（used for saying that although someone pretends to have one reason for something, there is in fact another reason）

A. 易于察觉地，明显地（in a way that is so obvious that it can easily be seen or known）

B. 自认；公然地（admittedly or stated publicly）

C. 看似；貌似；表面上（in a way that appears to be true but may in fact not be）

D. 据说；据传；据声称（If someone allegedly does something, another person says that they have done it, even though this has not been proved.）

句子大意：她出于同情而开始转移资金，从表面上看，是将富人的钱短期"借给"穷人。

2 D

snub sb. 冷落；怠慢（to insult sb., especially by ignoring them when you meet）

snub sth. 拒不出席；拒不接受；抵制（to refuse to attend or accept sth., for example as a protest）

A.（只有名词形式）势利小人；谄上欺下的人（a person who admires people in the higher social classes too much and has no respect for people in the lower social classes）
自以为优越的人；自命高雅的人（a person who thinks they are much better than other people because they are intelligent or like things that many people do not like）

B. ~ sb./sth. (from sb./sth.) 夺去；抢走；偷窃（to take sb./sth. away from a person or place, especially by force; to steal sth.）

C. ~ (at sb./sth.) 龇牙低吼（to show the teeth and make a deep angry noise in the throat）

咆哮着说；不耐烦地说（to speak in an angry or bad-tempered way）

D. ~ sb. 侮慢；冷落；轻视（to treat sb. rudely or without respect）

句子大意：不客气地讲，世界各国和各家企业都不敢不露面，生怕怠慢了这个态度往往生硬粗暴的强国。

3 A

perilous 危险的；艰险的（very dangerous）

A. 不稳的；不确定的；不保险的；危险的（not safe or certain; dangerous）

摇摇欲坠的；不稳固的（likely to fall or cause sb. to fall）

B. 不结实的；不稳固的；易折断的（not strong or well made; likely to break）

C. 摇摆的；摇摇晃晃的（moving in an unsteady way from side to side）

D. [prɪˈsɪpɪtəs] 陡峭的；险峻的；峭拔的（very steep, high and often dangerous）

突然的；骤然的；急剧的（sudden and great）

草率的；仓促的；贸然的（done very quickly, without enough thought or care）

句子大意：担任公司董事可能充满危险。但对于投资者而言，不担任这种职务往往更为糟糕。

4 C

erstwhile 以前的；先前的；往昔的（former; that until recently was the type of person or thing described but is not any more）

erst〈古〉以前，从前，往昔

A. ~ (to sb./sth.) 挚爱的；忠诚的；全心全意的（having great love for sb./sth. and being loyal to them）

B. [dɪˈspɪkəb(ə)l] 令人厌恶的；可鄙的；卑鄙的（very unpleasant or evil）

C. 先前的；以往的（happening or existing before the event or object that you are talking about）

D. [ˈpɒstjʊməs] 死后发生（或做、出版等）的（happening, done, published, etc. after a person has died）

句子大意：如同昔日的某些真正信徒一样，他也成为其原有信仰最有力的批判者之一。

5 C

sprightly 精力充沛的；精神矍铄的（full of life and energy）

A. [ləˈθɑː(r)dʒɪk] 嗜眠的；催人昏睡的（lacking energy and not wanting to do anything）

B. [ɪˈθɪəriəl] 优雅的；轻飘的；缥缈的；超凡的（extremely delicate and light; seeming to belong to another, more spiritual, world）

C.（动作）敏捷的，灵活的（able to move quickly and easily）

（思维）机敏的，机灵的（able to think quickly and in an intelligent way）

D. [dʒen'tiːl] 显得彬彬有礼的；假斯文的；上流社会的；装体面的（quiet and polite, often in an exaggerated way; from, or pretending to be from, a high social class）

幽静的；古朴单调的（quiet and old-fashioned and perhaps slightly boring）

句子大意： 他已经 67 岁了，但是精神矍铄，还定期到国外做体检。他说自己还不打算退休。

6 C

prescient ['presiənt] 有先见之明的；预见的；有预知能力的（knowing or appearing to know about things before they happen）

A. 有识别力的；有眼力的；有洞察力的（able to show good judgement about the quality of sb./sth.）

B. 审慎而明智的；明断的；有见地的（careful and sensible; showing good judgement）

C. [prə'fetɪk] 正确预言的；有预见的（correctly stating or showing what will happen in the future）

D. [ɪ'luːsəri] 虚假的；幻觉的；迷惑人的（not real, although seeming to be）

句子大意： 他对战争的无意义性和带来的痛苦进行的反思在今天看来特别具有预见性。

7 A

mothball sth. 封存；搁置不用（to decide not to use or develop sth., for a period of time, especially a piece of equipment or a plan）

A. ~ (doing) sth. 推迟；延缓；展期（to delay sth. until a later time）

B. ~ (with sb.) (on/about sth.) 商讨；协商；交换意见（to discuss sth. with sb., in order to exchange opinions or get advice）

~ sth. (on/upon sb.) 授予；颁发（奖项、学位、荣誉或权利）（to give sb. an award, a university degree or a particular honour or right）

C. ~ (sb.) (from sth./from doing sth.) 制止；阻止；威慑；使不敢（to make sb. decide not to do sth. or continue doing sth., especially by making them understand the difficulties and unpleasant results of their actions）

D. ~ sth. 减少，减缓（伤害）（to reduce the harmful effects of sth.）

~ sb. (against sth.) 保护；使不受……侵害（to protect sb. from sth.）

句子大意： 一直以来，默克尔夫人因推动修建现已被搁置的旨在连接德国和俄罗斯的"北溪二号"天然气输送管道而备受批评。

8 C

unenviable 不想要的；不得人心的；易惹麻烦的（not wanted or approved of; likely to cause trouble or problems）

A. （美好得）难以形容的，不可言喻的（too great or beautiful to describe in words）

B. 不可取的；不好的；不接受劝告的；不适宜的；不得当的；不妥当的（unwise; not recommended; not prudent; not to be advised）（可以与 unadvisable 互换，不过 inadvisable 更为常用）

C. 艰难的；讨厌的；不值得羡慕的（difficult or unpleasant; that you would not want to have）

D. 不可避免的；不能防止的（that you cannot avoid or prevent）

句子大意：欧洲央行面临一个棘手的两难选择：是为控制通胀而收紧货币政策还是为支撑日渐疲软的经济而继续实施宽松的货币政策？

9 C

half-baked 计划不完善的；考虑不周的（not well planned or considered）

A. 挖苦地；开玩笑的（spoken with gentle irony and meant as a joke; intended to be humorous and not meant seriously）

B. ['nɒnʃ(ə)lənt] 若无其事的；冷静的；漠不关心的（behaving in a calm and relaxed way; giving the impression that you are not feeling any anxiety）

C. 考虑不周的；构想拙劣的（badly planned or designed）

D. 不热心的；不尽力的；冷淡的（done without enthusiasm or effort）

句子大意：英国财政部本月在解释为什么小型机构对系统构成的风险可能不亚于大型机构时发表了一些考虑欠妥的观点。

10 C

rive 分裂；四分五裂（to tear something apart）

A. ~ with sth. 充斥，充满（坏事）（full of sth. bad or unpleasant）

B. ~ (about sb./sth.) 热烈谈论（或书写）；（热情洋溢地）奋笔疾书（to talk or write about sth. in a very enthusiastic way）

C. ~ sb./sth. 使产生分歧；使意见不一（to make two or more people disagree）

D. ~ sb./sth. 违抗；反抗；蔑视（to refuse to obey or show respect for sb. in authority, a law, a rule, etc.）

句子大意：由于该国有着欺诈和暴力的历史，有些人就担心最终会产生一个因冲突和混乱而陷入分裂的党派。

11 C

patronize ['pætrənaɪz] ~ sb. 屈尊俯就地对待；摆出高人一等的派头（to treat sb. in a way that seems friendly, but which shows that you think that they are not very intelligent, experienced, etc.）

patronize sth. 经常光顾（to be a regular customer of a shop/store, restaurant, etc.）

patronize sb./sth. 赞助；资助（to help a particular person, organization or activity by giving them money）

A. ~ sth. 赞助（活动、节目等）（to pay the costs of a particular event, programme, etc. as a way of advertising）

　~ sth. 主办；举办；促成（to arrange for sth. official to take place）

B. 接着发生；因而产生（to happen after or as a result of another event）

C. ~ sth. 常去，常到（某处）（to visit a particular place often）

D. ~ sth. 变卖资产；变现（to sell possessions in order to change them into money）

　~ sth. 为……提供运营资本（或资金）（to provide a company etc. with the money it needs to function）

句子大意：这家餐厅在20世纪20年代有许多艺术家和作家光顾。

12 C

recant sth. 公开宣布放弃（原先的信仰、观点等）（to say, often publicly, that you no longer have the same belief or opinion that you had before）

A. ~ sth. 不承认；否认；拒绝对……承担责任（to state publicly that you have no knowledge of sth. or that you are not responsible for sth./sb.）

B. ~ sb. (of sth.) 剥夺，夺去（某人的财产、土地、房屋）（to take sb.'s property, land or house away from them）

C. ~ sth. 宣布与……决裂；宣布摒弃（to state publicly that you no longer have a particular belief or that you will no longer behave in a particular way）

~ sb./sth. 宣布断绝与……的关系（to state publicly that you no longer wish to have a connection with sb./sth. because you disapprove of them）

D. ~ sth. 拒绝接受；不予考虑（to refuse to accept or consider sth.）

~ sb. 拒收；不录用；拒绝接纳（to refuse to accept sb. for a job, position, etc.）

句子大意：在70岁时，他在要被酷刑致死的恐吓之下被迫放弃了自己的观点。

13 A

auspice ['ɔːspɪs] 常用表达：under the auspices of (someone or something) 由……主办（主持、管理）；在……保护（赞助）下（under the protection, sponsorship, or patronage of; under the oversight, supervision, control, or management of）

A. ['iːdʒɪs] 保护；主办；（宙斯神的）神盾

under the aegis of sb./sth. 在……保护（或支持）下（with the protection or support of a particular organization or person）

B. ['dʒɔːndɪs] 黄疸；黄疸病（a medical condition in which the skin and the white parts of the eyes become yellow）

C. ~ (on sth.) 指导；引导；咨询（help or advice that is given to sb., especially by sb. older or with more experience）

D. [æŋst]（对形势、事态、生活的）忧虑，焦虑（a feeling of anxiety and worry about a situation, or about your life）

句子大意：在库克执掌之下，该公司去年的纯利润据估计翻了一番还多，达到570亿美元。

14 C

belie sth. 掩饰；遮掩；给人以假象（to give a false impression of sb./sth.）；显示（某事）不正确；证明（某事）错误（to show that sth. cannot be true or correct）

A. ~ sth. 构成……的基础；作为……的原因（to be the basis or cause of sth.）

B. 强调；突现（to emphasize or show that sth. is important or true）

C. ~ sth. 证明……是错误（或虚假）的（to show that sth. is wrong or false）

D. ~ sth. 不赞成；不同意；反对（to think that sb./sth. is not good or suitable; to not approve of sb./sth.）

句子大意：类似的例子打破了细菌是简单、寂静的独行者的观念。

15 C

miss sth. 未击中；未得到；未达到；错过（to fail to hit, catch, reach, etc. sth.）

A. 分支；（尤指）分支机构（a thing that develops from sth., especially a small organization that develops from a larger one）

B. ~ sth. 将……连根拔起（to pull a tree, plant, etc. out of the ground）

（使）离开家园（或熟悉的地方等）（to leave a place where you have lived for a long time; to make sb. do this）

C. 未达到目标 [to shoot short of or below (a target); to fail to achieve a particular result]

D. （使）溜走；（使）射出、喷出（to move or send something quickly）

句子大意：他们的通胀预期表明，美联储、欧洲央行和日本银行在今后10年都将无法实现预期目标。

16 C

emergency 突发事件；紧急情况（a sudden serious and dangerous event or situation which needs immediate action to deal with it）

A. 一致性；连贯性（the quality of always behaving in the same way or of having the same opinions, standard, etc.; the quality of being consistent）

B. 会聚，趋同（the act of moving toward union or uniformity）

C. 可能发生的事；偶发（或不测、意外）事件（an event that may or may not happen）

D. （河流的）汇合处，汇流处，交汇处（the place where two rivers flow together and become one）

句子大意：拜登指示手下官员制定应急预案以防形势有变。

17 A

affidavit [ˌæfɪˈdeɪvɪt] 附誓书面证词；宣誓书（a written statement that you swear is true, and that can be used as evidence in court）

A. 证实；确认书；证明书（a statement, letter, etc. that shows that sth. is true, correct or definite）

B. [səˈpiːnə]（传唤证人出庭的）传票（a written order to attend court as a witness to give evidence）

C. [ˈpɜː(r)dʒəri] 伪证；伪誓；伪证罪（the crime of telling a lie in court）

D. [ˈpenjəri] 贫困；贫穷（the state of being very poor）

句子大意：学生申请签证，必须要有人提供经济担保书，以保证该生的学业顺利进行。

18 A

diabolical [ˌdaɪəˈbɒlɪk(ə)l] 糟糕透顶的；烦人的；讨厌的（extremely bad or annoying）；道德败坏的；邪恶的；恶魔似的（morally bad and evil; like a devil）

A. [əˈtrəʊʃəs] 糟透的；十分讨厌的（very bad or unpleasant）

残暴的；残忍的；凶恶的（very cruel and shocking）

B. [ɪˈnɪkwɪtəs] 很不公正的；十分错误的；很不正当的（very unfair or wrong）

C. 极恶毒的；道德败坏的（morally very bad）

D. 尖刻的；讥讽的；激烈的（angry and full of strong bitter feelings and words）

句子大意：坦率来讲，交易状况已经糟糕至极。

19 D

cryogenic [ˌkraɪəˈdʒenɪk] 采用极度低温的（involving the use of very low temperatures）

A. [ˌembriˈɒnɪk] 胚胎期的；萌芽期的；未成熟的（in an early stage of development）

B. 密码的；用密码写的（relating to or using cryptography）

C. 体温过高的（of or relating to or affected by hyperthermia）

常考反义词：hypothermal 不冷不热的；体温过低的（relating to, involving, or typical of hypothermia, a medical condition in which the body temperature is much lower than normal）

D. 超低温的（having a very low temperature : extremely or extraordinarily cold）

句子大意：谈判也许已经脱离了深度低温冷冻，但在解冻后能否复活仍是个未知数。

20 C

visceral [ˈvɪsərəl]（未经过认真思考而）出自内心的，发自肺腑的（resulting from strong feelings rather than careful thought）；本能的（not intellectual, instinctive）；内脏的；脏腑的（relating to the viscera）

A. ~ (to sb./sth.) 漠不关心；不感兴趣（having or showing no interest in sb./sth.）

B. 有深刻了解的；富有洞察力的（showing a clear understanding of a person or situation）

C. 本能的；直觉的；天生的（based on instinct, not thought or training）

D. 有才智的；智力发达的（well educated and enjoying activities in which you have to think seriously about things）

句子大意：最令人吃惊的是人们对生食有着本能的厌恶感。在该国，人们传统上认为吃生食是一种野蛮的习惯，几乎所有食物都仍要烹调后才食用。

Practice 15

1 A

putative 推定的；认定的；公认的（believed to be the person or thing mentioned）

A. ~ sth. 设定；设想；假设（to accept sth. as true or existing and to act on that basis）

B. 减轻（疼痛等）的；缓和的（reducing the pain or other bad effects of a terminal illness one that cannot be cured）

C.（动词原形为 preclude）使行不通；阻止；妨碍；排除（to prevent sth. from happening or sb. from doing sth.; to make sth. impossible）

D. 惩罚性的；刑罚的；处罚的（intended as punishment）

（租税等）苛刻的（very severe and that people find very difficult to pay）

句子大意：秘密情报文件揭示，所谓的联盟之间存在着剑拔弩张的严峻气氛。他们可以在某一天一起喝茶，然后紧接着就互相开战。

2 D

damage sth./sb. 损害；伤害；毁坏；破坏（to harm or spoil sth./sb.）

A. ~ sb./sth. 诋毁；诽谤；贬低（to criticize sb./sth. unfairly; to say sb./sth. does not have any value or is not important）

B. ~ on sth. 违背（诺言）；背信弃义；食言（to break a promise, an agreement, etc.）

C. 谴责；指责；斥责（to strongly criticize sb./sth. that you think is wrong, illegal, etc.）

D. ~ sth. 损害，伤害，挫伤（信心、名誉等）（to damage sb.'s confidence, reputation, etc.）

句子大意：美国及其盟国离开了该国，落得个声名狼藉／名誉扫地的下场。

3 B

argument 争论；争吵；争辩；辩论（a conversation or discussion in which two or more people disagree, often angrily）

A. 一连串的提问；（尤指）盘问，责难（a series of questions that sb. asks you, especially when they ask them in an unpleasant way）

B. 争论；争辩；争吵（a noisy argument or disagreement）

C. 改进；改善；土壤改良（an act or instance of ameliorating or making better; the state of being ameliorated or made better）

D.（常因雨水带来的化肥造成水体的）富营养化（the process of too many plants growing on the surface of a river, lake, etc., often because chemicals that are used to help crops grow have been carried there by rain）

句子大意：她说做出如此仓促的决定是因为与警察发生了争吵。

4 C

heathen ['hi:ð(ə)n] 无宗教信仰者；异教徒（used by people who have a strong religious belief as a way of referring to a person who has no religion or who believes in a religion that is not one of the world's main religions）；未开化的人；不文明的人（used to refer to a person who shows lack of education; an uncivilized or irreligious person）

A. 宗教异端；信奉邪说（a belief or an opinion that is against the principles of a particular religion; the fact of holding such beliefs）

离经叛道的信念（或观点）（a belief or an opinion that disagrees strongly with what most people believe）

异教徒；异端者；邪教徒 [(= heretic) a person who is guilty of heresy]

B. [ˈhetərəˌdɒksi:] 异端邪说；非正统；非正统思想（an opinion, belief, or theory that is at variance with those that are established or accepted）

C. [ˈpeɪɡən] 异教徒；无宗教信仰者，寻求满足肉欲、物欲的人（one who has little or no religion and who delights in sensual pleasures and material goods; an irreligious or hedonistic person）

D. 作恶者；行凶者；犯罪者（a person who commits a crime or does sth. that is wrong or evil）

句子大意：欧洲殖民者认为新世界的人们都是未开化的野蛮人，因此强迫他们遵从欧洲的处世之道。

5 C

respite ['respaɪt] ~ from sth. 暂停；暂缓（a short break or escape from sth. difficult or unpleasant）；短暂的延缓；喘息（a short delay allowed before sth. difficult or unpleasant must be done）

 A. ~ (in sth.) 短暂的平静期或活动减弱的短暂时期（a short period of calm or diminished activity）

  （如：a lull in a storm 暴风雨的暂歇；during a lull in the conversation 在对话暂歇期间）

 备注：该词强调平静或活动的减弱，不符合该题目语境。

 B. 短暂的休息（a short pause for rest or to relax）

 C. 间歇；暂停（a period of time during which sth. stops before continuing again）

  常考近义词：interlude（两事件之间的）间歇；插入事件（a period of time between two events during which sth. different happens）

 D. 间奏曲，幕间曲（歌剧或其他音乐表演中幕与幕之间的过场音乐）（a short piece of music for the orchestra that is played between two parts in an opera or other musical performance）

句子大意：除了在公屋里待过短暂的一两年外，伦敦的街巷已成为他所知唯一的家。

6 A

exorbitant [ɪɡ'zɔː(r)bɪtənt] 过高的；高得离谱的（much too high）

 A. [ˌstrætə'sferɪk] 平流层的；极高的（relating or belonging to the stratosphere; very or excessively high）

 B. 使人兴奋的；令人激动的；令人高兴的（very exciting and enjoyable）

 C. 忙碌的；繁忙的（very busy; full of activity）

 D. 精力充沛的；热情洋溢的；兴高采烈的（full of energy, excitement and happiness）

  繁茂的；茂盛的；茁壮的（strong and healthy; growing quickly and well）

句子大意：相机确实不错，但就是太贵了！

7 A

flirt with 差点遭受……[to come very close to some outcome or result, often (though not always) a very bad one]

 A. 面临，必须对付（某情况）（If you face a particular situation, or it faces you, you have to deal with it.）

 B.（不及物动词）困难重重；艰苦挣扎（to have a lot of problems and to be in danger of failing completely）

 C. ~ sth. 公然藐视，无视（法律等）（to show that you have no respect for a law, etc. by openly not obeying it）

 D. 失败；破产（to fail because of a particular problem or difficulty）

句子大意：这位首席执行官因最近对媒体发表的即兴评论而一直处在灾难的边缘。

8 C

opprobrium [ə'prəʊbriəm]（众人的）谴责，责难，抨击（severe criticism of a person, country, etc. by a large group of people）

 A. 忧虑；担心；恐惧（worry or fear that sth. unpleasant may happen）

  逮捕；拘押（the act of capturing or arresting sb., usually by the police）

B. 认可；批准（approval or agreement）

C. ~ (of sb./sth.) 谴责；指责（an expression of very strong disapproval）

D. （尤指教会或大学的）大型正式会议（a large formal meeting, especially of Church officials or members of a university）

召集会议（the act of calling together a convocation）

（大学的）学位授予典礼，毕业典礼（a ceremony held in a university or college when students receive their degrees）

句子大意： 在华盛顿谈及"多极世界"就是在招惹非难。

9 A

botch sth. (up) 笨拙地弄糟（某事物）（to spoil sth. by doing it badly）

A. ~ sth. 笨拙地做；失败（to do sth. badly or without skill; to fail at sth.）

B. ~ sb. + *adv./prep.* 匆匆送走；推搡；赶（to push or send sb. somewhere quickly and not carefully）

C. ~ sth. (up) 用绷带包扎（to wrap a bandage around a part of the body in order to protect it because it is injured）

D. ~ sb. 使困惑；难住（to confuse sb. completely; to be too difficult or strange for sb. to understand or explain）

句子大意： 我们第一次尝试给洗手间贴墙纸贴得乱七八糟。

10 C

exhortation [ˌegzɔːˈteɪʃn] 规劝；告诫；劝告（something said or written in order to urge somebody strongly to do something; the giving of earnest advice or encouragement）

A. 勒索；强夺（a crime in which someone gets money or information from someone else by using force or threats）

B. 擦伤皮肤；严厉指责 [the act of scraping (the skin); the act of criticizing sth. harshly]

C. 鼓舞；鼓励；起激励作用的事物（the act of encouraging sb. to do sth.; something that encourages sb.）

D. 脱落；剥离；去角质（the removal of dead cells on the skin's surface in order to uncover new cells and improve overall complexion）

句子大意： 该社论的部分内容是劝诫人们减少发推特的时间，但更大的关注点则是太多的记者已经开始将推特受众作为公众的代理人。

11 A

duplicitous [djuːˈplɪsɪtəs] 欺骗的，奸诈的，两面派的（behaving dishonestly in order to trick someone）

A. 口是心非的，奸诈的，不诚实的（behavior by which you cheat someone, especially by pretending to do one thing while doing the opposite）

B. 可疑的；不可信的；靠不住的；不诚实的（probably not honest）

C. [ˈpaɪəs] 虔诚的；虔敬的（having or showing a deep respect for God and religion）

道貌岸然的；伪善的；假正经的（pretending to be religious, moral or good in order to impress other people）

D. ~ to sth. 不受影响的（not affected or influenced by sth.）

不能渗透的；不透气的；不透水的（not allowing a liquid or gas to pass through）

句子大意：今天，亚裔美国人不仅是搞两面派的CEO们的代罪羔羊。在市场驱动和竞争激烈的社会中，我们还为幸福感的日渐消退背锅。

12 A

restitution [ˌrestɪˈtjuːʃ(ə)n] 归还（真正物主）；归还（赃物等）（the act of giving back sth. that was lost or stolen to its owner）；赔偿；补偿；（通常指）赔款（payment, usually money, for some harm or wrong that sb. has suffered）

A. ~ (of sth.) 复原；复位；回归；归还（the act of returning sth. to its correct place, condition or owner）

B. 修复；复原；恢复原职（the process of re-establishing the status of a person, company or law）

C. 复苏；复兴（a new beginning for sth. which is old or which had disappeared or become weak）

D. ~ (for sth.) 补偿（或赔偿）物；（尤指）赔偿金，补偿金；赔偿（something, especially money, that sb. gives you because they have hurt you, or damaged sth. that you own; the act of giving this to sb.）

句子大意：资金归还的大部分流程受到世界银行监控，以确保资金流入国库而不是落入个人腰包。

13 A

insensitive（对他人的感受）未意识到的，漠不关心的（not realizing or caring how other people feel, and therefore likely to hurt or offend them）

A. 愚蠢、粗鲁、不顾及他人感受的（without refinement, delicacy, or sensitivity）

B.（言行）谨慎的，慎重的；考虑周到的（careful in what you say or do, in order to keep sth. secret or to avoid causing embarrassment or difficulty for sb.）

C. 有识别力的；有眼力的；有洞察力的（able to show good judgement about the quality of sb./sth.）

D. ~ (with sb.) 恼怒的；十分愤怒的；生气的（annoyed or quite angry）

句子大意：如果你特别有钱，跟比自己穷的人抱怨慈善机构吵着跟你"化缘"是多么让人讨厌未免有些矫情。

14 B

manifest（船或飞机的）货单，旅客名单（a list of goods or passengers on a ship or an aircraft; written document containing a detailed list of everything that is included in the ship's cargo）

A. 指纹；指印（a mark made by the pattern of lines on the tip of a person's finger, often used by the police to identify criminals）

B. 一览表；名单；目录；清单（a series of names, items, figures, etc., especially when they are written or printed）

C. ~ (on/to sth.)（尤指对财产、土地等要求拥有的）所有权（a right that sb. believes they have to sth., especially property, land, etc.）

D. 宣言（a written statement in which a group of people, especially a political party, explain their beliefs and say what they will do if they win an election）

句子大意： 国家档案馆收藏有从大约1820年到20世纪中叶由外国港口抵达美国的船只的旅客名单。

15 C

revive sth. 重新使用；使重做（to make sth. start being used or done again）；重新上演（to produce again a play, etc. that has not been performed for some time）

A. ~ sth. (from sth.) 垦荒，造田（to make land that is naturally too wet or too dry suitable to be built on, farmed, etc.）

be reclaimed by sth. 重新变为沙漠（或森林等）；沙化；荒漠化；抛荒（If a piece of land is reclaimed by desert, forest, etc., it turns back into desert, etc. after being used for farming or building.）

B. ~ (from sth.) 康复；恢复；恢复健康（to get back your health, strength or energy after being ill/sick, tired, injured, etc.）

~ sth. 收回；挽回（损失）（to get back money that you have spent or lost）

C. ~ sth.（为适合新用途）对……稍加修改，略微改动（to change sth. slightly in order to make it suitable for a new purpose）

D. ~ from sth./from doing sth. or ~ at sth. 对……做出厌恶（或恐惧）的反应（to react to an idea or a situation with strong dislike or fear）

句子大意： 在亚利桑那州，土地管理局已经启动一个项目，把垃圾掩埋场和废弃矿山转用于开发可再生能源。

16 C

redress (for/against sth.) 赔款；损失赔偿（payment, etc. that you should get for sth. wrong that has happened to you or harm that you have suffered）

A. 报复；报仇（something that you do in order to make sb. suffer because they have made you suffer）

B.（问题、分歧等的）解决，消除（the act of solving or settling a problem, disagreement, etc.）

C. [ˌrepəˈreɪʃ(ə)n]（战败国的）赔款（money that is paid by a country that has lost a war, for the damage, injuries, etc. that it has caused）

赔偿；弥补；补偿（the act of giving sth. to sb. or doing sth. for them in order to show that you are sorry for suffering that you have caused）

D. ~ (for sth.) 严惩；惩罚；报应（severe punishment for sth. seriously wrong that sb. has done）

句子大意： 这一法律草案只会迫使无辜的公司花钱私了，并阻碍被侵权方寻求赔偿。

17 C

destitute 贫困的；贫穷的；赤贫的（without money, food and the other things necessary for life）

A. ~ about/over sth. 苦恼的；沮丧的；泄气的；失望的（sad, without much hope）

B. 气馁的；垂头丧气的；心灰意懒的（having no hope or enthusiasm）

C. [ˌɪmprɪˈkjuːniəs] 贫穷的；不名一文的（having little or no money）

D. [ˈpetjulənt] 闹脾气的；爱耍性子的；赌气的；任性的（bad-tempered and unreasonable, especially because you cannot do or have what you want）

句子大意：许多抗议者表示，他们将毕生积蓄存入银行，现在一贫如洗。

18 D

excoriate [ˌeksˈkɔːrieɪt] ~ sth. 擦破，擦伤，剥落（皮肤）（to irritate a person's skin so that it starts to come off）

excoriate sb./sth. 严厉指责；痛斥（to criticize sb./sth. severely）

A. ~ sb. to do sth.（以法律、义务等）强迫，迫使（to force sb. to do sth., by law, because it is a duty, etc.）

B. [ɪkˈsaɪz] ~ sth. (from sth.) 切除；删除（to remove sth. completely）

C. [eksˈprəʊprieɪt] ~ sth. 征用，没收（私有财产）（to officially take away private property from its owner for public use）

D. ~ sb./yourself 痛斥；严厉指责（to criticize or speak angrily to sb. because you do not approve of sth. they have done）

句子大意：政府经常严厉指责企业数据管理不当。

19 D

expropriate [eksˈprəʊpriˌeɪt] 征用（私人财产公用）（to officially take away private property from its owner for public use）

A. ~ sth. 盗用；挪用；占用；侵吞（to take sth., sb.'s ideas, etc. for your own use, especially illegally or without permission）

B. ~ sth. 私吞；挪用（to take sb. else's money or property for yourself, especially when they have trusted you to take care of it）

C. ~ (sth.)（款项）盗用，挪用，贪污，侵吞（to steal money that you are responsible for or that belongs to your employer）

D. ~ sth.（尤指战时或紧急状态时）征用（to officially demand the use of a building, vehicle, etc., especially during a war or an emergency）

句子大意：工业资产被征用的现象如今在欧洲非常罕见。

20 A

dosh [dɒʃ] 钱（money）

swanky 摆阔的；时髦且豪华的（fashionable and expensive in a way that is intended to impress people）

pad 住所；（尤指）公寓（the place where sb. lives, especially a flat/apartment）

A. 华贵入时的；豪华的（looking expensive and fashionable）

B.（浪头拍岸后的）冲激，溅泼（the flow of water up the beach after a wave has broken）

C. 非常好的；十分愉快的（very good or enjoyable）

D. 怪异吓人的；阴森可怖的（strange and frightening）

句子大意：这些空壳公司可以为那些利用脏钱购买资产——往往是在伦敦和巴黎购买奢华公寓——的人提供掩护。

Practice 16

1 B

spunky 勇敢坚定的；劲头十足的（brave and determined; full of enthusiasm）

A. 暴躁的；易怒的（quickly or easily becoming angry）

B. [ˈfaɪsti] 充满活力、精力充沛、富有勇气的，精神饱满的（full of animation, energy, or courage; spirited）

C. 丰腴的；微胖的（having a soft, round body; slightly fat）

D. 上等的；豪华的；时髦的（of high quality; expensive and/or fashionable）

句子大意：她勇敢坚定，走起路来神气十足，就像个20岁的年轻人。她克服了重重困难才打造出一片天下。

2 B

badger n. 獾；v. 纠缠，烦扰（反复提出问题或要求）（to put pressure on sb. by repeatedly asking them questions or asking them to do sth.）

relent 终于答应；不再拒绝（to finally agree to sth. after refusing）；变缓和；变温和；减弱（to become less determined, strong, etc.）

A. ~ sb. 侵扰；骚扰（to annoy or worry sb. by putting pressure on them or saying or doing unpleasant things to them）

B. 打扰；纠缠；烦扰（to annoy sb., especially by asking them sth. many times）

C. ~ sb. 用短棒打（to hit sb. with a cudgel）

D. 用警戒线围住 [to form a cordon around (an area) so as to prevent movement in or out]

句子大意：她通过电话和短信不停地找居委会，直到他们做出让步。

3 D

submit to sth. 接受或屈从于……（to accept or give in to the authority, power, or will of another; to allow oneself to be subjected to something）

A. resort to sth. 诉诸；采取……的途径或手段 [to have recourse (to) for help]

B. turn to sb. 向（某人）求助；求助于（to go to someone for help when you are having difficulty dealing with a situation）

C. look to sb. for sth. 求助某人做某事（to hope that someone will provide something for you）

D. succumb to sth. 屈服，屈从于（to allow oneself to be overcome or overpowered by something; to submit or yield to something）

句子大意：从今日起，来访者必须刷脸方得进入。

4 **A**

recourse 依靠；依赖；求助（the fact of having to, or being able to, use sth. that can provide help in a difficult situation）

resignation 顺从；听任（patient willingness to accept a difficult or unpleasant situation that you cannot change）；**常用搭配**：resign oneself to sth. 放纵或听任（自己）于某事，顺从于……

A. 屈服，投降；归顺（the act of accepting that sb. has defeated you and that you must obey them）

B. （有条件的）投降；投降条约（a document that sets out the agreed terms of surrender）

C. ~ (from sth.) 背离；违反；逾越（an action that is different from what is usual or expected）

D. [dɪˈbɔːtʃ] 放荡，淫逸，沉湎酒色；暴饮暴食（an act or occasion of extreme indulgence in sensuality or carnal pleasures）

常考同义词：debauchery 道德败坏；淫荡；沉湎酒色（或毒品）（immoral behaviour involving sex, alcohol or drugs）

句子大意：对许多公民来说，求援渠道的缺乏让他们有一种无可奈何的感觉。

5 **A**

trusting 愿意相信他人（willing to trust）

A. （= trusting）愿意相信他人（willing to trust）

B. 值得他人信赖的，可靠的（deserving of trust, reliable）

C. （经过长期接触证明）可靠的；可信赖的（used for describing a person or thing that you have known or had for a long time and can depend on）

D. 值得信赖的（worthy of trust, able to be trusted）

句子大意：总的来说，人们对政府实体处理个人信息的方式更加信任，对企业部门的怀疑程度要高得多。

6 **A**

trade-off (between sth. and sth.)（在相互对立的两者之间进行的）权衡，协调（the act of balancing two things that are opposed to each other）

A. 妥协；折中；互让；和解（an agreement made between two people or groups in which each side gives up some of the things they want so that both sides are happy at the end）

B. ~ (to sth.) 补充物；补足物（a thing that adds new qualities to sth. in a way that improves it or makes it more attractive）

C. 赞扬；称赞（a remark that expresses praise or admiration of sb.）

D. 调味料；作料（a substance such as salt or pepper that is used to give flavour to food）

句子大意：许多居民把交出数据视为获得安全和方便的必要代价。

7 C

surreptitiously [ˌsʌrəpˈtɪʃəsli] 秘密地，鬼鬼祟祟、偷偷摸摸地（done secretly or quickly, in the hope that other people will not notice）

A. 迷信地，受迷信思想支配地（in a way that is influenced by superstitions）

B. 极大地；令人惊叹地（in a way that is extremely large or impressive, especially greater or better than you expect）

C. 偷偷摸摸；偷偷地；鬼鬼祟祟地（behaving in a way that shows that you want to keep sth. secret and do not want to be noticed）

D. 象征性地（using words not in their normal literal meaning but in a way that makes a description more interesting or impressive）

句子大意：该公司对待其商业机密非常谨慎，他只能用假名暗地里发表自己的研究成果。

8 B

extol 赞扬；颂扬；称赞（to praise sb./sth. very much）

A. （尤因强烈的情感或痛苦而）惊叫，呼喊（to say sth. suddenly and loudly, especially because of strong emotion or pain）

B. ~ sb. (to sth.) 提拔，提升（有时指不该得到的职位）（to make sb. rise to a higher rank or position, sometimes to one that they do not deserve）

~ sb./sth. 表扬；褒扬；高度赞扬（to praise sb./sth. very much）

C. ~ sth. (from sb.) 敲诈；勒索；强夺（to make sb. give you sth. by threatening them）

D. ~ sth. or ~ from sb. 流露，显露（感觉或品质）；（感觉或品质）显现（If you exude a particular feeling or quality, or it exudes from you, people can easily see that you have it.）

句子大意：一些对牛奶作为钙质来源大放赞美之词的研究背后都有乳品加工业的资助，至少是获得了部分资助。

9 B

incredulous 不肯相信的；不能相信的；表示怀疑的（not willing or not able to believe sth.; showing an inability to believe sth.）

A. 不可思议的；令人难以置信的（impossible or very difficult to believe）

  极好的；极大的（extremely good or extremely large）

B. 不相信的；怀疑的（feeling or showing that you do not believe sb./sth.）

C. 非常好（或坏、极端）的；惊人的（used to emphasize how good, bad or extreme sth. is）

D. 值得赞扬的；应当认可的（of a quite good standard and deserving praise or approval）

  道德高尚的（morally good）

句子大意：假如你造访一个处于动荡中的社会并告诉那里的人们，他们生活在一个幸福感不断提升、威胁不断减少的时代，人们可能会向你投来怀疑的目光。

10 A

precipitate [prɪ'sɪpɪtət] ~ sth. 使……突然降临；加速（坏事的发生）（to make sth., especially sth. bad, happen suddenly or sooner than it should）

precipitate sb./sth. into sth. 使突然陷入（某种状态）（to suddenly force sb./sth. into a particular state or condition）

A. ~ sth. 激起；引起；引发（to cause a particular reaction or have a particular effect）

B. 使行不通；阻止；妨碍；排除（to prevent sth. from happening or sb. from doing sth.; to make sth. impossible）

C. 宣布；宣告；声明（to publicly and officially tell people about sth. important）

D. [prə'feɪn] ~ sth. 亵渎神灵；亵圣（to treat sth. holy with a lack of respect）

句子大意：人们认为，随着制造业工作机会流向海外以及工会的衰落，工人阶级的稳定工作岗位受到侵蚀，这是突然引发西方民粹主义者强烈抵制的主要原因。

11 A

espouse [ɪ'spaʊz] 赞成，拥护，采纳（主义、学说等）（to give your support to an idea, principle, or belief）

A. 拥护；支持；提倡（to support sth. publicly）

B. 阐述；详解；详述（to explain something or to express your opinion about it in detail）

C. ~ sb. 使震惊；使大惊（to surprise or shock sb. very much）

D. ~ sb./sth./yourself (from sth.)（使）摆脱，脱离，脱出（to escape or enable sb. to escape from a difficult situation）

句子大意：该项目的一些反对者要么采用牵强附会的理论，要么使用被一些人认为是反亚裔的危言耸听的语言。

12 C

innocuous 无恶意的；无意冒犯的（not intended to offend or upset anyone）；无害的；无危险的（not harmful or dangerous）

nefarious [nɪ'feərɪəs] 罪恶的；不道德的（criminal; immoral）

A. 模糊的；不清楚的（not clear）

B. 脆弱的；微弱的；缥缈的（so weak or uncertain that it hardly exists）
纤细的；薄的；易断的（extremely thin and easily broken）

C. 恶毒的；邪恶的（enjoying harming others; morally bad and cruel）

D.（看望病人、祷告、抗议等的）不眠时间；（尤指）值夜，守夜祈祷（a period of time when people stay awake, especially at night, in order to watch a sick person, say prayers, protest, etc.）

句子大意：随着外交关系的恶化，美国官员质疑看似无害的俄罗斯投资是否会被用于邪恶目的。

13 A

percolate ['pɜrkə‚leɪt] 渗入；渗透；渗漏（to move gradually through a surface that has very small holes or spaces in it）；逐渐流传；传开（to gradually become known or spread through a group or society）

A. 渗透；弥漫；扩散（to spread to every part of an object or a place）

感染；传播；扩散（to affect every part of sth.）

B. ['pɜ:fəreɪt] ~ sth. 打孔；穿孔；打眼（to make a hole or holes through sth.）

C. [pə(r)'spaɪə(r)] 出汗；排汗；发汗（to produce sweat on your body）

D. ~ sth. 使永久化；使持久化；使持续（to make sth. such as a bad situation, a belief, etc. continue for a long time）

句子大意： 仇恨只会渗透——我叫它仇恨，人们觉得耸人听闻并且完全不喜欢这种说法——但仇恨迟早会浮出水面。

14 A

ludicrous 不合理的；不能当真的（unreasonable; that you cannot take seriously）

A. 荒唐的；极不合情理的（completely unreasonable, especially in a way that is shocking or annoying）

怪诞的；离奇古怪的（unusual in a silly or shocking way）

B. 肉欲的；色情的；甘美的，芬芳的（very attractive in a sexual way; luscious food looks, smells, and tastes especially good）

C. 汁多味美的（containing a lot of juice and tasting good）

肉质的；多汁的（having leaves and stems that are thick and contain a lot of water）

D. 十分舒适的；奢侈的（very comfortable; containing expensive and enjoyable things）

句子大意： 客观来讲，在登基70周年大庆中将要举行的相当一部分活动是不合情理的。

15 C

recoil from sth./from doing sth. or recoil at sth. 对……做出厌恶（或恐惧）的反应（to react to an idea or a situation with strong dislike or fear）

fuddy-duddy 守旧的人；老顽固；老古董；老古板（a person who has old-fashioned ideas or habits）

A. ~ from sth./from doing sth. 停止；结束（to stop doing sth.）

B. ~ sb./sth. (as sth.)（公开）谴责；（强烈）批评（to strongly criticize sb./sth., especially publicly）

C. [ə'bɒmɪneɪt] ~ sth./sb. 憎恨；憎恶；厌恶；极其讨厌（to feel hatred or disgust for sth./sb.）

D. ~ sb. (for sth./for doing sth.) 辱骂；斥责（to criticize sb./sth. in a way that shows how much you dislike them）

句子大意： 现在基本没有多少英国人对查尔斯三世登基存在抵触情绪，即便他有时看起来更像一位守旧的叔叔，而非一个国家的大家长。

16 C

dither 犹豫不决；踌躇（to hesitate about what to do because you are unable to decide）

A. ~ sth. 证实；确认；确证（to prove that sth. is true）；使生效；使有法律效力（to make sth. legally valid）

~ sth. 批准；确认……有效；认可（to state officially that sth. is useful and of an acceptable standard）

B. ~ sth. 证实；证明有理（to prove that sth. is true or that you were right to do sth., especially when other people had a different opinion）

~ sb. 澄清（责难或嫌疑）；证明（某人）无罪（责）（to prove that sb. is not guilty when they have been accused of doing sth. wrong or illegal）

C. ['væsɪleɪt] 观点（或立场等）摇摆；动摇（to keep changing your opinion or thoughts about sth., especially in a way that annoys other people）

D. ~ sth. or ~ that... 证明；证实（to show or say that sth. is true or accurate）

句子大意： 德国在向该国提供武器方面犹豫不决的态度已经损害了其国际形象。

17 B

galore [gə'lɔː(r)] 大量；很多（in large quantities, in abundance, in plentiful amounts）（作后置定语，例如：layoffs galore 大规模裁员；options galore 大量的选择）

A. 每人；每个；各（having, costing or measuring a particular amount each）

B.（通常作后置定语）大量；充裕；绰绰有余（being in sufficient quantity; generous in amount）

C.（指空间或时间）相隔，相距（separated by a distance, of space or time）

D.（用于名词后）除……以外（used after nouns to say that except for one thing, sth. is true）

句子大意： 这些恐怖电影的元素包括大量的血块、令人毛骨悚然的配音，当然也有大量的怪物。

18 A

flamboyant 炫耀的；卖弄的；艳丽的；绚丽夺目的（behaving or dressing in a way that deliberately attracts people's attention; brightly colored or decorated）

A. 炫耀的；卖弄的；夸示的（behaving in a way that is meant to impress people by showing how rich, important, etc. you are）

夸张的；招摇的（done in a very obvious way so that people will notice it）

B. 骇人听闻的；公然的；罪恶昭彰的（shocking because it is done in a very obvious way and shows no respect for people, laws, etc.）

C. 极讨厌的；可憎的；令人作呕的（extremely unpleasant, especially in a way that offends people）

D. 狂信的，狂热的，入迷的（behaving in an unreasonable way as a result of very strong religious or political beliefs）

句子大意： 他的生活方式与波斯湾的王室或炫耀招摇的寡头不相上下。

19 A

lure sb. into doing sth. 引诱某人去做某事

A. ~ sb. 使人放松或自信从而不会对不好的事情做准备（to make someone feel relaxed or confident so that they are not prepared for anything unpleasant）

~ sb. into sth. 让某人感觉安全从而误以为……（to make someone feel safe in order to trick them）

B.（尤指为做不正当的事而）埋伏，潜伏（to wait somewhere secretly, especially because you are going to do sth. bad or illegal）

（不好或危险的事）潜在，隐藏着（When sth. unpleasant or dangerous lurks, it is present but not in an obvious way.）

C. 唱摇篮曲催眠（to quiet with or as if with a lullaby）

D. ~ sth. 给……上润滑油；上油（to put a lubricant on sth. such as the parts of a machine, to help them move smoothly）

句子大意：安全专家对此表示担忧，因为这些系统允许司机放弃对汽车的主动控制，并可能让他们误以为自己的汽车在自动驾驶。

20 B

splendid 壮丽的；雄伟的；豪华的；华丽的（very impressive; very beautiful）

A. ~ about sth./over sth. 苦恼的；沮丧的；泄气的；失望的（sad, without much hope）

B. 辉煌的；灿烂的；华丽的（brightly coloured in an impressive way）

C. [dɪˈspɒtɪk] 专制的；暴虐的（using power in a cruel and unreasonable way）

D. 建立在错误的观念（或思想方法）之上的；谬误的（based on false ideas or ways of thinking）

句子大意：在威斯敏斯特教堂的这场为时两小时的盛大仪式开始时，查尔斯三世国王为这场华丽但对于王室加冕礼而言显得有些私密的典礼定下主题："我今日于此，非以役人，乃役于人。"